MISSOURI MYSTIC

JON MUNDY, PH.D.

*To
Mary Jean + Walt
Hubbard
with Love
Jon*

second printing

Royal Fireworks Press
Unionville, New York

A Note about the Footnotes:

All quotes from *A Course in Miracles* © are listed as ACIM.

Abbreviations used are as follows:

T: text, W: workbook, C: clarification of terms, In: introduction

A notation lists text, followed by chapter, section, paragraph and sentence.

I appreciate your feedback. Please visit www.miraclesmagazine.org

To order books and/or a subscription to *Miracles* Magazine

Write to: Box 1000 Washingtonville, NY 10992
Call 845-496-9089—Thanks

ISBN: 0-89824-971-6

Royal Fireworks Press
First Ave, PO Box 700
Unionville, NY 10988
tel: 845 726 4444
fax: 845 726 3824
email: mail@rfwp.com
website: rfwp.com

Printed and bound in the United States using acid-free paper, soy-based inks, and environmentally friendly cover coatings by the Royal Fireworks Printing Company of Unionville, New York.

Other Books by Jon Mundy

Awaken to Your Own Call
Listening to Your Inner Guide
The Ten Laws of Happiness

For a list of CDs and audio tapes, go to www.miraclesmagazine.org

Spare me the theology;
Just give me the story.

—Tim Winton, Australian novelist

To

My sister Ann & brother-in-law Glenn Phillips

About the Cover

The cover photo was taken by my wife, Dolores, in the backyard of my ancestral farm near Molino, Missouri. Now the home of my sister Ann and brother-in-law Glenn Phillips, the 160-acre farm was purchased from the United States government by our great-great grandfather Logan Mundy on May 16, 1857 for twenty-five cents per acre. Thomas Jefferson bought the land as part of the Louisiana Purchase of 1802 for three cents per acre. The pump house in the background draws beautiful, cold, clear water from an underground spring some sixty feet below. The tree on the left is a persimmon.

Acknowledgments

Thanks for opening this book! I hope you'll read it through.

Each of the following individuals enriches my life and thus this book.

My wife Dolores and daughter Sarah are the delights of my life.

With these two beautiful women I share my living, my learning and my loving.

My son Kristian is maturing into a fine young scholar and our monthly lunches and our philosophical e-mail exchanges and conversations are a delight for me.

My mother, Milly Mundy, sister Ann Phillips, and my high school sweetheart, Judy Femmer, were the first to read these pages, as I shared many of the experiences in this book with them.

Diane Berke, my partner in the foundation and development of Interfaith Fellowship, has been ever present in her love, devotion and commitment to the work we share.

Several friends offered their excellent editorial comments and suggestions. Dorothy Spelman did two complete edits. The first, a general grammatical clean up, and the second a more extensive process of helping me to refine, purify and thereby improve the overall quality of this book. I'm also appreciative of the editing skills of Irene Parcher, Nancy Donaldson, Susan Shapiro, Meribeth Seaman, Julianne Tyler, Sara Emrie, Zell Schwartzman, Heather Harris, Ruth Hanna, Toni Theodore, Jennifer Flagg, Mary Ishmael and Lois Chierico.

The following friends took the time to read this manuscript and offer their suggestions: Myron Blackman, Judy Halpin, Jennifer Kenney, John White, Rev. John Roming Johnson Jr. Ph.D., Therese Quinn, Carol Rollinger, Tom Gossett, Rev. Howard Westin, Rev. Bill Johnston, Terrie Anne Rafael, Richard Andrews, Vi Jefferson, Lorie Frisbee, Peter Fairchild, Helen Suckow, Audrey Lloyd, Sam Manheim Ph.D., Ed Foote, Jerry Jampolsky, M.D., Beverly Hutchinson Mc Nuff, Alan Cohen, Lee Coit, Nancy Glende, Odette Bigott, Dick Nye, Betty Whitis, Joan Lorenz, MaryBeth Scalice, Chuck Houser, Rudi Florian, and Ann Cortese.

Thank you to Judith Skutch Whitson, my friend since 1969, for your kind words, encouragement and support and, Dr. Kenneth Wapnick, my friend since 1975. Ken has consistently fostered my growth and understanding of *A Course in Miracles* by constantly challenging me to deepen my exploration of "The Course." Each time I followed his advice, I discovered he was right.

Thanks to Bishop John Shelby Spong for his wonderful book, *Here I Stand*. Though our lives took very different paths, we've both been committed to ministry and a pursuit of the truth, as we understand it. Thanks to Frank McCourt for *Angela's Ashes*. I read his book, as many people did, with amazement. It inspired me to talk about a good—seemingly ideal—childhood. The troubles came later.

Finally, thanks to the many mystics, masters saints and sages from all faiths and all ages who left us their inspiration and love.

Table of Contents

Foreword

Chapter 1—The Farm and the Family 1

Chapter 2—The Extraordinarily Ordinary
    (Mystical Moments of Childhood) 21

Chapter 3—Boyhood and Youth 28

Chapter 4—Gifts from My Parents 34

Chapter 5—Other Farms and Other Families 43

Chapter 6—Sneed School and the Field of Dreams 48

Chapter 7—Our Family Trip—Summer 1954 54

Chapter 8—Paradise Lost—Running Away from Home 61

Chapter 9—Going To Town—Mexico, Missouri 64

Chapter 10—The Highs of Adolescence 67

Chapter 11—Falling in Love 73

Chapter 12—The Call into the Ministry: The Universe's University 80

Chapter 13—College and the Move into Ministry 83

Chapter 14—Back to College 93

Chapter 15—Europe on a Vespa 98

Chapter 16—Southern California School of Theology—
    Marriage and Divorce 105

Chapter 17—Paris and Scandinavia 121

Chapter 18—New York City, College Teaching,
    Graduate School and The Tombs 126

Chapter 19—My Own Church—Brooklyn, New York
    and a New Judy 131

Chapter 20—The Atonement: The First Theological Debate 141

Chapter 21—The Seventies 144

Chapter 22—Which Guru? Adventures in India 150

Chapter 23—Edie and the Move Back to Manhattan 164

Chapter 24—Prague and Russia 174

Chapter 25—Finding What I'm Looking For 178

Chapter 26—Holy Hell—An Account of My Visionary Journey 191

Chapter 27—Postmortem 205

Chapter 28—High Rock Spring. 212

Chapter 29—Methodist Ministry and the Frustrating Eighties   219

Chapter 30—That Was Zen—This is Tao   228

Chapter 31—Three Failed Romances   235

Chapter 32—The Inn and the End of My Methodist Ministry   253

Chapter 33—The Birth of Interfaith Fellowship
            and *On Course* Magazine   266

Chapter 34—Why is the Church so Frightened by the Course?   275

Chapter 35—A Golden Year 1993   280

Chapter 36—Finally, Dolores—Love, Marriage and Family Life   283

Chapter 37—New Life in the Twenty-First Century   296

Chapter 38—The Classroom Called Cancer   302

Chapter 39—This is it!   308

Chapter 40—Something Wonderful Is Going to Happen   315

Postscript   324

FOREWORD

Mexican Shaman Don Juan, in Carlos Castaneda's *The Active Side of Infinity*, says that every warrior, in preparation for his entrance into the region known as the active side of infinity, begins his journey by collecting an album of pictures made of remembrances of moments that illuminated his path. The human mind longs to make sense of events that happen in time. *Missouri Mystic* is an archive of inner life, a chronicle of events, and an attempt to find meaning for a journey through the last half of the twentieth century, from a farm in mid-Missouri to a ministry in midtown Manhattan, to an itinerant ministry to the world.

> *God made man because he loves stories.* ——Yiddish Saying

My friend Alan Cohen once said that everyone needs to tell their story, otherwise they go crazy. Like *The Celestine Prophecy* by James Redfield or *Pilgrims Progress* by John Bunyan, all our journeys are adventure (sometimes misadventure) stories. My wife Dolores and I spend a good deal of time telling each other our stories. No matter how intricate the detail, there is always more that we can yet recall. We are all looking for peace of mind, a life worth living, meaningful work, enriching relationships and an assurance of life eternal.

Of all the writing and public speaking I've done in more than forty years as a minister, lecturer and magazine publisher, the most enthusiastic responses were to the messages in which I discussed my mystical experiences as a child on the farm in Missouri, the sixties and seventies, my travels in India, my work with a Mexican Shaman, a death experience, an ongoing love-hate relationship with the traditional church, and the co-founding of Interfaith Fellowship along with Rev. Diane Berke (inside Cami Hall across the street from Carnegie Hall in New York City), and my struggles with heart disease and cancer.

My last three books were essays on various aspects of *A Course in Miracles* (a self-study program of spiritual psychology which helps us release fear and achieve inner peace). The Course was scribed by Dr. Helen Schucman between the years 1965 and 1972 in New York City and published in 1976. This book is different. It is a story. It is your story and mine. It belongs to both of us, unique and divine. You have a story. You are a hero. You are a heroine. You are on a journey home. We are all also *already* home whether we recognize it or not.

On Writing

If you commit to it, writing can take you as deep as Zen.
—Katagiri Roshi in Natalie Goldberg's *Long Quiet Highway*

If you are born to write, you will find a way to do it. I write early each morning before showering, shaving, and proceeding into the work of the day. Morning is the most wonderful time of the day. It is quiet where we live—only the school bus stopping for our daughter, Sarah, interrupts the sound of the morning birds. I write religiously, like someone practicing the piano. In fact writing *is* my "practice." Something happens when you immerse yourself in any "discipline" and writing is a good one.

The only way to compose myself and collect my thoughts is to sit down at my table, place my diary before me and take my pen into hand. This apparatus takes my attention from other objects. Pen, ink, paper and a sitting posture are a great help to attention, emotion and thinking.
—John Adams, Second President of the United States

It's the same for me, except I sit in front of a computer. Writing is meditative therapy. It is a way of working things through, a time of soul searching. Writing is a voyage of discovery. To write is to see the whole of experience—why things happen the way they do. Writing helps make sense out of life. It helps me understand who I am now and once was. It helps me wake up, grow and belong.

Your "guilty secret" is nothing, and if you will but bring it to the light, the light will dispel it. —ACIM, T-13.II.9: 2

Writing *Missouri Mystic* helped me look within and I have had to face a few ghosts, and demons. *A Course in Miracles* encourages us to look at our dark side—not to affirm that reality. We look so that we might dispel our fears, "undo" the false and thus become open to that which is true. Some people are surprised that I "told so much" in this book. I have found that, if you tell "it," "it" can't hurt you. "It" can't jump out and surprise you.

I have, in the course of this writing, made assessments about various events. I do not claim objective truth. This is a subjective report. Others' memories are no doubt different than mine. Almost everyone mentioned in this book read it in manuscript form and then gave me their feedback. While this process has not always been fun, it has always been rewarding.

My struggle manifests itself in my willingness, or lack thereof, to look at my own shadow and my capacity for denial. The thing about denial is that, by definition, you don't always know that you are in it when you are. The very nature of the beast is to deny being in denial. I have had tremendous resistance to looking at the dark contents of my subterranean life. Life has thus been a series of many trials and revelations.

Trials are but lessons that you failed to learn presented once again, so where you made a faulty choice before, you can now make a better one, and thus escape all pain that what you chose before has brought to you.
—ACIM, T-31.VIII.3: 1

Over and over again, I made faulty choices. Like Abraham Lincoln, "I have many times been driven to my knees because I knew nowhere else to go."

The Myth of the Ministry

We must make the choices that enable us to fulfill the deepest capacities of our real selves. —Thomas Merton

At the age of nine, I announce to my family that I am going to be a minister. There was never any doubt about this. Destiny chooses us and I have always felt *called*. I believe that people know the purpose for their being early on. You must, however, cultivate it or lose sight of it. The Mundy coat of arms is inscribed with the saying, "God Provides." If we focus on what we are called to do, God will provide!

Psychologist Carl Jung once said that the most important question anyone can ask is, "What myth am I living? Am I living my own myth or that of another?" In 1961, at the age of eighteen, I began working as a minister with a circuit of three rural Missouri churches. I've always been a minister and a seeker and I've crossed paths with a number of saints, sages, and sinners. You can decide who is who. I've sat at the feet of gurus in India and twirled with sufi dervishes. I've gone on vision quests with shamans in the Tamaulipas Mountains and the jungles of Chiapas in Mexico. I visited parapsychologists in Eastern Europe and Russia. I've read through esoteric literature, Eastern and Western philosophy and modern psychology. I've meditated, practiced yoga and walked on fire. I've gone through Freudian and Jungian therapy, the Landmark Forum and Rebirthing, and participated in hundreds of workshops. I fell in love with several lovely women. I worked for many years on a doctorate which I did not receive until I was sixty. Most important, since 1975, I've been a student of *A Course in Miracles*.

Success is going from failure to failure with enthusiasm. —Winston Churchill

Stories are interesting when they are about struggle and the overcoming of difficulties. The rough road and rugged terrain make the journey meaningful and give us our strength. We who live in bodies, in time, on a specific planet—we who live in history—need stories that have beginnings and ends. My life has been a roller coaster ride; sometimes moments of incredible bliss, other times *almost* hell on earth. It has on the whole been "one wild and precious ride."

In 1976, I had a profound death experience, the description of which is central to this book.

In this experience it became clear that:

1. We are not bodies.

2. There is no such thing as death.

3. We are making up this world.

We could have done it many different ways. We are experiencing what I call the Western Twenty-First Century System of Glossing. As Einstein expressed it, our experience *is an optical delusion of consciousness.* This world—and the bodies we inhabit—are hiding places from God. It is a world of duality (subject and object) and thus not the real world. This is, if you will, "a dream world." The real world is God's World—Heaven.

4. There is no time. Everything is happening in a radically loaded now. Or, only that which is eternal is real. Heaven is eternal. The world is ephemeral.

5. The script is written. Or, "Things always happen as they should."
Or, "It has all—already happened."

Married at twenty-two and divorced at twenty-three, I vowed I would not marry again until it was a decision I could happily live with for the rest of my life. Twenty-seven years later, on one miraculous day, in my fiftieth year, Dolores, a loving, "firey," redheaded, creative, Irish Leo Lassie, *literally* rang my bell! Four years later, there were wedding bells! We have become progressively, comfortably, happily married, sharing a home, raising my step-daughter, Sarah, enjoying our mutual love of organizing and fixing our home, gardening, bird watching, reading, hiking, biking, river rafting, movies, cooking, eating, going to fairs, sharing our home with our friends, hanging out on our deck on cool summer nights, sitting before our fireplace in winter—still talking—still getting to know each other.

CHAPTER 1

The Farm and the Family

Life not in Heaven is impossible and what is not in Heaven is not anywhere.
—ACIM, T-23.II.19:6

The Parable of the Mustard Seed

And He said,

With what can we compare the kingdom of God, or what parable shall we use for it? It is like a grain of mustard seed, which, when sown upon the ground, is the smallest of all the seeds on earth; yet when it is sown it grows up and becomes the greatest of all shrubs, and puts forth large branches, so that the birds of the air can make nests in its shade.

He told them another parable,

The kingdom of Heaven is like leaven, which a woman took and hid in three measures of meal, till it was all leavened. All this Jesus said to the crowds in parables; indeed he said nothing to them without a parable. This was to fulfill what was spoken of the prophet: I will open my mouth in parables; I will utter what has been hidden Since the foundation of the world.
—Matthew 13: 31-35

Here is a story of something familiar yet hidden since the foundation of the world. There are many things we do not know. Why planet earth? Why space-time? Why human beings? Why consciousness? Why does anything exist at all? We experience consciousness—existence—life. Why? Why does a desire arise? Who knows how a thought is formed? What are we supposed to do here? How are we to live? Eighteenth century German transcendentalist philosopher Immanuel Kant observed that there are two characteristics to these questions: 1) They are always there and 2) We cannot answer them.

Speaking About the Unspeakable?

Unfortunately, even the mystic perceives no 'why'.
For, in that unitive vision, He alone is.
—S. Abhayananda, *History of Mysticism*, Atman Books, Olympia, WA.

Not being able to verbalize answers doesn't mean there are none. The first chapter of *A Course in Miracles* begins by talking about *revelation*. "Revelation," the Course says, is "literally unspeakable because it is an experience of unspeakable love." (ACIM, T-1. II. 2:7) At best we can paint a picture or tell a story which points beyond the surface. The heart knows things the lips can never utter. The mystics say that their experiences are ineffable—indefinable—inexpressible. Many questions lack obvious rational answers, yet answers come, though they have nothing to do with the accumulation of facts or what we call logical actualities.

Dr. Ken Wapnick says his "original" mystical stirring came while listening to the works of Mozart. I was once surprised when I burst into tears while listening to Chopin's *Polonaise*. Music lovers can tell of many such experiences. The following is just such rapture as described in the classic, *Samuel Pepys' Diary* from 1664.

> *The 27th. —Up and then with my wife and Deb to the king's house to see
> Virgin Martyr. That which did please me beyond everything in the whole
> world was the wind music when the angel comes down, which is so sweet that
> it ravished me and indeed in a word did wrap up my soul so that it did make
> me really sick just as I have formerly been when I fell in love with my wife.
> But neither then nor all the evening going home and at home was I able to
> think of anything but remained all night transported so that I could not believe
> that ever any music hath that real command over the soul of a man
> as this did upon me.*

My first stirrings came through a "mystical participation" with nature. My "call" came while watching a kaleidoscopic display of sunlight shining through prisms of dewdrops on leaves in the forest trees. There, an indescribable light shone inside and all around me, and I heard a voice calling me to be who I already am—who I always have been—who we all already are. On a sunny day in the springtime you can feel it. We all have felt it. Look directly with me now slightly past the picture to what it suggests. Let's take a look at something beautiful. It looks, I think, a lot like Heaven.

Home (1943—1961)

My first truly mystical experiences occur on the farm in Missouri with my immediate interest in and involvement with nature and the people I love and cherish, who also love and cherish me. They are my magnificent mother Milly, my fabulous father Sam, my sweet sister Ann, and my father's parents—grandfather Almer and grandmother Bessie Mundy, and mother's mother—grandmother Nettie Callahan. My great-uncle Estel and great-aunt Jessie live a half mile north, up the road from our farm. My great-aunt Bertha lives another mile up the same road in Molino. To the north, south, east and west are other farms, all with kids a little older or a little younger than I, though there is no one else in my grade at Sneed School, our one room country schoolhouse.

I spend the first eighteen years of my life on our farm, on a hill, by a dirt and gravel road in central Missouri. Our farm is a really pretty place that people drive by to look at. Daddy frequently puts fresh fine white gravel on the driveway and smoothes it out with a grader. The lawn is immaculate, the gardens stunning. The fences are in repair, the barn and house are painted often, and Mother has the flowerbeds in bloom spring, summer and fall.

The town of Mexico is some seven miles due south of our farm. Mexico takes pride in being the firebrick and saddle horse (a horse bred and schooled for riding) center of the world. The clay from around Mexico makes excellent firebrick—used for the lining of furnaces. My great-grand-father Jonathan Edward Mundy was one of several local breeders of saddle horses. The main crops in the county are soybeans and corn. There is a soybean festival every August with a county queen and a parade with floats and the local high school band. Our 4-H club, The Molino Musketeers, always has a float in the parade.

Our farm is quite isolated by today's standards. The front yard affords a bucolic view for miles, of nothing but fields, hills and trees. Looking south from the top of our hill, past Daddy's terraced alfalfa fields and a big oak tree in the center of the field in the valley below lies Paul West's cornfield. Crows come and sit in the oak tree in the evening, cawing to each other in the cryptic darkness. The cornfield below borders a wooded section we call "The Ten Acres" which in turn snuggles up against the west side of Salt River. A tree we call Old Hollow sits, in a bend in Salt River, radiating a gentle strength and a calming effect on everything around. The largest tree we know of in any of the surrounding woods, it is so cavernous that two kids can climb down inside at the same time. There is a cabin in the Ten Acre woods that Daddy let some hunters build, in ex-change for our use of the cabin.

Everyone has experienced what he would call a sense of being transported beyond himself. It is a sense of actual escape from limitations. If you will consider what this "transportation" really entails, you will realize that it is a sudden unawareness of the body, and a joining of yourself and something else in your mind enlarges to encompass it. It becomes part of you, as you unite with it. —ACIM, T-18.VI.11: 1-5

3

When I seek solace and a chance to listen to Spirit awakening within, I go into the woods behind our barn. There the trees open wide their branches and bid me welcome. I am particularly fond of a clearing in the middle of a black walnut grove overlooking the valley below. Here I sit under one of the walnut trees. There is such silence, such coolness below it. There is no one to disturb me, and I sometimes sit here till I disappear. The view invites the eye, and as the eye reaches the mind stretches. There is an expanse and emptiness in and around me. You can see all the different dimensions of consciousness in the woods. The forest is a place of calm, a holy space, a place where all day the animals play: a distant woodpecker drills away at a tree, squirrels jabber at each other and jays give off annoying calls. Here is a little world, in and of itself. It is "alive" and all a part of good-natured fun.

Molino, Missouri

We work two farms—the 120-acre farm we live on and my grandfather's 160-acre farm, two miles northwest of ours. Although Mexico is a big town of twelve thousand people, there is a village between our two farms, called Molino, that we identify with more than Mexico. Molino now hardly exists. At one time it boasted a general store, a bank, a small hotel, a post office, a blacksmith shop, a Baptist church and a baseball field.

As a child, opening the door to the general store in Molino brought me face to face with a glass display case, filled with candy bars and chewing gum. In the center of the store sits a potbellied stove. Farmers wearing overalls and dirty knee-high rubber boots sit around and talk, smoke and chew tobacco. Spittoons are provided here and at several stores in Mexico. All around are shelves crammed with canned goods. Women occasionally join in the circle. It's an adventure to go to Molino for soda, candy and ice cream, to see who is there and to hear the latest gossip.

Now, in the twenty-first century, Molino is practically a ghost town, only a few houses, the store, the church and the blacksmith shop remain, though the church is now a house, the store a shed and the blacksmith shop a garage. Molino is now filled with battered and broken farm equipment and junked cars. Small fenced-in lots contain too many cows, and everywhere there is manure. It's not the pretty place I experienced as a child. It was during the first half of the twentieth century *the* town around which the social life of the Mundy family and other local farmers revolved.

Mother's Family—The Callahans

We trace our family back six generations on each side of our family tree, covering three hundred years in the United States. Mother's family, the Callahans, fought in the Revolutionary War and with the Union forces of the Civil War. Daddy's family, the Mundys, were Confederates. Mother's hometown is Kirksville, which is one hundred miles north of our farm. Kirksville, like Mexico, is a county seat. The Fox Indians were once the primary inhabitants of this area, and it's said that grandmother Callahan's father, whose last name was Fox, came from the Fox Indians.

Mother is the youngest of three sisters. Dark-haired Marie, the oldest and childless, lives with her carpenter husband, Harold, in Kirksville. The next oldest, Lue, lives with her husband, Bill, and only son, Gary (my only first cousin), in Mexico. Lue is a beautician with a shop in the basement of her home. My Uncle Bill, a tall, good-looking guy with a knowing grin and cigarette almost always in his hand or mouth works in an office for the Wabash Railroad. I sometimes sleep at their house, and lie awake at night listening to the long, low, whisper-like whistle of trains coming through Mexico, a regular stop on the St. Louis to Kansas City line.

Mother was born April Fool's Day 1916, in Willmathsville, Missouri. Her father, Carl, suffered through the depression and lost his farm near Kirksville. He died of a heart attack in 1945 at the age of fifty-eight. It *seems* I inherited his heart. Fortunately, I live in an age when hearts can be mended. He did not. My grandfather's death greatly distressed my grandmother Nettie, who developed colon cancer shortly after his death. It *seems* I also inherited her disease. Again, I live in an age where it can be treated. After the death of my grandfather, Grandmother Callahan moved into Kirksville taking in ironing to support herself. The Mundys survived the depression better than the Callahans, as they owned their farm in full and were largely self-sufficient. For the Mundys and the Callahans frugality rules the day, and it is second nature to butcher your own meat, gather your own eggs, milk your own cows, and grow your own food on the land next to your house.

Daddy's Family—The Mundys

In Missouri a recognized superiority is attached to any person who hailed from Old Virginia. And this superiority was exalted to supremacy when a person of such nativity could also prove descent from the first families of that great commonwealth.—Mark Twain, in *Pudd'nhead Wilson*

5

The Mundys came to America from Wales during the early 1700's, settling in Albemarle county, Virginia, near Monticello, the plantation of Thomas Jefferson. In 1836, they moved west, down the Ohio, Tennessee and Cumberland rivers to St. Louis, and from there up the Missouri River to Audrain County. There, on October 10, 1845, in Santa Fe, Missouri, the next small town east of Molino, my great-great-grandfather Logan Mundy married Lucindy Creed. Logan and Lucindy Mundy raised thirteen of their own children and adopted four more. On May 16, 1857 he bought our ancestral farm from the United States government.

In 1864, Captain George Washington Bryson, a Missouri Confederate trooper, came to Audrain County to recruit soldiers. Here he met Logan and Lucindy's daughter, Josephine America Mundy, whom he married. Shortly thereafter, Captain Bryson's men encountered Federal troops. In the fighting that ensued Captain Bryson was wounded and taken to our ancestral farm.

My great-grandparents, Jonathan and Jenny Mundy, had eight children, seven daughters and one son, my Granddaddy Almer. My Granddaddy used to say of his seven sisters: "They all have a brother." All born during the 1870s and '80s, they had wonderful nineteenth century names. There was Ollie, Addie, Alice, Bertha, Jessie, Cora and Josie. Five of them live on farms near our own. Topping the list in importance in our lives is Aunt Jessie and my buddy, her husband Uncle Estel. I am named after both my great-great-grandfather Logan Mundy and my great-grandfather Jonathan Mundy, so I'm Jon Logan Mundy.

Jonathan Mundy's eight-day wind-up clock now sits on our fireplace mantle. His two canes lean against our fireplace, a basket he used to feed chickens and gather eggs and vegetables collects magazines on our hearth, a black metal box in which he kept valuable papers sits on my desk. Dolores thinks it interesting that inanimate objects exist so long and so well after the time of their owners.

Mother and Daddy

My father, Sam, was born on August 5, 1912. His only sibling, my Aunt Sue, was born four years earlier on January 13, 1908. Daddy spent his entire life either on our farm, Granddaddy Mundy's farm or in Mexico. I can't imagine him ever wanting to live any place else. Daddy is incredibly handsome. People frequently say so. He looks a bit like Henry Fonda. He stands tall at five foot eleven inches, with a sharp chin, clear eyes and discernible, delineated muscles. He is made, I think, of oak and rock. He is always slim. There is nothing he cannot do. He is a farmer, mechanic, carpenter, electrician, plumber, mathematician and real-estate salesman rolled into one well-rounded man. When he isn't busy doing one of these things, he is a fisherman, father and Mother's lover. Daddy and I never say "I love you" to each other in our early years, though I do so after he gets ill. Actions speak louder than words and there is never any doubt that Daddy loves Ann and me, and I love and respect him deeply.

Daddy graduated from high school in 1930. He immediately went to work educating himself by traveling around the United States, trying a number of odd jobs. Though he was bright enough, it was depression time and he didn't even think of college. After serving as a soldier during World War II, he took advantage of free university courses for veterans, at the University of Missouri. There he learned surveying and thus terraced the fields on our hill to prevent erosion. To this day, his beautiful terraces snake around the side of the hill giving symmetry to the fields.

In May 1998, Mother moves into King's Daughters' home in Mexico. She gives most of her possessions to her children and friends and sold the rest. Daddy loved to travel and, among mother's things, I find a scrapbook he put together in 1935 when he and another 23-year-old man, George Squires, took off in a Chevy pulling a homemade house trailer. They ventured down to San Diego, California for an exposition and then home again by a northern route. The scrapbook was put together four years before Mother and Daddy met.

In the album is a letter I wrote to him on July 31, 1975. Though Daddy and I got along well, I wanted to take the relationship deeper. I'm thirty-two, and it is written for his sixty-third birthday. My letter is an attempt to reach out to him. Our conversations always remained safely restricted to the things of the world. We talked about cars, money, the farm or other people. Our conversations never evolved into talking about women (a topic about which I could have used some help). We never talked about God or religion, why we are here or what life is all about. In my letter, I try to explain why I became a minister, something I don't think he understood. Daddy would have been happier if I had chosen some more profitable occupation. He never, however, objected to my decision.

Mother and Daddy Meet

Just after her twenty-second birthday on April 1st of 1938, Mother came down from Kirksville to Mexico to visit her sister, Lue. Mother had a date back in Kirksville to go see Walt Disney's first full-length movie, *Snow White and the Seven Dwarfs*. Daddy also had a date in Kirksville. Aunt Lue asked Daddy if Mother could ride along. When Mother came back to Mexico to see Lue a second time, Daddy and Mother had their first date. Two dates later Daddy took Mother for a drive in the country. He pulled off the main road onto a dirt road that led through the woods to a river and a place where one might have a picnic. There in the car he produced a ring and said. "I have a ring here. I was wondering if you might like to wear it?" They were married six months later. They began life together as owners of a new and used furniture store and antique shop in Fulton, Missouri, some twenty-seven miles south of Mexico. By buying, fixing, selling and saving as much money as they could, they were able to buy our farm in 1941. The house had no electricity or running water. They had no car, only horses. To get into town they caught a ride on the high school bus, which they again rode home.

In 1942, Daddy was drafted into the army so they rented out the farm and Mother went to live with her parents (Carl and Nettie) on their farm near Kirksville. Daddy spent most of the war years as a cook at Camp Hulen in Palacios, Texas. Daddy and Mother wrote to each other every day, dreaming in their letters of what life was going to be like once they have settled on their own farm with their new child.

I am born in Kirksville, on May 16, 1943. Franklin Roosevelt is president, and the world is at war. That same day a lot of souls left this planet. On May 16, 1943, resistance collapsed in the Warsaw ghetto. Fifty-six thousand Jews were killed, and Heinrich Himmler ordered the liquidation of everyone in the Warsaw ghetto. I've sometimes wondered if I might be a reincarnated Jew. Though born in a place where there are no Jews, many of my closest friends and colleagues are Jews. The same day I am born, my best friend, Myron Blackman, a Jew, is born in Brooklyn, New York. Once while participating in a Passover Seder, I had the feeling I was participating in something very intimate and familiar. My high school sweetheart, Judy Femmer, born one month after me on June 16, 1943, thinks that she too may be a reincarnated Jew. If in fact I did die during such a horrible page of history, I have awakened in a world of love, beauty and abundance.

The day I was born, my grandfather Almer purchased our ancestral farm from his father, Jonathan. Again, that same day, May 16, 1878, my great-grandfather, Jonathan, purchased our family farm from his father Logan. And, that same day, May 16, 1857, my great-great-grandfather Logan Mundy bought the farm from the United States government for twenty-five cents per acre. In May 1803, Thomas Jefferson bought the land from the French in the Louisiana Purchase for three cents an acre. The French stole the land from the Missouri Indians, whose name means "the ones with the big canoes." The Missouri Indians never claimed to own anything except their big canoes.

Missouri Farming Life

Missouri farms of the late nineteenth and early twentieth century were each little communes. Granddaddy's farm includes the wooden one story farmhouse built on fieldstone. There is a long front porch, kitchen, back porch, dining room, sitting room, and three bedrooms for a family of nine. There is a shed for tools backed by another for small farming equipment, the pump house (shown on the cover of this book) and adjoining grain bins. The water pump draws cold, crystal clear water from an underground spring. My sister, Ann, and her husband, Glenn, are now afraid to drink the farm's well water for fear of chemicals that adjoining farmers have poured into the soil. The farm is now in the soil bank. They get paid for not farming so the soil, covered with thick grasses and wildflowers, takes a rest and replenishes itself after 150 years of use.

Our farmhouse, two miles southeast of Granddaddy Mundy's farm, was built in 1919, or so it says in the cement of the outdoor cellar. It's a small, two-story house sitting on concrete blocks. Downstairs there is the breakfast room, a kitchen, a utility room, a living room, one bedroom, and eventually, though not initially, a bath. Upstairs there are three bedrooms. The back door opens out onto the top of a cement covered cistern framed by a trellis wrapped in blue wisteria.

Most of us come to our senses in the morning in the kitchen. Daddy fires up our black, flat-topped, wood-burning stove to cook breakfast. Ann and I come down the stairs to the rich aroma of burning wood, hot biscuits, fresh eggs, salt cured ham, sausage or bacon and coffee. My favorite breakfasts are biscuits covered with hamburger gravy or sweet cornbread covered with sorghum molasses and milk. There is warmth and energy, wonderful smells and Mother's hugs to greet us every morning.

Most majestic of all the buildings on any farm are the barns—colossal cathedrals filled with hay, corn, oats, wheat, cats, mice, hogs with piglets, sheep with lambs, cows with calves and horses with foals. Our barn is a deep ocher red with crisp white doors. In the barn there are horse stalls, pigpens, and a place to milk our one cow. All around is the smell of straw, feed and manure. The loft is filled with hay, providing winterfeed for the cows and horses, nests for kittens, and countless hiding places for playing hide-and-seek. I love to go up into the hayloft and sit and listen to the cooing of pigeons in the rafters above and tweeting of sparrows off in the sides of the barn. The outer sides of our barn are used to store larger machinery. On Granddaddy Mundy's and Uncle Estel's farms, one side of the barn is for horses, the other for buggies and horse-drawn wagons. Granddaddy Mundy's farm also includes a red three-sided cattle and horse barn, open on the south side where cows and horses come to eat hay in the evening and find shelter during inclement weather. There are also grain bins and corn bins with open slats to admit air to dry the corn. Even the pigs have pigpens and pig houses.

Daddy builds cement walkways, (a rare feature on most farms) down through the center of the barn so you can feed animals on both sides. He also builds cement walkways from the house to the cellar, smoke house, chicken house, garage and barn. Farming is literally a dirty business, and keeping clean is a chore. Daddy's cement walkways and boot washing station near the house are a great improvement over muddy paths.

That the world is, is the mystical. —Ludwig Wittgenstein

Mystical experiences develop initially in the senses, and I respond to each spring as naturally as sun-warmed seed. Fragrances warm me like music and poetry, their silent sensations rushing through my body and soul. Each spring the ambrosial smell of the earth becomes progressively more powerful and pungent. I stand on the cistern, the feeling of sun on my face, aware of the onset of spring, knowing I will soon be able to run and play with the soil and grass caressing my bare feet.

I am the life of all beings.
I am the fragrance of the earth and the light of the fire;
—Bhagavada Gita, 7:9-11, based on Juan Mascaro, 1962

When we break the earth with a plow, or disk or harrow, the earth's sweet breath pours forth. When we mow alfalfa, timothy, or lespedeza, again the earth offers up her wonderful aromas. Inside the garage, where Daddy has his workshop, there is the smell of sawdust, and the clean aroma of linseed oil.

Each farm has a chicken coop, open at the top of the south side. These windows can be shielded with doors, which provide shade in the summer when opened from the top and shut out severe weather in winter. Each farm has a smokehouse for smoking meats, which doubles as a tool shed. Inside it smells of smoke, maple and honey.

Butchering is done in the late fall and early winter. It is a hard, dirty job, often taking two days. We go from one farm to the next throughout December and January. Everybody shares in the labor and the meat. Ronnie West and I love to eat cracklings (pieces of hog skin boiled in oil). They are without doubt filled with thousands of grams of cholesterol per bite. No one knows or cares. The meat has to be salted down, and you pray it doesn't get too warm. One fall it does, and Daddy loses it all. In disgust we bury the malodorous meat. It is one of the few times I see him defeated to the point of depression.

The Garden and Orchard

A split rail fence separates our yard from our two gardens. We rotate between them each year, letting one lie fallow. We are, for all practical purposes, self-sufficient. There is always plenty of milk and a plethora of eggs and chickens. Mother is devoted to gardening and to canning. I go into the garden early in the morning. It is a magical, secret world. At the age of sixteen, I raise one hundred different vegetables for a 4-H project. We win several awards at the county fair for our vegetable displays.

Grandmother Callahan often stays with us. She is especially adept at wringing chickens' necks. It is not a pretty sight. There is a knack to it. You take the chicken by the head and, by twirling it, divest it of its head. The headless body then flips, flops and flails busily about for a minute or two, to everyone's fixed attention and the curious consternation of the dogs. Then, in order to make the feathers easier to pull out, the chickens are dipped in scalding hot water, providing a most disagreeable odor, and the feathers plucked—an unpleasant task.

The fencerows on the back of our farm are filled with blackberry bushes, and we love to go blackberry picking. You can eat all you want and there is still plenty. Each summer Mother puts up fifty-two pints of blackberry jelly, so that each week throughout the year a fresh pint of blackberry jelly is placed on the kitchen table.

On the back porch of most farms you can find a slop bucket into which leftover jelly, scraps from the table or canning and cooking, even dish washing water, is poured, and around which farm boys occasionally stand and relieve themselves. This bucket is taken to the barn each morning and evening mixed with feed and given to the pigs. They gobble it down with gurgling, guttural grunts, devouring each meal as though it is their last. Life is short for pigs. As soon as they are fat enough—it's over.

We have a large strawberry patch twenty feet wide and more than a hundred feet long running the entire length of the garden. In the summer of 1955, we gather fifty gallons of strawberries that we sell to the grocer on the square in Mexico for fifty cents a gallon. Gooseberry bushes surround our house, and blackberry or gooseberry cobbler is a frequent dessert. With no awareness of cholesterol, I fill a bowl with blackberry or gooseberry cobbler and drown the entire contents in whole cream.

All around our house are lilac bushes with heart shaped leaves. I climb in amongst the branches inhaling their sweet fragrance. Mother says it's her favorite aroma, and it is mine as well. It is the scent from Heaven. There are also cherry, plum, pear and apple trees whose flowers are filled with busy, bustling bumblebees. Their low humming chant hangs consistently in the air. I sit in a cherry or plum tree eating its fruit, spitting the pits on the ground until I just can't eat any more. There are two pear trees, one Bartlett, the other delicious little sugar pears. Granddaddy Mundy's farm has a persimmon tree (the tree to my right on the cover of this book), and there are neighbors with peach trees. On sultry summer afternoons we joyously eat fresh hot peaches with sticky, thick juice running down our face, fingers and forearms. Sometimes for fun in the evening, we raid our own garden for watermelons.

Canning

Each farm has a cool underground root cellar where the canned goods are kept. Our cellar has a dinner bell on top used for calling everyone in for lunch. Each summer, our cellar fills with the produce from our garden. As soon as the garden starts generating vegetables, Grandmother Callahan comes to help Mother do the canning. By October our cellar is full of quart and pint jars of everything: tomatoes, corn, green beans, beets, beef (yes, beef), pickles, pickled peaches, plums and pears, apricot preserves,

12

blackberry and grape juice, and all sorts of jellies. Ann and I help, chopping up tomatoes, snapping green beans, or cutting corn off the cob. Mason jars are placed in a pressure cooker and boiled under pressure until they "pop" and no air is left inside. From one day to the next throughout the summer, our kitchen fills with the prodigious aroma of the fruit or vegetable being canned. Grandmother Callahan also makes soap from lye and fat drippings in flat pans.

Once a week or so you can watch a good old rip-roaring thunderstorm with corpulent gray and black clouds, lightning flashing, thunder roaring, cracking and crashing, leaves swinging and branches swaying, barreling its way across the prairie. We run to the cellar on blustery, tempestuous nights when heavy storms portend possible tornadoes. On the way, Mother grabs her stash of pictures of Ann and me. Daddy lights a kerosene lantern. He stands guard at the cellar door, now and then looking out to see. Is it safe to go back to the house? As long as he is there, everything feels safe. Years later, in the early '90s, a storm comes through and takes the roof off the barn. Sadly, the new farmer replaces our beautiful barn with a large metal structure.

The Animals

Every spring there is new birth. Inevitably, with so much birth, there is the mystery of death. I love the musty smell of earth and stone under our house, and I crawl through the cement blocks with a flashlight to watch a mother cat give birth to kittens. Elmer Kotsenburg stops by and he's talking to Daddy while sitting in his car. He starts to back up and runs over a kitten. Daddy has to ask him to please drive forward a little to finish the job. It is all an enigma, an amazing riddle, a miraculous puzzle—and I want to know more.

Cats live in the barn and are infrequent visitors to the house, coming in only when invited and then usually only as kittens. A pregnant mother cat comes crying to the door. Mother, Ann and I are sitting on the couch while Mother reads a book about ponies. Ann puts the cat in her lap, and she almost immediately starts having kittens. Mother puts the cat on a towel and as each kitten is born, we name it after one of the ponies. We have cats, cats and more cats—big cats, little cats, cats in the hayloft, cats in the smokehouse. At one time we total eighteen cats.

We have cocker spaniels, Candy and Knight and collies, Lady and Butch. Candy likes to chase cars on the gravel road out front and she is hit and killed. Ann goes out to the road and cries, "Get up, Candy! Please, Candy! Oh, please, Candy! Get up, Candy!" Lady lies with her head in my lap, periodically turning her velvet eyes upward into my face, wagging her long tail and looking at me as though there is some question she wants to ask. I'm hoeing the garden when a group of boy scouts come by on a hike. Lady starts to run after them. When I call her name, they start calling her name so she will go to them. Despite my calls, there are more of them and she follows them until they disappear. Lady never comes home again. Later a boy scout from the Methodist church in Mexico tells me she followed them all the way back to town where they piled into their cars and left her standing in a church parking lot. This does not endear the Methodists or the boy scouts to me.

I have a billy goat and Ann has a nanny goat. By jumping on boxes and barrels, the goats go up and walk around on top of the chicken coop and we go up and joyously join them. I playfully butt heads with Billy and we play who can push whom backwards while I hold on to his horns. We have big sheep with curly black hair (not wool) that is used in making women's coats. The sheep birth huge lambs that often have to be pulled. Daddy holds the sheep while Mother does the pulling, because her hands are smaller and she can reach inside.

Taking care of the animals requires over an hour of chores each morning and an hour and a half or more each day after school. Daddy milks in the morning. It's my job after school. It's true for all farm boys. As Daddy or I milk, we practice shooting milk into the cats' mouths. The cats stand on their back legs batting at the milk with their front paws. The barnyard is full of swallows that swoop and dive and fly around looking for flying insects in the early evening. Barn swallows make mud dauber-type nests on rafters inside the barn. I stand in the barnyard, looking at the pasture and woods out to the east and call "pig, pig, pig, pig" or "su cow, su cow, su cow." The pigs come a'grunting and the cows come a'running, cowbells dangling, clicking and clanging, their full udders sloppily swinging and swaying.

Cows love to be caressed on the head. They line up at the back of the barn door steps, each nuzzling and snorting up, cold air erupting from their nostrils, each looking for a chance to be petted. We have a milk cow whom, because of her creamy red color we name Strawberry. Like lady, she too has big, sad, inquisitive eyes. Eyes are the windows of the soul and there are souls in there. The cow is a poem of empathy; one reads pity in the gentle animal. The milk is processed in the upper part of the cellar through a hand-driven separator which, by spinning, discharges the cream from the milk. Mother churns butter from cream with a hand churn inside a large glass jar. Just by sloshing, splashing, and splattering around, cream magically turns into butter. Mother also makes cottage cheese, and Daddy is a great lover of buttermilk. As there is always too much for a family of four, the extra milk is given to the many cats or poured into the slop bucket and given to the pigs.

One of the more grueling jobs is the castration of the male pigs. Jody Mongler is best at it. He brings along a whetstone to sharpen his pocket-knife. It just takes a couple of minutes per pig. My job, or Clifford Mongler's job, or any boy's job, is to hold the screaming piglet up by his two front legs, our knees tenaciously holding on to the sides while Jody, or Daddy, or another farmer performs the operation. Some antiseptic is then poured on the poor pig. Once removed, these testicles called Rocky Mountain Oysters are served for dinner. All the animals are "free range:" they wander about as they please. There is a saying, "Pigs follow cattle, and chickens follow after pigs." Each roots around looking for nourishment in the other's manure.

Granddaddy Almer and Grandmother Bessie Mundy

After Mother comes into the Mundy family she starts calling Granddaddy Mundy, "Daddy Mundy" and it sticks for everyone. Daddy Mundy has a full head of fine hair as white as an Easter rabbit. Although he owns our ancestral farm, Daddy Mundy lives on Love Street in Mexico with grandmother Bessie. He works as a policeman. He "enjoys," I think, carrying a gun, and he likes to tell stories of how you are supposed to drive the police car in order to capture bad guys. It is like walking through Heaven to walk through Grandmother Mundy's garden filled with snapdragons, hollyhocks and sunflowers. I love her creamed pearl onions. It seems she's frequently in the hospital undergoing some kind of operation.

Uncle Estel and Aunt Jessie

Uncle Estel and Aunt Jessie live a half mile north from our house, up the road to Molino, on their own forty-acre farm. Jessie is one of Daddy Mundy's seven sisters. As Uncle Estel and Aunt Jessie have never had any children, Ann and I become their surrogate grandchildren. Uncle Estel has a wonderful simple love for Ann and me. A small slim man, he always

15

wears blue shirts, blue overalls, and a golden straw hat. He carries a gold pocket watch with a blue and white face. Aunt Jessie never cuts her long dark hair, which she keeps in a braid wrapped around her head. At night when she lets it down, it falls all the way to the back of her knees.

Uncle Estel and Aunt Jessie live a simple life, hardly ever venturing off their forty acres. Uncle Estel never pays income tax in his entire life. He is not trying to cheat the government. Social security numbers were not always given out at birth. They were given to you when you got your first job and thus began paying taxes. Uncle Estel never had a first job. He never worked for anyone, except as a day laborer where he was paid in cash. He also never earned more than $600 in any one year.

Uncle Estel and Aunt Jessie are largely self-sufficient and truly love the land they live on. They have a generous garden in which they spend time every day that weather permits. Their root cellar fills each summer and there are always eggs, chickens and plenty of milk, ham and potatoes. Though he no doubt has his challenges, Uncle Estel is, from my perspective, a free man. He chews cinnamon sticks and, in imitation of him, I get into the habit. He can stand all day talking to you, moving a stick of cinnamon from one side of his mouth to the other, while jingling change in his pocket. He loves witticisms and cowboy stories. Whenever I go to their house, we go out to the barn where he shares his secret stash of butterscotch and chocolate chips, hidden in a horse-drawn corn planter.

Uncle Estel and Aunt Jessie's closets are as full as Fibber Magee's. Everything, however, is neatly arranged. Topping off the list is Uncle Estel's metal train set from the nineteenth century. His tool sheds are filled with remarkable, well-kept tools. No newspaper, magazine or postcard is ever thrown away, postcards being the closest thing to e-mail in the early part of the twentieth century. The cards from various relatives, kept in shoeboxes and filed in chronological order, make for interesting viewing and reading.

When we get television in 1956, Uncle Estel comes up to our house, goes into the living room, turns around a straight-backed chair, casts his arms across the back, and watches in fixed amazement. He will never own a television. He doesn't have electricity. He is always at our house on Christmas morning, usually walking the half-mile in the dark. Uncle Estel and I are somehow connected. We take care of each other.

16

One of the most difficult parts of Uncle Estel's life is the unending job of trimming the hedge that surrounds his home and barnyard. Much of the work has to be done on a stepladder. He no sooner gets the job done than it's time to start over. Aunt Jessie's biggest job is ironing with heavy metal flatirons she heats on the wood-burning stove in her kitchen.

Their toilet is an outhouse, out near the chicken coop. The chickens take their pickings from the droppings in the bottom of the privy. Ann is afraid to use their toilet for fear that the chickens will peck her bottom. Ecologically, it all works out pretty well. For toilet paper there is a Sears catalogue from which we tear pages or, better yet, soft, recently shelled corncobs. The Sears catalogue makes for interesting reading while waiting to do one's business.

Uncle Estel is forever saying, "Why don't you come up and spend a week some day?" Sometimes I do stay, and they treat me like royalty. For entertainment each evening, we sit in rocking chairs on the front porch and watch cars go by. The porch is the only reward they need after a long summer's day. Whenever a car passes, Uncle Estel or Aunt Jessie has a comment. "Jennings Talley is late getting home. He'll have to do his chores in the dark."

At bedtime Uncle Estel carefully takes off his socks, ritualistically folding each one and flattening it out. He then dons a sleep shirt, a night cap and earmuffs before going to bed with a western novel. Uncle Estel and Aunt Jessie sleep in a Murphy bed that folds up against the wall in their living room revealing a mirror hiding underneath.

Their kerosene lamps give off a sweet smell and cast dancing shadows on the walls. For heat there is a coal-burning stove in their combination living room/bedroom. Uncle Estel lifts the lid to drop in coal. I stare in at the red-hot glowing embers. As he pours in more coal, we watch the sparks jump like little rockets, and a pan of water on top of the stove pops and hisses and gives life to their house. Furnaces today are quietly hidden away in the basement. Their stove stood in the very heart of their home.

Uncle Estel and Aunt Jessie live just as great-grandfather Jonathan Mundy and his family did. An hour or so after dark you go to bed and you're awake before dawn. Morning birds serve as your alarm clock. For entertainment in the evening, they have themselves, cards, board games, crocheting, knitting, reading, and Great-grandmother Jenny playing a small accordion known as a concertina. Mostly, they like to sit on the porch and watch cars go by. Almost everyone honks a knowing hello.

When Uncle Estel gets sick, Daddy, Paul West and other farmers each take turns plowing, disking, planting, cultivating and harvesting his crops for him. No one expects any payment or reward. I hear Daddy, Paul West and Red Coose talking about how they are going to take care of things for him. Farmers just help farmers. Men on tractors can take care of his forty-acre horse farm in short order. Maybe he'll be well enough to harvest the corn himself in the fall. Uncle Estel might, on a good day, shuck a hundred bushels of corn, throwing each ear into a wagon. His horses walk slowly along the side. No one holds the reins. When Uncle Estel tells them to "giddy-up," they move forward. When he says "whoa," they stop. His horses are his familiars, and he talks to them throughout the day. I assume that they understand everything he says. It *seems* like they do.

One day when he was still fairly young, a model-A Ford, with curtains drawn, pulled up to Uncle Estel's house. Uncle Estel got his gun, and walking out on the porch was instantly shot in the chest. No one knows what happened, and Uncle Estel refused to talk about it. The bullet lodged in his chest and eventually contributed to lung disease and his death at the age of seventy-six.

Our farm and Daddy Mundy's farm still exist, though many of the outhouses are now gone. Many of the other small farms are now completely gone. Except for one lonesome tree in the corner of the field, there is no indication that Uncle Estel's farm ever existed. It's also true for the Talleys who lived up the road, and Ella Baker's farm. All around, the little farms have vanished and the land is now part of some megalithic farmstead. There is now more open space on which nobody walks. Twice a year, perhaps, a huge air-conditioned tractor with radio or CD blaring out some country music or rap tune quickly passes over these backfields. In the fall colossal corn-picking combines slither across these fields like monstrous dinosaurs gobbling up the crops, harvesting and shelling 25,000 bushels of corn in a single day. On the positive side, deer, coyotes and wild turkeys have returned to mid-Missouri. Hunting is better than when I was a kid. Back country roads are now often the scene of mishaps between animals and the swift moving cars and trucks that traverse these country roads.

Aunt Bertha

Next in time, attention and geography (to Uncle Estel and Aunt Jessie), there is Aunt Bertha, a small, wonderful, feisty woman with large protruding ears. She and Aunt Jessie are buddies and usually go shopping in Mexico together. Bertha is the last of the Mundy girls to marry. She marries Forest Weaver, a tall man with deep-set eyes and an enchanting smell of garlic. Bertha does not marry Forest till she is in her mid-forties. She asks her oldest sister, Ollie if she might invite recently widowed Forest, and the pastor from Mt. Zion Baptist Church, for dinner to Ollie's house on Sunday afternoon. After dinner, to everyone's surprise, including even Forest it seems, she announces that she and Forest are to marry. That is what the preacher is there for. So, they are married.

Bertha fancies herself an artist and does her works of art on brown paper bags. Bertha, Jessie and a few other local ladies publish *The Molino Enterprise*, a newsletter filled with jokes about each other, funny sayings and local gossip. Their motto is, "If the shoe don't fit, don't wear it." Each edition is copied by hand in pencil on tablet paper and passed from one to the other. For the privilege of reading the paper you have to pay two cents.

Parking meters in Mexico are a penny for twelve minutes, five cents for an hour and ten cents for two hours. With Bertha driving, she and Jessie go into town to shop. When they get back to the car, rather than taking off for home, Bertha just sits there. When Jessie asks her why they are not leaving, Bertha points out that they still have time left on the meter.

Aunt Bertha reads the Bible through nine times and is working on her tenth reading when she dies, at the age of ninety-six. She insisted she be buried on the left side of Forest. His first wife, Daisy, is buried on the right. To bury her on the left of Forest would mean killing a Catalpa tree, and there is much debate. After her death, the church keeps the tree and buries Bertha to the right of Daisy.

That's the farm and the family. I love them all.

Mark Twain—A First Hero

On tourist maps of Missouri, the area north and east of Molino is marked as Huckleberry Finland. A favorite outing as a child is to take visitors to nearby Florida, Missouri, to see the log cabin where Samuel Clemens was born. It sat out in the open until, in 1960, a massive wing-shaped structure was built to house the cabin and a museum. Still later, a larger man-made lake is built, creating what is not surprisingly known as Mark Twain Lake. *The Adventures of Tom Sawyer* and *Huckleberry Finn* are among the earliest stories I read and the song of Tom Sawyer's soul still beats in my heart. Like Mark Twain, my father and my boyhood friends, I spend as much time as I can outdoors hunting in the woods, working in the fields, walking in the pastures.

It is through some of these same woods hiked by Samuel Clemens that Clifford Mongler, Ronnie West and I go hiking and horseback riding, looking for arrowheads, buzzards' roosts, hollow trees, underground caves and similar enchanting places. As Mark Twain expressed it, "There comes a time in every rightly constructed boy's life when he has a raging desire to go somewhere and dig for hidden treasure." Mark Twain was a bit of a mystic. He had a *keen* eye for everything. As he said, "A soap bubble is the most beautiful thing and the most exquisite, in nature." In a similar way I am transfixed watching rainbow colors in oil pools under the tractor.

Mark Twain was clearly a character, and therefore an easy caricature. He was also a curmudgeon and a clown, and for this I love him. In *Letters to Earth,* Mark Twain also proves himself a splendid theologian. His de-mythologizing of Adam and Eve bears interesting similarity to that of *A Course in Miracles.* Just as Hannibal, Missouri, and life on the Mississippi never left Mark Twain, so Mexico, Missouri and life on the farm will never leave me.

CHAPTER 2

The Extraordinarily Ordinary

Mystical Moments of Childhood

*Listen, perhaps you catch a hint of an ancient state not quite forgotten;
dim, perhaps and yet not altogether unfamiliar, like a song whose name is
long forgotten, and the circumstance in which you heard it completely
unremembered. Not the whole song has stayed with you, but just a little wisp
of melody, attached not to a person or a place or anything in particular.
But you remember, from just this little part, how lovely was the song, how
wonderful the setting where you heard it, and how you loved those who were
there and listened with you.* —ACIM, T-21.I.6: 1-3

Philosopher William James, father of the psychology of religion, describes in his classic text *The Varieties of Religious Experience* four characteristics of a mystical experience:

1. **Ineffability**—the experience defies description.

2. **A noetic** quality—we come *to know* something with a depth of truth not normally accessible.

3. **Transience**—the experience is fleeting and cannot be sustained.

4. **Passivity**—our own will is suspended and a higher power is in control.

The difficulty with the mystical is being able to talk about it at all.

*Words are but symbols of symbols.
They are thus twice removed from reality.*

—ACIM, M-21.1:9-10.

The Extraordinarily Ordinary

I have a friend, Tom Baker, an ex-priest, now a therapist and *Course in Miracles* leader in Virginia Beach, Virginia, who tells a story from the time when he was a young priest. There was a special event where Catholic dignitaries had gathered. A type of Catholic bishop known as an Ordinary, Tom and another young priest are sitting at the altar during the religious ceremony. Suddenly the Ordinary produces a prodigious amount of gas and a suspicious odor fills the altar area. When an opportune moment presents itself, the other young priest leans over to Tom and observes that something rather extraordinary has come out of the ordinary!

Dolores gets three weeks off from work each year, and one of them was the last week of July 1998. Dorothy Spelman, a member of our church in New York City, and her husband, Larry, have a home on the beach at Fire Island and they were going to be gone for a few days, so they offered us their house. Dolores, a beach lover, said, "Say yes!" I did so, and we spent five rather remarkably ordinary days on the beach. I went for four days without shaving or wearing shoes, and I read two books. Sarah and I built sandcastles, flew kites, and played in the waves. Each day we hiked a couple of miles up and down the beach.

As the spider weaves its thread out of its own mouth, plays with it, and then withdraws it again into itself, so the eternal, unchangeable Lord, who is formless and attributeless, who is absolute knowledge, and absolute bliss, evolves the whole universe out of himself, plays with it, and again withdraws it into himself. —Srimad Bhagavatam, XI. Iii

Our first day on the beach I find a tennis ball bounding about in the ocean waves. I pick it up and begin a game of toss with Sarah. Then we play monkey in the middle with mommy as the monkey, then I was the monkey in the middle and then Sarah took her turn. After we exhausted this game, Sarah asked if she could throw the ball back into the ocean. We said yes, and she no sooner threw the ball back than she looked at the ocean and playfully yelled, "I want my ball back!"

After three or four waves the ocean gave the ball back. This began a whole new game called *I Want My Ball Back*. Sarah threw the ball into the ocean and yelled, "I want my ball back!" And the ocean played with her, eventually returning her ball. This led to another game. We would throw the ball into the ocean and, at the same time yell out the number of waves it would take for the ball to come back. Depending on how far we threw it, would it be three waves, or four, or five or six, or maybe only two. And who could retrieve the ball first by splashing into the ocean to get it? We played this game well over a hundred throws, all the while walking a mile or more along the beach.

With seagulls calling and circling above, with the air filled with a salty tang, with sun and sand and fun, with our joyous involvement in play, it occurred to me how rather wonderfully ordinary this game was. It didn't involve much competition. It was active and exciting. We were all laughing. The crashing of the waves, the giggling, the bright sunshine, competing to see who could get to the ball first, was pure fun. The whole experience was elementary, wonderful, and completely ordinary. Nothing was more important than this moment, this rare and precious moment together with family. If Dolores and I had taken this vacation by ourselves, we would no doubt not have built any sandcastles or played "I Want My Ball Back!" We would, however, have taken several walks along the beach. On the last day there, Sarah and I took a final walk on the beach. She threw the ball in saying nothing. The ocean kept it, and we watched, as more than twenty waves came and went, and came and went again carrying the ball away.

> . . . *There is a Child in you, who seeks His Father's house, and knows that He is alien here. This childhood is eternal, with an innocence that will endure forever. Where this Child shall go is holy ground. It is His holiness that lights up Heaven, and that brings to earth the pure reflection of the light above, wherein are earth and Heaven joined as one. It is this Child in you your Father knows as His Own Son. It is this Child Who knows His Father. He desires to go home so deeply, so unceasingly, His voice cries unto you to let Him rest a while. He does not ask for more than just a few instants of respite; just an interval in which He can return to breathe again the holy air that fills His Father's house. —ACIM, W-182.4: 3-6:5:1-4*

Infancy—Innocence—The Cradle

> *Every child is a born mystic, Then we draw him toward the school and the education and the serpent. The serpent is the civilization, the culture, the conditioning.* —Osho, *Osho on Zen*, Renaissance Books, p. 43.

Returning to Heaven requires innocence. Thus Jesus says: "Bring the little children to me and forbid them not, for of such is the Kingdom of Heaven." If you believe in reincarnation, you may well agree that we each carry a bag of karmic predisposition. I've come to believe, as a result of my death experience, that the death/birth cycle is a purification process. While children are not wholly innocent, we all recognize that there exists within the child a 'relative' innocence. The young child cannot remember any past and there cannot as yet be any guilt. The ego, however, is developing. Defenses soon appear in more definite forms than crying—soon there will be lying.

There are moments that we can remember, if we choose, when we were innocent. The further we go into eternity, the less there is of this world, and the more innocence there is. Eternity is purely innocent. These moments remain for anyone who has ever dreamed a happy dream, who has been truly happy, felt completely whole and safe, and able to rest in the arms of God. It can happen any day. It happened on the farm in Missouri.

Can you remember times in the cradle? I don't mean with great clarity, just a soft and gentle laying down of the head, on clean flannel blankets with a satin strip sewn along the edge. Mother and Daddy or other adults are talking in the background; their words are of no particular importance—just a strong, gentle reminder of their presence.

When I receive a new toy I cherish it, take it to bed and hold it. Born before plastic became popular, it is not unusual to take a tin toy to bed. It doesn't matter that the edges are hard. What matters is the color and the fantasy with which I might hold a tin water pump with colorful images of Jack and Jill going up the hill and then plumping, tumbling, down together. I have a red and yellow tin chicken with a crank. She clucks and lays wood and marble eggs. My life is filled with adventure and fantasy, silliness, laughter, curiosity and play—simmering with fun, ready to bubble up. I'm part of something bigger. I merge with whatever immediate experience brings.

As water becomes one with water, fire with fire, and air with air, so the mind becomes one with the infinite Mind and thus attains Freedom.
—Maitri Upanishad, VI.24.

There are mystical pieces of childhood for all of us—if we choose to remember when we were completely cared for and free, moments when colors took on brilliance, when every "thing" had its mesmerizing charm. Children are as happy to play with pots and pans as they are with expensive toys. As a child, for me everything is mystically, magically, teeming with life. I'm sitting alone in a load of creek gravel beside the roadway of my grandfather's farm. Creek gravel comes from riverbeds and is made up of stone, sand and mussel shells washed clean and smooth by the stream. This intrigues me. I'm transported into these stones. I am completely whole. I am completely taken care of. Soon Mother comes looking for me. She has only love in her heart for me.

Mother is the name for God in the hearts and lips of children.
—Jewish saying

Mother's oldest sister, Marie, has no children, and it is fun to stay with Aunt Marie a few days each summer in Kirksville. Aunt Marie has a collection of salt and pepper shakers that she keeps in a big tin box under her bed. Ann and I are delighted to get out the salt and pepper shakers and play with them. No other toys are needed, though I always carry my black cloth doll, Joe. Aunt Marie's salt and pepper shakers, shaped like a

24

Dutch boy and girl, or penguins, or houses, have personalities and life in them, though they lack their salt and pepper.

Imagination disposes of everything: it creates beauty, justice, and happiness, which are everything in the world. —Blaise Pascal

Jacques Lusseyran

You say, "I see color." Do you see it as you did when you were a child? Colors are fascinating for me. Even people have different colors. Our neighbors, the Wests, for example, are for some reason blue and yellow. I listen to Andre Gregory's reading of *And There Is Light*, the autobiography of Frenchman Jacques Lusseyran. At the age of seven, while running in a schoolroom, Jacques crashed into the corner of a desk, driving shards of glass from his spectacles into his eyes, blinding him.

Jacques was incredibly bright. He learned several languages, and knowing no fear, became a leader of the French resistance during the Nazi occupation. Captured and taken to Buchenwald concentration camp, he was one of its few survivors. His is an incredible story of a truly mystical man, who lived under the most miserable of human conditions. Yet, he knew nothing other than happiness because he knew nothing other than God.

Lusseyran's description of color is remarkable. He was blind, yet he could see magnificent colors which he described as a great miracle of light. Nothing throughout his life was as precious to him as his experience of light by which he could see—not the way you and I do. Yet, he could see. Each person vibrated with different colored lights in front of him, as he smelled, listened to, and received intimations from that person.

After he went blind, he had an experience of enlightenment that he described as *Radiance.*

Of the experience he says:

I felt indescribable relief and happiness so great it almost made me laugh. Confidence grabbed me as though a prayer had been answered. I found light and joy in the same moment. And I can say, without hesitation, that from that time on light and joy have never been separated in my experience. I either have or lose them together. I saw light and went on seeing it though I was blind. I was not the light itself but was bathed in it. I could feel light rising, spreading, resting on objects and giving them form. Withdrawing or diminishing is what I mean, for the opposite of light is never present.

For every waking hour and even in my dreams I lived in a stream of light. I saw the whole world in light, existing through it and because of it. All the col-

ors of the rainbow also survived. For me, the child who loved to draw and paint colors, this makes for a celebration so unexpected that I spent hours playing with them. Light throws its color on things and on people. This gives me an impression of them as definite as any impression created by a face.

Before his blindness, Lusseyran says he loved to play with colored blocks, diving into the colors as one would into water. Everything had its color vibration, including moods and feelings. While in the concentration camp he became a counselor to many because of his great serenity and empathy.

Just for the Fun of it: Running—Playing—Dancing

Zen master Eihei Dogen when asked, "What is the awakened mind?" replied, "The mind that is intimate with all things." Running, playing, and dancing are fine activities in and of themselves. The more primitive the religion the more dancing there is—around bonfires, at weddings, at harvest time, and just dancing for the sake of dancing. When truly present, there is no dancer; there is just the dance.

Mother and Daddy are active square dancers. In the summer just before baling hay, whatever bales were left from the previous summer become benches around card tables; the space opened in the middle of the hayloft. They sweep it down, fix broken boards and hold an old-fashioned barn dance. Mother does square dance calling for 4-H, school and church parties. It's hard to square dance and not smile at the same time. Even the old people sitting around watching are all smiles.

Dolores and I are on one of our late afternoon walks, and we stop to watch Chelsea, a four-year-old neighbor girl, prancing around in her back yard as carefree as a colt in a pasture. It is springtime, and she is free to run to her heart's content. She runs to look at a daffodil, and then she flops down and watches some birds. She jumps up and runs and stops and looks out into space—just looking. Do you not remember such moments?

Looking

To see the world in a grain of sand and Heaven in a wildflower, hold infinity in the palm of your hand and eternity in an hour.
—William Blake

You can see so immediately into things on the farm, the details of a flower, the intricacies of an anthill, the cracks in snow and ice. Snow brings its dazzling mystical silence all around. One winter there is a generous snowstorm followed by an ice storm. Every drop of rain freezes fast to whatever it lands on. The back yard is a magical forest with ice-encrusted snow the brightness of burnished silver. Icicles on every branch and twig shimmer with the sheen of diamonds. The whole world is a glitter of precious jewels; every tree and bush a chandelier of cut glass. Ann, Mother and I dance around breaking ice off low hanging tree limbs. In the same way, Sarah and I joyously dance on and destroy the sandcastle we constructed at the beach.

While vacationing on Fire Island in '98, I read Leo Tolstoy's *Childhood, Boyhood, and Youth.* I love Tolstoy because of his great descriptions, as in this one sentence:

The chatter of the peasants, the tramp of the horses and the creaking of the carts, the merry whistle of quail, the hum of insects hovering in the air in motionless swarms, the smell of wormwood, straw and horse's sweat, the thousand different lights and shadows with which the burning sun flooded the light yellow stubble, the dark blue of the distant forest and the pale lilac of the clouds, the white gossamer threads which floated in the air or lay stretched across the stubble, all these things I saw, heard and felt.
—Childhood, Boyhood, and Youth (page 33)

And on the farm in Missouri, all these things I saw and heard and felt and now remember.

CHAPTER 3

Boyhood and Youth

1945-1947—Age Two—Four

1945 is a busy year for birth and death in the Mundy family. My sister Ann is born on February 24th. With a farm, an infant, and a small child Mother has her hands full. Still, she loves every minute of it. Daddy and Mamma are making their dream of independent living come true. Mother's father Carl dies on November 23rd and my great-grand parents, Jonathan and Jenny Mundy die at Christmas time. Jonathan could not attend the burial of Jenny on December 23. When the family returned from Jenny's burial, Jonathan was dead. He was ninety-one, she, eighty-five.

Medical Intuitive Carolyn Myss says we remember our wounds best of all. I'm four and Ann is three. We're both on the back of our pony Billy. Suddenly the saddle slips and we turn over and tumble upside-down under the pony's hooves. The pony is frightened and prances impatiently. Ann and I are temporarily terrified, as are Mother and Daddy. We are not seriously hurt. Yet, it is so horrifying that a permanent memory trace is laid down. Afterwards, Daddy pulls the cinch up extra tight.

We go into town to see President Harry Truman standing on the back of a train, campaigning on one of his "whistle stops" across the United States. Ann and I are waving small American flags. After the train pulls out of Mexico, we're climbing up an embankment on our way back to our Studebaker (a car that looks as if it could go either way). Daddy Mundy has a Lark Studebaker. Daddy has a Hawk Studebaker. Aunt Cora has a Studebaker. It's the family car. I put the stick on my flag into the hillside for support. It breaks. I begin to cry.

1948-1949—Ages Five and Six

I'm five and standing behind Mother. She is on her knees tracing the outline of a picture with the page of a book pressed up against the window on the second floor of our house. We are in a yet-unfinished room which will later become my bedroom. She is going to all this trouble so I will have something to color in school. It's my first visit to Sneed School. Next year I'll begin the first grade. Mother is a whiz at teaching nursery rhymes.

She knows them all and repeats them often. Ann and I soon memorize *Little Jack Horner, Jack and Jill, The Owl and the Pussycat* (I can still recite it.), and all the many others. Mother also reads book after book after book including all the Bible stories to us. I especially enjoy the golden books, *Johnny and the Monarch,* and *The Little Engine That Could.* It becomes an encouraging motto: "I think I can, I think I can, I think I can." Though she is incredibly busy, Mother finds time for reading for herself. At Christmas 1948 we go to Sneed School for the annual Christmas party and I'm invited to come sit on Santa's lap while everyone watches. He asks me if I've been a good boy and I tell him that I have. However, I add, the same cannot be said for Ann. Everyone laughs and I'm embarrassed.

1950–1951—Ages Seven and Eight

I resolve that beginning on January 1, 1950, from then on I will be perfect. We don't stay up until midnight on December 31, 1949. Still, I want to celebrate. I have a little bomb-like dart in which you insert one cap from a cap pistol. When Daddy starts down the stairs on January 1st, I throw the dart and yell, "Happy New Year!" It scares him and he scolds me.

Ann and I catch the measles near the end of my second year in school, and I'm disappointed that I'm going to miss the dollar you get, at the end of the year, for perfect attendance. The measles go to my eyes, and I stand in front of a mirror in the morning and literally pull my encrusted eyelids apart. The good thing about the measles is the warmth of Mother's care.

1952—Age Nine

Nine is innocent. Nine is brilliant. —Jerry Lewis

In a deep dream I find myself falling off the side of a huge round orange-red sphere that I identify as the earth. The earth is getting smaller as I become bigger until I can hardly hold on. I am afraid that I am going to slip off into emptiness. I get out of this situation by gaining control of my vocal cords and screaming. My screams bring Mother and Daddy running into my bedroom. I awake, in a cold sweat, unable to explain what has happened. Twenty-four years later I will go through something similar in my death experience. I come back from that experience also by regaining control of my vocal cords and screaming. The words "person" and "personality" come from the Etruscan, *per sona*, "through sound." It refers to the masks that had built-in megaphones that players wore in the dramas. Language is a tool for bringing the world into existence. What is the first thing that a baby does when it comes into the world? What is its first defense? Is it not a strike back through sound, through crying? Through sound we regain our persona, our mask, our personality, our defenses.

I have my first encounter with anesthesia when my tonsils are removed. I'm wheeled in under bright lights. As the ether takes effect, I watch blue and white lights, balls and stars as I am hurled through space. It is all perfectly clear. There is something familiar about this experience. Coming to, I am horribly sick from the ether.

While visiting Aunt Marie in Kirksville, I am given the privilege of going to the movies by myself for the first time. I go to see Gene Kelly in *Singin' in the Rain.* When I come out of the theater, it starts to rain just like in the movie, so I start singing and dancing down the street swinging on the parking meters, pretending they are lampposts. I am on my way to Woolworth's to buy some watercolors. The rain stops, the sun breaks through, and as I skip down the wet sidewalk and cross the rain-soaked streets, a rainbow arches itself over the town. Everything is beautiful. Kirksville, like Mexico, is built on a square with the courthouse in the middle, a bit like the town in the movie *Back to the Future.* Skipping down this magical street on this beauteous day, I notice adults looking at me sternly. I understand, expeditiously, that one does not impishly and impulsively break into song and dance on the streets of Kirksville. I sober up.

Joe—My First Familiar

Joe is a black cloth doll made for me by Aunt Marie when I am four. Joe is named for the famous black boxer Joe Louis. He has big round eyes, fuzzy black hair and muscular arms and legs, like Popeye the sailor man. Joe and I will be inseparable for the next five years. (In fact, he is with me still.) He goes with me everywhere and we are the best of friends. He gets sick and receives get-well cards from my aunts and grandparents. Now, I'm nine and it is an early summer day and I'm sitting on the toy chest in my bedroom looking out the window watching Daddy working in the field. I am holding Joe. It has slowly become clear to me that Joe is not in fact alive, as I had thought. On some subtle level, it doesn't make any difference if he is *actually* alive or not. The spirit of Joe plays an important role in my life. Joe will always be with me whether his body or my body exists or not. Love clearly extends beyond the obvious.

> *There is a time when childhood should be passed and gone forever.*
> *Seek not to retain the toys of children. Put them all away, for you*
> *have need of them no more.* —ACIM, T-29.IX.6:1-3

I'm going to have to put Joe away and not play with him anymore. I am, after all, nine and it is embarrassing to still be playing with a doll. When Daddy comes in for lunch, I tell him that I want to go back out to the field with him that afternoon. From then on I work. Mother puts Joe in her cedar chest and I do not look at him again for thirty years. Mother gave Joe back to me as a Christmas present when I was forty. When I opened the box with Joe inside, I nearly broke into tears. Joe now sits on the bookshelf above my computer. Every now and then I look over and ask his advice, or say something like, "What do you think of that, Joe?" He says he thinks I'm lucky to have grown up and had so many adventures. I think he's lucky. He got to remain a kid and live in the wonderful world of imagination.

> *It is a pity that we cannot escape from life when we are young.*
> —Mark Twain

Segregation

Missouri of the forties and fifties is racially segregated. Audrain County is known as "Little Dixie." I grow up accepting segregation as part of life. It's not that I like it or approve of it. I am, however, just a kid, and it's the way things are. There are separate grade schools, segregated churches, separate toilets and drinking fountains at the country fair. There is a separate entrance for blacks at the Liberty Theater. White people go in the front. Black people go in a side door. Black people can only sit in the upper right part of the balcony with a barrier separating the two sides of the theater. If you're a black person who can't climb stairs, you cannot go to the movies. Having grown up loving a black doll gives me a different outlook and attitude toward my black brothers and sisters.

When there is extra work to be done on the farm, Daddy and I go into town early in the morning to the jail, where we get African American prisoners released in Daddy's custody. If no prisoners are available, we go to a part of Mexico called "niggertown." We walk around knocking on doors, or wake up men who are sleeping in cars and take them out to the farm for the day.

Elementary schools are segregated. High school is not. When I go out for track, I am pleased with the goodhearted bantering and camaraderie that develops with black friends on the track team. I am, for a time, the only white boy to run in the 220, and I thoroughly enjoy this fact.

I announce to Mother and Daddy that I no longer want to share a room with Ann. So they fix up the other upstairs room as my bedroom. The floor is covered with red and black checkered linoleum tiles like a big checkerboard. Only one window looks out to the west, out past the catalpa trees. Though our farm sits on top of a hill, the land to the west is as level as any land you'll ever see. The catalpa trees have big heart-shaped leaves and grow long spindly beans. There is often a lilac cast to the sunsets; at other times the sunsets are so brilliant it looks like the sky is on fire. I take pride in my room, decorating it with a map of the world, a map of the United States, a picture of Jesus entitled "The Savior," and a goose neck lamp for my desk. There is a place for everything and everything is in its place. Here I go alone to read, to listen to LPs and to study. I lie in bed and memorize the state capitals, the multiplication table and the presidents of the United States.

Playing Church

While attending a Baptist children's camp, I have an overwhelming experience and I start crying after watching a film designed to convert us to become Christians. With the support of the inspirational film and the aid of ministers at the camp, I dedicate my life to Christ. The ministers are thrilled and take me aside for counseling. What does it mean to dedicate one's life to Christ? I'll need to rededicate my life to Christ again and again.

I still have the worship bulletin from the Christian Church in Mexico from July 20, 1952, the day I was baptized. I think that after you are baptized, you are perfect and I get to make up for my failure at perfection back on January 1, 1950. I try rather mightily to be perfect. It's a hard job. During the years when I am nine, ten and eleven, I hold regular church services for my family each Sunday, after our standard meal of fried chicken, corn-on-the-cob, and mashed potatoes with gravy—yummy. I make worship bulletins, read scripture, serve communion (grape juice) in little communion cups (liqueur glasses) and play a tin organ with a crank handle with the picture of a big church organ with a stained glass window on it. Along with Joe and other toys, the tin organ now sit on my bookshelf.

The organ still works just fine. Mine is a complete ministry and I am called upon to perform wedding services for Ann's dolls and funerals for baby rabbits, cats, birds and other creatures, which we bury in wooden cheese boxes.

CHAPTER 4

Gifts from My Parents

Self Reliance—Independence—Confidence

There is nothing that Mother and Daddy cannot do. Mother can hang wallpaper, upholster, paint, decorate and arrange flowers. She is a wonder at crafts and tries every medium—sculpture, painting, jewelry making, cutting patterns in copper and bronze with acid, and weaving. She is the quintessence of what a 4-H leader should be. 4-H stands for heart, hands, head and health, the equivalent of boy scouts and girl scouts for farm kids. Our club is The Molino Musketeers. Mother has a bunch of us boys gathered on the front steps of the house, showing us how to build birdhouses. I'm impressed that it is she and not one of our fathers who is helping us with woodworking. Over the years, Mother teaches more than thirty different 4-H projects. We are deeply involved in 4-H on a local, state and national level, exhibiting cornucopia vegetable displays at the 4-H fair, and going on expeditions with the club to Chicago and Washington, DC. Mother will receive numerous awards as a 4-H leader.

Daddy and I work a great deal together, and because we do, we develop a bond that inevitably occurs when you spend many hours laboring with someone to complete a task. If Daddy is going someplace he asks if I want to ride along and I almost always do. I enjoy being with him whatever we are doing. He is so tall and strong, mature and smart, and so competent and capable. I always feel comfortable in his presence. I am, after all, "his" son and Ann is proud to be "his" daughter. As with all farm boys, I am expected to be available to do whatever work I can. It seems we own every kind of farm animal there is. Daddy also experiments with a variety of crops.

Dawn on the Farm

Morning is when I am awake and there is a dawn in me.
—Henry David Thoreau

In February 2000, Mother has a second heart operation, and I return to Ann and Glenn's farm, to be with her. I awake at five-thirty. I look out the bedroom window to the west. There near the horizon is a silver daybreak moon. It is the biggest, brightest moon I think I've ever seen. The angle at which the morning sun is shining on the moon, and the fact that it is so near the horizon makes it look like a big bright spotlight. It's so clear I can see the details of the surface of the moon. I understand what it means to be moonstruck, and I sit for half an hour watching light creep back upon the earth.

A love for his native soil wholly mystical. He used to say that healthy feet can hear the very heart of Holy Earth. Up always before dawn, he liked to bathe his bare feet, walking about in the morning dew.
—A biographer writing about Sitting Bull

At dawn on the farm, you are greeted with bird song. I wonder if the birds have been off practicing their concert in the woods. At precisely that moment when dark turns to dawn—depending on the time of the year—birds gather around our house, greeting the day with their morning arias. Each bird responds to another in an attempt to sing more brilliantly than his neighbor. Dozens of birds begin to twitter and tweet and thus usher in the light. The Wren sings *tea-kettle, tea-kettle, tea-kettle.* The Bobolink sings, *Bob-o'-link, bob-o'-link, spink, spank, spink.* The Cardinal sings *purdy, purdy, purdy - whoit-whoit-whoit-whoit.* My favorite, the Red-wing Black Bird, also sings at dusk, hanging on the side of cattails down around the pond bank. They sing like a tinkling fountain, *o-ka-lee, o-ka-lee, o-ka-lee.*

Dawn is the sweetest time on earth. Morning frost makes grass look as though it's covered with the white shavings of coconut. We do the chores, then head for the fields, gassing up the tractors, with the smell of gasoline drifting into the sweet dew-filled morning air, often as the sun is coming up on the horizon. A point in the sun resonates with a point in my soul. Daddy tells me what I am supposed to do that day. I am to plow, disk or harrow a particular field. Maybe I'm to mow, cultivate or rotary hoe. I'm often left alone while Daddy goes into town to work. It's more fun when we work together, Daddy, Daddy Mundy, sometimes Mother and sometimes Ann. As Daddy works in town until 3:00, often it's just me. When we work on Daddy Mundy's farm, Mother brings lunch out to us in the pickup truck. We sit around in the shade enjoying her delicious sandwiches, fried chicken with blackberry, peach or gooseberry cobbler and gallons of sweet iced tea.

Daddy and I go into business together. He owns the tractors and supplies the gas. He has an excellent six-foot mower. It's a new invention that has lots of little knives instead of a big swinging blade. The summers I'm fifteen, sixteen, and seventeen, I mow, every two weeks, three ten-acre estates just outside of Mexico, for ten dollars per estate. Daddy gets half. It takes two full days. It's a forty-minute drive on the tractor down along Sunrise Christian Church Road. You go through a little valley and across a bridge right after the church where, for 4-H Sunday, I gave one of my first sermons on the 4-H motto "to make the best better."

Crops are rotated each year, plowing under different nutrients so as to not too quickly deplete the soil. When you plant soybeans in a field which last year was corn, corn grows up in the soybeans and you have to get the corn out before the combine comes through for the soybeans. Daddy hires Clifford and Ricky Mongler for fifty cents an hour to help me, and we walk through half-mile rows of soybeans cutting out corn stalks and weeds. You don't see farmers cultivating crops any more and you drive past soybean fields where you don't see any cornstalks or other weeds. It's all because of genetic engineering and spraying. Genetically engineered seeds can't come back up the next year because they are sterile. Monarch butterflies are now dying off by eating pollen from genetically modified corn which produces its own pesticide that bites back.

Spring is a busy time for plowing, disking, harrowing and planting. In summer we cultivate and combine wheat and bale honey colored straw. Straw has no food value. It makes, however, excellent bedding in the barn. Daddy terraces the ten-acre field next to our house. There he grows emerald green alfalfa. Thus, one massive ten-acre yard curves its way up the hill to our house. You can get at least three, and in a good year four, cuttings of hay from the alfalfa field. The bales have to be bucked (picked up and thrown up onto wagons). Freddie and Ronnie West, Clifford Mongler and I go from farm to farm helping in this task for five cents per bale. It's hot, dirty work. When you throw the bale up onto the wagon the loose hay falls down and sticks to your sweaty head, back and chest. By the end of the day our muscles are sore from all the lifting. After work we race to the pond, taking off our clothes on the way. If it's only us boys, underwear stays on the bank.

In the fall we harvest corn and soybeans. It is my job to drive the truck up to the combine to get the soybeans, and I sit in the back of the truck eating raw soybeans while I wait for the combine to fill again. The soybeans are taken to the Missouri Farmers Association plant in Mexico where they are ground like coffee. Much of this grinding is done in the evening, giving the whole town a most wonderful aroma—a little fuller and richer than peanut butter.

One of Daddy's credos is, "There is always work to do on the farm." I've adapted that motto to my life as a minister. "There is always work to do in the ministry." I have many clear memories of working with Daddy baling hay, cultivating corn, and cleaning tools in the garage. I loved his capriciously whimsical smile and his distinctive cough.

After he retires, Daddy spends many years in his workshop making fine furniture, including lots of doll furniture. My doll Joe now sits in one of Daddy's chairs. Daddy never just farms. During the winters when there is less farm work, he buys old farmhouses and refinishes them. He modernizes the houses, putting in electricity and plumbing. He then rents them out or sells them at a profit.

I am trying to help him plaster the ceiling in a house he is remodeling. It is a tough job making plaster stick to the ceiling; he is getting stressed with the plaster which keeps falling. In disgust he throws some plaster at the ceiling and says, "Damn!" It sticks. "Wait a minute," he says. He takes some more plaster and throws it at the ceiling again saying, "Damn!" It sticks. Now he grabs more and more plaster and keeps throwing it at the ceiling, saying, "Damn!" "Damn!" "Damn!" It works, and he is soon able to smooth out the ceiling.

Farmers are inevitably independent entrepreneurial types, and this self-sufficiency of spirit stays with me, making it frustrating trying to work in a church where ideas have to be run through the crunch and chew of committees. Daddy, Daddy Mundy and his father Jonathan before him were all entrepreneurs. If Daddy has a good idea—he just does it!

Though a dryer is added later, Mother prefers to hang clothes out to dry. I go searching for her and find her in the sunny breeze with white sheets fluttering and flapping all around her. She is wearing a white apron on top of a white dress, and the way the early morning sun is shining behind her; it looks like she is an angel. The clean sheets, blue jeans and shirts smell so good. I bury my face in the sheets inhaling their fresh aroma.

Our house does not have a bathroom, so Daddy adds on an extra room and puts the plumbing in himself. One winter morning I am standing by the oil stove in the living room, when the plaster ceiling falls. Daddy takes this as a sign that it is time to redo the whole house. He completely redoes every room in knotty pine, including built-in beds, dressers, closets and built-in wall-mounted wooden telephones upstairs and down.

The phones have a crank on the side for placing calls. We are on a party line. Our number is two short rings followed by a long ring. The West's are two longs and a short. Monglers are two longs. For people outside the party line you have to ring Mrs. William, the operator in Molino—that is just one long ring. Everybody on the line knows when the phone rings for someone else. It is Aunt Jessie's calling in life to keep track of the movement of others, and it is assumed that Aunt Jessie is listening. Daddy occasionally disconcerts her by asking her opinion on the topic at hand when he is on the line. Sometimes she just chimes in.

As Daddy's "gofer," I learn the name of every piece of pipe, electrical part and tool there is. "Go get me a 3/4 inch copper coupling." He works for a time in the laboratory at the A.P. Green Brick plant in Mexico, where he tests the quality of clay. He takes me with him on occasion. The plant contains huge, hellishly hot brick baking ovens. The flames are fierce, the smell intense and sterile. These bricks will themselves become the lining of furnaces.

Mother and Daddy are lovers of the outdoors, of nature and gardening. Mother knows the name of every tree, bush, flower, weed and insect. What she doesn't know she finds out. Mother instills a fascination and allure for nature in Ann and me. She joins and becomes president of Mexico's Garden Club.

Mother becomes a Deacon and an Elder in the church and when she is eighty-four they make her Elder Emeritus. Mother brings God into our house. She takes us to church, Sunday school and vacation Bible school. Daddy comes along for church socials and for mingling with neighboring farmers. Mother, Ann and I go to church every Sunday beginning at Mount Zion Baptist church in Molino. However, Mother's home church in Kirksville is the Christian Church (Disciples of Christ), so with time we switch to First Christian Church in Mexico. Sometimes go to both churches. We go to First Christian on Sunday mornings. We go to Vacation Bible School, youth meetings and Sunday evening sing-a-long services at Mt. Zion Baptist. I join the Royal Ambassadors for Christ, and we get pins for memorizing the Ten Commandments, the Twenty-third Psalm, the Be-atitudes, the names of the disciples and the books of the Bible.

Daddy prefers to spend his Sundays working or communing with the surrounding prairie. He keeps the pond on the back of our farm stocked with bass and the pond near the house stocked with catfish. The compost pile behind the chicken coop is filled with worms for bait and we sometimes catch buckets full of catfish. All around the ponds you find dragonflies, snakes and frogs. While walking on the bank of the bass pond, I nearly step on a moccasin. The moccasin strikes, leaving small holes in my combat boot. I kill the moccasin and take it home. We skin it and dry it and Mother makes a belt out of it for me. Daddy likes to go alone early on Sunday morning to the bass pond. His favorite motto is "My rod and my reel they comfort me." At least twice each year we go down to the Ozarks for some serious trout fishing.

Many men go fishing all of their lives without knowing
that it is not fish they are after. —Henry David Thoreau

Each evening birds and insects sing light operas in the fields and along the pond banks. There is the chickadee's "dee, dees," cicadas buzzing like carbonation, chirping crickets and the "ribbit, ribbit, ribbit" of the frogs at night, especially enchanting when they are mating in the spring. There is something restorative about these repeated refrains of nature like the certainty of dawn after dark and spring after winter.

Daddy and Mother are both horse lovers. The first gifts Daddy ever gave Mother were a horse and saddle. My horse, Flicka, named after Flicka in the movies, has a white mane that hangs down between his ears and along his long black neck, making him quite handsome. Ann's horse is larger and named Dinah. Dinah is all white with clear glassy eyes and a back so wide; it was easy to stand up on her.

Mother and Daddy share a love of antiques. The older and more unusual the object, the more fascinating it is. We frequent auctions, antique shows and junk piles with equal relish, often finding and fixing some ancient artifact. Daddy is a master carpenter and Mother is a master seamstress. There is little thought of buying clothes. Mother makes most of what we wear, including clothes for my doll, Joe, Ann's dolls, and later my niece Erin's dolls. And there is quilt after quilt after quilt, including the queen-size quilt that now hangs over the upstairs banister in our family room. It is all Mother's own design, with twenty-four large blocks, each with a different religious scene or symbol.

There are wonderful dinners of corn bread and navy beans, roast beef with potatoes and carrots and gravy, hominy cooked in heavy cream, fried breaded okra, chunky potato and leek soup, chocolate pudding, and chocolate cake with chocolate frosting and chocolate chips on top. Daddy can make dinner and dessert out of bread, butter and molasses. Our table is a cornucopia of nutrition and variety. Thanksgiving and Christmas dinners are wonderfully big Norman Rockwell-style events, with grandmother Callahan, grandmother Bessie and Daddy Mundy, Uncle Estel, Aunt Jessie and Aunt Bertha and Uncle Forest, Aunt Cora and Uncle Harry, and Aunt Sue and Uncle Sam all coming to our house. We fix a prodigiously big table by placing a four-by-eight board on top of our regular table. I peel potatoes and help clean the turkey. Aunt Cora brings delicious salsify (a white root vegetable) which tastes like oysters. Mother makes a pumpkin pie with my name spelled out on top with piecrust, and Daddy and I make homemade ice cream in a hand crank ice cream freezer. I get to do the stirring, turning, churning, churning, turning, stirring, and testing (tasting)—to see—is it ice cream yet?

Grandmother Bessie Mundy has cancer and is released from the hospital for Thanksgiving of 1953. I am down at the barn playing with the cats. When I see my grandparent's Studebaker, I come running in the back door of the house only to get a shock. There sits Grandmother Mundy with a mighty bandage wrapped over the side of her head where they have removed her cancerous eye. She is staring straight ahead in a bewildered trance. I never forget her devastated appearance. In less than six months she is dead. She knew it even then. This starts a long process of wondering about death. My first book in 1973 is entitled *Learning to Die*. Mother says it is strange that such a young man should develop such an interest in death.

There is always something wonderful under the Christmas tree. Ann and I come scurrying down the stairs. We are told to wait. We can hardly contain ourselves with excitement. Daddy gets as much into my toys as I do. He is fascinated with my Erector Set. One morning there is a complete train set built around the surface of a four-by-eight board.

I get a Daisy BB gun when I'm twelve. The next spring I'm out back trying it out. I see a mother robin with a nest in a row of lilac bushes. I try several shots in different directions, just to see what I can hit. I turn and focus on the robin. I'm quite a long way away. I probably can't hit her from this distance. If I did hit her, it would probably just scare her. More likely, I would just hit the bushes and scare her away. I pull the trigger. I hit her square in the chest and she falls over dead. I cannot believe what I have done. I scream "NO!" and run up to her. She is quite dead. I have done an awful thing. I have taken a life. The eggs will never hatch. I go into deep guilt over this. I will never again shoot any living thing unless we intend to eat it.

Daddy is excessively organized. I have in our garage the pigeonhole compartments that once lined the wall of his garage. There is a place for everything, and everything is in its place. No job is ever left undone. No tool is left outside. At the end of the day you clean whatever tools you are working with, putting a protective coating of oil on shovels, hoes or other metal instruments which might otherwise rust if they are left lying out. Each tool is then returned to its appropriate spot.

In an age before calculators, Daddy enjoys teaching me the use of a slide rule, which he moves back and forth with lightning speed. He loves to help with math, and we sit at the kitchen table going over my homework till it is done correctly; the more challenging the problem, the more interesting.

Daddy whips me only once. Ann and I are trying out new (to us) bicycles. I'm showing off and losing control of the bike. I crash into Ann causing her to fall over. That is the only time I remember his lifting a hand against me. I was greatly surprised that he did. He rarely raises his voice, and with the exception of an occasional "hell" or "damn," he never used profanity, though profanity can easily be found on the lips of Missouri farmers. Daddy never lowers himself to profanity. He doesn't need to. He's too clever for that. There is rarely a quarrel or raised voice in our household. One evening Mother and Daddy are fighting over money at the supper table. I yell, "Stop it!" And they do. I never see Daddy drink any alcohol though he keeps beer in the refrigerator to offer to visiting farmers.

Daddy gives Mother a diamond ring inside a box that is inside a box that is inside a box that is inside a sewing machine box. Though she handles it well, mother is hoping for a sewing machine. Another Christmas he gives her a yellow Volkswagen station wagon with a big red ribbon tied around it.

The first time Daddy finds condensed whipped cream in a spray can he brings it home, eager to give it a try. He's trying to figure how to make the can work. It goes off and shoots across the table, hitting Mother. Mother gets up and takes the can away from Daddy and shoots him back! Daddy takes the can away from Mother. Before long the breakfast room is a mess.

One Leghorn rooster wakes us with an annoying "cock-a-doodle-doo" each morning, till one morning we awake to discover that Daddy has fixed mister cock-a-doodle-doo as roasted rooster for breakfast.

Daddy could have worked longer and retired with more money. He retired at the age of fifty, to spend the rest of his life doing what he wanted. He died in 1984 at the age of seventy-two. In his early sixties, he began to show signs of early onset Alzheimer's disease, though that's not what killed him. A nurse who was feeding him left him lying down, and he choked on some food. No one complained to the nurse. In some ways it was merciful. Daddy was very far-gone with the disease. There are things we didn't share that I needed to learn from other guides. Daddy did what he could, what he knew how to do. It is significant that he was trying to be a better human being. Mother was always magnificent, always the example of love personified. As Abraham Lincoln said of his mother, "All that I am or hope to be I owe to her."

CHAPTER 5

Other Farms and Other Families

The Axis Mundy

The Incas thought that their capital, Cusco, was the navel of the universe. The Chinese teach that the farther you travel from China, the farther you go away from civilization. The Japanese believe that Japan is as close as you can get to Heaven on earth. New Yorkers think that the sun rises on the east side of Manhattan and sets on the west. There are five states west of Missouri: Kansas, Colorado, Utah, Nevada and California—and five states east—Illinois, Indiana, Ohio, Pennsylvania and New Jersey. There are two states north of Missouri: Iowa and Minnesota and two states south: Arkansas and Louisiana. I take a yardstick and place it on a map of the lower Forty-eight States on a wall in my room. It is twenty inches from top to bottom and the ten-inch mark falls just north of Mexico, Missouri—exactly where our farm is. Mid-Missouri lies halfway between the North Pole and the Equator, making it the seasonal battleground between climates of the north and south. Sometimes the cold Canadian wind comes down and we see ten degrees below zero. Sometimes the warm air from the Gulf of Mexico comes up and we see temperatures in excess of 100 degrees. Though the actual center of the lower forty-eight states is somewhere in Kansas, I assume that we are living in the center of the world.

The Monglers—Clifford, Dee, Ricky (Jody and Lillis)

Although I'm the only one in my grade at Sneed School, there are neighborhood boys and girls a year or two older or younger than I am on each of the surrounding farms. Using our home as the center of the compass: due east down through the barn and the barn lot, out through the pasture and the woods, through the grove of indigenous black walnut trees and on through another pasture are the Monglers. Jody and Lillis have three children. Although, Clifford is only a few months older than I am, he's a year ahead in school. Dee is Ann's age, and Ricky two years younger than Dee.

Lillis, once a professional swimmer, teaches us all to swim. There is a pretty picture of her as a young woman on the wall. Jody is rather big. He served in Europe during World War II. He has souvenirs from the war,

43

and he tells gruesome stories like knocking the teeth out of dead German soldiers to retrieve the gold. He's the best at butchering and once killed and butchered a bear. He uses language I never hear from Mother or Daddy's lips. When he sneezes, he says as loudly as he possibly can, "Hooorseshiit!"

Jody has coon dogs, and it's an adventure to go coon hunting with the Monglers in the dark woods down by Salt River, perilously pressing forward through scratchy bramble bushes, with no idea where your next step will bring you. With the Monglers we also hunt for frogs at night on Salt River in flat-bottomed boats. Frogs freeze as if hypnotized when you shine a flashlight in their face. You can then spear the immobilized frog before it comprehends the danger and springs into the river.

Breakfast at the Monglers is a treat. After pancakes or eggs with ham, sausage or bacon, Jody and Lillis toast bread, cover it with butter and jelly and pass it around. You then dip the toasted butter and jelly bread slices into milk. You can eat all you want, and we do.

People just automatically like Clifford. He is kindhearted. He is everyone's friend. He certainly is one of my best friends. He marries his first girlfriend when he is eighteen and gets a job working for the University of Missouri in Columbia building scientific apparatus. He has two daughters, and becomes a family patriarch and grandfather by the time he is forty.

The Condemned Bridge

A dirt road runs along the south side of Mongler's farm, a half mile east, to the condemned bridge, our favorite meeting place. The road across the bridge is blocked with a steel beam welded to each side of the bridge. Many of the boards on the bridge are missing and it is a challenge to see who is brave enough to cross the bridge by jumping from one board to another. All of us boys do it, and some of the girls. Or, more daring, who is willing to walk up the side of the iron trellis and, in a graceful balancing act, walk across the very top of the bridge. Clifford does. I never try. It looks way too dangerous. There is a bluff and a bend in the river near the condemned bridge where the water is deep and a wire cable hangs from a tree, so we can swing out over the river and drop into the water below.

A board from the condemned bridge is jammed into the side of the cliff to act as a diving board. It has no spring to it. You can, however, walk out and jump off. Ricky Mongler swings out. He doesn't let go and comes back and hits the pointed end on the diving board, driving fragments of splintered wood into his back. With nothing better, we grab my underwear to stop the bleeding, jump on our horses and ride as fast as we can back to the Monglers so Lillis can dispatch Ricky to town for stitches.

Ricky and I go down near the condemned bridge, where there is a long flat area of rocks next to the river. We strip off our clothes and throw mud at each other till we are completely covered; then we take a swim to clean up.

We're all swimming naked when a couple of teenage girls show up on the riverbank and start making fun of us. There is no way we can get out of the water without exposing ourselves. Clifford decides to make a run for it. He will grab our clothes and meet us down river. He starts running up the steep muddy riverbank and almost makes it. He slips, falls and slides back down on his belly. Everyone roars with laughter!

Salt River is so shallow in places that we can ride our horses down the middle. Clifford is on his pony, Macaroni, ahead of the rest of us. Suddenly, Macaroni and Clifford disappear under the water. Fortunately, they swim safely to shore. We were all scared for them. We are riding on the road to the condemned bridge when we come upon a couple wrapped in a blanket. The girl holds her clothes up to cover herself and screams, "Get your dumb farm animals out of here!"

The Wests—Kay, Freddie, Ronnie and Meribeth (Paul and Irma)

To the south is the West family. Daddy and Paul sometimes rent fields and farm the land together. Sometimes they work on each other's farms. Paul and Irma are Catholic. There are two pictures of Jesus in the West's house. One shows Jesus on a cross with his head thrown back in agony, his eyes in anguish, his mouth afflicted and twisted in pain. Another picture shows Jesus smiling while holding a shining bleeding heart in the middle of his chest.

Ronnie and Freddie are small of stature, muscular and gregariously active. Ronnie and I slept in the same crib when we were infants, so it's natural that we develop a bond. I sometimes beg Mother to call Irma and ask if I can play with Ronnie. There is a playful Huckleberry Finn quality to Ronnie, and a delightful mischievousness. He likes to play tricks on me and often succeeds. He convinces me that he can play the violin even though he doesn't own one. He and Freddie are more than occasionally into some impish trouble. Freddie puts his pinkie finger into a whirling belt on the motor of a water pump under the windmill to see what will happen. He is immediately divested of his finger. He picks it up, looks at it and throws it away. Ronnie and I are tramping around in the woods. He has to go to the bathroom. So he drops his pants and does his business. Lacking paper, he reaches behind and grabs poison ivy leaves. You can image the result. Perhaps you'd rather not.

Ronnie, Clifford and I like to stay in the hunter's cabin in our Ten-Acre Woods. Going out into the woods in the middle of the night to pee, we see a ghost in the forest. We carefully move up on the glowing object, speculating about the source of the illumination. It is a rotting tree stump giving off phosphorescent light. In these same Ten-Acre Woods, we attempt the building of a hut similar to what Ronnie saw in a *National Geographic* magazine. We dig a round hole, around which we plant poles from trees we cut down in the woods. While Ronnie and I are busily digging away, Clifford observes that the three of us work like our dads. Ronnie is spear-heading this adventure. I'm the one most intent on actually getting it done. Clifford is taking his time. We never finish. What we created was not a hut. A hut like this should be built on highland, not in the low lands in the Missouri woods. What we have created is a pond with rather strange looking poles arising from it. We do not brag about our hut, i.e., our hole in the ground.

The Cooses

Due west are our closest neighbors, the Cooses. Theirs is the only farm visible from our own. Red was stationed in England during World War II. There he met Queenie, whom he brought back to the States as his bride. Mother helps Queenie make the transition from Bristol, England, to life on a Missouri farm, and Daddy helps Red make the transition from soldier to farmer. Mother and Daddy and Queenie and Red soon become close friends. Queenie and Red have two daughters Pat and Susan both younger than I am.

The Fosters

Farther to the west are the Fosters. Jim and Rose have four children. They have two huge silos for the storage of silage made from corn, cut when it's still green. As it ferments, it gives off a sweet, pungent smell *dis-stinktive* of their farm.

The Banisters—Marilyn, June and Richard

On past the Fosters' is Sneed School, and on past Sneed School are the Banisters. Marilyn is a year older than I am, and the first girl I ever spend any serious time kissing, all done at the age of thirteen on the bed in her room while her younger brother, Richard, stands guard at the door.

All of our parents are in their thirties and forties, all enjoying the euphoria of the post-World War II boom of the 1950s. We kids have a wonderful time riding horses, swimming in Salt River, playing baseball, catching fireflies at night and putting them in glass jars, playing hide-and-go-seek in the dark, and busying ourselves with innumerable 4-H projects, school and church activities. The Monglers have a pool table in their detached garage, and it is a frequent gathering place. One of our favorite activities is to go arrowhead hunting—on the back of the Mongler's farm where the arrowheads are particularly abundant. I wonder why there are so many arrowheads here, and I want to know more about the Fox Indians who so freely roamed this land prior to the nineteenth century.

Our favorite activity is riding our horses to explore abandoned farms, their barns and houses. We find a cave by Santa Fe, Missouri. It's nothing like the cave that Tom Sawyer found. There is no Indian Joe and no Becky Thatcher to get lost with. Some passages are so narrow; I get a little panicked about getting caught. We find skeletons of dead coyotes and other animal bones. When we get out we're covered with mud, so we abandon our clothes and joyously jump into nearby Salt River.

CHAPTER 6

Sneed School 1949-1957
The Field of Dreams

You have not lost your innocence.
It is for this you yearn. This is your heart's desire.
This is the voice you hear, and this the call which cannot be denied.
The holy Child remains with you. His home is yours.
—ACIM, W-pl. 182. 12:1-6

Whenever I'm home in Missouri, I drive past the farm and adore every-thing. In May 1998, Mother gives up her house and moves into King's Daughters Home in Mexico. Ann calls and asks that I come and help in the sale of Mother's things. Mother goes from a three-bedroom house with a full basement and a nice yard to one fairly small room. With the exception of a few things, like Daddy's first gifts to her, she gives Ann, her grand-children and me whatever we want. We hold an auction for everything else. Uncle Estel and Aunt Jessie's collection of old postcards are among her most valuable possessions. Mother's auction is on the Saturday before Mother's Day, so I get to be with her on Mother's day, holding her hand in church and walking with her to lunch, and joining her and her friends for tea in the afternoon at King's Daughters Home.

Once everything is loaded on the U-Haul to take back to New York, I head out to Ann and Glenn's farm. On the way, I pass Sneed School, the one-room country schoolhouse where I spent eight years of grade school. I was the only student in the first, second, third, fourth, fifth, sixth, seventh and eighth grades. In 1949, my first year in school, there were eight stu-dents. When I graduated in 1957, we had grown to twenty-four. It wasn't until junior high school, when I was able to board a bus into town that, I was in a class with students my age.

I slow down in front of the old schoolhouse and stop. Sneed school now sits boarded up in the corner of a cow pasture on a gravel road. The schoolhouse is still intact, though the chimney is beginning to crumble, and some of the shingles are missing. The outhouses, pony barn, shed and playground equipment are gone. I get out of the car and stand looking at the school. No student or teacher has graced its steps in more than forty years. Yet it is the home for many. Raccoon tracks are clear near the well.

They lead from there to holes underneath each side of the building. Swallows fly in and out of the attic where missing shingles provide neat little doors, and hundreds of bees are flying in and out of holes in the side of the building. On the southeast corner of the school is a well-worn section where cows obviously stand, trying to protect themselves from northwestern winds that sweep across these prairie lands in the winter. There is such loneliness and peace in this prairie. Above, a chicken hawk swoops and dives with beautiful symmetry.

It is a gorgeous May evening, about an hour before dark. The sun hangs indolently over the western horizon, casting long shadows on the school and surrounding hedge trees. The lighting is perfect. The land drips with richness. The air is filled with butter-colored sunlight, crisp and clear, so that every object is set off against the background of every other object, with a penetration of light into solid substance. Everything looks sharper and more highly defined than usual. The song of the birds, the shape of the trees all blend into a magical evening. Over in the field, the hide of white cows caught in the evening sunlight glistens against shadows in the rich green pasture.

I walk around to the back of the school and stand at the spot that was once second base. I look across to home plate, and then over to first and third base, then over to where the girls' outhouse was. I look back toward home plate as Ronnie West hits a highflying ball back toward the fence. I run as fast as my legs will carry me across the path that leads to the boys' outhouse and back to the fence, and I catch the ball at just the last second.

I walk up to the back of the school and look at a hole in the foundation, the size of a missing concrete block. To think, I once crawled through that hole to the middle of the school where I buried a box containing a valentine and light blue plastic pop-beads, a popular item for girls during the fifties. I had secretly given the valentine to June Banister. She, however, had refused the gift. To cover up my embarrassment, I buried this testament to young love. I suppose it is still under there. I paid a dollar for the valentine from the Hallmark store on the square in Mexico—the most expensive one in the store. The saleslady noticing my extravagance said, "She must be quite some young lady!" I assured her that she was. June rejected me and there was nothing I could do except bury my love.

I walk around to the east side of the building next to the well. The pump is now gone and the well is covered. Each of us kids had a tin cup with our name painted on it with red fingernail polish. The cups hung on wooden pegs in the back of the school. At recess and lunchtime we gathered around the pump taking turns filling our cups. The cold clear water tasted wonderful. We often had lunch sitting around the well. My favorite sandwich was sliced radishes on buttered bread. One April Fool's Day I bite into my sandwich thinking it is cheese. There is, however, a piece of paper in the middle—an April Fool's note from mamma. April Fool's is her birthday.

I look over to where the swings, seesaws, trapeze bar, balancing rings and slide once were and then the spot where the shed stood that held tools for shoveling snow and coal for the potbellied stove. On the west side of the school was the pony barn. Most of us had horses. In good weather, we either rode or walked to school.

Standing, looking at the old school, I find myself worshipping at this shrine. In my heart it is a holy place. I suspect that's also true for the others who once knew this place as their school in a far more innocent and seemingly peaceful time. I first went to school here when I was five. I am now fifty-five. Fifty years have gone by, and I have come home to help Mother move into a home for older women. It is a quiet, peaceful evening like so many evenings on the farm. In the distance I hear a dog barking and the white cows start mooing, as cows often do in the evening.

After school I sometimes rode Flicka to the woods on the back of our farm—my Heavenly Spot. Here I would lie on a spongy, moss-laden rock, I called my "thinking rock" in a clearing in the woods amid big rocks and tall trees. Here an incredible world lay silently about. I would lay back and gaze up through an opening in the oak canopy, watching cotton candy clouds passing over the branches of the trees high above. Sometimes I lay in a small ditch about a foot deep. The sides of the ditch block my view to the left or the right so I can only see straight up into the blue sky. There are no limits to the sky. It stretches endlessly in every direction, never beginning and never ending. My mind merges with the tranquility of the blue sky and I am lifted beautifully, buoyantly beyond the body. It's hard to describe in human words.

The sudden expansion of awareness that takes place with your desire for it is the irresistible appeal the holy instant holds. It calls to you to be yourself, within its safe embrace. There are the laws of limit lifted for you, to welcome

you to openness of mind and freedom.
Come to this place of refuge, where you can be yourself in peace.
Not through destruction, not through a breaking out, but merely by a quiet
melting in. —ACIM, T-18.VI.14: 2-6

Here, I experienced what I think the Course means by a holy instant. It was a space where I felt complete safety, love and freedom. It was a place where, for a moment, I disappeared.

It is springtime, and I'm standing alone in the woods when I become aware of a world of beauty and majesty. The skunk cabbage is oh-so-green and the forsythia is oh-so-yellow, and I hear birds singing like I have never heard them before. There are white dogwood trees all about. I'm seeing everything for the first time. I hear the trickle of a nearby stream and I feel as if I'm in Paradise. A sense of awe comes over me. A flood of ineffable bliss overwhelms my heart and I kneel in the presence of something divine. I have to dedicate my life to something more than working for money and raising a family. I have to help unfold this majestic moment.

I stop to get as close as I can to watch a bee wandering about the face of a flower, or ants officiously going about their business. Who among us has not stopped to look at the beauty of a flower and wondered about it for an hour? There is an amazing, complex delicacy to the woods. All things come together to form a perfect presence here. When I need to think about things, I run into the woods and stand protected by the trees and, in silence, I inevitably find serenity.

Hunting includes a kind of meditation which involves freezing in the woods. You stand or sit perfectly still and just look and wait a while. Without a doubt, the animals come out and parade about, oblivious to your presence. You then just observe life happening around you. This process requires becoming objective instead of projective. I pretend that I do not exist. I'm just eyes on the world, nothing more—with no need for interpretation. It is a matter of *seeing*. You get very quiet and observe. Standing in the sunshine in May, a cool breeze blowing, taking in the air, just looking—looking—looking. I would do this even when I was not hunting. I would go into the woods and stand or sit and observe. Have you not been there? Have you not followed this route? Have you not felt what I'm talking about?

51

One day I write:

Immediate involvement with Mother Nature
Eternal connection with Mother Soil.
Lying in the woods—touching earth.
Listening—talking to myself
Standing in the field
Bright sun—warming my exposed torso.
Occasional white clouds
Many May flowers—bees busily moving
My youthful body set to run for no apparent reason.
Alive—alert—awake to the moment.
Everything is mine—everything is okay.
Such feelings—so long ago—forgotten—remembered
I'm free—so is everyone
Free to be human—here now
On a sunny morning in May on the farm in Missouri.

I freeze by myself on the back of the Mongler's farm and a young possum walks right up to my boot. I drop my jacket on him, catch him and bring him home as a pet. He gets loose in the house and makes a home for himself in the space between the downstairs ceiling and the upstairs floor. We finally catch him climbing on a curtain in the living room. Mother makes me let him go.

Although I cannot now bring myself to kill anything, I was like all farm boys, an active hunter and fisherman. Rabbit, quail, duck, frog legs, fish and other game frequented the table. There was a competition among us boys to see who could succeed in getting the most squirrels by tacking their tails on a rafter in the barn. Clifford was always the winner—the most skillful and devoted hunter and trapper.

I walk around to the front of the school where the flagpole used to stand. We gathered round each morning and saluted the flag. On May first, we did a Maypole dance, walking around the pole with different colored ribbons. I turn and look back at the front of the school. I start to cry. I cry profusely. I bend over and back up as if I'm in the presence of something holy. I cry so hard the insides of my glasses get wet and I have to take them off and wipe them on my shirttail. It is a mournful cry of sorrow. I'm crying for lost youth, for a time of purity and innocence. The day before, we dispensed all of Mother's possessions. My crying is a letting go and mourning for things once cherished—now seemingly lost. I am recapitulating previous decades and bringing them to a close. I cry for those peaceful days of innocence when things were what they were, and were without question.

Mother's dining room set and couch, the pigeon hole compartments from Daddy's garage, love letters, scrapbooks, photo albums, high school albums and innumerable reminders of life on the farm are in the U-Haul over on the road. I have just visited Mother's house for perhaps the last time.

I get back into the Jeep and drive on over to our old farmhouse. The new family is home. They welcome me and invite me to tour the house. Daddy's knotty-pine walls are now all dark from age and too many coats of varnish. The house is a mess with toys and clothes scattered about. It is also beautiful. I'm still crying. I try to explain to the two young boys who live there how lucky they are.

CHAPTER 7

Our Family Trip—Summer 1954

All I know or feel is that I am wild with impatience.
All I want to do is to move, move, move.
Curse the endless delays.
I wish I never had to stop anywhere a month.
—Mark Twain in a letter to his mother

Daddy's Wanderlust

Though his feet are permanently planted in Missouri soil, Daddy dreams of visiting any place he has not seen. Traveling is Daddy's college. He wants to "strike out," to go just for the sake of going. He enjoys studying maps and planning trips, cutting through unfamiliar territory. He knows backcountry Missouri roads as well as a spider knows her web. We've no more completed one adventure, than he has another one in mind. He wants to go someplace different; someplace he's never been before. He also wants to keep his feet on the ground. Daddy absolutely will not fly. From 1953 onward he owns a motor home, sometimes more than one, trading up, until they get as big as they can get.

During the spring of 1954, when I'm eleven and Ann is nine, Daddy buys a Cree Coach, one of the first aluminum campers to fit on the back of a three-quarter ton pickup truck. This contrivance is such a novelty that people often come up to us at campsites and ask if they can see inside. In the camper there is a table with benches on each side that turns each evening into a bed where Mother and Daddy sleep. Above the bed is a roll out hammock for Ann. I sleep on the floor on an air mattress. The camper includes a stove, a sink, an icebox, closets and drawers. There is no bathroom. A telephone connects the cab of the truck with the camper in the back. You have to bang on the glass of the cab's rear window to get Mother or Daddy's attention so you can talk.

Daddy rents out the farm with an advance payment of $500 for the summer, and we pile in and take off for a three-month adventure around the United States. Mother keeps a daily journal, including a listing of all our expenses. Eating bacon, lettuce and tomato, grilled cheese, and peanut butter and jelly sandwiches for lunch and cooking corn on the cob, fried chicken, hamburgers and such for dinner, we keep our expenses down. In an age before McDonalds and Burger King, we eat out only on Father's day and a few special occasions. On the stove in the back of the Cree Coach, Mother makes apple pies and cherry pies from farm stands. Our biggest expenses are gasoline and tires. Gas varies from nineteen to twenty-nine cents per gallon. Most days our expenses never exceed six dollars. With cheap gas, free maps, viewing towers you can climb for ten cents each (kids admitted free), miniature golf and drive-in theaters, we have a great time.

Most days Mother and Daddy are up and on the road by four or five a.m., I get up and crawl into their bed so they can move about. Around seven, no later than eight, we stop and fix breakfast. Ann and I then join them in the cab. By ten or eleven we reach our destination. We have lunch, then spend the rest of the day playing, exploring and engaging ourselves in some new adventure. By nine, no later than ten, we are back in bed.

You will find angling to be like the virtue of humility, which has a calmness of spirit and a world of other blessings attending upon it.
—Izaak Walton, *The Complete Angler*

We leave home at 7:30 on the morning of May 25, 1954. We arrive in the afternoon at Bennett Springs state park in the Ozarks of southern Missouri. Daddy catches and prepares six trout for dinner. Every chance he has, Daddy goes fishing. It is part of what this trip is about. Fresh fish is frequently our fare for dinner. During the first month there are perpetual flat tires until Daddy buys new ones in Louisiana. Each Sunday I give a brief Sunday service, usually around a picnic table. Once each week we find a laundromat. We look for places where we can go swimming, so we can also get a good shower.

We stop at the Hermitage, President Andrew Jackson's home, near Nashville, Tennessee. The bold white columns, the stately trees and the French wallpaper pictogram of the Odyssey inside the hall and entranceway are impressive. We drive through the Great Smoky Mountains of Tennessee and North Carolina—smoky because of the heavy fog of clouds that hangs in the valleys till late in the morning. Then down to Atlanta to visit Daddy's sister, Aunt Sue, and Uncle Sam. They take us to see Stone Mountain (a carving of Robert E. Lee and other soldiers on horseback)—more than three football fields wide and ninety feet high. We visit the zoo and the cyclorama depiction of the Civil War battle of Atlanta.

Aunt Sue has a living room that is a showplace of what a really fancy living room should look like. You never sit in or actually use this room, though you can go look at it. Uncle Sam has an ability to talk to almost anyone in an interestingly intimate and connected way. He remembers the names of every person he ever met, and he always has a joke. He dies in 1985 and I'm given several of his quality sports coats. There is something in an inside pocket. Reaching in, I find three-by-five cards with jokes on one side and a list of people to whom and places in which he told the jokes on the other side.

Each December, Uncle Sam and Aunt Sue come up from Georgia with his bird dogs, and we go hunting for the beautiful bobwhite quail. Uncle Sam regularly supplies our family with quail and sometimes pheasant for Thanksgiving and Christmas dinners. They bring along Georgia pecans and fruitcake, which I submerge in whole cream before devouring.

We travel to Warm Springs, Georgia, to see Roseanne Foster. She is from a neighboring farm in Missouri. Roseanne suffers from polio and is living in an iron lung in a sanitarium founded by Franklin Roosevelt. I like Roseanne and fancy her as something of a possible girlfriend. I once hid with her in tall grass while playing hide-and-go-seek with my arm around her tenaciously holding on to her back brace. We drive through cotton fields and cheesecloth covered tobacco fields, and Mother gets Daddy to stop so she can pick her first magnolia.

We venture down to Jacksonville Beach, Florida, for our first-ever experience of the ocean. My air mattress now becomes a contrivance on which I ride the mighty ocean waves. In St. Augustine, Florida, the first town in America, we hire an African-American cabby for three dollars for the day and he takes us to the sights including the old fort where the British and the Spanish fought over this northern Florida land. In Pensacola, Mother, Ann and I get so sunburned on a cloudy day on the beach. We are so sick we are unable to eat. I look like Mr. Tomatohead. That night, we lie in the back of the steamy camper and moan.

We travel on through Alabama and Louisiana, where late one afternoon, in a noisome oil-refining town on the gulf of Mexico, the jack slips off the truck while Daddy is changing a rear tire. The truck comes crushing down on top of Daddy's left hand, trapping it between the truck and the tire, breaking the bones and throwing him into incredible agony. Mother and I run as fast as we can to a nearby garage and get men to come and lift the truck off of Daddy's smashed fingers. Even I try to help. There is no hospital nearby and the doctor who cuts Daddy's wedding ring off and puts splints on his broken fingers seems none too adept. Journal entry for the day reads, "doctor, three dollars twenty cents." That terrible night, Daddy cannot sleep, and we lie awake in the camper listening to his groans.

There is no air-conditioning in the cab or the back of the truck. It is June and throughout much of Texas and New Mexico we roast. Despite this fact, Mother irons clothes in 105-degree heat. We stop on hot afternoons or sultry evenings to go to the movies just for the air-conditioning. I want a sombrero so we venture into Juarez, Mexico. Daddy and Mother both are excellent in the art of bargaining. In a trailer camp that night, we hear screaming and gunshots. Daddy gets up and we get out of there.

We drive on through Arizona, the painted desert, and the Grand Canyon. Here is nature on a scale that is intimidating. How small and insignificant we human beings seem. Pictures do not describe it. Mother and I take long walks, learning the name of every tree, flower and shrub. In the evening we listen to a naturalist's talk. We enjoy our first view of jackrabbits hopping through the desert and tumbleweeds rambling around the highway. We head up through Utah and cut across Nevada to Reno, amazed that you can gamble at every filling station. At Harrah's in Reno, Mother and Daddy try five- and ten-cent slot machines. Ann and I cannot go inside, so Mother and Daddy take turns staying with us outside. Daddy comes out with a handful of nickels. Mother goes in and comes out with a handful of dimes and gives a dime each to Ann and me. Daddy goes back in and comes out with five nickels. They stop while they are a quarter ahead.

In Donner Memorial State Park in California an inextricable feeling is made on this young mind. The Donner party of pioneers tried to winter over here in 1846-47. With snow up to twenty-two feet deep, it was impossible to proceed and the party resorted to cannibalism. Thirty-nine people perished. Fifteen were eaten.

In Chico, California, we visit my only great aunt who does not live in Missouri, Aunt Josie, and her husband, Wayne, who owns a one-man barbershop attached to their house. Mother is elated to find oranges, grapefruits, figs, and bay leaves she can gather from Aunt Josie's yard. As his own boss, Wayne can close shop any day and take off fishing. According to Aunt Josie, he's often fishing. Daddy has found a kindred spirit in Wayne. Wayne is a tall-tale storyteller, especially about fishing. He comes to camp telling our camping neighbors about the big fish he caught. When Aunt Josie later challenges him, he explains proudly that it never hurts to lie an inch or two. While fishing with him, I catch my first trout in a culvert under the road. I see the fish go for the salmon egg on the end of my hook. It's a big trout, and I'm proud. Mother makes a fuss and takes pictures. At Aunt Josie's, we receive letters from home. Folks are roasting in Missouri. There is no rain and a formidable infestation of grasshoppers is devouring the crops.

With Wayne and Aunt Josie, we venture up Mt. Shasta where on the Fourth of July we take pictures in snow more than twenty feet deep, while folks back home are scorching. On Fisherman's Wharf in San Francisco, we eat delicious shrimp fresh out of cauldrons handed to us in cone-shaped newspapers. We venture into Chinatown, where everything is written in Chinese. I feel like an intruder in this city within a city. We try fresh-baked fortune cookies, and we buy firecrackers.

We travel up highway 101 through the magnificent Redwood forests and I take notes on the tallest tree in the world: 364 feet tall, 200 feet to the first limb, 47 feet around, 1,200 years old. Big lumber trucks barrel down the highway, and we are frightened to see four accidents in two days. We pull off along the northern coast to watch the chaos of waves slapping against huge heaved-up rocks. We spend an afternoon at Agate Beach where, with the beach to ourselves, we gather multicolored, smooth agates, and Mother finds driftwood suitable for her flower arrangements. Where can we find room for driftwood in the Cree Coach?

At Crater Lake in Oregon, the lake lies mirror-still before us like a picture postcard. Through southern Oregon, Mother makes notes of the onion, chard and potato fields. I'm taken with the beauty and cleanliness of Boise, Idaho. It seems so peaceful in Boise. In Yellowstone National Park we watch old faithful and over two hundred other active geysers hissing and bubbling, spitting and sputtering their sulphurous steam. To think this has been going on for millions of years! All about there are alluring opal- and sapphire-colored pools. Yellowstone has the largest ecosystem in the lower forty-eight states. It's pure wilderness; rugged, beautiful; the way it used to be. Daddy loves it. We take horseback rides, see elk, bear, buffalo and caribou and listen to lectures about the park. Here, too, we receive more bad news from home. For ten days it's been in the 100's and throughout the entire month of July, it's been in the nineties every day. There has been no rain in weeks. The crops have died.

Each Sunday morning, Daddy drops Mother, Ann and me off at a local church. He then goes and cooks lunch—usually fried chicken and corn on the cob. It is all ready when we return to the camper. I collect worship bulletins from each of the churches we visit. The one from the Episcopal service in Yellowstone on July 28, 1954, has the following confession of sin:

Almighty God, Father of our Lord Jesus Christ, Maker of all things,
Judge of all men; we acknowledge and bewail our manifold sins and
wickedness, which we, from time to time, most grievously have committed,
by thought, word and deed, against Thy Divine Majesty provoking most justly
Thy wrath and indignation against us.
We do earnestly repent and are heartily sorry for these our misdoings:
the remembrance of them is grievous unto us; the burden of them is
intolerable. Have mercy upon us most merciful Father;
For Thy Son our Lord Jesus Christ's sake, forgive us all that is past;
and grant that we may ever hereafter serve and please Thee in newness of life
to the honor and glory of Thy name.

There is nothing like this confession in the Church back in Mexico. I have to ask Mother, what does the word *indignation* mean? Is God really angry with us? Is it true? Are we so wicked? I appreciate the openness and tolerance of the Disciples of Christ Church. This Episcopal service is disturbing. After the confession, we sing, "When I survey the Wondrous Cross." The minister gives a sermon titled, "My God, My God, Why?" and we sing "Rock of Ages." There is something disturbing about this most morose minister, something hard and disquieting, and I'm perturbed by this confession of sin. Is it really true?

At our campsite, I make friends with two brothers. The older one suggests a rock throwing battle. I'm not in favor of this potentially dangerous exercise. He is, however, bigger and older, and when his brother agrees, I'm outnumbered. I aim at the ground so I will not hit the boy. I also don't want to be hit. The older brother tosses one that smashes into his brother's eye. There are screams and the boys' mother comes running. The older boy blames it on me. I'm dumbfounded. No one has ever told a lie about me. I straighten up, look the mother in the eye and tell her with confidence that I'm going to be a minister, and I would not lie. She looks at me for a long accusing moment. Apparently deciding to believe me, she grabs her son by the ear and hauls him off to their campsite.

We venture into the Tetons and Jackson Hole, Laramie, and to the rodeo in Cheyenne. Then it's on through Nebraska, where Daddy gets our truck stuck in a funeral procession—and there is a woman hanging out the window of her black Cadillac limousine shaking her fist and yelling at Daddy telling him to "Get your damn truck out of our procession." Through southern Iowa, we are finally back in Missouri where, at Ann's insistence, we stop the truck, get down on our knees and kiss parched Missouri soil. Our last stop is Kirksville and a visit with Grandmother Callahan, Aunt Marie and Uncle Harold. The experience has been incredibly bonding for the four of us. Every family who could, should make a trip like this.

There has been no rain in mid-Missouri during the entire month of July. The last time it was this bad was during the dust bowl days of 1930. Cows have stopped giving milk. Salt River is so low that Uncle Estel and other farmers have walked along the river bottom, scooping up catfish in small muddy pools. Missouri farmers have lost their crops, and there is little to feed the cattle. One of the few wells still working is the spring on Daddy Mundy's farm. Uncle Estel and other farmers have taken advantage of its bounty by hauling water from it to fill their own cisterns. Because Daddy has rented out our farm and been paid in advance, and living as we have on sandwiches and much free entertainment, the summer costs us less than $600. Daddy figures we saved money by going away. If we had stayed and worked the farm, it would all have been for naught. Uncle Estel, Aunt Jessie and Daddy Mundy are delighted to see us. "Lord it's good to be back home again. This old farm seems like a long lost friend." The grass is dead so Daddy plows under and replants the entire yard. In August it begins to rain again. It's too late to save the crops.

CHAPTER 8

Paradise Lost

Running Away From Home

1955—Age Twelve

Till the age of twelve, I experienced a peaceful unruffled life loved by all, safe and secure. In the summer of 1955, the ego raises its ugly head and things get a little twisted. I'm to meet Clifford, Ronnie and Malcolm over at the Mongler's to go arrowhead hunting, then down to the condemned bridge for a swim. When I get there, Dee Mongler and Roseanne Foster are playing pool in the garage. I don't know where the boys are. Dee and Roseanne tell me they have gone on without me, as they don't like me and don't want to play with me. There has never been any indication of this before. Still, the boys are gone and I don't know what to do. I limp home through the woods like a wounded animal. The other boys don't like me? Is it possible? Is it true? I'm horribly upset and profoundly injured for the first time in my life. The thing to have done is to have shrugged it off and said it didn't matter, "no big deal." It *is* a big deal. These are my *closest* friends, my *only* friends.

I decide I no longer want to live in this community. I love my folks. I love the farm. I don't want to live where I'm not wanted. I resolve to run away. No one is home when I get back to the house. I get together essential items, a pellet gun, a pair of binoculars, a canteen of Kool-Aid, some raisins, carrots and marshmallows for food. I take off. Going through the barnyard, I see Daddy coming up the hill in our blue Plymouth station wagon. I duck into a pig house. Once he is in the house, I take off, first to the hunter's cabin down on the ten acres. I then make my way along Salt River and through the woods back over to the Monglers and up into the loft in the barn where I'm sure Clifford will show up to throw hay down for the cows. I know Clifford isn't responsible for this. He is just too kindhearted and too good a friend. I can't imagine that Ronnie is behind this either, which makes it all the more complicated. When Clifford comes up into the loft, I call him aside and tell him I'm running away and ask him to keep my secret. He is so kind; he says he would run away with me, except he really doesn't have a reason to. He agrees not to tell.

With the help of my binoculars, I watch the Monglers come out of their house, get into their car and take off. Clifford told me they were going to the Fosters that evening to play cards. After they leave, I take off. I'm thinking maybe I will go to Grandmother Mundy's sister, my Great Aunt Suzy Fry in Auxvasse, Missouri. I will get her to agree, like Clifford, not to tell. I will work my way on down to St. Louis. Somehow I will make it on my own. Walking along the gravel road I can hear cars coming before they get too close and thus have time to run and hide in a cornfield or culvert or ditch. I feel like a thief in the night. I walk the three miles from the Mongler's back to the Foster's.

There I lie in a ditch and, again with my binoculars, watch people walking around in Foster's house. I go around behind their house and put my ear up to what I know is an unused outer door, with missing steps, off the dining room. I can hear people talking inside. The phone rings. "Jonny Mundy has run away from home!" After some commotion, Clifford confesses that he knows about it. He ran away because Roseanne and Dee played a trick on him, telling him the boys don't want to play with him. I can hear much of what is being said. They decide they will go out and look for me. Everyone comes out of the kitchen door on the other side of the house, piles into cars and in a hail of dust takes off. I'm standing behind the house only a few feet away. Suddenly, they are all gone, and I'm alone.

It is now about nine at night. It's dark and I'm missing Mother and Daddy and Ann, and I am sorry about what I have done. I begin running toward home, crying, telling God how sorry I am about hurting Mother and Daddy, uncles and aunts and grandparents. I want to get home on my own. I don't want anyone to find me. Every now and then I hear a car coming and run and hide. No one sees me. At the base of our hill, only about a quarter mile from the house, I hear a car coming. This time there is no place to hide. I try running into the multiflora rosebushes that surround the pasture on the south-facing hill, where someday I would like to be buried or have my ashes scattered. Right now, there is no way of getting through the densely packed multiflora roses. I have to hold my arm up to cover my eyes from the bright lights of the car which are now shining on me.

Of all people, it is Mike Foster and some older boys. Mike is fifteen. All Missouri farm boys drive by the time they are fifteen, often even younger. You have, after all, been driving a tractor since you were nine or ten. It is not legal till you are sixteen. Highway patrolmen, however, rarely venture into these backcountry roads, so you are not likely to get caught. Mike once stole a 7-Up from my lunch box at school. I knew he did it. So did the other kids. Miss Mills, the teacher, herself only eighteen, had all of us lay our heads down on our desk and close our eyes, and put our hands up over our heads. She asked that the person who took the 7-Up, get up and go out and get it and return it. It didn't work. Nobody got up. Mike already drank the 7-Up out behind the pony barn. From then on, I didn't like Mike. Now he is the one who has heroically found me. There is not much choice. I get into his car, and he speeds up the hill, honking his horn, letting everyone know of his glory and my shame. (At the age of fifty, Mike will be found sitting straight up dead in his United Parcel truck.)

I jump out of the car. There are people gathered all round. I run into the house, up the stairs and into my bedroom and straight to bed crying. Fortunately, only Mother and Uncle Estel come up to my room. Uncle Estel sits beside my bed, not talking, just looking curiously with his head tilted to one side like the scarecrow from the *The Wizard of Oz*. After he says goodnight to the neighbors, Daddy comes in and says good night. He doesn't scold me—just says never scare them like that again. All I can do is cry. Roseanne and Dee get spankings. This does not, of course, endear me to either Dee or Roseanne. I have lost a certain amount of innocence. I have called attention to myself in an embarrassing way. By the time school starts that fall, the incident seems forgotten. I doubt it.

CHAPTER 9

Going to Town—Mexico, Missouri

Our favorite activity is going to town on Saturdays for groceries, seed and feed, hardware and other needs. We always visit family. A trip to town is an adventure. Ann and I are excited. Aunts and grandparents will make a fuss over us. We'll probably get some sort of treat. We usually take the all-gravel, old Molino road that runs due north and south past our house. Sometimes we make the three-mile trip to the west past Sneed School to Highway 15, a smooth macadam road. This way it's ten miles to town. The four of us sit in the front seat of our pickup truck. There is an iron bridge on old Molino road just before we get to Mexico, then a hill, and then we're officially in town. As Daddy gears down to pull up the hill, Ann and I jump up and down on the truck seat saying, "Almostie to town." This becomes a habit and a tradition until we are simply too old for it.

Daddy is forty-three. We are standing next to the counter in the kitchen talking to Mother. Daddy has been offered the opportunity of taking over ailing Uncle Jim Mundy's real estate office. They want to keep the office in the Mundy name and, as Daddy has had some success in buying, fixing up and selling old houses, and, as Daddy Mundy is a landlord, it seems a natural. Daddy says he has recently read an article in *Reader's Digest* which said that by the time he's in his mid-forties every man needs to feel as though he has had at least one really good break. Daddy thinks this is his break.

Mexico, Missouri

Mexico, like many county seats, is built on a square with the courthouse in the middle. Cars slant park around the square. You can walk into the center of the courthouse from the north, south, east or west to a rotunda open to a domed skylight on the roof. There are various county offices in each corner, convenient bathrooms in the basement, a wrap-around balcony and a courtroom on the second floor. Out the north door directly across the street is Daddy's real estate office. To the right is Rexall's Drug Store with a soda fountain. There are stools bolted to the floor around a counter and booths off to the other side with jukeboxes on each table, all with the latest rock-n-roll music. It is rocking and rolling time, and Elvis is King!

Once I'm in high school, the nice thing about Daddy having an office in town is that after school, rather than riding the bus home, I can walk downtown with other kids where we visit the Rexall Drug Store. I have a malt with two eggs and a banana, to help make me extra strong. To the left of Daddy's office there is a record store, a Singer sewing machine store and, on the northwest corner, a little grocery store with produce sitting on the sidewalk. This grocer often buys produce from our garden; strawberries in June, sweet corn and watermelon in July and August.

On the west side of the square is JC Penny, Western Auto, a Hallmark card shop with a bell which *tinkle-tinkles* when you open the door, an electronics and large appliance store, a men's clothing store, and a shoe store. On the south side is Montgomery Ward, Mexico Savings Bank, Kroger's grocery store and the Royal Cafe. Opening the door to the Royal Cafe you are met with the aroma of coffee, hamburgers on the grill and fruit pies baking in the oven.

On the east is Fredenall and Wilkin's department store. The salesclerk does not exchange money here. She puts it into a tube that carries it on a little track to a balcony on the second floor, which then whisks the tube back your way with a receipt and change. There is Cline's furniture store, F.W. Woolworth's 5 & 10-cent store, Safford's shoes, Hagen's men's store and my favorite, Craddock's books and stationery. Inside is the aroma of books, paper, ink, crayons and paints. And there are all sorts of wonderful desk accessories.

Just off the square you can find Eardle's hardware. There is a smell of oil and sawdust and a display of beautiful screwdrivers with clear plastic bright yellow and red handles—a wonderful display of hammers and axes, saws, and, well, absolutely everything. I walk slowly around in the hardware store looking at all the new tools. I'm going to have the latest tools someday, all neatly arranged in my garage—just like Daddy. Daddy is definitely a "tool man."

There are also pool halls with spittoons still in use, barber shops, women's dress shops, Hassen's Creamery with wonderful rich ice cream, Crown Laundry, Talbot's News Agency, the Ringo and the Hoxey hotel, Wonneman's Greenhouse, the Liberty and the Rex theaters, Mexico's Evening Ledger, the post office and the public library. Everything is available on or just off the square in Mexico. You park your car on the square, walk around the block and take care of your needs. You'll probably run into a few people you know. As with most small towns, there is not much left of the square in Mexico. Most of what you want is now found at Wal-Mart or one of the mini malls on the edge of town. The courthouse is busy with many legal matters. There is a cafe and the *Evening Ledger* thrives.

CHAPTER 10

The Highs of Adolescence

1956—Age Thirteen

I make two discoveries at thirteen, classic comic books and chess. By reading classic comics, I figure I'll have some idea about what the classics are about before I have to actually read them in high school and college. They are colorful early versions of Monarch notes. They are more expensive than regular comic books, fifteen cents each instead of ten. They are all numbered, and I am determined to collect and read the entire set. Each time we go to town, I go by Talbot's news agency to see if they have any new classic comics to add to my collection, perhaps also a paperback book and a *Popular Science* magazine.

With certain jobs like plowing, you can read while working. Our two-bottom plow behind the Ford tractor moves at two miles an hour. You can actually walk faster than it moves. As the Ford is a four—instead of a three—wheel tractor, you can put the front right wheel in the furrow and the tractor will pretty well steer itself. You just have to touch slightly on the steering wheel, holding it a little to the left, so it gently hugs the side of the furrow. Plowing this slowly on bright cloudless days you think about everything. There isn't much to see or hear—maybe the oboe call of crows, their black iridescent wings flopping lackadaisically out over the field or a coyote running across the terrain, his tail trailing out back like a whiff of silver gray smoke.

Plowing half-mile rows at two miles an hour, you can get a lot of reading done. I love stories about the sea, *Robinson Crusoe*, *Swiss Family Robinson* and *Treasure Island*. I begin keeping a log of each book I've read. When we go on vacation, or we visit one of my aunts, I take along a book and several classic comics to read in the car. Broke, in my early forties, I venture into New York City where I find a dealer who trades in old comic books. My nearly complete set of ninety-five classic comic books, all from the 1950s, all in good to excellent condition, brings about $200, several dollars for each book.

Once I get the chess bug, I play the game as often as I can with whom-ever will engage me. Frequently, I lose because I get so fascinated with the task of capturing my opponent's pawns, that I invariably forget my king. This becomes a metaphor: how easy it is to become fascinated with the world, the play, the soap opera; concerned about the pawns, we forget about the King.

Coming out into the Light

On Saturdays, while Mother and Daddy are shopping and visiting with family, I'm dropped at the movies. From there I can walk to Daddy's office, or over to Aunt Lue's to wait for Mother or Daddy to pick me up. Aunt Lue has a beauty parlor in her basement, and it is fun to go there and have her and the other ladies gush over me.

Mexico boasts two theaters, the upscale Liberty, which offers blockbusters and the Rex which shows black and white gangster and cowboy movies. Saturday afternoon the Rex has matinees with serials of *Buck Rogers, Flash Gordon, Tom Mix, Roy Rogers, The Lone Ranger,* and *Superman.* The serial always has a heart stopping, cliffhanger conclusion with a promise of a more interesting adventure next week. Stay tuned! There are also cartoons, newsreels, and popular science shows with futuristic things like fancy cars, modern trains and airplanes.

The main show is some black and white action adventure such as Gregory Peck in *The Gunfighter,* Jimmy Stewart in *Broken Arrow,* or Humphrey Bogart in *The Enforcer.* There are gifts and toys and unusual treats in Cracker Jack boxes. One Sugar Daddy lasts the length of an entire show, and Necco Wafers are good for a double feature. The Liberty has a well-lit marquee with moving lights on the front side where white people go in and a smaller marquee with lights on the side of the building at the "black" entrance.

Inside the Liberty there is a wonderful smell of buttered popcorn, thick red carpets, the dark and the silence and the ushers with little red flashlights who lead you to your own sanctified seat. Mine is just left of center five or six rows down from the back, not too far down, just at a good angle where you can catch the whole screen and let it catch you. The screen is not on the wall. It is rather on a stage where plays and piano recitals were held in earlier days. The Rex also has a stage that was once a boxing ring. At one time Mexico was the home of Rex Rodenbaugh, a golden glove champion.

The best movies are the blockbusters at the Liberty, Cecil B. De Mille's type, kinescope productions of *The Ten Commandments, Ben Hur, The Robe, Gone with the Wind* and *Bridge on the River Kwai*. I get lost—so involved I forget where I am. Sometimes in the middle, I might remember that I'm sitting in the movie and am not, in fact, one of the characters. Movies are like dreaming out loud. You're there in the middle of it—watching everything that is going on, yet removed.

There are also the first 3-D movies with the comical, colored cardboard glasses. It's fun watching *Bwana Devils* and *The House of Wax* with Clifford and Ronnie! There is also that memorable first "3-D" moment when an Indian spear comes off the screen and pierces my heart. I had forgotten that I'm not a cavalry soldier who lies wounded on the ground only to look up and see an Indian on horseback throw his spear right through me. I'm saved. Something miraculous happens. I'm not killed. I'm still alive. Divine grace, I guess.

Then comes that dreaded moment. Just when I have totally forgotten who I am or where I am, I am up out of my seat and walking with other people out of the building into the street and the brilliant sunlight of a hot summer afternoon. The theater is the only air-conditioned building in town. Air-conditioning has not yet found its way into our churches, our homes or our cars. You are so comfortable, and then suddenly there is bright light and heat. Now you need sunglasses and your straw cowboy hat. Every farm boy has a straw cowboy hat to protect his eyes from the ungentle sun. Besides, it makes you look cool in an age before there is the word "cool."

Coming out of the theater you have to hold your hands over your eyes to protect them from the light. Then the light embraces you. Coming out of the Liberty is like waking from a magnificent dream, and I'm filled with incredible and often improbable inspiration. I *too* will have a life of adventure. I will prosper. I will visit exotic places and do all the things the heroes and heroines do—someday. Most important of all, I will fall in love.

In 1955, the Williams in Molino get a television. We go to their house and sit around on the floor and watch. We get a television ourselves in 1956. There are only three stations that broadcast between three in the afternoon and ten in the evening. I find a local religious show that's on each afternoon after school and watch it faithfully.

We're playing baseball at night under the lights in Mexico when a car comes speeding up the gravel road throwing up dust all around. It comes right up onto the baseball field. It's our neighbor the Cooses with news. Mother's oldest sister, my Aunt Marie in Kirksville, has died of a heart attack at the age of fifty-one. In an age before by-pass operations, there was nothing that could be done. Grandmother Mundy has died and now Aunt Marie. I get to look at death again. I really don't think there is such a thing as death—only life. Still, Aunt Marie is too young to leave us. It is a tragedy, and Mother is grief stricken.

1957—Age Fourteen

I graduate from grade school and start taking the bus into Mexico to the junior high school. I go a bit crazy that first year. I have never seen so many girls. I try out for football. Huge Ray Lineberry comes crashing through the line laying me out flat, knocking the air out of me. I roll around in pain, holding my sides wondering why I'm doing this. Suddenly tennis seems like a much more enjoyable and reasonable sort of sport.

For the first time, I have some choice about which classes I want to take. Most farm boys take woodworking or mechanical shop. I choose public speaking. My speech teacher, Richard Rea, becomes my first true guide. Under his tutelage, I begin to win public speaking and debating contests. I discover another deeper voice, one that enables me to win a state award in radio announcing. "And now for the latest news from the Associated Press and the KXEO news room!"

On my fourteenth birthday, the *Mexico Evening Ledger* prints a picture of Daddy, Daddy Mundy and myself, and writes an article about our family. As of today, May 16, 1957, our ancestral farm has been in our family for one hundred years.

What is it that repels us about a bug climbing up a wall, except that it is a will which is not our own. —Feodor Dostoyevsky in The Possessed

Meadowlarks build their nests on the ground, and a number of them live in the alfalfa field next to our house. The song of the meadowlark, often delivered from a roadside fence post, is one of the loudest, most common and prettiest songs heard around the farm. It consists of a plaintive, down-slurred whistle with a tempo sounding like *spring-of-the-year, spring-of-the-year*. I'm walking with a neighbor girl (to remain nameless) through our alfalfa field when we come upon a nest of meadowlarks, full of baby birds. Immediately, my companion jumps on them, stamping the baby birds

70

to death. I am for a moment traumatized. It all happens so quickly. I look at her aghast. What happened? Why did she do this thing? Why this disrespect for life? Human beings are strange creatures, loving at one moment, capable of insane cruelty the next. Human beings, it seems are sometimes angels with assholes.

Mother and I are working in the field. I'm driving the tractor, and she is standing in a trailer attached to the tractor. I start the tractor with a jerk. She falls face forward on to the trailer hitch. She has to get several stitches in her mouth. She is bleeding so badly the nurse who is helping the doctor faints. She looks awful, and I'm crestfallen and apologetic for days.

1958—Age Fifteen—The County Fair

I get a book on chess strategy and figure out how to win. In high school I find a new group of opponents, often meeting John Ringo after school at the town library.

The Audrain County Fair runs for two weeks each August. There are many exhibits of vegetables, horses, cows, pigs, sheep, goats, woodworking, leather, photography and more. There are exhibits of the latest in farming equipment, cars and trucks, and old tractors, steam machines and thrashers—absolutely everything. I love the smell of sawdust on the paths to the grandstand. There is also the aroma of the animals and the smell of the numerous food stands grilling hamburgers, hot dogs, onions and french fries. All the kids are there, farm kids from the entire county. Mexico boasts a huge amphitheater and racetrack, and there are activities all day long and well into the evenings. As the saddle horse capital of the world, harness races are a popular attraction, and horse judging is a serious matter. There are also automobile races, demolition derbies, tractor pulls and rodeo events.

During the summers when I'm fifteen, sixteen, seventeen and eighteen, I work at the fair directing cars with the twirl of a cane to the appropriate places to park. Red Coose is in charge of hiring, so Freddie, Ronnie, Clifford and I always get these jobs. The pay is one dollar an hour. Once we're finished we can run around the fairgrounds, and we have our own money. 4-H is a big part of the fair. We learn how to judge animals. And, of course, there is the colorful carnival with super rides and games.

Back to the Fields

I'm working by myself on the half-mile rows at the back of Daddy Mundy's farm when I notice that the oil cap on the bottom of the tractor has fallen off. Rather than stopping the tractor immediately—the smart thing to have done—I drive it back up to the barn, spilling critically necessary oil. By the time I get back, the tractor is a goner. When Daddy comes home and finds out what has happened, he is, needless to say, upset. He has a few pointed questions to ask me. He does not punish me. He just fumes. I'm miserable.

Daddy buys me a saddle for my fifteenth birthday. I go with him to bargain over the saddle. Daddy and the seed and feed salesman go back and forth on the price. Finally, Daddy says, "No deal. Let's go, Jon." We get into our blue Plymouth station wagon. Daddy begins an awkward process of slowly backing up and turning around. I ask why he is going so slowly and he says, "Because that guy's going to come running after us and accept my last offer." He does.

Back home, I'm standing on the big flat stone at the back door of the barn while Daddy is putting the saddle on Dinah. I'm holding her reins. Dinah blows out her belly when you put the saddle on so that, after the cinch is fixed, she can let the air out and have more room. Daddy, knowing Dinah's tricks, pulls the cinch up extra tight; Dinah impetuously reaches around, takes the whole of my upper arm in her mouth and bites down hard. No bones break. I am, however, black and blue and sore for days.

I am walking from high school to Daddy's office in downtown Mexico with Connie, a girl from one of my classes. Suddenly, we see five flying saucers straight up in the air in front of us. They are maybe a quarter of a mile away. They are huge. There are two on top and three underneath. There is no other possible explanation. There is nothing else they could be. They are football shaped and each glows with a bright red-orange light. Connie turns and says: "What is that?" I say, "I don't know." I look over at Connie. Her mouth is open and her eyes fixed. Time stands still for a moment. I look back at the flying saucers. Suddenly they disappear. Within seconds they are gone. We look at each other dumbfounded. When we get to Daddy 's office, we tell what has happened. Our story seems incredible. I keep assuring people that we are not making it up. No one knows what to make of it.

CHAPTER 11

Falling in Love

The Holy Spirit knows no one is special
—ACIM, T-15.V.5:1

1959—Age Sixteen

I arrive home from town with Daddy and notice a white '53 Ford sitting in our driveway. I ask Daddy if he knows whose car that is, and he says, "Yes, it's yours!" I love my white Ford. I fix it up with chrome exhaust pipes and mud flaps and add whatever accessories are convenient. The nicest thing about the '53 Ford is that it is the place where Judy and I discover the wonders of necking.

Relationships are the reason we are here. They provide us with our greatest joy and our deepest pain. Of all mystical experiences, love is the most wonderful, expanding and exciting. We all have a great desire to melt, merge and fall back into oneness. During my sophomore year in high school I notice a tall, beauteous girl named Judy Femmer in my art class. She has long flaxen hair; two rabbit type front teeth, a beautiful overbite, large luscious lips, and a cute laugh. She is beauty and grace and womanhood personified. Whenever she passes, my eyes fall on and stay with her. I sit behind her in class and stare at the nape of her neck. A sun worshipper, Judy always has a golden tan. I position myself in the hall so I can walk behind her—just to get a whiff of her scent, and to watch the way she walks down the hall and navigates the stairs.

We are busy working the farm the summer of 1959. At the end of the summer, I take a train to Atlanta, Georgia, to spend a week with Aunt Sue and Uncle Sam. It is the first time I have gone a long distance by myself and I'm enjoying my independence.

Whether you like it or not, history is on our side. We'll bury you!
—Nikita Krushchev

I'm trying to read *Inside Russia Today* by Joseph Gunther, a best-selling book on communism. Joseph McCarthy frightens everyone in the early fifties, then sputnik is launched in 1957, a U-2 spy plane is shot down over the Soviet Union, Cuba becomes Communist under Castro, and the Berlin Wall goes up in Germany. The cold war has everyone frozen in fear. I begin a diary on January 1, 1960, and write in it every day through the middle of 1966, so I've got a record of what has happened on a day-to-day basis. Diary entry for April 18, 1960 reads: "Communism is such a formidable problem. It now seems clear that it will take over the world in the next twenty years." Such is the terror and trepidation with which we are indoctrinated.

Reading the book on communism is difficult. My mind keeps drifting to Judy. I can hardly wait to get home and call her. Back home, I immediately call and ask her out. Now that I have a car, dating is possible. We are young, innocent and naive. The major excursion for dating is the drive-in theater, where we have the opportunity to learn about necking. I'm ready to learn, and Judy's kisses are oh-so-sweet. And then there is her fragrance. There is something distinctively wonderful about her aroma!

> *Only the eternal can be loved, for love does not die.*
> —ACIM, T. V. 9:1

Falling in love is like being hit over the head. Something uncontrollable happens. It is overwhelming, mystical, incredible—the most inconceivable experience of my life. There is a sensation of merging with Judy, of boundaries breaking down, of becoming one with her. My experiences on the farm involved a merging with nature. This is something new, a merging with another human being. This is better—bigger—grander—deeper—more exciting. I'm overwhelmed, aghast, dumbfounded and thunderstruck. Words are inadequate. No matter how much I tell Judy I love her, it never seems enough. My love for Judy is eternal and will clearly last forever. In fact it does. Falling in love is beautiful, free and flowing. Like a spring breeze, it brings fragrance and beauty. I *fall* in love, tumbling into the experience, dropping my defenses and allowing for a union with Judy. When love first comes, it seems we have touched something eternal. I go to see her. Her mother will not let me go into her room alone with her. I want to explain, "You don't understand. I *am* Judy. We are *one* soul."

1960—Age Seventeen

Our junior year of high school, Judy and I start going steady and we become an item. I drive by and pick her up each morning and drop her off each day after school, often finding time to make out. We start a photo album of our life together. Like other couples in Mexico, at night we drive around the square. I'm not sure why we do this. I guess because it is the center of town. We go downtown and cruise around, listening to KXEO

74

with Elvis, the Everly Brothers and the incessant repetition of *It's an itsy-bitsy tiny weeny yellow polka-dot bikini* on the car radio. Driving around the square is "the thing" to do. I wonder if kids still do this. I doubt it. There's not much left of downtown Mexico. We also drive in the country at night with the windows all rolled down. When we aren't driving, we're parking in Elmwood Cemetery and Apple Tree Orchard in the woods on the huge A.P. Green estate. Petting is all there is; no serious sex is ever considered. We're going to wait till we get married.

One evening, on the way home after a date with Judy, I fall asleep at the wheel of the car and go off the road. I wake up with the car still moving—knocking down corn in Banisters cornfield. I turn the wheel, step on the gas so as not to lose momentum, go back up the embankment and on to the gravel road without stopping. The next day I go back and look. It is clear that somebody went off the road, made a U-turn in the cornfield and came back up on to the road again.

The train tracks go through the middle of Mexico right behind Judy's house next to a huge pile of coal used for the electric power plant only a hundred yards away. Her father works as a mechanic on road graders and is, unbeknownst to me, an alcoholic. Her mother is very overweight. Judy once asked her mother why she ate so much and she said, "because I'm so unhappy." Judy's mother often threatens that she is not going to be there when Judy returns from school. Judy must thus find an excuse to call home in the middle of the day, just to see if she is there. Judy is in some sense "from the wrong side of the tracks." I don't care. All I know is that I love her. I feel that this wonderful feeling I have with Judy I can have with no one else. Judy is absolutely perfect. She is wonderful, naive, and innocent. She can do no wrong—she would not know how. And we share two common passions—reading and chess. I'm keeping track of the books I read. Now it's George Orwell's *1984* and *Animal Farm.* Judy is a junkie for the printed word. She devours books like a person taking vitamins. She still does. By this time she has read thousands. She was the second person to read this book.

Daddy Mundy dies of cancer on December 5, 1960. I'm lying awake in bed when I hear Daddy come home from the hospital. Going into the bedroom he says to Mother, "He's gone." I don't think he is really gone. His body, however, is gone. I inherit his silver Bulova wristwatch. I still have it. And I get the use of his Lark Studebaker, which has a unique feature. The back of the front seat goes down, and combined with the back

75

seat, turns into a bed. You can imagine the possible uses. Although Judy and I have not made love, we have explored each other's bodies.

Daddy begins building a house in Mexico. Christmas of 1960 is the last on the farm, the only home Ann and I have ever known. After twenty years of farming, Daddy is tired of all the work. Farming is a risky business. He wants to come home at the end of the day and have nothing more complicated to do than mow the lawn on a riding mower. No more animals, no more milking, no more fixing broken tractors, no more dirt, no more messy mud and stinky manure. Daddy wants to relax a little bit; besides, he is having some real success in selling real estate.

At Christmas, Mother gives me The Oxford Red Letter Edition of the *King James Version* of the Bible with a complete index. The floppy leather cover and the golden gilt-edged, tissue-thin pages mean it is a real proper Bible. I am thrilled. I will rely on it many times in the composition of sermons. Its poetry is magnificent. It still holds a place of honor on my desk.

1961—Age Eighteen

In January, we move into our new ranch style home in Mexico. Our new home is clean and well organized, and there are no chor . We've moved up the social scale just a little. Our nearest neighbors are doctors. Daddy installs a modern intercom system that works from the kitchen into each of the bedrooms. The radio can be played throughout the house. The morning of our first day in our new home, Daddy wakes us with a "Rise and shine, Jon and Ann" over the intercom. We hold an auction for all of our farm equipment and accessories, including my Lionel train set. Daddy builds a workshop for himself in the basement. Mother wanted to stay on the farm. I did too. I loved it so much. Daddy wants to be free of it. Besides, I'm graduating from high school in five months and I'm going to take off.

During our senior year, I begin to notice other girls. Judy is reserved, quiet and bookish. I love those features. I'm also attracted to girls who are more outgoing. I love being in love. Still, I have found my love too soon. Things begin to get rocky. We break up in February and I begin dating other girls. Entries in my diary read: "I had a date with Susan Botts" or "a date with Nancy Sterner." Then I add, "It's not the same as being with Judy." The other girls are nice, fun to talk to. Still, it isn't like the bonding that comes with being in love. They do not have that freshness,

76

that sweetness, that laugh, that aroma that *is* Judy. There is something eternal in Judy, something beyond anything I have ever known. By March we are back together again. Diary entry for the 5th says, "I missed her so. It is so good to be back." In April we are off again.

I read *Robinson Crusoe* by Daniel Defoe, and I'm taken by the conversation between Crusoe and Friday on the topic of hell. Hell is a new idea to Friday, and he doesn't get it. In diary entries of April 12 and 13, I'm struggling with the question of Hell. Is it so? If it is so, why such a horrible idea? Why would an all-powerful, loving God permit the presence of Hell? Life is so short. We come here, we get maybe eighty years. Then it ends. We get one time around. That's it! During that time we either make some faulty decisions that land us in *the eternal* fires of Hell, or we make right decisions and go to Heaven forever. Why would an all-wise and loving God punish someone because they are not as wise as He is? Do we go to Hell because we are naive and immature? I don't get it. I want to be a minister. This doctrine, however, seems excessively cruel. I will never preach fear. I will never try to scare people into being good.

Diary entry April 30: "Judy and I broke up. We love each other so much. Still, I have a college education to get through—and traveling to do. It really hurts. We will not go together anymore. I will go on to do all the things I can and she will, too."

Diary entry May 10: "I went to see Judy after school today. All the things I wrote on April 30th are not true. I cannot possibly leave her."

Diary entry May 17, the day after my eighteenth birthday—we have broken up: "I don't have much to do. There is little homework. It is so near the end of school. There are no more sports—only lots of time to think about Judy—what is she doing? Are other guys asking her out? Is she going?"

I send away for a positive-thinking record by Earl Nightingale entitled *The Greatest Secret in the World.* The greatest secret in the world is: "We become what we think about." I find the book *Yoga for Americans* by Indra Devi at the library and begin to put into practice, as much as I can, each of her suggestions, getting up early each day to do yoga and meditate. I am very attracted to the East. The colorful rituals, the romanticism of far off lands pulls me in. Someday I will visit India. I'm talking with a group of boys about nicknames. They ask me what I would like to be called, and I say, "Yogi."

77

I date Lynn Van Matre, the daughter of a local lawyer. Lynn will later become the music editor for the *Chicago Tribune* and remain a lifelong friend. We'll have a date again in 1985, when she comes to New York to review a concert. I enjoy going with Lynn to Christian Science services. I'm impressed by their emphasis on the power of the mind and the use of prayer.

I go to revival meetings to watch passionate preachers pounding the pulpit. There are lots of women fanning themselves with fans with pictures of Jesus on them and singing, singing, singing. Mother's favorite hymn is "Beneath the Old Olive Tree." My favorite is "Whispering—whispering hope, O how welcome thy voice." Diary entry of June 4 indicates going to a Jehovah's Witnesses meeting. They are predicting the imminent end of the world.

There are a number of Mennonites who live near Mexico. I'm intrigued by these people's apparent hold on the inner life and love of the Missouri countryside. I drag Judy or some other girl off on Sunday afternoon jaunts to visit them in the country. These people believe you should do nothing worldly. They don't vote or hold public office. They have only horses and buggies, nothing with rubber tires. They do not smoke, drink or go to parties. We buy butter brickle, fudge candy and straw hats from them. Sometimes there are so many flies on the fudge and butter brickel that we can't bring ourselves to eat it. Their yards, filled with barefoot children, are often lacking in grass and, on rainy days, turn into a messy muddle of mud.

While I'm flirting with other girls, other guys begin to notice what I had seen before anyone else—Judy is the most beautiful and truly enchanting girl in our school. Other guys start asking her out. Yet we are in love. It is all very painful. Somebody else asks her to the senior prom. I wind up asking Pat Adams, the local judge's daughter. There is nothing wrong with Pat Adams except that she isn't Judy. Judy is the only one who matters. It is too late.

I'm truly miserable. Mother, seeing my sorry state, comes sits on the edge of my bed, holds my hand and we talk. She is my steady raft on a rampaging river—the only one who has any idea what I'm going through. At the senior prom I see Judy dancing extra close with her date, and my heart sinks. I nearly faint. Pat asks me why I'm so upset. I cannot explain it. All I can do is wait for the next day when I will run to Judy, fall on my knees, beg forgiveness and implore her to come back to me. That is exactly what I do. I'm unable to sleep after coming home. Is she off with her date making love for the first time? Truth is, she has her first taste of orange juice and vodka, gets sick and is home by three a.m. At seven a.m. I call and implore her to come out and talk. We go to a lake, near KXEO radio station, get a rowboat and go out into the lake. Though I had no such intentions, years later Judy told me I was so despondent and in such a desperate state, she thought I was going to swamp the boat and kill us both. Diary entry June 17, the day after Judy's eighteenth birthday: "Judy and I are going steady again. I gave her my ring. I love Judy so much and she loves me. We'll be happy."

CHAPTER 12

The Call into Ministry
The Universe's University

After a church service one Sunday morning, a young boy suddenly announces to his mother, "Mom, I've decided to become a minister when I grow up." "That's okay with us. What made you decide that?" "Well," says the boy, "I have to go to church on Sunday anyway, and I figure it will be more fun to stand up and yell, than to sit and listen." I'm too religious not to go to church and as long as I'm there I should be working.

We may choose a career. A vocation chooses us. My decision to go into the ministry has nothing to do with some wise old preacher pulling me aside for a talk. It comes not as a conversion experience at a revival, nor does it come at the encouragement of family or friends. I don't think Daddy ever quite knew how he came to have a son who is a minister. More than anything, it's my walks in the woods, which draws me in. I keep feeling there is something more—something calling—something invisible, something imponderable, something imperceptible—something very real. I have read the scriptures of the verdant pastures on the back of our farm. I have been an avid reader. Nature is, as Thoreau once said, "a place where much is published but little is printed."

Watching the cows grazing in the pasture behind the barn I'm overcome with a sense of the interconnectedness of all beings. There is a dimension within and beyond where awareness saturates every particle. I look at the meadows, the woods, the small lake and the pond. I look at one particular field. In the evening, there is often a crimson glow stretching its colors out across the flatlands to the west as the sun, like a big pat of butter, melts on the horizon. At night how clear the stars are in the big, black sky! When the weather is absolutely beautiful, we sometimes sleep outside on canvas cots. One evening I write:

Sitting outside on a summer evening, after a hard day of work, our bellies full of mother's supper, daddy smoking a cigar, talking about nothing consequential sometimes not talking at all; listening to the katydids, tree frogs and crickets, watching evening fall, and then the stars and the fire flies. Sleep comes so peacefully these summer evenings.

I keep asking: What's behind everything? What is really going on? The church, it seems, is the only place dealing with these questions. Nature prods, and so begins the quest—the church, books, classes, professors, travels. More than anything else, I keep coming back to one pasture out behind the barn, high on a hill overlooking the valley. When I have been too long without this awareness, it is time to take another walk, to hear again this inaudible voice. Most every year, I return to this pasture, usually in August. August holds the deepest feeling. In August you find the detailed Queen Anne's lace, the yellow yarrow and the blue cornflowers. August has all the music of nature—bees, katydids, tree frogs, crickets and locusts. August has all the smells—the newly mown hay, the sun, the sweat, the dry earth— the energy of nature.

Walking the pastures, sitting in the woods, you can't help noticing something behind the obvious, something that itself causes everything to grow, to breathe—something that *animates*. Walking is a powerful spiritual process. Pilgrims get where they are going by walking. Walking with our soles, we engage our souls. In walking, I listen, and to this day I walk to get an answer.

I went to the woods because I wished to live deliberately, to confront the essential facts of life and see if I could learn what it had to teach, and not, when I come to die, discover that I have not lived. —Henry David Thoreau, *Walden*

German esoteric philosopher Rudolf Steiner once said when it comes to developing a taste for spiritual things, "one is especially fortunate to grow up within the context of nature." Here clearly in the daily events—in death and new life—a mystery unfolds and a story is told. With every new spring comes new hope, new sunshine and flowers; with every winter comes the quiet blankets of snow, shorter days, longer nights and rest for the soul.

A province for the beautiful must be celebrated outdoors where there is no house and no housekeeper. —Henry David Thoreau, *Walden*

To know the essence of things, the ancient alchemists say, it is necessary to know the process by which things grow, ripen, rot, decay and turn over into new growth. If you want to know about God's Kingdom, say the alchemists, study the working of a compost heap. From the alchemical point of view, Heaven is *a happening*. We don't have the exact word for it in English. The ancient Greeks called it *automate*—that which produces of itself.

We need not force anything. We need only allow Spirit to spring up and grow. Heaven is something fine and seemingly hidden. Jesus says it is inside, working subtly like the rebirth of nature in springtime. Spirit is always stirring deep within. It's like leaven in bread. It changes everything. It expands and grows, we know not how. With proper nurturing, it matures into something wonderful. In archeological digs, seeds hundreds of years old have been found which, when planted, came back to life. Deep within is the memory of God. Though buried for centuries, it can be brought back to life. It just needs some light, a little encouragement, a bit of nourishment, and a willingness not to be afraid of the dark. We only need to gently push aside the dark soil that has kept everything hidden.

To plant seeds and watch the renewal of life, this is the commonest delight of the human race, the most satisfactory thing that one can do. —Charles Warner

Growth occurs at first as a process of inward turning, of becoming more and more concentrated. Then there is expansion. Then there is a turning inward again, then another expansion. That's how things grow. It's like watching cells divide. Pierre Teilhard de Chardin says it is the way all things grow, including awareness. The most natural way for something to grow is logarithmically, or exponentially. A chambered nautilus (a sea creature with a coiled shell) is a perfect example of exponential growth outward from the center with ever-increasing natural expansion on the previous dimension. The shell grows as the organism focuses on inner growth. As we grow aware of our mission, as we focus on cultivating inner life, so does the exterior develop naturally, without distraction.

The earth produces of itself, first the blade, then the ear,
and then the full grain in the ear. —Mark 4:28

Jesus' parables tell us of the sureness of Heaven and the inevitability of its coming. First there is a turning inward—first the grain, then the ear, then the full corn. "The extension of God's Being is spirit's only function. Its fullness cannot be contained, any more than can the fullness of its Creator. Fullness is extension" (ACIM, T-7.IX.3: 1-3). The full corn is the meaning of the grain and the ear. As we grow in awareness, as we fulfill our function, we enter Heaven. The parable of the mustard seed and the leaven suggests that the discovery of Heaven is something subtle. There is something there and hidden. Deep inside the earth itself, deep inside our hearts, ourselves, somewhere there is an answer. Do you not know it? Have you not heard it?

CHAPTER 13

College and the Move into Ministry

I quit school because I didn't like recess.—Robert Duval in *The Apostle*

No Mundy or Callahan has ever gone to college. Gung-ho to get on with life, I see no reason to wait. A week after graduating from high school, I'm off to Culver-Stockton, a small Disciples of Christ college in Canton, Missouri, a small town on the Mississippi River a hundred miles northeast of Mexico. Judy cannot afford to go to college, at least not yet, and has to stay home and work. I have a 4-H scholarship and enough money for college, provided that I also have a part-time job.

The summer of '61, I share a room with James Wafula, from Kenya. James is a unique character, with a wide grin and big teeth. He loves chess and beats me nearly every time. Halfway through the short summer session, Mother, Daddy and Judy come to see me. Judy is wearing a black summer dress with little red dots with thin straps over her tan shoulders. God, she looks so good! She is so beautiful. I want her so badly.

After summer classes, I take off with a 4-H group to tour our nation's capital. I take up photography and capture the best pictures I can for a 4-H photography contest at the County Fair. Then it's off to Camp Miniwaska near Muskegon, Michigan, by way of train to Milwaukee and an all-night boat, the 4,000 ton Milwaukee Clipper, across Lake Michigan.

I dare you to be the strongest boy in this class. —William H. Danforth

Camp Miniwaska is based on the works of a well-known Missourian, William H. Danforth, who wrote a book for boys called *I Dare You.* He says there are four basic areas of life, the physical, mental, social and spiritual. The idea is to live a well-balanced life by developing each of these areas. There is a four-year program and this year I graduate. Each morning we run into lake Michigan. There is a competition to see who can do it every day for the two-week duration. The lake is freezing even in August. You must run in till you are up to your neck in the water. We close each day sitting around a campfire singing. Every day I write Judy. Every day my diary mentions how much I miss her. We are required to spend time alone meditating in the sand dunes. This is not what I'm to later learn as the quieting of one's mind. It is rather a time for self-reflection, and, for an eighteen-year-old, thinking about the future. I'm convinced my life is to be in the ministry. Mostly, I'm thinking about Judy.

I volunteer for a week as a helper in an orphanage in St. Louis. I'm given the job of spending the evening with a half dozen six and seven-year-old girls sleeping on the orphanage grounds in a tent. It rains; water seeps in under the tent, and the girls, seeking refuge, climb on me like a log in the middle of a river. Two of them are calling for "Daddy." I get no sleep. During the night someone breaks into the orphanage and rapes a retarded teenage girl.

I return to Mexico to work at the county fair. While I'm directing cars, I read *The Autobiography of Benjamin Franklin*. I'm impressed by all he was—Renaissance man, lover of books, printer—father of the American Philosophical Society. I want to create a magazine like his *Poor Richard's Almanac* with wise sayings and seasonal information. He is also one of my hero's heroes. Mark Twain also admired Benjamin Franklin. They were both typesetters and printers. They both were humorous and cynical writers who wrote for the papers they worked for under a pseudonym. Someday, I'll busy myself with typesetting, printing, humor and writing.

Having no car the first months of my freshman year, I hitchhike home each Friday to see Judy. Bob Adams, an older student from Mexico, has a car and comes home on Saturdays, so I have a ride back on Sunday evening. Then Daddy gets me my own car, a metallic blue-gray '56 Volkswagen convertible. One Sunday evening, on the way back to college, Bob Adams' car goes off the road. He is decapitated, and the other boys in his car are each seriously injured.

I join Tau Kappa Epsilon fraternity, though I do not move into the fraternity house during the first year. I enroll in classes in *Beginning Preaching* and *Public Speaking*. I become a varsity debater and I win the Kuntz Trophy in public speaking.

Small rural Missouri churches cannot afford to hire seminary graduates and are thus served by lay speakers, retired pastors or pre-ministerial college students. These jobs are only given to juniors and seniors. I become friends with Bill McGill, a junior serving a circuit of three rural Missouri churches. I'm so eager to get into the ministry I coax Bill into letting me go with him to preach at Hawk Point Community Church. On November 19, 1961, I give my first sermon titled *Happiness Is*. I have five points.

84

Happiness is:

1. Good health.

2. An active, curious and investigative mind always engaged in learning.

3. Good relationships with friends and family secured through being a good friend oneself.

4. A vocation that you love and feel committed to.

5. An active spiritual life of reading, prayer and meditation.

It still makes a good message. I'm not concerned about converting people to Christianity or trying to save people's souls. My heroes are Norman Vincent Peale ("Change your thoughts and you change your world,") author of *The Power of Positive Thinking* and Dale Carnegie ("Flaming enthusiasm, backed up by horse sense and persistence, is the quality that most frequently makes for success"), author of *How To Win Friends and Influence People*. I'm going to be an optimistic positive-thinking preacher.

At home after Thanksgiving dinner, I'm talking with Daddy, Uncle Sam Carter and Uncle Estel when Uncle Sam tells a story of a hunting expedition in which he shot a deer, shattering its front leg. Despite its crippled condition, the deer manages to limp off into the woods. They never found it. The thought of the poor crippled deer with a shattered leg going off someplace in the forest to die is too much. Though I tell no one, I vow that day that my hunting days are over. I will never again kill an animal—mice and insects being an exception.

During Thanksgiving vacation, Bill McGill gets beat up in a barroom brawl. He is fired immediately by big bellied, balding, Rev. Charles Crank, the district superintendent. Apparently, it doesn't matter whether Bill is guilty or innocent in this; the fact that he is in a bar is sufficient grounds for dismissal. I call Bill. As far as he is concerned, he has had it with the church and is happy he is out, or so he says. I go to see Rev. Crank. (His name is the butt of many jokes.) I ask for Bill's job. He tells me they do not give these jobs to freshmen. I tell him, "I have already preached at Hawk Point, and the people like me." He has no one else to fill the position so he says I can substitute till he finds someone. I begin the first Sunday in December of 1961. I'm licensed (not ordained) by the Disciples of Christ and begin serving Hawk Point Community, Ariel Christian and Fairview Christian Churches.

I buy Bill's books on sermon illustrations, wedding and funeral services, ministers' prayers and so on. I type up the prayers on three-by-five cards, cutting out what I feel are overworked words and phrases, including removing "In Jesus' name" from a lot of prayers. Though I love Jesus, there's an "Isn't Jesus wonderful?" language that seems to miss the point. Is it not our task to see what he saw and do what he did, or are we just to worship him? I work as a minister throughout my college years, driving my '56 Volkswagen beetle convertible around a circuit of nearly 200 miles every Sunday—preaching and conducting worship services, baptizing in the river, performing marriage ceremonies and funerals. My salary is thirty-five dollars per week—not bad for a college student.

1962 —Age Nineteen—Back to Judy

Judy and I are together every weekend throughout the spring, summer and early fall of 1962. I'm either studying, writing a sermon, conducting a worship service, working on a debate, or spending time with Judy. I'm spending lots of time in varsity speech contests.

Judy comes to Culver-Stockton, and we go to a TKE dinner dance on a Mississippi river boat in Hannibal, Missouri. While we're eating, Judy takes off a shoe under the table and reaches under my pants cuff and caresses the side of my leg with her toes. It's incredibly exciting to think we have this little secret thing going on. We have such a great connection. We get back to Mexico at two a.m. I drop Judy off and go home and find the phone ringing as I walk in the door. It is Judy. Her mother is having a heart attack. Her father, apparently drunk, is out of his mind—wandering about in a delirium. Mexico doesn't really have an ambulance. We only have a hearse with oxygen. The driver says I will have to help him put her mother in the "ambulance" and hold oxygen on her while we go to the hospital. Judy is now also hysterical, along with her poor father. Judy's mother later says I saved her life.

Judy spends the night at the hospital. She works the next day and then goes back to the hospital. At nine I pick her up and bring her back to our house, and we fall asleep together on the living room couch. We have never slept together. It all seems so natural. Holding her in my arms, I think how wonderfully sweet she is, how close we are. I could never leave her. Although Judy's mother recovers she is never as strong after her attack.

There is not much in the way of inspiration in Rev. Crank's class in Beginning Preaching. It is pretty matter of fact. Interestingly, Jesus never taught his disciples to preach—only to pray. Culver-Stockton has required chapel at eleven each Wednesday morning. Few enjoy or appreciate this prerequisite. On my nineteenth birthday, I give one of my positive thinking addresses to the entire student body. I decide that each birthday thereafter I'll do something significant on May 16.

I baptize seven people in the Cuivre River. The crowd spreads out all along the riverbank so everyone can see. Everyone is dressed in their Sunday best, some with hats, others with fancy hairdos. Two young women are wearing white blouses, and when I dunk them in the river and bring them back up again, the water makes their blouses cling to their bodies, revealing the details of their breasts. I can't help noticing. Still, I look away lest anyone notice my noticing. As they emerge from the water, their mothers notice and run forward screaming, wrapping towels around their daughters, and escorting them to their cars.

One Sunday, at Ariel Christian, right after the offering is placed on the altar in front of the pulpit, ceiling plaster falls, catching the front of the offering plates and throwing the money back out into the congregation. Though startling, it was in fact quite funny.

One wintry Sunday morning, I awake to a white wilderness. A foot or more of snow has fallen during the night. I'm not sure if I should try to drive or not. I have never missed a Sunday. I leave an hour early. The rear-mounted motor on the VW Beetle digs into the snow, and off I go. I almost lose it on a curve on a cliff that would have taken me over a precipice into the Mississippi river. I stop with the front wheels in a ditch, hanging over the edge of the road and slowly, very slowly, back up, catch my breath and start out again. I make it to the church on time. Only one family shows up, a man, his wife and two young daughters. Their farm is conveniently located just across the road from the church. I ask the farmer what he wants to do, and he says that he has come to church, so he expects we should "do church," so we "do church." The four of them sit on the front row and we go through the service. I give my sermon and take up a collection. After it's over, I go down front and ask him what he thought of the service, and he says that when he goes out to give hay to the cows, if only one cow shows up, he doesn't dump the whole load. (This story is true up to the punch line, which I couldn't resist. I don't remember exactly what he said.)

87

The First Pilgrimage

I make my first pilgrimage to New Mellery Abbey, a Trappist monastery near Dubuque, Iowa. During my college years and for many years thereafter I make regular retreats to New Mellery. Here are truly religious men. The monks get up at two-fifteen each morning to sing the night office, a collection of Psalms and prayers the monks recite in a monotone or chant in Gregorian plainsong. (Some thirty years later, these Gregorian chants hit the top of the charts in the New Age music category.) They have only enough time to splash cold water on their faces before they are to be in their seats in the chapel ready to sing. Day in and day out, month after month, it's the same routine. None of them owns any material possessions beyond a razor, toothbrush and one change of clothes. Those who are priests each own a chalice. They eat no meat and sleep on straw mattresses on wooden platforms in individual stalls. After five years they make a vow that they will never leave the monastery. There is something incredible going on here, something I haven't experienced in the Protestant church—a resolute singleness of purpose exemplified by carefully preserved perpetual silence, which enables the inward process. These men seem centered, and content.

Aldous Huxley, watching his house burn down in the Bel Air fires of 1961, said the experience provided him with *a marvelously clean feeling.* Freed as he was by everything external, he was open even more keenly to the mystical dimension. Trappists have none of the worries that beset breadwinners. They have plenty of time for God.

At spring break each year, lacking the money to go to Florida and needing to take care of my churches on Sundays, I venture to New Mellery. There I befriend the gray-bearded guest master who comes to my room after supper and talks about inner life. Only the guest master and those who have a relationship with the outside world—the clerks in the gift shop who sell honey, whole grain breads, woodcarvings, candles and such—are allowed to speak. Even this is kept to a minimum. I'm enchanted with their simple, peaceful way of life. I get to eat with them in their cafeteria, sharing their all-natural communal meal. It is a pleasant diversion to walk about on the monastery grounds. The most wonderful thing is sitting in the mornings and evenings listening to their singing of the divine office.

The fall of 1962 is rocky for Judy and me, on and off again. I'm constantly torn between wanting to make a deeper commitment to Judy—as in asking her to marry me—or getting on with my education and my growing desire to travel and see the world. Like Daddy, I have the wanderlust. The problem is, I'm only nineteen.

All students are to make a chart showing how we spent each hour of the week. The professors are interested in how much time we allow for study. My chart is all right, my professor says, except I should not go home every Friday. Judy wants to get married. More importantly, she needs to get away from home. By this time, even I'm aware of the fact that her father, though not abusive, is nevertheless an alcoholic. While Judy is home alone in Mexico, and I'm off in college, the wolves move in. Judy begins to date other guys. Diary entry of November 25 says, "I called Judy. She has a date tonight. I can't stand it."

For Thanksgiving vacation I go to Chicago with Bob Newsome, a college buddy. Bob is planning to become a psychologist, and I'm majoring in psychology. Bob and I visit patients in the Cook County mental hospital. With the benefit of a guide we go from locked ward to locked ward, seeing people in the most miserable of circumstances. In a ward of severely regressed women, one of them pees all over herself when we walk into the room. No one makes any attempt to clean up the mess. I notice a woman holding onto the side of a door talking to herself. I go close to her. She says, "I'm scared. I'm scared." She repeats it over again and again. A nurse says she's been doing that for twenty years. This scene of human wretchedness tears at my heart. This is the closest I've been to hell on earth.

1963—Age Twenty

I make a note in my diary that starting this year, we must now use zip codes. Judy commences college part-time at the University of Missouri in Columbia and begins to commute there with Jim Reynolds. I never liked Jim Reynolds, buzzing around town as he did in his fancy blue and white Corvette. Then comes the fateful days of Saturday and Sunday, June 1 and 2. Judy and I spend Saturday afternoon together, and she tells me she is going to elope with Jim on Sunday evening. I beseech her not to do this. Try as I might—no matter how much I profess my love for her—there is nothing I can do to dissuade her. Sunday at church, I can hardly keep my mind on what I'm doing. I hurry back to Mexico. It is evening when I arrive at her house. I park a couple of blocks away so I will not be noticed. I walk to her house. Her mother will not let me see her and closes the door in my face. I start walking around trying to think of a way to stop her. Suddenly, I see Jim Reynolds' car. I run behind Judy's house onto the mountainous pile of coal that separates her home from the train tracks. Hurriedly, clambering up the pile of coal, I stumble and fall, getting coal dust on my good white shirt. Jim turns into the lot beside the house. The headlights of his car sweep over me standing on top of the pile of coal like a madman in a black and white Montgomery Clift or Marlon Brando movie. No doubt he has seen me. He drives around to the front of the house. Judy runs out. They leave.

I get into my car and start driving back to college, crying out loud to Judy, begging her to hear me—to turn around and come home. My heart is beating like a machine gun, and I'm banging on the steering wheel. I have lost the love of my life. I'm so deeply afflicted and in such a miserable state, I feel as if I know what those crazy people in the mental hospitals are going through. If this is life, I'm not much interested. I never think of suicide. I decide it's not a good idea to have children. If this is the kind of suffering human beings have to go through, why subject another soul to such despair? This is the bottom of the bottom of the pit of despondency. I have fallen into an abyss—nothing can save me from this unhappy state. How can this possibly be for my own or Judy's greater good? We are one soul in two bodies. There is no meaning in this. This is not the way things are supposed to turn out. We are supposed to be happy together. We are supposed to get married and have kids. Life doesn't make sense. I cry and cry till I'm numb.

I'm too dejected to return to the fraternity house and let anyone see the sorry state I'm in. I stop at a cheap motel in Monroe City. Sleep is impossible. Judy and I have never made love. We were going to wait till we were married. Now she is actually giving herself to another man. How can she? She belongs to me. I belong to her. While I'm alone in this dirty little old motel, crying and trying to wash the coal dust out of my white shirt—she is making love for the first time, with another man in another motel. This thought is so insufferably incomprehensible, so unfathomable, that I cannot think about it. Try as I might, I cannot *not* think about it. I lay awake wide-eyed in the dark—crying throughout the night. It is easily the worst night of my life. I determine that, if I ever get free of this green-eyed monster called insane jealousy, I will never visit this state of mind again.

Diary entry for June 5: "My soul cries out for the love of you and receives no answer." Then, tragedy of tragedies, I read *Wuthering Heights*. The love that Heathcliff and Catherine have for each other is, I feel the love Judy and I have, and I weep till I nearly die. There are many dark clouds in my mind. The task of letting her go is formidable, and I'm not successful. Many years will pass before I realize any success in this endeavor. You can't go back to what you were before, after you have loved somebody. This woman from Missouri has left a scar on my heart.

Six years later, Judy will divorce Jim and we will renew our relationship. Judy will go on to earn three college degrees. She will become a schoolteacher and grade school principal. Over the years, we remain friends. We call each other on our birthdays and at Christmas. Judy calls to tell me of her struggle with the death of a friend. I call to tell her I've had open-heart surgery and cancer. We send jokes and notes to each other over the Internet. Our lives take different paths. We still love each other. She has her own life now, and though it is many years in coming, I wind up happily married.

Failed Romance

Romantic love is both a many-splendored and a many-splintered thing. If we feel possessive or jealous, then the *attraction of love for love* becomes something different—a reinforcement of guilt rather than the bringer of oneness. We can all tell about the experience of pain associated with failed romance. In the coming years, I'm to have my share. Read romantic novels, watch movies or listen to popular songs—how full of illusion and pain! "I can't live without you, I can't laugh and I can't sing. I'm finding it hard to do anything. If you only knew what I'm going through . . . " There are tens of thousands of such songs. Most love songs are not about real love. They are about the pain surrounding romance. Plato called romantic love *divine madness*. I listen to one line from a popular song on the radio that says: "I must be living in a fantasy world," and I think, "Yes—no doubt a fantasy."

> *Fantasy is a distorted form of vision. Fantasies of any kind are distortions because they always involve twisting perception into unreality.*
> —ACIM, T-1.VII.3: 1-2

Why did I have to learn such a tough lesson at such an early age? Why does anyone? Love comes with great ado. It fills our whole being. Like all mystical experiences, it isn't something we have much control over. It is not in our hands. It never was. You can feel the coolness and the freshness of love across your face. Try to capture it, to define and describe it—and you lose it.

Judy is gone and that part of my life is over. Try as I might, I cannot forget her. There is nothing I can do but go ahead and do the best I can despite my dreary state. One positive thing has happened. I have actually fallen in love. I know what love is and it is incredible—so big, so beyond me, so ineffably wonderful. Someday, hopefully, it will happen again at a better time, under better conditions.

CHAPTER 14

Back to College

Onyango Josiah

During my first summer at Culver-Stockton, I'm delighted to meet two young men from Kenya, James Wafula, my first roommate, and Onyango Josiah, who becomes my best friend. Onyango is six foot four with dark black skin, scholarly looking round glasses and short-cropped hair. He is the brightest, most interesting man I have ever met. A few years older, he is twenty-four to my nineteen. He dresses impeccably. He is a man of the world. His father is a Provincial Governor in Kenya, and Onyango travels with him in his upscale Land Rover throughout the province that he over-sees. He is royalty. Having received his high school diploma in England, he speaks an eloquent "Queen's English." He is a true gentleman.

I bring Onyango home to meet Mother and Daddy and take him to preach in each of my churches. We arrive early one Sunday morning at Hawk Point while Sunday School is still going on in the one-room church. Not wishing to disturb the class, we go to the coffee shop next door to wait. The waitress looks at us nervously. Pointing her pencil at Onyango she says, "We can't serve him in here." I ask, "Why not?" Her boss walks over and tells us to get up and get out. Onyango is a foreign dignitary, far more cultured and refined than those who now refuse to give him a cup of coffee. I do not know what to do. I'm abashed and confused. I get coffee for the two of us and we go and sit in the car. Onyango seems to take it pretty well. Later, he tells me how much it hurt him. When we go into the church, some of the parishioners get up and walk out.

I take Onyango to Ariel Christian Church near Mark Twain's Home in Florida, Missouri. There he gives a brilliant talk in which he tells the story of a father who, wishing to busy his son in some useful play takes a picture of the world and cuts it into pieces like a jigsaw puzzle. He asks the boy to put it back together, thinking it will occupy the boy for some time. The boy finishes the puzzle in only minutes. How is it possible, the father asks, seeing how he knows so little of the world? It's easy, the boy says. On the back there is a picture of a man, so he put the man together and the world came together automatically. At the end of the service Onyango and

I stand at the front door greeting people. One of the men, an elder, in whose home I have been a guest for Sunday dinner grasps my hand rather firmly, leans forward, pulls me toward him, and says slowly and distinctly into my ear, "You're just like Kennedy and all the other Goddamned nigger lovers, aren't ya?"

My VW Beetle has been giving me trouble, and I'm not sure what to do, when Daddy comes up with a great solution and trades the Beetle in for a new beige 1963 Valiant convertible. For the next five years it will serve me well, crisscrossing the United States many times.

Seeing how dejected I am after Judy's elopement, Onyango decides it is time for me to lose my virginity, and he has a plan. There is a black girl at Culver-Stockton from Jamaica named "Celia"; she and Onyango are friends—not lovers. Jamaicans and Africans have a more relaxed attitude toward sex than we do here in mid-Missouri. During a school break, we are all going to St. Louis to visit some of Onyango's African friends. While there, Onyango makes arrangements for Celia and me to have a date and spend the night together in a hotel. We start the evening by going to see *West Side Story*. There are many stares at a white boy and a black girl obviously out on a date, and I enjoy this moment of rebelliousness. The love between Maria and Tony is so poignant. Still mourning the loss of Judy, I start to cry. Celia asks me why I'm crying. It is impossible to explain to her. How can I tell her how much I still constantly think about Judy? Celia and I make love all night long. There is no sleep. I'm filled with hurt and pain and energy, and I just want to do it again and again and again, and we do. (Judy, upon reading this manuscript, writes in, "Damn it Jon! That should have been us!")

During Onyango's senior year, he falls in love with, a white girl and the daughter of a Disciple of Christ minister. This is a big mistake! It is impossible for them to be together except in secret. Their trysts are very exciting to Onyango. It is hard for them to conceal their affection for one another. The lady in question, thinking her parents are open-minded, tells them and her mother attempts suicide.

Onyango graduates a year ahead of me and goes to Howard University in Washington D.C. to begin his doctorate in African politics. Diary entry for June 19, 1963 reads: "I just said good-bye to the best friend I have ever had, Mr. Onyango Josiah. We have spent a lot of time together; Chicago, St. Louis, Burlington, Iowa, Mexico, and my churches. I plan to visit him in Kenya some day."

The year after he left, my social psychology professor says, "This College has known only one true genius and that was Onyango Josiah." "Onyango is a genius!" I thought so! Now a professor has confirmed it. Yet, he could not get a haircut in our town. He could not openly date a woman he loved. He couldn't be served in local coffee shops and restaurants. He is a kindhearted, handsome genius snarled in the morass of a mid-western jungle, and in Africa he is a Governor's son.

I spend my senior year in the fraternity house. I'm made editor of the fraternity newsletter. It's my first taste of writing which will actually be printed. Three of us share one small room in the third floor walkup. Roger Innes, a kind, gentle man who works hard to understand algebra, becomes a good friend and buddy. He will later be listed as MIA as a Navy fighter pilot in Vietnam. Roger's body is never found. A TV Documentary is later made about Roger.

Then there is Ted Buhl, a bright, handsome, beer-loving, playboy from St. Louis. Ted's idol is James Dean, and he looks like him, with squinted eyes, raised eyebrows, a turned-up jacket collar, a pack of cigarettes rolled up in his T-shirt sleeve and a cigarette dangling from his lips. He has a "Whatever" attitude. Ted will also go to Vietnam. He will return, though a bit affected by the disaster. Ted is not happy about having to room with "the preacher kid," and barely talks to me unless it is necessary. One evening he explores the fraternity house looking for someone to go out and have a drink. He returns dejected. No one wants to go out. I have finished my studies, so I say I will go. To my surprise, he accepts. (There was no alcohol in our fraternity house and absolutely no drugs. I will not encounter someone smoking marijuana until I'm a twenty-three year old graduate student in California.)

Sitting in a boathouse bar by the Mississippi river, Ted begins to tell me his troubles. His girlfriend has broken up with him and he is feeling wretched. I'm also dejected. The day before, I took the big, beautifully colored picture I had of Judy from our high school graduation out to the trashcan behind the fraternity house, set it afire and watched it burn. So Ted and I cry together, and in that crying, we become friends and remain so—the preacher kid and the playboy. Ted is a fan of Dean Martin, whom he thinks is unappreciated as the finest singer in America. He puts Dean

Martin LPs on the record player and sits and rocks back and forth while he listens through the length of an entire LP. My favorite singer is Nat King Cole. His voice is three parts fog, one part frog.

A new hero, Henry David Thoreau, soon enamors me. I'm smitten by *Walden*. Thoreau's love of solitude and his mystical communion with nature means everything to me.

> *I hearing get, who had but ears, and sight, who had but eyes before: I moments live, who lived but years, and truth discern, who knew but learning's lore. I hear beyond the range of sound, I see beyond the range of sight, new earth, and skies and seas abound and in my day the sun doth pale his light.*

I'm determined to spend the summer of '63 in a cabin in the woods between Mexico and Molino. I will do independent studies in this summer before my senior year. I'll write my senior thesis and spend the summer reading on the porch, meditating and raising vegetables. Miss Kaump, my major advisor, refuses my request. If I want to go to summer school, I'll have to stay on campus.

The United Nations and the Death of JFK

Each November Culver-Stockton sponsors a trip to the United Nations for four students. You have to write an essay on why you want to go. The essays are judged and a selection is made. Four of us students and one professor drive from Missouri to New York City where we tour the UN and sit in on various committee sessions. Onyango comes up from Washington, D.C., so we can spend some time together. He takes me to visit African friends in Harlem. They make a delicious African meal of couscous, chicken, carrots and garbanzo beans. Then, we go to a nightclub in Harlem where I see dancing like I have never seen before, including one woman who seductively rides a man's leg till she—well, you know. I'm feeling very grown up. (In 2003 I enter the name Onyango Josiah into a search engine, and I find a heading from a newspaper saying "the late" Provincial Governor, Onyango Josiah).

We return to Missouri via a visit to Niagara Falls, arriving in Niagara, Canada on the morning of November 22, 1963. In a tower overlooking the falls I overhear a couple of tourists with strong Russian accents talking about our President, John F. Kennedy, about how he has been shot. This is more than a little strange—Russians talking about the assassination of our President! I go to our professor to tell him what I have heard. Suddenly, we are all aware of the fact that something *has* happened, and we rush to our car to turn on the radio for the reports of the shooting in Dallas. It is so impossible—so unbelievable. We take off for Missouri—our ears consistently tuned to the radio. We stop only for gas and bathroom breaks through Ohio, Indiana, Illinois and finally home. The only televisions are in the lobby of the dormitories, fraternity and sorority houses. The biggest space is the main dorm for girls. There we gather round on the floor and watch in tears—Jackie Kennedy in her blood-stained suit, Ruby shooting Oswald, the funeral march with the horse-drawn hearse and little John Jr. saluting. It is indeed the end of an age of innocence.

With the help of the guest master, I get permission to get the life stories of some of the monks at New Mellery Abbey and write a paper for Social Psychology on why men become monks. I put a picture of a monk on the cover with the simple word "Why?" underneath. I tell the story of several men, describing the circumstances that led to their decisions to enter the monastery. My Social Psychology professor is delighted. I have understood, he says, what Social Psychology is all about.

1964—Age Twenty-One

I petition the college to offer a course in The Psychology of Religion. I now have the opportunity to try to understand the meaning of prayer, conversion experiences, belief and mystical experiences. I'm like a pig in mud heaven! I find what is to be the central focus of study for the rest of my life.

I gradually move farther away from friends in the fraternity house and start hanging around with a small group of Onyango's friends, all girls except for Tom Martin and Mike Dixon, two other pre-ministerial students. There is also Celia, Wanda Russel and Diana Weber, all "independent" non-sorority girls. We are a little group of "intellectuals" and poets. Diana is a fine, cute brunette with almost no bridge for her nose. We start to date. People say we look good together, and friends are asking—are we going to get engaged?

I apply to Southern California School of Theology in Claremont, California, which has a four-year program leading to a Doctorate in Religion that sounds perfect. I am accepted and thrilled to know what I'll be doing that fall. I'm going to go someplace really different. I'm going to California. By carrying extra hours each semester and going to summer school every year, I have completed college in three years.

CHAPTER 15

Europe on a Vespa

Like Daddy, I've got an itch to roam. As much as I wanted to wed Judy, I want to wander. I want to see and experience that which is beautiful while I'm young. You cannot settle down and take off at the same time. Judy is gone, so I begin to travel. Ted and I take off for a summer in Europe. I take along a good supply of paperback books. I am determined to read everything that John Steinbeck and Aldous Huxley have written. Right now it's Huxley's *The Doors of Perception*. Huxley is my new hero. He writes intensely and deeply about mystical experiences.

Ted and I take a train to New York City and we go to the World's Fair in Flushing Meadows, Queens. They're cleaning up after a performance by the Beatles, who played there the night before. I love the futuristic shows. Will we some day live under the sea? Will everybody some day have their own computer and their own portable phones?

We board the Auralia, a former troop transport converted to student ship, bound for Southampton, England. Our compartment, consists of four bunk beds with an aisle in between. The room is so narrow you can only stand, sit or lie on a bed. Life on ship is carefree and Bohemian with lots of music, drinking and, although I do not get in on it, sex. I try my hand at Ted's favorite drinks, rum and coke. Combined with the rocking of the ship, it makes me sick and thereafter I can't stand the stuff. Every afternoon and evening there are black and white avant-garde French and Italian films in a small theater in the bow of the ship.

If I take the wings of the morning, or dwell in the uttermost parts of the sea, even there shall Thy hand lead me.—Psalms 139

There is no place you can go to be completely alone. I love standing on the deck looking out at the pewter sea, the wind blowing in my face, the sound of the ocean splashing against the sides of the ship, my soul filled with emotion. There is nothing out there—just the vast emptiness, the great void and enormous openness. This is the kind of feeling I've had on the Missouri plains. Strange—lonely—also connected.

The last night before docking in Southampton, Ted, with nowhere else to go, brings his date back to our room. They climb up onto the bunk above me, and with drunken muffled giggles, make love all night. They moan and groan and I'm afraid they're going to fall down on top of me. I don't know how Ted is feeling the next morning. I am, however, exhausted.

Queeny Coose, our nearest neighbor back on the farm, is a World War II bride from Bristol, England, so our first stop is Bristol to stay with Ivy, one of Queenie's sisters. It's strange to drive on the "wrong" side of the road. Ivy treats us like royalty. Every afternoon we *must* have tea with scones, butter, jam and cream. Everybody is a *mate*. We enjoy eggs, beans and fries for breakfast. We buy two used Vespa motor scooters, one red, and one dark blue. We buy helmets, goggles and gloves.

We head down to London, where we arrive so late at night, we cannot find a place to sleep and we wind up trying to sleep on the steps of an office building. We find lodging in a flophouse next to London Bridge. For a dollar each, we are given clean sheets and shown to a huge old brick dormitory where we pick out a bed for ourselves. In the middle of the night, some drunk comes over, belching and burping, and pees into a pot near my bed. I lie awake the remainder of the night. Two nights now without sleep.

We take a ride around Parliament and Big Ben, and on Sunday afternoon stroll through Hyde Park. Speaker's Corner fascinates me, with everyone offering their opinions; everyone convinced they are right; everyone making up the world to their own specifications. Three rules prevail. You cannot beg for money, you cannot entice to riot, and you cannot insult the royal family (even though people do insult the royal family). Why is it that most every question and many declarative statements end with the word "then?" "Are we going over to Robert's then?" Or sometimes it's "what?" After my first-ever disgusting try of kidney pie, we venture down to the white cliffs of Dover, where we ride our Vespas to the edge of the cliff looking across the English Channel. There, facing Europe, we raise our arms and shout like victors at battle.

The next day we're on the ferry across the Channel to Calais and then Paris. An hour outside of the city we stop and spend the night sleeping on a farmer's haystack. In the morning I awake to see the farmer headed toward us on his tractor. I wake Ted, fearful that the farmer is upset with us. He drives right past, waving and yelling "bon jour" over the clamor of his single cylinder tractor.

I now make an interesting discovery. My college French is almost use-
less.

*In Paris they simply opened their eyes and stared when we spoke to them in
French! We never did succeed in making those idiots understand their own
language.* —Mark Twain, *Innocents Abroad*

In Paris, we find a great little hotel on the left bank, where for three
dollars a night a matronly concierge gives us a room and breakfast of cafe
au láit and fresh croissants with orange marmalade. The bathroom is a
unique affair. There is no toilet such as we have in the States; rather, in
a closet in the hallway, there is a hole in the floor with two metal plates
where you plant your feet and squat to do your business. You then pull a
chain to flush everything down the drain, below your feet. I have read in
Indra Devi's book, *Yoga for Americans,* that this is the most natural way,
not sitting on a seat as we do in the West. Squatting is a more unconstrained
position for elimination of the bowels. It's the way man did it for many
thousands of years prior to the modern era.

We sleep for the remainder of the summer in sleeping bags, on haystacks,
in the woods, at campsites and on beaches. Every few days, we find a
youth hostel or, better, a cheap hotel, just for the pure joy of a hot shower
and the wonder of clean sheets. Ted likes to drink, so it makes for an
interesting summer. I'm not a serious drinker, so while he drinks and sleeps,
I read T. Lobsang Rampas, and Somerset Maugham's *The Razor's Edge.*

Unless you leave room for serendipity, you will never find your way.
—Joseph Campbell

Our planning is not the best; we sometimes wander around like dogs
that have lost their scent and find ourselves in the middle of nowhere at
bedtime. We leave Paris at midday and head south toward the French coast.
We pass through a vast carpet of beautiful mustard-colored flowers in bright
sunlight. It gets cloudy. When it gets dark, it is impossible to see anything.
Ted runs out of gas leaving us to feel our way around like blind men in
a ditch on the downside of a sharp mountain curve. Suddenly, a car appears
around the curve, shining its lights on us. Seeing our desperate condition
they stop. It is a group of French university students celebrating the end
of their school year at a mountain chateau. Their English is much better
than my French. We are rescued! They will help us get gas in the morning.
With the aid of outdoor lighting, we swim nude in a nearby stream, swinging out on ropes—yelling as we drop off into the cold water. Afterward
at dinner, one of the boys points to his stomach and says something in

French. I say, "Oui, tres bon." Another says in English, "I don't think you understand. He's not saying it's good. He's saying you're eating bull's intestines." Soft, squishy, spongy chit'lins, we're hungry. It's scrumptious.

Ted's Vespa starts giving him trouble and dies completely near Clermont, France. He kicks and kicks and kicks it, offering up a variety of invectives. It does no good. This inanimate object couldn't care about his remonstrating against it. Finally, we walk it into Claremont, where the mechanic simply says, "Il kaput, kaput." We sell the Vespa, take one change of clothes that we stuff into our sleeping bags and ship our suitcases, with our clothes, books we've read and other supplies back to the States. We spend the remainder of the summer sharing one Vespa and washing out our one change of clothes in the sinks of cheap hotels.

In Genoa, Italy we find an inexpensive hotel with clean sheets and a shower. Nothing could feel better, not even sex. The next morning, with the sun pouring through the window, I awaken to see sheer white curtains blowing into the room, with sunlight all around and the sound of a loud-speaker announcing the price of various goods as so many "cinque lire." We climb the Leaning Tower of Pisa. I emerge at the top and, to my surprise, have to hold to the wall to keep from falling. (There are actually three leaning towers in Pisa, each sinking into the soil below). In Rome, Ted enjoys sitting in the piazzas listening to live music, drinking wine and eating pizza and gelato (ice cream). I'm amazed at the pathologically aggressive driving in Rome. As Bill Bryson once expressed it, "Italians should not have been let in on the invention of the automobile." At each traffic circle we plunge into a maelstrom of horns honking, arms waving, hoping to exit this vortex, on the right artery. How many people must die this way!

We ride around the Coliseum. To think this place could hold 80,000 people! How many people died here? Did the crowd enjoy watching people die? We go to the catacombs dug into the volcanic soil. The Vatican is a treasure trove of art, luxurious superfluity and extravagance. It's like nothing I have expected—the high bronze altar above St. Peter's tomb looks like a canopy of a four poster bed made for a giant, the Pieta is so smooth, the Sistine chapel so magnificent. Everything is inlaid with gold, silver, ivory, granite and fine marble. Would Jesus be at home here? I guess Jesus would be at home anywhere.

We move on down to Naples, a visit to the blue grotto at Capri, and the city of Pompeii, forever frozen in time when Vesuvius erupted August 24, 79 A.D. Everything is so well preserved by volcanic ash, even graffiti on the walls. It is as though we are there the day after the volcano erupted. Ted wants to go to the top of mount Vesuvius. The road is paved in the beginning. Then, the pavement ends and the weight of the two of us digging into the volcanic ash makes driving nearly impossible. Halfway up, and fearful that we are about to burn out the motor on the second and only Vespa, we give up and coast back down.

We cross Italy to the east, to the Adriatic coast, to Venice and a visit to the Basilica of San Marco with its golden mosaic tiles and the four bronze horses. We drink coffee in Piazza San Marco and tour the back paths where laundry hangs out over the streets. After our usual dinner of pizza, we sleep on the floor in a youth hostel. After swimming on the coast, we arrive at the Yugoslavian border wearing only bathing suits. We have to put our clothes on before we're allowed into this proper Communist country. We then speed in and spend the night in Ljubljana.

Buzzing down a road in Austria, I decide to change over to the Unitarian church when we get back to the states. Ted is driving, so I lean forward and shout my decision into his ear. "That's nice," he says, nodding in approval. My reading of Huxley and my growing interest in world religions calls for a more open approach than that offered by traditional Christianity.

We make friends in Munich, Germany and they take us to the Hof-brauhaus where we sit on long benches around tables covered with red-checkered tablecloths, listening to "oompah" bands and eating big sausages with sauerkraut. Amazingly, our waitress is able to carry twelve beer mugs at once, wrapping her fingers around six mugs in each hand. Our escorts try to steal their mugs at the end of the night and are caught and required to cough up their booty.

Sleeping next to a lake in Zurich, Switzerland, we awaken to swans maliciously biting our ears and arms, even trying to bite us through our sleeping bags. What is all the fuss about? Little did we know—we're sleeping on their breeding ground. We go north along the Rhine to visit with Ted's relatives in Ludwigshafen, Germany. The children are nice and view us with curiosity. The father, a Nazi soldier during the second world war, wants nothing to do with us. The children tell us he absolutely will not speak about the war, and we are not to ask him any questions. In Ludwigshafen, we go to see *Rebel Without a Cause*, in English with German subtitles. Walking out of the theater we turn up the collars on our jackets and light up cigarettes like James Dean. Ted revs up the Vespa like it's a Harley, eliciting a few stares before we take off with a sudden jolt.

Out and about by myself in Amsterdam, I hear a song being played. It is in English, and the announcer says it is the number-one song in the United States. It's Dean Martin singing, "Everybody Loves Somebody Sometime." I run back to the hotel to wake Ted and tell him his hero has a hit.

Finally, it's on to Luxembourg, where we sell the Vespa and board an Icelandic turboprop jet back to the United States via Iceland. It is a very long all-night flight. Fortunately, I meet a young woman on the plane who enjoys smooching and snuggling under the covers. Ted and I have not met any girls during our entire stay in Europe, so this is fun. Again, I don't get any sleep, and we arrive in New York as exhausted as when we arrived in England.

We have very little money left. At Penn station we count out our money, though I'm still hoarding a few dollars in my sock. We ask how far west our money can take us. We are told Pittsburgh. Ted has relatives in Pittsburgh, so he makes a call and we are on our way. After one night with Ted's relatives, I'm anxious to get home. Ted wants to stay. I ask them to please take me to the nearest highway-heading west. I will hitchhike back to Missouri. I get a ride, and then another, and then in Ohio I get a ride with a man, a little older than I am. He has skinny arms and legs and a big belly. After a few miles he announces he needs to go off the road for a quick visit to his home in a nearby town. He assures me we will soon be back on the road heading on west toward St. Louis.

A half-hour later, we are still headed north from route 70. We finally arrive at a house where he has an upstairs apartment. He asks me to go up with him, and then announces that he is tired, and wants to lie down for a nap. Locking the door from the inside, he takes off his shirt, lies face down on the bed and asks me if I will give him a back rub. It is clear where this is going and I'm not going there. I'm trying my hand at smoking. I don't inhale, so I won't become addicted. I have a pack of English Player cigarettes. I go over, unlock the door and announce that I'm going to go downstairs and have a cigarette. If he is not down there by the time I'm done, I'm going to leave, though I have no means of transportation other than my legs.

He gets down to the car before I finish the cigarette. All the way back to highway 70, he keeps nervously apologizing for the delay. Once back on the highway, he dramatically announces—after only a few miles—that he has forgotten his billfold and has to go back for it. He stops and demands that I get out of the car. Making a quick U-turn he expeditiously disappears. It is nearly dark. I begin walking—trying to hitchhike. No one stops. I have my sleeping bag and think perhaps I should go off into some farmer's pasture and sleep. I have done this many times in Europe where I couldn't speak the language. Now, here in my own country, I'm apprehensive. Maybe it's because I'm alone. I walk for five hours. Finally, about eleven p.m., I come to a rest stop. I go around knocking on car windows asking for possible rides west. Eventually, I come to a guy driving a small European car. He says he is going to Albuquerque, New Mexico, by way of St. Louis. He is planning on driving all night. If I want to come along and share the driving, it's fine. We arrive in St. Louis early the next morning. He drops me at the train station. I have just enough money for a ticket home to Mexico.

I'm filthy dirty. I have not showered. I have not slept. I sport a fuzzy youthful beard. From the train station, I walk home rather than call and ask someone to pick me up. I cross the tracks, past the pile of coal behind Judy's home, stopping to take a nostalgic look at her house. Her mother now lives in the local projects, and the house looks as forsaken as my heart. At home, I knock rather than just walking in. Mother opens the door and screams with delight. I'm exhausted. Though I'm eager to tell everyone about my adventures, all I can think about is a shower and my own clean bed.

CHAPTER 16

Southern California School of Theology
Marriage and Divorce

In late August of 1964, I pack my Valiant convertible with my most essential possessions, stick my college degree in the glove compartment, and with two hundred dollars take off for Southern California School of Theology in Claremont, a Methodist seminary affiliated with the Disciples of Christ. I like John Wesley, the founder of the Methodist church. He was after the real stuff, the essence of the spiritual life. The nature of Methodism, as he created it, was a method of deepening the sense of the presence of God. John Wesley didn't want to found a church. It happened despite his protestations and his work got overlaid with organizational and doctrinal encrustations.

It is a 2,000-mile journey to Claremont—three days at 600-700 miles a day. Passing into Kansas, I look back and see Missouri in my rearview mirror. I'm leaving Missouri but Missouri will never leave me. I shall return often and always think of Missouri as home. Right now, my eyes are on the far horizon. I'm going to California.

Southern California is nothing like the mid-west. To start with, it's hot. It's September, and it's in the upper 90s. The new seminary buildings are in the A. Quincy Jones style of architecture, in a tamed desert with palm and eucalyptus trees with aromatic evergreen leaves, cactus and rock gardens. Palm trees line the spacious boulevards. Behind the Seminary, in the San Bernardino Mountains is the sometimes snow-capped Mt. Baldy looking like a charcoal drawing smudged up against a smoggy sky. My room opens directly onto the parking lot. It is a cell the size of a small motel room with one large window and a bathroom I share with the guy next door.

I call the Unitarians and begin the process of switching over. I need a job right away. While the Unitarians are processing my application, I'm offered a job as the assistant minister of Central Christian Church in Glendale, a large church near Hollywood. For fifty dollars a week, I'm to put in two days a week at the church. I decide to introduce the youth in the congregation to a study of world religions. After a few weeks, the parents

105

take me aside and tell me they want me to take the kids bowling and to teach them the importance of church membership, tithing and weekly attendance. The emphasis is to be on fun, food and games. We are not to study cults.

Rita—My First Woman Guide

I begin classes in Hatha yoga and meditation with Rita. Sixty-year-old Rita has the body of a thirty-year-old. Only her face betrays her age. She has been to India and tells us of her adventures. My first attempts at meditation are more "thinking" about meditation than actual meditation. Meditation is, however, a knack that gets better with time, like a muscle that has to be exercised to grow strong. Meditation, as I now come to understand it, opens me to a more expanded and centered dimension. Spirituality is not taught in seminary except insofar as an individual teacher may inspire you. Seminary is an academic institution. For inspiration and guidance I go to Rita. I trust her. When it comes to the inner life, she has been and is, there.

In the nonviolent army, there is room for everyone who wants to join up.
There is no color distinction. There is no examination, no pledge.
Just as a soldier in the armies of violence is expected to inspect his carbine
and keep it clean, nonviolent soldiers are called upon to examine and burnish
their greatest weapons—their heart, their conscience, their courage and their
sense of justice. —Martin Luther King Jr. *Why We Can't Wait*

Dr. Martin Luther King, Jr., is awarded the Nobel Peace Prize, and one of our professors persuades us to become members of the NAACP. After what happened to Onyango, I'm happy to help. I'm actually eager to belong, hungry for participation in a significant social effort. I call home with pride to tell Mother. She is thinking about what happened during the McCarthy witch-hunt in Washington D.C. and isn't sure it is a good idea to be a card-carrying anything.

Three professors are impressive: Howard Clinebell, Ph.D., professor of pastoral care, is particularly sympathetic to the students. He is an active supporter of Alcoholics Anonymous and admired for his books on counseling alcoholics and another on counseling techniques for ministers. There is also John Cobb, Ph.D., now a well-known theologian. Best of all, I get an assistantship, with the man who becomes my mentor, David Eitzen, Ph.D., professor of the psychology of religious experience. A mystic himself, he speaks poetically about watching a sunset from the roof of his house. He has us read *The Little Prince*. He pushes at the edges of the metaphysical and finds those things that lie beyond the ordinary. He is trying to get to the important stuff—not just academics. He provides more than knowledge. He provides inspiration. I come to love Dr. Eitzen very much. One day he comes to me and he says he does not think that any of his students understand him as well as I. I ask him what I'm supposed to do for him. He doesn't know. I catalogue his journals and newsletters, and clean up the piles of magazines, and papers that clutter his office. He is absolutely delighted and brings his wife to the seminary, just to show her.

I write a paper in which I try to prove that Martin Luther was a true mystic and not "just" a theologian and reformer. Our teacher in world religions says on Saturday he is going to climb nearby Mt. Baldy and does anyone want to come along? Mt. Baldy is just over 10,000 feet high. You drive as far up the mountain as you can (about halfway) then hike the remaining distance. At the top we look down at the San Bernardino Valley. You can't see anything except smog. Everything has disappeared from view. Standing, looking at the heavy smog below, our teacher says, "All is Maya." I get what *Maya,* i.e. *illusion* means.

Marriage

There are few women around the seminary. Those who are here are older, unattractive or married. There are also no available young women at church. I hang out with two single guys, Jim Wooden, from England, four years older than I, and Takayo Yamada, a naïve, dedicated Japanese student who is trying to perfect his English. He has a huge smile and teeth as big and neat as piano keys. You can't help smiling at his permanently fixed grin. Jack, the fellow who lives in the cell next to mine, is getting married and his fiancée is a frequent visitor. They seem happy. I'm corresponding with Diana Weber, now in her senior year at Culver-Stockton. Diana asks me if I think she should accept a scholarship to do graduate work in another state. In the back of my mind, I think, "Or . . . am I going to make a better offer?" There is a nice apartment with great views of Mt. Baldy becoming available in the complex. I can have it—if I'm married.

My sex life has been confined to petting with Judy, the one night stand in St. Louis, and the event under the covers on the flight back from Europe. Sex is admittedly a driving force for a twenty-one-year old man. Diana and I decide to get together for Christmas in Missouri. When I get back to Southern California, I'm admittedly lonely. I call Diana and ask her to marry me. I don't have enough money for an engagement ring. That will have to come later. I immediately feel as though I've made a mistake. I pick up the phone to call her again and take it back—the decision is so final—I put my hand on the phone—I dial—then—impetuously—before she can answer—I hang up. What have I done? My inner voice is actually quite clear. Yet, I ignore it. Have I done something stupid? Guilt sets in like an old wet hen, stinky, awful guilt. I think I've made a mistake.

1965—Age Twenty-Two

Monday, February 15, I'm headed out to dinner when I hear on the car radio that my favorite singer Nat King Cole has died from lung cancer at the age of 45. His songs just kept uncurling from his cavernous mouth, each vowel savored, as he flashed those yard wide smiles.

Before long, Diana's family is spending money in preparation for the wedding. I hope my fears are misplaced. Maybe I will enjoy it. I'm still thinking about Judy. I know what love is. In May, at the end of my first year of graduate school, I drive home to Missouri, and then down to Jeffersonville, Kentucky, where Diana and I are married in her local Baptist church. Ronnie West comes to be my best man. I go to Diana's house a few days early to get measured for a new suit. I pick up the suit the morning of our wedding and find that the pants have not been taken in at the crotch as I had requested. There is a great distracting area of cloth that hangs between my legs and I feel like I'm waddling when I walk. I'm disgusted with the pants and with myself for having so impetuously asked Diana to marry me. Nevertheless, she is a nice girl. Maybe it will work. For both of us, it is an adventure.

There is no reception after the wedding. That would be too expensive. Daddy runs over to Diana and gives her a big kiss. He seems so happy. Then, it's down the church steps, into the car, and off to California. Diana is wearing a girdle, and when we get to the Holiday Inn, we have an awful time getting her girdle off and my condom on. It is the first time for the two of us, and we have fun. For our honeymoon, we drive to Southern California, where we settle into playing house. I have my fifty dollars a week job at the church. We have a few wedding presents. That is it! Until Diana begins teaching that fall we have almost no money. As a joke, some people from Glendale Central Christian give us a wedding present of a box of canned food with the labels missing. For several days whatever is in the can is our dinner. An older man from the church gives us a 1954 Desoto, through the church as a tax write-off, so we can have a second car for Diana.

Diana and I often spend the weekend in an over-the-garage apartment in Glendale belonging to Irv and Penny Currier. They have four delightful sons. The Curriers become the main supporters of the youth group and our closest friends. The bloody race riots are in full swing in Watts, the black section of Los Angeles. People are concerned that events in Watts are going to spill over into the surrounding communities. We watch the reports on television each evening. Thirty people have been killed, hundreds injured, thousands arrested and there are many millions of dollars in property damage. Each evening the helicopter reports on television show what looks like a ravaged war zone.

1966—Age Twenty-Three

As part of our training in seminary, we are required to participate in a therapy group, partly so we can lead such groups in the future. The group is refreshing; people are talking about what is going on with them. I'm relieved that I have an opportunity to say something about what is going on inside, and I confess the whole mess I have fallen into with Diana. She is wonderful. This is not, however, a romance. I truly respect and care for Diana. Still, the relationship lacks the exotic romanticism and deep heart bonding I experienced with Judy. There is something of the infinite in Judy, something I still hunger for. I have been in love before. I know what it is. This isn't it. What an idiot I am! There is also an incident in the Pomona college library. While doing research, I look across the top of the card catalogue drawers and notice a beautiful, petite, dark-haired young woman looking back—smiling. What an enchanting smile; I fall in love in an instant. A look can tell you everything. A look can penetrate your face and eyes and go right inside you. I smile back. There is nothing I can do. I have a ring on my finger. And I'm only twenty-three.

I spend the summer of 1966 as a chaplain-intern at Southern California Institution for Women, in Frontiera, the largest prison for women in the United States. The work is exciting, and I find considerable assistance under the tutelage of Reverend Gerald Walcutt, the head chaplain.

One Sunday afternoon, a little less than a year after we're married, we are driving home from church when Diana starts to cry. I ask her what is wrong, and she says she doesn't know. Something is wrong. I tell her she is right, and I have to confess that I do not want to be married. On Monday morning, Diana and I split, and she goes to Long Beach to live with Wanda Russell, a member of our little gang from college. I'm so ashamed and humiliated by this event and so sorry that I have hurt Diana and our families that I vow to never marry again until I'm sure I can make a lifetime commitment. I will not marry again for thirty years. Mother later tells me that when she received my letter telling of our separation, she felt as though she was kicked in the stomach and walked around feeling that somehow it was her fault, that somehow she had failed me. This is exactly what I was afraid of. She has not, however, failed me. I failed her.

When the seminary gets wind of our separation, they decide I should go into therapy, both individual and group. This proves to be a good idea. On the one hand, I think, "well, here I am being really honest about my situation, so why do I need therapy?" On the other hand the therapy is helpful—insightful. My therapist, a Freudian, focuses on my relationship with my parents. I love my parents dearly, easily and unequivocally. They were never abusive. It is fun talking about them. Right now, I'm more interested in the future than the past.

Every relationship is an experience in forgiveness. Each relationship continues until we have learned what we need to learn together or all that we are ready to learn at a given time. Holding on to a relationship does not make it a success. It may be necessary to separate to gain perspective and become clear about one's destiny and identity. Separating means the lessons I have to learn with this *special* person are in some sense complete. Letting go of the false allows the truth to come to the fore. Love is a fresh, flowing experience. We want to keep it, to hold onto it, not to lose it. We want to love the beloved forever. Fearful of loss, we feel compelled to codify and define it. We bring in the law; we bring in society. We turn choice into obligation answerable to guilt. Now the fresh breeze is gone. We have love, and we want to hold it. We want to freeze a holy instant. How can we freeze eternity?

> *Love is freedom. To look for it by placing yourself in bondage,*
> *is to separate yourself from it.* —ACIM, T-16.VI.2:1-2

Diana and I were frugal and managed to save $500, which Diana withdraws from the bank. As something of a statement about her new freedom, she takes the money and our second car and buys a newer car and a blonde wig.

On Monday morning after my confession to Diana on Sunday, Reverend Walcutt, the other two intern-chaplains and I sit in his office. I have my head down on my arms, on the table in the center of the room. Rev. Walcutt points out my labored breathing. It is as though I have just come up for air. I had not realized it. He is right.

Rev. Walcutt is in the process of selling his sleek black 350cc Honda touring motorcycle, and I buy it from him, paying him in installments. It is my way of expressing freedom, as well as a replacement for walking on the farm. I go to the back roads on the open desert. There is a natural tidiness about the desert and I work through the divorce by riding and riding and riding, letting the breeze make a mess of my hair. I'm cruising along over a roller coaster-like hilly section. Suddenly, Hell's Angels surround me. They are on my left and my right, in front of and behind me. They point at my touring bike and laugh, making jokes to each other, mocking and taunting me. I look straight ahead, keep going, and pray for the best. When we get to a long flat stretch, they speed up suddenly and disappear in a matter of seconds.

I have an experience with a woman prisoner. Nothing physical happens. That would have been impossible. A bonding does occur with Linda, aptly named Big Linda by the Hell's Angels bikers with whom she rode. Linda has long blond hair, freckles, and a smile that will not quit. She is not big in size—rather in reputation. She was arrested with a pound of cocaine in her possession. We aren't supposed to give any advice, just be a sympathetic ear. I ask her what she thinks about mostly, and she says that mostly she thinks about me. That's strange. I've been thinking about her. Linda looks like Judy. She is pregnant and, as the chaplain in charge of hospital visitations, I spend a little time with her every day prior to and after the birth of her baby boy. She asks me for a name. I like the Scandinavian name Lars. She loves it, and so the baby is named Lars. Later, I see some papers for the baby. Someone changed the name to Larry. Linda awoke feelings in me once again. Given the right opportunity, I might love again.

I'm given the job of delivering death notices. I show up in the prison garment shop. The moment I walk in, the sewing machines stop and a hush falls over the factory floor. Everyone knows why I've come. No one likes to see the chaplain coming into a work area in the middle of the morning. When the guard goes and gets the woman in question, there are gasps and cries. What a job!

I start an evening class on world religions. A petite, beautiful young Mexican woman with large dark eyes and long black hair faints at the end of each class so she will have to go to the infirmary instead of back to her dormitory, where she is afraid of being molested. Word gets out that attending my class is the thing to do, so the room fills each evening. In the three short months I'm there, I develop a small following. I get close with one older woman named Margaret, who acts as a mother to the younger women. It makes parting at the end a bit more wonderful.

I'm put in charge of eight women in a weekly therapy group, where we talk about whether or not they should feel guilty for their crimes and seek forgiveness. One woman who has killed her lover works hard on the issue. On the last day of our time together, she tells us that she has decided that if she had to do it all over again, she would still "kill the son-of-a-bitch." Prison is better than living with him.

I'm eating dinner in a coffee shop in Claremont, when I notice a young woman at another table obviously looking at me. In fact, she is blatantly flirting with me. Mary Rose is an attractive, dark haired, second-generation Italian. She has just come out of a convent after a two-year stay during which time she was trying to decide if she wanted to become a nun. She has decided that she does not and is now coming out—so to speak. She is a virgin. She wants to change that. She thinks I'm handsome. I think she is the most charming woman I have ever met. I think I can help her. In fact, I'm happy to help. We ride the motorcycle in the desert—her arms wrapped around my waist, holding on tight. It feels so good! We go for picnics and swim in Arrowhead Lake state park. This is the best sex ever. We moved together in a way I had never experienced before. Mary Rose rolls her eyes back in her head and she goes into a multiple orgasmic state of ecstasy. This screaming stuff is a whole new experience!

I can no longer live in married student housing, so I move out of the seminary altogether. I find a small house in Pomona next to the San Bernardino freeway. The sound of traffic is so thick twenty-four hours a day; it sounds like flies buzzing against the windows. This is far removed from the peace and serenity of Missouri. I find a note on the bulletin board at the seminary from a retired minister, a Dr. Merlo Heicker. He wants a seminary student to be his live-in companion. This is a much better situation.

112

Dr. Heicker's wife has died. He has had a heart attack, and his family is afraid he might have another with no one there to help him. Dr. Heicker is the author of an annual manual for ministers, filled with illustrations and sayings one might use in a sermon, newsletter tidbits, jokes suitable for sermons, and so on. It is my first experience with a collector of facts and funny stories. I love Benjamin Franklin, and Dr. Heicker is a Benjamin Franklin for ministers. He spends each day in his study, reading magazines and doing research for his journal. Three walls in his office are lined from floor to ceiling with books. There is also a large bulletin board on which he tacks notes. A fourth wall contains a sliding glass door opening onto a small garden. In many ways, his life seems ideal. He has a lady friend over for dinner each evening, and he appreciates my not being there when she is. This idea of a companion is more his son's doing than his. He is usually sleeping by the time I get home in the evening. I'm paid three dollars a day, which is a lot better than paying rent. There are a few drawbacks with Dr. Heicker, however. I'm not allowed to have friends visit. Mary Rose is living with her parents, and our opportunities for intimacy are greatly diminished.

Girls' Collegiate School

Reverend Frank Cron, the senior pastor, at Glendale Central Christian is fired and forced into early retirement. While he is not a dynamic speaker and the church is not growing, he is nevertheless a kindhearted, gentle man. The severe manner in which he is dismissed leaves me wondering about this thing that we call Christian love. I support Rev. Cron rather than those who seek his ouster and he is grateful. In light of my divorce and my support for Rev. Cron, my own situation is now also on shaky ground. I look for and find a position as a chaplain and instructor at Girls' Collegiate School, a private girls' high school in the midst of orange groves just a few miles from the School of Theology in Claremont. My salary nearly doubles, from fifty to ninety dollars a week. At Girls' Collegiate, I teach Ancient History, World Religions, Public Speaking and Debate. I'm also the chaplain. This means conducting a combination midweek chapel service/general school meeting where the headmistress gives a little talk about school activities. We observe the holidays. I pray. We sing and call it chapel.

Pierre Teilhard De Chardin

I now have Sundays free, so each week I visit different churches in the area. I finally choose my favorite, a Unitarian church in Pomona. A variety of symbols from different religions are displayed on the wall behind their altar. Here I am inspired by a slide lecture sponsored by The Phenomena of Man Project based on the works of French Jesuit Priest Pierre Teilhard de Chardin. His work, predicated on the spiritual evolution of consciousness, makes incredible sense. I become a disciple, join the American Teilhard Association, and resolve to read each of his books, in French, if possible.

Pierre Teilhard de Chardin (1881-1952) was a Jesuit paleontologist, archeologist, geologist, anthropologist and evolutionist who held to an optimistic view of the future. Because of his belief in evolution, the Catholic Church censured Teilhard's message and prohibited the publication of his books. Eventually, his message got out. In similar fashion, Father Matthew Fox will later be expelled from the Catholic Church. As with Galileo so many years before, censorship brings popularity to an author. Everyone wants to know why the church opposes his teachings.

Teilhard outlined what he called the *law of complexity consciousness*. As a system rises in complexity, it also rises in consciousness from nonlife to life; from atoms to molecules; from molecules to megamolecules; from megamolecules to single cell life; from single cell life to multi-celled organisms; from multi-celled organisms to plants; from plants to animals; from animals to humans. At each stage, there is a jump in consciousness, and something wholly new comes into being—something not previously imagined in the preceding stage. The jump from animal to human consciousness, of course, is immense.

Along with the complexification of consciousness, there comes a growing awareness of *within,* or the consciousness of spirit. This leads us to the discovery of the heart of God that has always been buried deep inside, in the spiritual, not the physical, world. According to Teilhard, as there are more and more people on the planet, we begin to experience, through what he calls *supersaturation*, a *noospheric* link of consciousness that covers the whole planet. The earth, he said, is a living system that is becoming ever more complex through communications, cultural systems and mobility.

Teilhard died in 1952. He could not have known about the advances we are now experiencing in the amassing of information via the internet, supersonic transport, rapid transit, super highways, satellites, cellular telephones, CD—ROM's, interactive television, and more. In Teilhard I find everything genius, spirituality, and mysticism. Teilhard now becomes my hero. Theologically, I would have done better to choose Tillich, or Barth or Bultman—or one of the theologians my professors find interesting. No one is interested in Teilhard. Yet, for me, Teilhard "is it" and will remain so for years.

I read *The Collected Writings of Saint Hereticus,* in which the author facetiously puts forth the idea of developing a religion based upon the best of all the world's great faiths. He also doesn't think it will work. I find the idea fascinating though I agree—it doesn't seem workable. I read *Kabbalah: The Secret Names of God* by Abraham Ben Samuel Abulafa. In 1280 this bold visionary addressed Pope Nicholas III in Rome to convince him of the unity of all religions. For this he was thrown into prison and sentenced to death. I read the works of Sri Ramakrishna (1836-1886), founder of the Vedanta societies in the West. Ramakrishna claimed that "God consciousness" could be reached through Judaism as well as Christianity, Islam or any religion. I read the following lines from Ramakrishna:

> *I say that all are calling on the same God. It is not good to feel that my religion is true and other religions are false. All seek the same object.*
> *A mother prepares dishes to suit the stomachs of her children. Suppose a mother has five children and a fish is brought for the family. She does not cook the same curry for all of them. God has many religions to serve different aspirants, times and countries. All doctrines are only so many paths.*

When I read this passage, I shout, "Yes, yes, it must be so!" How arrogant is Christianity to think that it is the only true religion! Our personalities, our backgrounds, our temperaments, out interests are different, so why not different religions? To claim that I have the right way and you are a lost soul is supercilious. The French have a saying, "No matter what road you take, you will eventually get there." Vivekananda follows Rama-Krishna's path of universalism. The Bahai faith teaches that it is only through an unwavering consciousness of the ones of mankind, that world peace can be realized.

At Girl's Collegiate I meet the fellow who is about to become my best friend. Myron Blackman is a charming; tall, dark-haired young man with a strong, long angular face and a neatly cut mustache. Myron is working on his master's in history at Claremont Graduate School and teaching classes in government and American history. We share the same birthday exactly. I'm about an hour older than Myron. Myron finds a house for rent in Claremont. He needs a couple of housemates to make it workable. It is a sprawling, one-story ranch with a spacious central living room—a great place for parties. I agree to go in on the house with him, so Mary Rose and I will have a place to rendezvous. At the same time, I continue to spend each night sleeping at Dr. Heicker's.

I soon develop an appreciation for Myron, a goodhearted, gentle man with a great smile. Everyone loves Myron—and no wonder. He's a great guy. As a twenty-three year old farm boy from Missouri, I have never met anyone who is Jewish. I'm so naive that it doesn't occur to me that someone with a name like Myron Blackman from Brooklyn, New York, is Jewish. We have known each other for several days before I turn to him and say, "You're Jewish?" Myron is surprised that I have just figured that out.

Myron and I share our ranch house with an extremely wealthy, handsome, sports car driving guy from New York City named Bob Durst. Bob's father, head of Durst and Company, owns several skyscrapers in New York City. A brilliant fellow, Bob earns his Ph.D. in economics the same year that Myron and I earn our master's degrees. Strangely, Bob will later be accused of killing his wife. Her body is never found. He can afford expensive lawyers and he is not arrested. Twenty years later he is accused of killing two other people. The story of his life becomes a documentary. He is now in prison.

My First LSD Experience

Now that I'm no longer married, I have more free time, and I'm back to doing yoga with Rita. Yoga has not, however, carried me to the inner landscapes my soul so strongly desires. I long for the deeper experience I have read about in the mystics' descriptions of rapture. I'm enamored with St. Francis of Assisi and St. Theresa of Avila. Aldous Huxley's experiences with mescaline suggest something very interesting. Rita has brought me to meditation. It is peaceful and comforting. It is not truly transcendental. Through friends of friends, I'm given the opportunity to try LSD. This is in a time when it is pure and made by the Sandoz pharmaceutical company of Switzerland. Although it is not yet illegal, it soon will be.

One Friday afternoon I venture up a windy mountain road leading to the top of Mt. Baldy to a cabin near the end of the lane. I'm to spend the evening with Phil and his wife, Judy, each of whom has experienced LSD. They are willing to guide me, as much as one can be guided, through this adventure. They will not take LSD themselves. I take the first amount at four in the afternoon. After a half-hour, I tell them nothing is happening. Shortly thereafter, I'm sitting on the couch in their living room when the shade on the lamp begins breathing, slowly pulsating in and out like lungs. I sit in front of the fireplace and, with fascination, watch complex fractal (structures that duplicate the flow of nature in complex patterns) type designs, three-dimensional colored balls, stars, diamonds, triangles and other objects slowly rise out of the flames of the fire, flicker and flutter up the chimney. They are each perfectly clear. They are immensely complex. Why don't we see these things all the time? Or, is it purely of my own making? How can I possibly dream up such incredible detail?

Phil comes and tells me it is time for dinner. I cannot talk. I get up and follow him to the table. I have no desire to eat. Eating is such a base, gross activity. I can't do it. I look at the food and shift it around on the plate. I take a cooked carrot and slowly slice it open, meticulously examining the intricate delicacy of its magnificent inner structure. Why don't we see this all the time?

I go back and sit on the couch. I have brought along a tape recorder to tape my experience. I pick up the microphone, bring it up near my mouth and slowly bite down on it. There is no way I can put this into words. My mind is going way too fast. Let's say that, under normal circumstances, we think at one hundred words per minute. I'm now thinking at a thousand words a minute or perhaps ten thousand words a minute. Words and minutes are too difficult to get a hold on. They soon lose their significance. It seems I've been here before. My life is part of a dream, and I'm remembering things I've always known.

Phil and Judy check to see if I'm okay. They are letting me have an inner experience. I assure them that I'm fine—in fact, wonderful. Phil builds up the fire with fresh logs. They ask again how I'm doing, and I assure them I'm fine—in fact, getting more clarity by the second. Sitting around campfires is for centuries ancient man's first introduction into the invisible. It's TV for tens of thousands of years before TV. There is something fascinating about a fire. The fire Phil has now built for me turns into a kinescope display. A movie now presents itself in the flickering flames and I find myself sitting around a campfire, watching the glow of eyes on the other side of the fire.

The script is written. When experience will come to end your doubting has been set. For we but see the journey from the point at which it ended,

117

looking back on it, imagining we make it once again; reviewing mentally what has gone by. —ACIM, W.pt.i.158.3:5-7

My mind soars in a spiral into higher and progressively more ineffable realms. I'm riding the spiral that Teilhard so beautifully described. It all makes such incredible sense. It is as though I'm seeing the "order" of all things—the DNA of the universe. Matter is so malleable in relationship to spirit. Higher and higher levels of consciousness await each step, and I take one step and then another. I see, for the first time, that mind exists independent of the body. This is incredible!

I'm enjoying where my mind takes me. On another, basic level I begin to need to pee. I am not at all sure that I can move. Like eating, moving is a gross activity. The pain gets more intense, as it does when you're sleeping and you need to get up to go to the bathroom. Finally, it becomes so painful; I decide that I'm going to have to let go even if it means urinating on the couch. I give in and say, "Well, here it comes." To my surprise, my legs move, and I automatically get up and walk outside. There is an outdoor light on next to the door on the deck. From there steps lead into the woods. I go into the woods to pee, feeling the most incredible connection with the earth. I come back to the house and gaze with fascination at a large moth with spotted iridescent gold and blue-black wings on the wall next to the light. I get close to its wings. There is a magnetic allure in the tiny fibers that make up this magnificently complicated and beauteous creature—a world unto itself!

I come back and sit on the couch. I'll be awake all night. It does not matter. This is too wonderful, too outstanding, and too stupendous to miss. Phil and Judy begin to make love. I can hear their sounds getting louder and louder through the wall that separates me from their bedroom. The more I listen, the more I find myself sharing this wonderful experience of man and woman making love together. Judy's moans are long and deep and low, and her climax is magnificent. I'm with Judy, except it is my Judy, not the Judy in the other room. I'm man, and she's woman, and we are in a lovers' ecstatic embrace. The next morning, I ask them if they realized how much I shared in their experience. They said, they did.

It is all quite astonishing, exhilarating and inspiring. I spend most of my time quietly sitting on the couch watching the fire. I have plenty of opportunity to go within. It rains before morning and the sound of the rain falling gently on the cabin roof gives the feeling that everything is being washed clean and given new life and vitality. There is a fog in the morning.

Then it clears, and the morning sun comes dappling through the trees as the last bit of rain drips off the leaves. Everything has an expectant shine about it. A purification has taken place within me—I can feel it—a making new—a rebirth.

I want to tell someone what has happened. The only person I can think of who will be appreciative and not judgmental is Dr. Eitzen. He too has been interested in the work of Aldous Huxley. I seek him out in his office. He is captivated by my description. It is something he has always wanted to do. He looks at me with fascination and says, "Who are you now?" He wants to do it himself. He feels he is too old. He has missed his opportunity. Years later in New York, I have the honor to meet Dr. Walter Houston Clark, author of the textbook we used on The Psychology of Religion. He too wants to try it, though he is in his mid-sixties. He does, and it opens him up in surprisingly exciting ways.

This wonderfully deep religious experience arouses within me an even more profound respect for nature. I am not advocating the use of hallucinogens for recreational purposes. I was a twenty-three year old theology student at the time of my experience. I had not experienced marijuana or any drug other than alcohol. I spent my time alone sitting on a couch, going within, not without. Ten years will pass before I will have another experience like this night in the cabin.

1967—Age Twenty-Four—The Death of Dr. Heicker

Early one morning in April, I awaken with a start. I sit straight up in bed—something has happened. I know that Dr. Heicker is dead. Dr. Heicker usually gets up early and turns up the heat. There is no heat. I go to his bedroom and knock. There is no answer. Slowly, I open the door and go in. He is lying like a monk in adoration with his arms clasped across his chest as though in reverent prayer. There is great serenity and calm in his face. Clasping his hands over his chest was no doubt his last gesture of grabbing for his heart before he died. I call his son in Australia. He tells me to see to it that the authorities are notified and his father cremated. He is moving back to the states in June. We will hold a memorial service for his friends at that time. I'm to continue to live at the house for the same pay. And, oh, by the way, I can have his library. "I can have his library!" Is he serious about this? Dr. Heicker has some library! "Yes, you are a theology student, aren't you?" "Yes." "Well, then, you can have his library."

In the house next to Dr. Heicker, lives Alan Hunter, a writer and pacifist during the Second World War. Alan doesn't believe it's right to kill, ever, for any reason. Being a pacifist during a popular war had not been easy. Alan takes pride in the fact that though he and his wife are both in their seventies, they still make love. He was a friend of Aldous Huxley, and Alan shows me a letter that Huxley sent him describing the death of his first wife, Maria. At Girl's Collegiate I meet Huxley's second wife, Laura, who comes to speak to the girls. Laura has written a book called *You Are Not The Target.*

The Sixties

What we call the sixties did not begin, for me, till the late sixties and played itself out for about a decade ending in the late seventies. *Time* magazine ran its first article on hippies, Haight-Ashbury and the psychedelic generation in January 1967. I read Richard Morris Buck's book, *Cosmic Consciousness,* and discover even more people who have had contact with the same inner world I've experienced. Inspired by Teilhard's thoughts on the evolution of consciousness, my own experiences with LSD, Buck's book on *Cosmic Consciousness,* and what is beginning to happen with the birth of the psychedelic generation, I write my master's thesis on *Consciousness Expansion and Religious Experience.* I have enrolled in the Rel.D. (Doctorate of Religion) program. However, at the end of my third year in seminary, I elect to take the Th.M. (Master of Theology) degree instead and graduate a year earlier so I can get to work on a Ph.D. degree. I think it silly to waste another year on the Rel.D. What I really want is a Ph.D., so I might as well get started. Had I stayed in the program one more year, I would have graduated with a professional doctorate at the age of twenty-four.

CHAPTER 17

Paris and Scandinavia

Myron and I complete our master's degrees in May 1967 and we take off for Europe. Beginning this fall, I'm going to start working on a doctorate at the New School for Social Research in New York City. They have a Ph.D. program in phenomenology (a philosophy that concentrates on what is consciously experienced), which looks very interesting. Myron invites me to come to the city with him. First, we drive to Missouri where Myron gets a taste of rural life. We arrive on June 7th just after the death of Uncle Estel whose last words were, "I guess I'm not going to get to see Jon." Myron is moved by the simple funeral in the one-room country church and adjoining graveyard. He writes a poignant poem about his images during the farewell to this man who meant so much to me. I shall never forget the craggy landscape of Uncle Estel's face. He was my first polestar. Through him, somehow I am connected to the Universe. Like Mother, his love was simple, uncomplicated—unconditional.

This same week my nephew, Sean, is born. It's funny how when one goes, another comes. Sean has grown into a handsome man who looks a bit like Tom Hanks. Hardworking, good-natured, and a wonderful father, Sean will one-day take charge of the farm. Missouri is in his blood as it is in mine. Fortunately, my niece Erin's husband, Michael, also loves the silence and beauty of the farm. He is, however, a fisherman and a hunter—not a farmer. I'm the last of the Mundys.

In New York, I get my first taste of "The Big Apple" by staying with Myron and his family in the projects of East New York, Brooklyn—where people live stacked on top of each other. There are long corridors, swinging doors and a lot of racket from people hollering in the not-so-hallowed hallways. After dinner each evening, Myron's family sits with other residents in a screened-in cage, overlooking a noisy courtyard several stories below. It is a clangorous, chock-a-block atmosphere—and a long way from the open plains and quiet nights of Missouri farm life.

I put my Valiant in storage in Manhattan, and we fly to London. As I had been there three years earlier, I'm able to guide us around a bit. We take a train to Dover, where we spend a night in a quaint attic bedroom before taking the boat train across the English Channel and down to Paris.

The man who goes alone can start today but he who travels with another must wait till that other is ready. —Henry David Thoreau

As much as Myron and I enjoy each other's company, we decide to go our separate ways. As I have already traveled through Europe, I'm less interested in touring than staying put. I want to get the feel of a place and the people. I want to learn something and enjoy the view. Knowing I will someday have to pass an exam in French for a doctorate, I spend my time studying French at the University of Paris. Myron takes off for Rome. We agree to meet at the end of the summer and return home together.

I'm fortunate in finding the same little hotel as before. It is still three dollars a day with café au láit, orange marmalade and a croissant for breakfast. The concierge remembers me and is extremely helpful, sitting with me at breakfast—quizzing me on my French lesson. My room is on the top, fifth floor, with a little balcony that overlooks a small park. By leaning out and looking to the left, I can just see the Seine and the back of the noble and majestic Notre Dame cathedral, a vast symphony of stone and the quintessence of early Gothic religious architecture.

I enjoy watching Paris wake up—shops opening, the smell of fresh bread and whiffs of strong coffee floating out from sidewalk cafes; motorbikes sputtering by, and barges whistling as they move up and down the Seine. I go to eat in the underground caves (old wine cellars) where I enjoy French onion soup and steak au poivre. Hemingway once explored these same caves. Was he in the one I'm in now?

With little time for the Louvre in 1964, I go back several times now, enjoying a different wing each day, wandering through the endless corridors. The marble statues seem to breathe. Illuminated manuscripts speak of the purity of the monks who worked on them. And there is painting after painting, by Leonardo da Vinci, Rembrandt and El Greco. I take a tour of the sewers. Used by the French resistance during the Second World War, this 373-mile underground labyrinth contains millions of rats. This is a good thing, as the rodents reduce the solid waste fifty percent by eating it.

Paris is hopelessly romantic. I've got no one to share it with. I walk along the Seine. How wonderful it would be to share this experience with Judy. I make up a little song: "One night and I—I walked along the Seine.

One night and I—I was alone that night.—Then, I—I had a dream that night—and we—we walked along the Seine." It's been six years since she ran away, and I'm still in love with her.

In French class, I meet Ann McGovern, a children's book author, who has separated from her husband and is in Paris to get over it. Ann lives in Edna St. Vincent Millay's house, the smallest house in New York City. She is older than I am, and our relationship is strictly friendship. It is a good one. She is someone to hang with, to accompany me to dinners and to museums. I am forever grateful to Ann for introducing me to the Sufi mystic Rumi. He penetrates so clearly, so simply and so deeply into things. Thirty years later I will sponsor a concert at St. Peter's in New York City based on Rumi poetry. Ann will attend.

Myron returns briefly to Paris, then takes off for Hamburg following some girl. I "get away from it all." I have never been to Scandinavia, so with a Eurailpass, I take off for Oslo. The city feels fresh and unspoiled, and I eat shrimp right off boats—as we did in San Francisco in 1954. Then, I'm off to the Viking Ships Museum and the Grand Café. Interestingly, Norwegians eat only two meals a day, brunch and dinner.

I take a train to Stockholm, one of the most beautiful train trips in the world! In Stockholm, I catch the train to Narvik, Norway, two hundred miles north of the Arctic circle. This will give me a chance to read amid trees in the mountains, literally on top of the world. The train trip is super scenic—and exactly twenty-four hours from noon one day to noon the next. There is plenty of time to enjoy the scenery and tasty meals like breakfast with filmjolk (a sort of buttermilk) mixed with corn flakes and honey. The train winds its way up through Lapland, where you see Laplanders in brightly decorated red and blue costumes, with hats looking something like a court jester's. (So this is where Santa Claus comes from!) They are riding sleds pulled by reindeer or Siberian Huskies. Sitting in the stopped train, I stare at a white snowy owl staring back from a nearby pine. On the way I read Herman Hesse's *Siddhartha*.

Narvik is the land of the midnight sun. About ten p.m. there is a red glow in the west. The light never completely goes out. By two a.m. it begins to get light. This land, called Nordland, is farther north than much of Alaska, Iceland and Siberia. It is not dissimilar to Mexico, Missouri, with an abundance of American cars, magazines and soft drinks. The air is crystal clear. A recipient of the Gulf Stream, it is also surprisingly warm.

It seldom gets below ten below zero even in the winter, an event not unusual in Missouri.

The day after I arrive, I take a skiers' cable car up the side of a mountain. There is no one else on the tram. There is no snow, just grass and flowers, though I can see snow on the mountain caps. I take off on a hike till I find a thick moss-covered rock. I sit down on the rock, bare my torso, and let the sunshine gently warm my body. Nearby is the ripple of melting snow and the beginnings of a little stream. Listening to its gentle roll, I repeat the twenty-third psalm over and over again. Suddenly, I'm overwhelmed with the most incredible feeling. I experience a melting and merging into the mountain, and an amalgamation with the green, green grass and the yellow butter flowers. Life is good—beautiful—to be enjoyed. I open my eyes. Filled with energy, I start running along the side of the mountain stopping to look at some small robin's eggs, blue, bell shaped flowers; and, bending over to smell them, like a lamb, I open my mouth and eat them.

I continue running along the side of the mountain, through these beautiful Elysian Fields, till I stop from sheer exhaustion. I've rarely felt as completely free as I do this beauteous day. I am happy and as free as the mountain winds and the sky above me. My enthusiasm is such that I think I can do anything that man can accomplish. Everything is clear. Everything is possible. The whole of life is before me. I have no major cares, no worries, only the fun of the future to look forward to. This is the most natural of highs. I am so blessed!

Back at the cable car, I meet a young, red-bearded Norwegian journalist, with small dark rimmed glasses. He has also escaped for a day of solitude in the mountains. He is the only other person on the tram. He's just a little older than I am. He invites me to his home for dinner—to meet his friends. He makes a few calls. Soon his apartment is filled with young people. Everyone speaks excellent English—many of them have visited America. One nice girl keeps asking me lots of questions about my life in America.

I meet Myron in London, and we come back to the states together. Over the years, we remain friends. Myron takes off for Hawaii for several years. He gets married and divorced and lives in a number of places, while I stay in his native New York City. In the early seventies, something strange begins to happen to Myron's body. His gait becomes heavy and labored. It is difficult being around him, as he falls frequently, crashing into things, often hurting himself. He is in denial for a long time about what appears to be the onset of multiple sclerosis. Finally, in 1989, he consents to a doctor's analysis of what many of his friends know is most likely MS. When he first hears the diagnosis, he laughs. Once Myron accepts the reality of MS, he does so with dauntless courage and fortitude. He continues to be active. He goes back to school, gets a master's in social work and secures a position, working with the handicapped for the city of New York. No longer with the city, he continues to do counseling and run workshops for people suffering from a variety of disabilities. We will celebrate our 40th and our 60th birthdays together. It is the same day. He will be best man at our wedding in 1997.

CHAPTER 18

New York City, College Teaching, Graduate School and The Tombs

I return to New York filled with energy and enthusiasm, determined to pour myself into my studies and learn as much as I can. I enroll as a graduate student in philosophy at the New School for Social Research with classes in the evening. Again, I contact the Unitarians and begin the process of switching over. With no place to go, I get a room at the Y on 34th Street in Manhattan. It is not a good place for me. I pass rooms with doors left open or partly open to reveal some guy playing with himself and beckoning others to come in. While I feel people should be free to follow whatever sexual orientation they want, I'm not interested in a homosexual encounter.

I have just read Orwell's *Down and Out in Paris and London,* and now I'm in New York City with almost no money. I get a job at the original Barnes & Noble shelving and helping people find books in the philosophy, religion and psychology sections. It's great getting to know the books. I get an interview for a position with the probation department for the City of New York. I explain to my supervisor that I'll be late the next day. When I come in, he says he has no memory of my asking to come in late and fires me on the spot. I leave swinging my new leather briefcase in the air, singing as I walk down the street. Since my experience on the mountainside in Norway, I have incredible faith. Somehow it will work out. It has to. I call home and ask Daddy for another loan, so I can have a deposit for an apartment once I find one. He sends $400.

I find a studio apartment on 16th Street near 6th Avenue for $200 a month. It's on the ground floor with its own entrance to the street. The room is so small the door touches the bed to the right when I open it. There is just enough room to walk past the bed to a refrigerator, card table and chair. A door at the other end leads into a little vestibule and a bathroom I share with another guy I never see. There is only the occasional sound of a flushing toilet.

New York is big and lonely and I love it. —James Dean

Aside from a visit home for Christmas, September 1967 through February 1968 easily qualifies as the loneliest time of my life. I never felt lonely on the open Missouri plains. Now, here in the city with people all around, loneliness descends like a plague. I have no dates and make no male friends. I am longing for conversation. There are people, people everywhere and not a conversation to be shared. There is much I come to love about the city. I like getting up early and going to the corner deli for breakfast. I love the smell of fresh blueberry muffins as you open the door. I like watching people hurrying to their jobs. I enjoy the sharp-edged, hard-charging pace of New Yorkers. Who is that girl standing on the corner selling newspapers on top of a cardboard box? She cannot be more than nineteen or twenty. She always has such a big smile and friendly "Good morning!" And I never buy a paper. I am convinced, as the Dalai Lama has said, that the basic underlying nature of human beings is gentleness, even here in this close and crowded city. Still, conversations are nothing beyond what is said at work or in one of my classes.

Now I land my first real job in the Big Apple as a part-time instructor in psychology, industrial psychology and sociology for Interborough Institute, a business college on Park Avenue. The director wasn't going to hire me because I'm too young. He later tells me he was impressed with the sharp looking new leather briefcase I purchased in Amsterdam. He thinks I'm neat, clean and smart.

The Tombs

For two dollars and seventy-one cents an hour, I also secure a full-time position with the Office of Probation of the New York City Court at 100 Center Street in what is known as the tombs, a gloomy netherworld in the bowels of the earth, in the basement of the courthouse in lower Manhattan. In 2001 a dramatic A&E television series is released called "100 Center Street," based on the activities in this incredible place. As I teach two afternoons each week, I agree to work on Saturdays to make it a full-time job. My task, along with others, is to interview everyone who is arrested during the night and write up reports, which the judges will have in front of them at the time of each individual's arraignment. This will help the judges decide if these people can be released on their own recognizance. I go to the tombs at eight o'clock each morning, first interviewing the prostitutes, most of whom give fictitious names and addresses. Interestingly, none of the Johns have been arrested. Then I interview the drunks. Unless they are also involved in a more serious crime, the prostitutes and drunks are released. I see the same ones over and over again. Some of the prostitutes have been arrested as many as one hundred times. One prostitute tells me she has been arrested more than two hundred times. What an undecorous and ridiculous system. This bizarre process has been going on for hundreds of years. It continues to this day! Once finished with the prostitutes and drunks, I help my colleagues work on the more serious cases.

Though not always fun, this is certainly interesting work—and an amazing way to be introduced to life in New York City. I wear a gold badge at work and carry it on the street. This enables me to ride free on subways and buses.

In November of 1967, there is a march against the war in Vietnam, called The Whitehall demonstrations, and a number of intriguing personages are arrested. I interview baby doctor Benjamin Spock and poet Allen Ginsberg. Ginsberg is one of my heroes and it's all quite strange. Here I am sitting on one side of a table wearing a golden badge while a man I admire sits across from me following his arrest. He has a thick black and white speckled beard and round black-rimmed glasses. With his head bent down a bit, looking over the top of his glasses he says sternly, "You ought to be ashamed of yourself," meaning that I should have been outside protesting, instead of inside working for the establishment. I'm reminded of the story about the American Transcendentalists, Thoreau and Emerson. When Thoreau was arrested for failing to pay taxes to support the Mexican-American War, Emerson went to see him in jail and asked: "What are you doing in there Henry?" Thoreau responded, "What are you doing out there, Mr. Emerson?"

I see things in the Tombs I do not want to see. By placing his hands around a crossbar that runs about eight feet from the ground, correctional officers hang an unruly man by his handcuffs, in such a way that only his toes touch the ground. I go to my supervisor, who goes to the judge's chambers. The judge in turn goes to the supervising correctional officer who has the man taken down. This does not endear me to the correction officers. This is the time of Serpico and massive corruption in the New York City police department.

Someone is needed to work Thanksgiving Day, and, as everyone else has families and wants to be with them, I agree to work alone. There are more people arrested this day than any other day in the year, mostly because of domestic violence. It is impossible to interview everyone. I just take down as much information as I can. A huge black man sits across the table from me with flat bloodshot eyes that bulge from his head with an eerie numbness. He is arrested for bludgeoning his own son to death with a bicycle chain while the boy was sitting on the toilet. There are many sad tales. The Tombs is one hell of a place to be—Thanksgiving Day 1967.

I'm gullible and frequently taken advantage of. Just before Christmas, I interview a sixteen-year-old boy. When I ask him what he is charged with he says, "stealing a Christmas tree." He tells me how his mother has said that they were not going to be able to afford a Christmas tree that year. As I listen to his story, I resolve to get him released. First, I have to find the arresting officer. The officer's response: "He stole a Christmas tree all right. He was unloading a boxcar of trees and putting them on a truck."

Home in Missouri for Christmas, I call Diana in Kentucky to wish her Merry Christmas, and she says she told me that if we left California separately she never wanted to talk to me again. I don't remember her having made such a statement. I will not speak to her again for more than twenty years. I would happily have stayed friends with Diana, as I have with several girlfriends.

I remember Judy's number and call her mother. She gives me Judy's number. I call. We talk. Though she is married, we decide to meet. We are to have an hour together. She is late for our meeting, and when she finally arrives, she tells me she only has fifteen minutes. It has been six years since I have seen her, and we have fifteen minutes laden with memories, pregnant with hopes. We hold each other and kiss. I hold her away from me, so I can look at her. I keep telling her how much I love her. And then—she is gone!

1968—Age Twenty-Five

Back in New York, I resign my position with the probation department in order to have time to study for final exams. If I'm going to do well, I will have to cram; so I cram and do well. Finally, in February, I make a friend. Tom Hovland is a bright A-level student from St. Louis, also in the philosophy department. Tom is living in the East Village next to the

Electric Circus nightclub. This is the center of hippiedom and the psyche-delic generation. His apartment is horribly infested with cockroaches, and he has been robbed several times. We decide to get an apartment together. To find something affordable, we go out of Manhattan to Woodside in Queens. Once in Queens, I can get my car out of storage. It is great to have wheels again and I begin exploring New Jersey and the Hudson River Valley.

I've seen the Promised Land. . . And I'm happy tonight. I'm not worried about anything. I'm not fearing any man. —Martin Luther King, Jr., April 3, 1968

1968 is a year of rebellion and restlessness. On April 4th, Martin Luther King, Jr. is assassinated. Why can't our nation grow up? Why this ongoing insanity? I feel he died for an ideal to which we still aspire. I'm just turning onto Queens Boulevard when I hear the announcement on the car radio. Funny how space and time converge and form permanent memory traces when dramatic events occur.

Somebody help Bobby! Somebody help Bobby!

Exactly two months later, on June the 4th, Bobby Kennedy is assassi-nated. The war in Vietnam is escalating; there are innumerable protests and, in August, riots at the Democratic National convention in Chicago. Much of the world seems to have gone crazy.

CHAPTER 19

My Own Church

Brooklyn and a New Judy

Windsor Terrace

More than anything, I want my own church. Not much progress is made in switching over to the Unitarians. I'm still a member of the Disciples of Christ, so I call them. There are only three Disciples Churches in all of New York City, one on Park Avenue, and two Hispanic speaking congregations. None of these churches needs a minister. I like the Disciples of Christ, as it is one of the more moderate and open-minded of the Protestant denominations. The Disciples of Christ Church is the only church I know of, that holds as doctrine that someday it will not exist, being founded with the intention of one day dissolving back into the larger body of the church. It has also been one of the fastest dying of the Protestant denominations, losing half of its membership in the last half of the 20th century.

I call the Presbyterian Church, the United Church of Christ, and the Methodist Church looking for a position. I do not care too much about whom I work for, though I could not work for the Baptists or one of the more conservative denominations. The Presbyterians offer me a position as an assistant pastor in charge of evangelism in Teaneck, New Jersey. While I'm thinking about it (evangelism does not seem like my thing), the Methodists offer me my own parish, Windsor Terrace United Methodist in Brooklyn.

Windsor Terrace is a small section in Brooklyn between Prospect Park and Greenwood Cemetery. The red brick church with its tall white steeple looks like something from the New England countryside plopped down in the middle of one- and two-family row houses. The church even has a small yard, something unusual in this neighborhood. It was built in 1954, after an earlier building was destroyed to make way for the Prospect Expressway. It thrived fairly well during the fifties. Now there is an exodus of Protestants to the suburbs. There is a large Catholic parish and a synagogue nearby and the community is becoming progressively Italian Catholic and Jewish.

131

I take one course in early summer on The Trial and Death of Socrates. Prospect Park is near by so I go there, find a large tree and, resting my back against it, read Plato. The Methodist hierarchy intends my move to Windsor Terrace to be a stopgap effort to keep the church alive a little longer—maybe five years. My salary is eighty-six dollars a week, and I'm given a parsonage, half of a two-family house. The street looks exactly like the opening scene from the Archie Bunker sitcom, *All in the Family.* I ask permission for Tom to come along, and he moves into the basement.

When Myron and I left Southern California the previous summer, I left behind a number of belongings, including Dr. Heicker's books. It was impossible to bring Myron, his possessions and my possessions all back in one trip. During the summer of 1968 I drive back across the United States, stopping to visit with family in Missouri, both coming and going. The first night heading west from Missouri with the threat of tornadoes, I stop at a roadside park in Oklahoma. When the lightening flashes, a bizarre snapshot is imprinted on my mind. I see a tornado, and I wish it would go away. The convertible roof on the car is whish, whish, whishing up and down. For a moment the whole car lifts off the ground and then settles back down. Though the tornado passes. I cannot sleep.

I'm amazed to see how many dead armadillos there are on the highway. I drive on nonstop till I'm exhausted—finally stopping in the desert near Barstow, California, to sleep in the car. After a couple of hours I wake up. The sun is coming up. It is already getting hot. It is only a couple more hours to Claremont. I get out of the car and start running across the hardscrabble desert. Extending my arms in the air, I scream as I run, trying desperately to wake up enough to continue my journey. I run smack into a barbed wire fence. I never see it. Instantly, I'm enfolded in the fence. Cut and bleeding badly, I limp back to the car and drive to an emergency room in San Bernardino. I still have the scars.

The Dream of Fear

I stay with Donna, a friend from Glendale Central Christian. She is short with short-cropped blond hair and a frisky, impish quality about her. Though I do not know it, she is given to epileptic seizures. At Donna's insistence, I sleep in her bed while she sleeps on the couch. I have a dream. I'm with two other young men. We are walking and come upon a peninsula with an amusement park on it. On the edge of the park is a tunnel—like a tunnel of love—only this is the *tunnel of fear*. One of the young men is particularly eager to show us the inside of the tunnel. The other is resistant to going through. The two of them go through while I walk around on the outside. When they come out the other end, the hair of the fellow who was resistant has turned white. He falls on the ground in a fit, frothing at the mouth.

He recovers and my companions proceed farther onto the peninsula. I stay back and climb into the top of the tunnel through a loft-like door, much like the one on our barn in Missouri. It is my intention to expose the inside of this place and show that it is just a bunch of machinery to frighten people. As I enter the loft, I find that indeed the place is filled with demons, just as one would see in a book on demonology. As I walk into the room, they back away respectfully. As long as I'm not afraid, they are powerless over me. I'm not afraid and keep moving forward. They keep moving back. I stop, and a larger bellied, somewhat human-looking demon approaches me. She asks me if I would like to see the devil himself. I say I would, and she leads me into a side room.

The devil is a young boy sitting in an aluminum lawn chair with his arms resting regally on the arms of the chair and his head bent down to his chest as though he is pouting. I walk over to him, kneel down beside him, put my arms around him and say, "I love you. I love you." He starts shaking violently screaming, "No! No! You can't say that!" And, puff! Like a wisp of smoke, he disappears. I'm instantly awake and in the living room next to Donna on the couch, wrestling with her, trying to keep her from choking on her own tongue, as she is having a grand mal seizure. She looks like the young boy in my dream. After the seizure ceases, I drive her to her mother's house.

I retrieve my things and head back to Missouri. Judy is now divorced, so I call and ask if I can see her on the way back. She says yes. We meet and make love for the first time. It is as I had expected—wonderful. I am so in love with her. I melt into her like butter on a hot muffin. It has been seven years since she ran off with Jim. I want to take her back to New York. She has two young children, whom I cannot support; and Judy is not interested in New York City.

A New Judy

In the fall, I take a heavy academic load. A delightful problem now presents itself at Windsor Terrace. Her name is Judy Halpin. Judy is eighteen. I'm twenty-five. Judy is almost unbearably cute. She is, as Uncle Estel would say, "as cute as a speckled pup under a red wagon." She is blond, with lambent blue eyes and eyelashes so long you think they would scrape the inside of her glasses. She has a wonderful smile, a delightful silly chuckle, nice legs and perfect breasts. Judy lives with her parents in a railroad flat on the second floor of a group of row houses across from the Fort Hamilton Parkway subway stop. She is all Easter and apple pie and as straitlaced and methodical as Methodism itself. It is all conformity and uniformity and white. Everything is white—white clothes, white shoes, white furniture—everything. She is also incredibly kind, simple-hearted and naive. I have seen a bit of the world. I have been married and divorced. I'm doing graduate studies. Judy has just graduated from high school. She has lived an insular life with her mother and father with whom she is incredibly close—so close it is hard to get her away from them. It's safe to say I've never met anyone as tied to her mother's apron strings as Judy, and she will agree with that assessment. It's also safe to say I've never met anyone who grieved so much for the loss of a mother. I used to say of Judy that she is a square and I'm a circle.

There are interesting similarities between Judy Femmer in Missouri and Judy Halpin in Brooklyn. Both are beautiful blondes. Both had an older brother who died in infancy. Each grew up as an only child. Each has an irrational fear of snakes, spiders, mice and such. If either of them even sees a picture of a snake in a book, she will scream and slam the book shut. Both of their fathers are alcoholics who work in repair and mainte-nance of large equipment. Due to the alcoholism, neither family has much money. Judy Halpin's father, Jim, has given up alcohol and is an active member of Alcoholics Anonymous, though he now has a new addic-tion—playing the ponies. While Judy in Missouri is one month younger to the day than I, Judy Halpin and I share the same birthday—she is exactly seven years younger. It is inevitable that Judy and I will start dating. She is at church every Sunday. There are no other young women around, and she is beautiful! Judy is a virgin, and her mother is very clear; there is to be no hanky-panky. Judy is also clear about this. This makes for an inter-esting, frustrating time. She is not the kind of girl I can ask to spend the night.

If, while growing up on the farm in Missouri, someone had said I would spend ten years in Brooklyn, New York, I would have said, "No way!" That is precisely what happens. Life at Windsor Terrace is like living with one big family, and I soon become part of the church's family system.

134

I'm the prince and Judy the princess. They are happy to have their own energetic young minister, and I'm happy to have found a home, my own parish and loving friends with whom I can share my life. I'm now given a new name, which everyone uses to address me. I'm called *Pastor*. I'm the sole pastor. However, this is not a full-time position, so I'm free to do graduate studies and part-time teaching.

One of my first acts is to raise money to plant six sycamore trees around the perimeter of the church, between the sidewalk and the street. Five are now large trees still growing in Brooklyn. A drunken motorist felled the sixth. Because of my active academic life and involvement in parapsychology, there is always some idea I want to try out in a sermon. Being a minister for me is as easy as a walk in the park. A good part of ministry is just being nice to people, and that is simple enough. The older ladies love me, and I love them like my great aunts and grandparents in Missouri. On Sunday afternoons, I call on the "shut-ins," taking communion to their homes. A half-hour or so is enough to show them that someone cares and will pray with them. I sometimes resist calling, yet, I always enjoy it and feel richer for it.

One older woman, Mrs. Voescht, has a permanent live-in nurse. I make several calls to see Mrs. Voescht because the nurse calls and says she is dying. Mrs. Voescht's only living relative is a retarded nephew named Buster who lives by himself in his deceased parent's home four blocks from the church. Buster regularly drops by and puts out the garbage. One morning I notice that Buster has not put out the garbage and intuitively I know he is dead. I call his house. There is no answer. I am so sure that he is dead that I call the police. They pick me up, and we go to Buster's house together. There is no answer at the door. Going around behind the house to the kitchen door, we can see him lying face down on the kitchen floor. It's the first time I've heard a policeman say we have a DOA (dead on arrival). Mrs. Voescht tells me I should take whatever I want from the house, so I take the piano, which we roll down the hill on a dolly and into the parsonage. I also pick up a 1901 leather-bound edition of the *Encyclopedia Britannica*, which has never been removed from its boxes. This is the second time I've been left valuable books.

One day I'm called to Mrs. Voescht's home when she really is dying. The nurse and I are standing next to her bed, and she is moaning and muttering, "I want to go home. I want to go home." The nurse leans over Mrs. Voescht and says, "Now, nonsense, Mrs. Voescht, you are home." I

135

ask the nurse if she will leave us alone, so I can say some prayers for Mrs. Voescht. It is clear what she wants. She wants to go home. She has had it with this old, tired, diseased body of hers. She wants to go home. I say a few prayers, and Mrs. Voescht goes home.

I've put a lot of miles on the Valiant, from Missouri to California, to Missouri, to New York, to Missouri, to California, to Missouri, to New York. I'm making some money now, so I sell the Valiant to Tom and buy a new dark metallic blue 1969 Dodge charger with a black top, and an incredible eight-cylinder, 200+ horsepower engine, all for $2,995.00.

Each year, Windsor Terrace holds an annual fall bazaar. This requires the publication of an annual journal. It occurs to me that we can save money if I do the paste-up work myself. I enjoy thinking about how things are going to look in the journal. This first taste of publishing will eventually lead to *The Mustard Seed, On Course, Inspiration* and *Miracles* magazines.

1969—Age Twenty-Six

I apply for a position as an instructor at the New School. I want to teach a course on The Psychology of Religion. When they accept, I literally dance around the parsonage. I'm going to get to design my own curriculum at a university in Greenwich village. For the next ten years the New School lets me teach two or three courses each semester on whatever topic I choose. I make up what I think are fun courses with titles like Consciousness Expansion and Religious Experience, Creative Force Philosophies, Theories of Religious Experience, Religion and Society, Jung, Teilhard and the Future of Consciousness, Oriental Philosophy, Esoteric and Mystical Philosophies, and many more.

I develop a growing interest in the works of psychic Edgar Cayce. I wake up in the middle of the night. There is a light coming from the hallway. I see Edgar Cayce standing at the foot of my bed. It seems very natural. I'm not at all scared of this apparent apparition. I say, "Why are you here?" There is no response. In the middle of the afternoon the next day, I remember the incident and wonder, "Was I awake or was it part of a dream?"

I join the American Society for Psychical Research. Upon receiving my membership application, Dr. Karlis Osis, head of the society, invites me to visit his office on Seventy-third Street and Central Park West. Afterwards, I become a guinea pig for parapsychological investigation. I start attending lectures at the American Society for Psychical Research. Here I meet Judith Skutch, a mover and shaker in the psychical community. Judy looks a lot like Elizabeth Taylor. Both Jews, they were born the same year. Both petite in their younger years, they will both struggle with weight in their later years. Judy's mother wanted her to try out for what became Elizabeth Taylor's role in the movie, *National Velvet*. Judy is always energetic, glad to see you and excited about new developments in parapsychology. She frequently has friends over to watch Uri Geller bend spoons without touching them or to look at slides on the latest in Kirlian Photography, showing one's aura or light energy extending from the body. At Judy's, I meet Ingo Swan and other famous mediums and psychics from the United States and England.

At the New School I also meet Bob Brier, a tall, lanky guy who is fascinated with the study of Ancient Egypt. He will later become a well-known Egyptologist and produce a number of specials for *National Geographic, PBS,* and *Arts and Entertainment* television. I also meet David McKnight, a young minister from Canada. He, his wife, Rosie, and I share an interest in parapsychology, which leads to seances in the basement of the parsonage. Dr. Osis' secretary, Vera Feldman, a good friend of Judy Skutch, soon joins us in our seances. Before long, Rosie and I are going into trance and doing what we call "soul rescue work." We allow what we think is a soul that has died, and not yet made a complete transition (i. e. has not yet realized it is dead) to come through and talk to us. The others then persuade them that they have, in fact, died.

Houston, Tranquillity Base here. The Eagle has landed. —Neil Armstrong

David and Rosie and I are doing a seance on the evening of July 20, 1969, when we stop, and, along with Tom watch TV pictures of Buzz Aldrin and Neil Armstrong, all shimmering in light like angels walking on the moon. We also get interested in spiritual healing. We stand with our hands over a seated person's head, until we can feel energy moving back and forth between the palms of our hands as we move them over the person. I become involved in the work of Spiritual Frontiers Fellowship, and their exploration of the unexplained and the relationship between psychic phenomena and spirituality. I become vice president of the metropolitan New York chapter and start putting together the annual conferences. I start working with Hilda Charlton, another polestar about thirty years my senior and a well-known spiritual teacher in New York City.

137

At one of these conferences, I receive a free consultation by a psychic, who looks at me with surprise and says, "You're going to have three business failures. You will, however, bounce back from each." I wonder if this is a curse or a blessing. What am I to make of this? Am I to assume there is some truth in this, or shall I just ignore it? I once had a friend who, engaged for the first time, was told by a psychic that she would be married twice. I'm wondering about the ethics of psychics.

One Saturday afternoon, David, Rosie, Vera and a psychic friend, Rosemarie De Simone, and I are invited to go up to Riverdale, New York, to meet John Lennon and Yoko Ono. We are going to demonstrate the trance work we've been doing, some of our healing work, and to provide John an opportunity for a psychic reading from Rosemarie. I'm excited about getting to meet John. He is just two years older than I am, and he is one of my heroes. I do love his songs. They are saying so much of what needs to be said—*all you really need is Love—Imagine*. While the others go into a bedroom to do the reading with John, I'm left sitting at the kitchen table with Yoko. I try to find things to talk about, mostly to no avail. Yoko, I sense, would rather be in the bedroom listening to John's reading than having to deal with me.

New Mellery Abbey

I get three weeks off in August, so I take off. There is only one vacation I think of making each summer—back to Missouri, to my family, back to the farm to remind myself what I am here for.

> *The Holy Spirit can indeed make use of memory, for God Himself is there.*
> *Yet this is not a memory of past events, but only a present state.*
> —ACIM, T-28.I.4:1-2

Walking precipitates memories, and I need to hear again and again the Voice that first spoke to me in the back pasture. (At Thanksgiving 1999, Mother tells me it is the same pasture she visited for solitude and solace). I venture home to Missouri and then to Dubuque, Iowa for my longest stay at New Mellery. It's a good time to read Alan Watts and Thomas Merton. Though the Trappists observe silence, they have developed the ability to talk in sign language. I see a couple of them doing what you might call *silent laughing*—literally, holding their sides. I realize that one of them told a joke in sign language. While I'm there, a monk dies. There is no embalming. He is placed in a simple wooden coffin in the chapel, and for twenty-four hours monks take turns sitting with the body, praying.

138

The next day, at the grave, the monk is taken out of the coffin, lowered into the grave and buried with only a white sheet wrapped around him. it could hardly be more natural than this.

I've been taking flying lessons at La Guardia Airport in New York City so each day I venture to the Dubuque airport to take lessons. It is here that I first solo, though I do not fully understand the radio controls, and I never notice a large airliner that has priority in air space, and I land ahead of him, forcing him to slow his approach. Though scolded by my instructor, we celebrate my first solo experience.

Back in New York, friends from the New School invite me to go with them to a rock concert near Woodstock, New York. I have obligations at church, and I want to see Judy. Woodstock proves to be a pivotal point of transformation for many friends. Four hundred thousand people show up for the festival and despite endless traffic jams, food and water shortages, and torrential downpours, the weekend is a fantastic success. There is an experience here of oneness. Thirty years later in the summer of 1999, when another generation seeks to duplicate the event, there are riots, fires, looting and reports of police misconduct.

I busy myself in the fall with graduate courses on the Phenomenon of Life and the Philosophy of Art, running the church, teaching at the New School, and working with David and Rosie. I'm still teaching psychology at Interboro Institute on Park Avenue. When the New York Miracle Mets win their first World Series in October, the ticker-tape parade passes six stories below our classroom. We cease teaching and open the windows so students can throw out their old test papers, their version of confetti.

Spiritual Frontiers sponsors a workshop by author Allen Spragett. At the end of the afternoon, we are invited to Connecticut, to meet an amazing man named John Hay. John has worked as an engraver for the U.S. Mint. He is now retired and spends most of his time tinkering in his basement. John, a serene-looking older man with a full head of white hair, comes out to the car to meet us, wearing an unassuming button-down blue cardigan sweater. Ostensibly, we are there for Allen Spragett to meet John. His basement looks like an alchemist's laboratory. John says he knows how flying saucers work and, to our amazement, demonstrates the fact by flying a small saucer-shaped object around in his basement without any obvious means of propulsion. It has something to do with magnetism and anti-gravity achieved by the spinning of an internal gyroscope. It's all beyond me.

I'm taken aside and told that the reason we are here is so John and I can meet. I'm not quite sure what my companions are talking about. It is all very esoteric. John gives me a book he has channeled called *The Magic of Space*. It was written in ten days, he says, not by himself rather, by someone named Triton. The book provides a correlation between metaphysics, the physical science and the power of the mind. It talks about separation, and the subjective-object problem. It proves fascinating reading. Many years later, I will realize that it was an important precursor to *A Course in Miracles*.

God gives no special favors, and no one has any powers that are not available to everyone. Only by tricks of magic are special powers "demonstrated."
—ACIM, M.25.3: 7

I'm doing more and more psychic work when one day, at the New School I'm talking with Dr. Lawrence Le Shan, author of *How to Meditate*. Le Shan asks me if I want to become known as a psychic and a healer. I immediately say, "No." That doesn't seem like me. Though I continue to be involved in psychic work through the mid-seventies, I eventually quit, as I'm not sure where the information we receive in trance is coming from. I'm hopeful that we are not making it up, not even on a subconscious level. Lacking clear evidence, for the sake of integrity, I let it all go. I want to be the *message*—not the *medium*. I've seen too many people misuse their psychic abilities.

CHAPTER 20

The Atonement
The First Theological Debate

During the first two years at Windsor Terrace, the Methodist hierarchy pretty much leaves me alone. They are glad to have filled the position, and everyone is happy. Although licensed by the Christian Church, I have never been officially ordained, so it is necessary to go through the ordination process with the Methodists. I think this is just a formality, as it is clear that I am committed to the ministry and now actively doing what I always wanted to do. Believing that the Methodist church is open-minded, I think this is a good opportunity to explore some questions. As it turns out, my questions cut into the heart of traditional theology. One question in particular presents a problem.

To be ordained, you have to answer in writing a series of questions, and then undergo an individual interview, which is followed by a group review by the Board of Ordained Ministry. In my initial paper, I raise the question of the doctrine of the atonement. You might think that any good seminary graduate would be able to understand the atonement. In traditional Christian theology, the atonement is defined as the effect of Jesus' suffering and death in redeeming mankind. I have a book of illustrations for use by Christian ministers. It has twelve illustrations of what the atonement is. Each illustration describes the agony of a suffering, bleeding, dying Jesus on the cross, a *sacrifice* he makes because of our sins. Being washed in blood sounds like a messy affair. Not exactly the kind of thing a God of Love would come up with.

If I understand it correctly, according to traditional Christian theology an all-wise and loving God killed his only Son, who was innocent, because I am innately sinful, i.e.; we are saved because Jesus was killed. I don't get it. How could Love (God) devise such a horrible system? In a Lenten retreat for ministers, the leader hands each of us spike nails and asks us to contemplate the misery of Jesus on the cross. Christianity uses a cross as its symbol, an instrument of torture and death; the Catholic church puts a bleeding body on the cross. What we have is vicarious salvation. According to traditional Christian theology, we are saved not because we are able to see what Jesus saw. We are saved *because we believe* he suffered and died for us.

Belief is weaker than *knowledge*. The BBC did an interview with Dr. Carl Jung shortly before he died in 1961. The interviewer asked Dr. Jung if he believed in God. Jung hesitated for a moment then said, "Believe in God? No—I know!" Is it not better to *know* God than to *believe* in God? Is it not better to see what Jesus saw and do what he did than to believe that he has vicariously atoned for our innate sinfulness? Because we are sinners, he suffered on the cross? If Jesus knew who he was, if he knew he was not a body, did he suffer? I watched a TV show entitled *Rome: The Power and the Glory*, where they point out Ancient Rome's strong belief in sacrificial blood. Is this where the idea comes from?

According to *The Encyclopedia of Religion*, the theme of all Christian doctrines of the atonement can be expressed in the sentence, "Christ died for our sins." In Judaism as well, Yom Kippur, the Day of Atonement, the most solemn holiday of the Jewish year, is a day of fasting and repenting of sins. The way the atonement process is understood makes sin real. When it comes to the question of our innate sinfulness, I say, "Maybe we are innately good and just forgot it." This does not go over well. After we make sin real, we must then try to forgive sin or seek to overlook what we have made real. Many years later, *A Course in Miracles* is to answer these questions for me. At this point, I have questions with no answers. The *Course* asks how you can overlook something you make real? The fact that you make it real means you cannot overlook it (ACIM, T. 9. IV. 4:5-6).

My consternation over these issues is received not as a play of ideas, as I had naively hoped. It rather raises some questions regarding my readiness for the ministry. I have put myself in an awkward position. Though I have a theological degree and have nearly completed the course work for a doctorate, and though I have already been a minister for nine years, there is some question as to whether or not I should be ordained. This is not at all what I expected. I thought they would be glad to receive me. As far as the Board is concerned, I do not understand the atonement. Another minister, Rev. Evelyn Newman, has similar questions, and she is also eyed with suspicion. Evelyn will later go on to lead workshops on mysticism. Evelyn and I are ordained in the United Methodist church in June of 1970.

Daddy is already beginning to show signs of Alzheimer's disease and he absolutely will not fly, so Mother and Daddy take a train to New York to attend the ordination, which is held at the University of Bridgeport in Connecticut. The doctrine of the atonement remains a point of difference for me. Eighteen years later it will be *a* pivotal point in my leaving the Methodist church.

CHAPTER 21

The Seventies

1970 - Age Twenty-Seven

I have only two more courses to complete for the doctorate so I cut my academic load to one course on Kant's *Critique of Theoretical Reason*. I'm determined to thoroughly understand Kant and make an A. I'm teaching three different courses at the New School.

My next-door neighbor in Brooklyn wants to sell his house and move to Florida. The asking price is only $16,000. With a small down payment even I can afford, I proudly follow in Daddy's footsteps and invest in real estate. I have the basement of the house refinished with an additional apartment and rent the house to three nuns from a nearby parish. I also rent the house next to the parsonage and sublet the rooms to students. With the church in Brooklyn, teaching at the New School, and income from the rental property, I'm able to save ten percent and give away ten percent of everything I make and still have enough money to be generous with friends. On the whole, life is good.

Joyful Dog—My Second Familiar

I want to get a dog. Now I can. I have a home, I have a back yard and it's fenced in. It has to be a cocker spaniel, and so it is I find my little blonde female, Joyful Dog, who pees all over the pet shop counter while I pet her. Joyful Dog is one of the best things that ever happened to me. She obeys so well. I'm clear with her from the beginning that she is not to be a barker, and she gets it. She is almost barkless. She is also good about not making messes in the house. I don't dare, however, leave potential "toys" lying about, and I lose several belts and shoes.

There is lots of drug activity in the neighborhood, and I befriend the kids who hang out at the corner deli across the street. One day they come to me in a panic. Alberto has shot air into his arm while trying to shoot up on heroin. I take him to a doctor, who immediately lances the skin to let the air out. A few days later Alberto, along with the others, breaks into the parsonage through a back window and steals my stereo, television, and IBM typewriter. I know they did it. They all know Joyful. She probably just wagged her cute little behind when they came, as if to say, "Hi! Hi! Hi! Help yourself!" Surprisingly, my goods are retrieved when the police stop a suspicious car and find them in the trunk. It takes several weeks and lots of red tape to retrieve my possessions.

In March, a horrific explosion devastates a townhouse across the street from the New School killing three radical terrorists of the Weathermen ultra-military faction. We are traumatized to think it can happen so close to our classrooms. In April, I help John McConnell raise money for the first celebration of Earth Day. In May, National Guardsmen fire into a crowd of Kent State University student protesters. Two young women and two young men are killed, and eight others are wounded. American students are now being killed because of the Vietnam War. On this day, a lot of hawks turn into doves. This really is, I think, *the* experience that, more than any other, ended this war.

With lots of Beatles music, I try sponsoring dances in the basement of the church for the kids in the neighborhood. It's an adventure trying to get Judy to loosen up and do some fast dancing. The kids I'm trying to help steal a few items from the church, and that's the end of the dances.

I take one last course, in the summer of 1970, on philosopher Alfred North Whitehead. Though I continue to teach philosophy courses to this day, this is the last of my experience with philosophers. When Whitehead was once asked, "Why don't you write more clearly?" he replied, "Because I don't think more clearly." Why am I studying this stuff? There are so many philosophies and all of them think they are right. One thing, though: I have fallen in love with Schopenhauer, Nietzsche, Kierkegaard and William James. Schopenhauer and Nietzsche were both cynics, who pointed out before Freud how deeply buried and how malicious the ego can be. Still, why not study something that is clear—something that is freeing—like the mystical experience—like what the Zen Buddhists are talking about? Like something logic says is not clear.

Tom, my housemate, needs money and decides to drive a taxi. He asks me to come with him, so we get taxi-driving permits together. It is tough work. Being low men on the totem pole, we are given the worst cabs with broken seats, broken shocks, and broken springs. By the end of the night, our backs and butts are also broken. The second day out Tom is held up at gunpoint. The robbers take him to an empty lot in the Bronx, put a gun to his head and demand his money. He is sure that he is dead. He cannot believe they let him go. A number of men have lost their lives this way. Tom quits the next day. Despite fare beaters who jump out of the cab and run when we reach their destination; despite a lady in a fur coat who screams obscenities when I'm unable to turn down a one-way street the wrong way, despite what has happened to Tom, I continue to drive. There are also many nice passengers, particularly inquisitive out-of-towners, and it's fun to tell them about the Big Apple. I soon know the streets of Manhattan, the Bronx, Brooklyn and Queens.

Though Judy and I have been dating for a couple years, though I have fallen in love with this lovely young woman, things do not always work well for us. While we truly love each other, we seem to live in two different worlds. We have not developed a sex life, and I'm frustrated. In the summer of 1970, another woman comes into my life. Vera Feldman, Dr. Osis' secretary at the American Society for Psychical Research, and I become lovers. Vera is Jewish with a thick head of black hair. She is perky and cute and very interested in parapsychological phenomena. Somehow we overlook the fact that I'm twenty-seven and Vera is forty-one. Age doesn't bother us. Neither of us thinks of our relationship as anything other than an intimate friendship. There is never any talk of marriage, and that makes it all the more comfortable.

Firewalking

I take the month of August off to visit the Sivananda Yoga ashram in Val Morin, Canada, for a month of intensive training to obtain credentials as a yoga teacher. Vera is going to join me during the last two weeks. The last week there they plan a firewalking demonstration during a week-long festival sponsored by Swami Vishnudevananda. I think it will be fun to interview the participants before and after the firewalking and see if I can write an article on the experience. I go to the man in charge and tell him what I want to do. He says if I really want to know about it, I should do it myself. So, with cold feet (later to be warmed), I sign up. We go through a week of training: long daily meditations, two hours of yoga each day, fasting and lots of pujas (worship services) with chanting. We are to remain celibate. Mostly, we practice going into trance.

I awake early the day of the firewalk thinking that before the day is over I'm either going to walk on fire or burn the hell out of my feet. At two in the afternoon, we watch the building of the bed for the fire. A thirty-foot-long pit is filled with logs, gasoline is poured on and the fire begins. All afternoon two young men with long metal rakes beat down the logs. By early evening there is an intense bed of glowing hot coals, so hot you cannot walk within several feet of the pit. I'm feeling nervous about this potentially dangerous exercise, so I go into the mountains to meditate. I sit down and simply say, "Help! What's going to happen?" I then think I hear a voice that says, "You are going to do what the others are going to do." This provides a sense of relief. I suppose it means that I'm going to be all right or we are *all* going to burn the hell out of our feet.

Just before the firewalk, we do another long puja and I fall into the same kind of trance as what happens when I work with David and Rosie. When I reach the other side of the pit, I fall on the ground shaking. All of us who have completed the walk join together in one large ball of arms wrapped around each other and we go into one long *"OM!"* lasting several minutes. Coming out of this experience, I'm thinking, "My goodness, if you can walk on fire, think of all the other things you can do if you let your mind do it." The next day there is a feature article in the *Montreal Star,* and there is my picture, front and center; just as I'm about to step on the fire. I have a straggly beard, eyes closed, hands clasped together in a prayerful mudra position. Below the picture is the caption "Young mystic walks on fire."

Vera goes back to New York. I drive back to Missouri via an overnight at New Mellery Abbey. I want to see Mother and Daddy and, of course, show off the cover page of the *Montreal Star.* I go out near the condemned bridge, leave a tape recorder on a rock and rest on a sandbar watching the playfulness of the fish while listening to the gentle roll of the water over smooth rocks and sand in a little rapid. I take the tape home to listen to at night when I'm falling asleep in the City.

I write an article about the firewalking experience and send it along with pictures to *Fate* magazine, and they publish the article. I notice an ad for a position as an instructor at Highland, a private high school for well-to-do Jews in Jamaica Estates (Queens), New York. I call the school at eight-forty-five on Monday morning and let the phone ring until someone picks up at nine. I secure the first interview and thus the job. I teach at Highland each morning, and then return to Manhattan to teach or take classes each evening at the New School. At Highland, I teach World War II and Ideology, Public Speaking, Psychology, Comparative Religions, and Yoga. I am a Christian minister, teaching Oriental religion in a Jewish high school.

1971—Age Twenty-Eight

According to 16th Century Mystic St. John of the Cross, only by transcending the intellect can Divine Essence be achieved. As he was to express it, "I entered where I was not and remembered not knowing, all knowledge transcending." I have completed the course work for the doctorate in philosophy at the New School. The philosophy department focuses on Phenomenology and German Idealistic Philosophy. No one is interested in the Psychology of Religion, Parapsychology or Mysticism.

The Holy Spirit, seeing where you are but knowing you are elsewhere, begins
His lesson in simplicity with the fundamental teaching that "truth is true."
This is the hardest lesson you will ever learn, and in the end the only one.
Simplicity is very difficult for twisted minds. —ACIM, T-14.II.2: 1-3

This *is* the hardest lesson any of us has to learn. I have spent four years studying philosophy. Philosophers spent a lifetime figuring "it" out. Hegel had an elaborate dialectical system. No matter how much we "figure it out," we are not going to do it. Freud figured out the ego. He didn't, however, see any way to be free of it, and he was himself an atheist. Mystics say it is not a matter of trying to figure anything out. It's a matter of letting things be—or just being present. What is important is revelation.

Tom is a dedicated A-level student working nearly full time on his doctorate. He takes his comprehensive exams ahead of me. I'm surprised when he fails; he is completely dejected. He goes to visit a girlfriend in Queens and later calls and asks if I can pick him up. I agree. On the way home, he abruptly asks me to stop the car. He wants to get out and walk. I say, "How will you get home? When will you come home?" He says he doesn't know. "Just go! Just go on!" I leave him standing on a street corner in Queens. He never comes home. Tom is an exceptionally gifted man with a beautiful, brilliant mind. He lives, eats, drinks and thinks philosophy. Failing the doctoral comps hits him hard. Later I'm to learn he has gone home to Missouri and then on to spend time on an Indian reservation. Two years later he returns to New York and takes the master's degree in philosophy. Then he disappears. I never hear from him again. (After a lecture I give in Gainesville, Florida in January 2002 a lady tells me she is Tom Hovland's sister. Then, just like Tom, she disappears.)

After Tom fails, I know I will not succeed. Fewer than one in a hundred actually get the doctorate at the New School. To succeed, you have to develop a close relationship with a sympathetic mentor who is willing to shepherd you through the program. And you have to have a passion for nothing except philosophy. I have not developed a close relationship with any of the professors. There are several highly honored men and women here like Hannah Arendt, Arron Gurwitch, and Hans Jonas. With Hans Jonas, I share an interest in Gnosticism. That's about it. They have their favorite protégés and I think they are too famous for the likes of a preacher boy like me. There is no Dr. Eitzen at the New School, no one willing to put his arm around me and shepherd me on through.

I have completed the course work with A's and B's and one unfortunate C-. In the fall of 1968, Tom and I took a course on Predicate Calculus Logic of the First Order taught by a professor from Yugoslavia with a heavy accent. He was hard to understand and everyone complained. From the original forty students, eighteen take the final exam. There is one A, one B, one C- and 15 F's. Tom was the B. I was the C-. Thank God I had Tom to help me. With no more classes to take and wanting to clean up my record, I ask if I can take Predicate Calculus Logic over to see if I can do better. I get Bill McKenna, the student who got the A, to tutor me through the course. As time goes by, I figure out what the professor "has to ask" on the final. Sure enough, there is one major question and I'm thoroughly prepared. Finally, I get it! The C- turns into an A+.

In May, I drive down to Washington D.C. with friends to protest the war in Vietnam. There I meet Philip and Daniel Berrigan, two Catholic priests earlier convicted of destroying draft records to protest the war. The event is disorganized. There are lots of people. There are not a lot of activities. We look around for something going on. I see a long line of people and think it must be something important. When I get there, I see it's a queue for the portable toilets. Back in Brooklyn, I write an article for a local Brooklyn newspaper about the event, and I mention the portable toilet experience. One of my parishioners is outraged that her minister has written about toilets.

Academically, I'm in the wrong place so I look around for an alternative and am admitted to the Th.D. program at General Theological Seminary in the fall of 1971. There I meet Dr. John Johnson, Jr., a specialist in Jungian psychology and a teacher of the Psychology of Religion. Finally, I've found someone who speaks the same language.

149

CHAPTER 22

Which Guru?
Adventures in India

The experience with firewalking has deepened my interest in yoga and Hinduism. I begin a more serious study of the Vedanta System of Hinduism as derived from the *Upanishads*. According to *Vedanta*, nothing except God—the indescribable Brahma—really exists. The physical universe and our individual egos are all ephemeral, all Maya or illusions. The world of maya represents a lower order of knowledge. To know that our separate selves are identical with the one Self, God, or Brahma-Atman is to apprehend reality and have true revelation. In reality there is only God, only that which is spaceless, timeless and eternal.

Western philosophy has not given me many answers. Philosophy stretches the mind. Theology stretches the soul. I'm looking forward to my new academic adventures at General Theological. In the meantime, I have to go to India to find out some things for myself. What if I can meet a living avatar? Would it not be a more immediate and authentic experience than reading the works of a dead philosopher? I decide to do a backpacking guru search through India to spend time with Sai Baba, Muktananda and any other gurus I might find. Hilda Charlton is planning a trip to India to see Sai Baba. I already have tickets. She says she is coming along in about ten days. We agree to meet at American Express in Bombay and go see Sai Baba together. I want to make a couple of stops in exotic and truly unusual places like Kabul, Afghanistan. Istanbul is, however, a more "civilized" and thus a more convenient stopover and Teheran, Iran, will serve for a five-day stop on the way back. Vera wants to accompany me. I feel it important that I do this trip solo. I want to do some inner soul-searching. A companion will provide too many distractions.

Istanbul

The air is thick with perfume and enchantment in Istanbul. I go to the mosques and the museums, and I walk the bazaars, first built during the 1600s. The aroma of cinnamon lingers in the air. There are men smoking a hookah, a pipe designed with a long tube passing through an urn of water that cools the smoke. Everywhere street urchins are trying to sell something: nuts, candy, spices, candles, wool blankets, and Turkish coffee. There is brass and copper ware of every sort imaginable. Live chickens are for sale in cages. There are too many shops and too many people—I'm overwhelmed. I visit the aqueducts of Valens built during the Roman period, still in excellent condition. The most impressive part of Istanbul is Santa Sophia's. Built by Constantine around 320, it is the oldest and one of the greatest churches in Christendom, nearly as large as St. Peter's in Rome. Few buildings are so overwhelming in their sheer beauty. Even with the old tarnish, the building is one of the wonders of world religion. Then I go to the Blue Mosque, symbolic of the blue sky. You have to remove your shoes and leave them in a comical heap of dozens of others. I pray inside that my Frye boots will still be there when I come back out.

I stay at a hotel on the coast off the Bosporus, the opening to the Black Sea. The Bosporus is all shimmering and blue. Seagulls swoop and dive on the air currents above, calling out their ceaseless cries. Across the bay, only a couple of miles away is Asia. I'm alone and lonesome in Istanbul. Traveling alone in eastern countries, staying in hotels without television, or with television in foreign languages, provides lots of time for reading. I have asked Dr. Johnson for his reading list for a course I'm going to take with him this fall on Ways of Liberation, East and West, Ancient and Modern. Off on a pilgrimage, I read John Bunyan's *Pilgrim's Progress;* Paul Burton's account of Meher Baba; *The Way of the Pilgrim;* St. John of the Cross's *Dark Night of the Soul,* and the mystical *The Cloud of Unknowing.*

Initiation in India

Exiting the plane in Bombay, I'm struck by dust and heat. I'm surprised at how widely English is used. I hail a taxi and ask the driver to take me to a nice hotel. I want to work into Indian culture slowly. He takes me to the Taj Mahal hotel right on the coast of the Arabian sea. Here, for fifteen dollars per day, I'm given a large room with big shutters that swing out offering an enticing view of the ocean. The hotel is a marbled marvel with huge fans constantly whisk-whisk-whisk-whisking clear the thick Bombay air. There is also a courteous, smiling, turbaned staff eager to please.

I go upstairs, unpack and come down for a walk. Stepping out the front door of the hotel, I'm hit with a blast of warm air filled with a salty tang coming from a breeze off the ocean. I take a deep breath and look about. People are everywhere. I've only gone a block when a beggar asks for some money. I make a classically naive American mistake by giving him some. This brings a barrage of beggars. Trying to give a little here, a little there, I'm soon overwhelmed by the crowd pressing itself upon me. I drag an old lady, who will not let go of my pant leg, several feet before a strong looking young Indian man intervenes and chases the others away. He offers, for a price, to keep the others off of me. I agree and go back to the hotel to regain my composure. I change into the roughest looking clothes I can find and come out the back door of the hotel, where I meet this young man. Govinda will act as my bodyguard and tour guide. He is a bit taller and more muscular than most. He is twenty. He has thick, dark, shiny, black hair, big teeth and a wide smile. It's an intriguing experience getting to know the psyche of this young man. He has been an orphan for as long as he can remember. He is like so many others struggling to make it in this desperate place. I try to think of some way I can take Govinda back to the states with me. This is an impractical idea.

A rupee, the main currency in India, is worth about fifteen cents. The average Indian earns about thirty rupees a day. Walking down these scorching streets, it is obvious I'm a Westerner, a target, and beggars approach me on every block. I feel as if I have the words "easy mark" tattooed on my forehead. It is nearly impossible to give money away without being mobbed; still I look for ways to do so. I get on a bus, carrying a good bit of change. As the bus pulls away, I throw a few rupees or a bunch of parsies, a smaller unit, out the window. There is a scurry for the money while I'm safely moving away from the crowd.

Bombay is filled with movie theaters playing B-rated American and Indian movies. There are animals—cows, dogs, cats, and rats—everywhere. Little girls are collecting cow dung to be dried and used as fuel. There are women in multicolored saris, their bangles and anklets tinkling. There is the clink of cymbals, the lusty blowing of conch shells and the beat of drums. The music that fills the streets is a strange mixture, sometimes enchanting, sometimes nerve racking. India is blindingly colorful. There are people, people everywhere and parades and festivals with amazing vibrant reds, deep yellows and soft blues.

Rajneesh and Chaotic Meditation

I'm given the name of a family in Bombay I should contact. I call, and the father comes to meet me at the hotel. When I tell him I'm in India on a guru search, he tells me there is considerable excitement about a relatively new teacher named Rajneesh. He is willing to drive me to Rajneesh's ashram for my first visit. I meet several gurus in India. Rajneesh is by far the most erudite and scholarly, and therefore the most interesting. He was a professor of philosophy who had an experience of enlightenment in 1952. He now speaks daily to a growing group of Indians and young Americans and Europeans who come to his lectures. He has a sharp, insightful, humorous, metaphysical mind. Hilda says she will leave word for me at American Express. Each day I go there first, looking for a message from her. Day after day there is none, so off I go to Rajneesh's ashram, where I participate in "chaotic" meditation and listen to his lectures.

Our eyes covered by a bandana, we do heavy breathing for ten minutes, until a gong sounds, then, for ten minutes, we are to behave as crazily as possible: fall down, beat on the floor, let out all the donkeyish noises we want. The gong sounds again, and we jump up and down for ten minutes with our arms over our head saying "Who, Who, Who, Who." At the next sound of the gong there are two options available to everyone: freeze in the position you find yourself in or collapse on the floor and freeze. Now, exhausted from thirty minutes of vigorous energetic exercise, the real meditation begins.

The last day there, I collapse on the ground only to have an immense Indian standing with one foot next to my chest, under my right armpit, and the other foot near the left side of my head. He freezes immediately above me with his head bent over the top of my head below. He begins emitting deep belching and burping sounds as though he is about to divest himself of his breakfast. Fearful he is about to lose it on top of me, I have a less than meditative experience.

I'm given an interview with Rajneesh. We sit cross-legged together on his raised platform bed. I feel very comfortable with him. He feels like an old friend. We talk for half an hour. There is a force and clarity about this man that stops me. I don't remember the content of our conversation. I do remember our laughing together. I do think that he *has it*, that he is enlightened. I've never experienced anything like this in the presence of Christian *dignitaries*. I trust this man and I think that he loves me. I could not say that about my bishop or district superintendent. Rajneesh has an irreverent and cynical attitude toward traditional religionists and stuffy dogmatic zealots. His openness toward sex is also refreshing. The establishment doesn't like him. He likes to call it as it is. His life takes strange twists and turns. Deceased now for several years, he is currently known and re-

153

spected as Osho. I still enjoy his books and tapes. He helped me see the similarity of *A Course in Miracles* and Zen Buddhism.

Bombay by Night

There isn't much to do in Bombay at night except eat, take walks and read. With copious amounts of time for reading, it is soon clear: I'm going to get through Dr. Johnson's entire reading list before the summer is over. There is a nightclub in the basement of the Taj Mahal Hotel patronized by wealthy young Indians, a minority in this country. I go and feel out of place. I notice a placard on the counter of the hotel advertising "Bombay by Night." Why not try a tour? I sign up. We meet in the hotel lobby at eight. Two middle-aged men show up, a big-bellied German salesman and a slim mustachioed Englishman. The three of us hop into what is apparently our guide's own little taxi, and we take off on a tour of Bombay. We go to a nice restaurant for dinner, then to a nightclub. To top off the evening, we go to a strip show. The place is full of thick smoke. None of the strippers are appealing. Most of them are overweight, and none of them strip all the way, getting down at best to a bikini. Indian men, obviously inebriated, are banging on the tables, shouting, and apparently enjoying themselves. I find the whole thing surrealistic, like a scene from some old black and white Middle Eastern movie. I wonder where our guide would have taken us if women had shown up for the tour.

One of Rajneesh's disciples tells me about yet another swami who lives outside Bombay. I leave a message for Hilda at American Express, and on a rainy afternoon, load up my backpack, check out of the Taj Mahal, and head off. I have a small collapsible umbrella that works only poorly in the strong winds. When the bus lets me off, it is pouring sheets of rain that hits and bounces. Looking about, I step off the bus. The wind is strong, and the trees are all dancing in the rain. I run as best I can, slipping, swish swashing, and splashing in the mud, to the swami's ashram. I'm drenched. Inside I'm greeted, given a dry towel, and told the swami will see me later. I spend the entire afternoon sitting in wet clothes reading in a damp, slate floor lobby.

Finally, another man with dark black hair and all white clothes appears and says the swami will not be able to see me. He says he, too, is a swami. He says he has an ashram on the other side of Bombay and invites me to go there with him. He seems charming, and since I have nowhere else to go, I agree to go along. First we have to take a train back to Bombay, from there, another train to his ashram. At the station, he asks if I can buy us both third class tickets. Third class means that you get to ride wherever you can find a seat, and if you cannot find one, you stand up. I stand with my companion and others between two railroad cars for several stops before we are able to secure seats from those who have departed. You don't dare look at the floor, which is crawling with cockroaches. The onboard toilet is approached with trepidation. As a man, you can stand, but, my God, you wouldn't want to sit on the thing. I hope the women's room is cleaner.

This guru now asks me many questions about life in America. Where do I live? Do I have a girlfriend? Do I own a car? What kind of car? How much horsepower does it have? When I tell him the horsepower of my Dodge Charger, he makes quite a commotion. Horsepower seems to be something he understands, and 200 horsepower is impressive!

When we get to Bombay, he asks me again if I will buy us tickets, this time first-class. I do. I offer to buy him an ice cream cone, and he is pleased to receive it. Two shapely, Swedish-looking girls with backpacks, long blonde hair in braids, ample breasts and long legs come walking by. I'm getting nervous about my companion. He seems less and less like a swami and more and more like a con-artist. Where is he taking me? With his attention focused on the girls, I step behind a thick support column, turn and walk quietly out of the train station, and into the back of a waiting cab. I have the driver take me to a small (more economical) hotel I had seen near the Taj Mahal hotel. I go around to the Taj Mahal hotel looking for Govinda, my young tour guide and bodyguard. He is nowhere to be found. For the next two days, I spend a lot of time reading, of all things, *The Godfather*.

Sai Baba

I finally give up on Hilda and go to see Sai Baba by myself. Sai Baba is perhaps best known for his apparent materializations. He simply waves his hand in the air and something appears—*vabhuti* (sacred ash), flowers, candy, gold rings, and more. I take a turboprop to Bangalore, in the mid-central part of southern India, where I'm to take a bus to Putaparthie to see Sai Baba. Bangalore has many beautiful parks and public gardens. The next day I have a taste of Indian time, as the bus, scheduled to leave at nine a.m., leaves at noon, and no one complains or thinks there is anything unusual about the late departure. Little importance is given to *time* in the sense of punctuality.

Seats designed for two people have three. There are crying babies, sleeping babies, sleeping bags, bunches of bananas, and chickens cackling in boxes on the roof. With no air-conditioning, dust rolls in the open windows as we rattle through the sweltering Indian countryside, speeding down a progressively rougher road. Other seekers who share the bus are excitedly talking about how we might get to Putaparthie in time for *darshan*, which means we will be able *to see* Sai Baba come out and stand on his verandah. One is thought to receive a blessing from this viewing, something like viewing the Pope.

On the bus I meet a turbaned Sikh (Sikhism is a faith that attempts to blend Islam and Hinduism) and a young Indian, and we decide to get a room together when we arrive in Putaparthie. We are the first customers in a "hotel in the making." For three rupees a day for the three of us, we get a room. That is all there is to it—no beds, no dressers, and no lights, just a bare room. The "hotel" is still being built from cement blocks. The windows have no glass, and there is no bathroom. To go to the bathroom, you stand in line for an outhouse, or as some Indians do, you might go to a "latrine" area behind the building where you can do your business and cover it with dirt. There is a public shower, for which you have to stand in line and shower quickly, as the water is only one temperature—cold. A shocking experience in the morning, it feels great in the hot afternoon.

> *A master may purposely make a test of one's eagerness to meet him.*
> *This ruse is frequently employed in the West by doctors and dentists!*
> —Paramahanasa Yogananda, *Autobiography of a Yogi*,
> Self Realization Fellowship.

Sai Baba has a huge Afro haircut. He is the only guru I meet who is still alive more than thirty years later. He lives in what looks like a Greek revival southern plantation mansion. He comes to stand twice each day on the porch of the second floor where he can wave to the thousand or so who fill his yard below. There is no lawn—only dirt. I understand now there are tens of thousands of people and many buildings, temples, and paved streets. Every morning, we sit in the yard around Sai Baba's house, and he comes out and walks among the crowd pointing to different individuals. If he points to you, you get an audience with him that day. I sit for several days. One day he stops and stares at me. I stare back. I could reach out and touch him if I wanted to. He does not pick me. He walks on down and then back behind me and just as he comes to my back, he trips and puts his hand on my shoulder to steady himself. After he goes back into his house, people run up to me and tell me that putting his hand on my shoulder was intentional. They say he never does anything "accidentally." I am amazed by the whole experience.

I sit for several more days and he never picks me. There are, however, a lot of people here. I have a business card that indicates I'm a minister and college instructor. I write a note on the back, saying I would have enjoyed an audience with him. I have decided to go see Muktananda. I pass the card to one of his lieutenants, pack my backpack and start walking to the bus station. As I arrive at the bus stop, only a few hundred yards from the ashram, a young Indian comes running up behind me, taps me on the shoulder and says, "He will see you now."

I see Sai Baba along with five Indians. We sit in a semicircle on the floor. I'm on the far left. He spends time with each person beginning on the far right, doing materialization for each. The guy two down from me gets rock candy. He immediately takes it up in both hands and ravenously devours it. The fellow next to me is a wealthy young Indian wearing a beautiful white shirt with an embroidered collar. He receives a gold ring, which Sai Baba puts right on his finger. I cannot help thinking, "My goodness, he got a gold ring, and I'm next." When he comes to me, he waves his hand through the air and hands me a plastic button with a picture of himself on it. The button has a scratch on it. I feel like the boy in the classic Christmas movie, *The Christmas Story,* who fails to get his BB gun for Christmas. The others are dismissed, and Sai Baba asks me if I will come with him into an adjoining room for a private talk. I remember only one thing he said. He asks me if I know the difference between good and God. I do. I once heard a minister use the illustration. The difference between good and God is (o) a zero. Nothing is missing; God and good are one and the same. I say nothing, so he can tell me what I already know.

A crowd is waiting when I come out, and they want to know if he has materialized anything for me. I hold up the button. Someone grabs it from my hand, and it begins to make the rounds from hand to hand, and mouth to mouth as they take it to their lips and kiss it. Finally, someone intervenes, rescues my button, and returns it to me. I ask one of his people why, if he materialized the button, does it have a scratch on it? He explains he does not really materialize these things, he telaports them from his storehouse. That explains it! I do not know what to make of Sai Baba. I have friends who admire and respect him and think him a great avatar, a living Christ. I don't know. Perhaps he is. Who am I to judge? I go to see Muktananda.

Muktananda

Muktananda's ashram in Ganispuri is an hour-and-a-half train ride from Bombay. It is the most beautiful ashram of all. Day and night, all the time I'm there, it is being worked on. Marble and granite are being laid around on the inside of the ashram, and new apartments are being built. There is a garden in the middle of the ashram, with magnificent flowers and princely peacocks parading their blue and gold fanned-out tails. A rear garden contains jackfruit, mango, and plantain trees. There are dozens of young Indians, Americans and Europeans busily taking care of the grounds, cooking the meals, and cleaning the apartments. Everything is upbeat and immaculate. Lunch each day consists of *chai,* strong tea with milk, rice and curried vegetables served on banana leaves pinned together with sticks, ecologically, an excellent method. There are no utensils. Everything, even rice, is eaten with your hands. After lunch, you throw your plate into the compost and wash your hands.

Here, the main approach is meditation, and, after a few days, I begin to have the experience of *shaktipat* (spiritual energy transmission) where my body shakes uncontrollably. I suspect this experience is similar to what the Quakers and Shakers felt when they got together and sat until they "quaked" or began to dither, quiver and shake. Letting go to this experience is marvelous. I don't feel like I'm making it happen. I have never experienced anything like this. Although Rajneesh was the most intellectually inspiring, something is happening with this release of energy beyond what I experienced with his chaotic meditations.

Seeing that I'm getting into it, Muktananda's disciples suggest I become a more permanent member of the community. "Write back to New York, have someone sell your things (I think of my brand new Dodge Charger), send the money over here, spend your time meditating, and you can reach enlightenment in one lifetime." I'm thinking maybe I should stay, that it is *just* my ego refusing to surrender. But, what about Judy, Brooklyn, my life as a minister, my doctorate, and my life as a college instructor, not to mention the new Dodge Charger?

158

I'm given a private audience with Muktananda. I discover we have the same birthday, and he assures me I'm a true seeker, something I feel I already know. Still, I appreciate his affirmation. Finally, after several days in Ganispuri, I go to a manmade cave to meditate on my predicament. The cave is several feet underground, with no light or sound, so it is a perfect place to meditate. You take a flashlight, walk down and find a pillow on a cement ledge to sit on. There is no one else there. I sit down and ask: "Am I supposed to stay here?" I have no sooner asked this question, than I think I hear a voice say, "No!" which echoes throughout the chamber. A rush of thoughts follows it. "Go back to New York. There you will find what you are looking for." I can hardly get up out of the cave and back to New York fast enough. I immediately go to Muktananda and tell him what has happened and he says that what I heard was right. I will find my path in New York City. Several years later, as I'm preparing a slide lecture on the life of St. Francis of Assisi, I discover that on the first night he was a knight, he had a dream (vision) in which he was told to return to Assisi. What he was looking for would be revealed to him there.

On the plane to Delhi, I meet Bill, another American, five years older than myself. He has been a Peace Corps volunteer and is back in India visiting the people he worked with in the sixties. He suggests we get a hotel room together in Delhi. That evening, he wants to change some money on the black market, as you can get a lot more for your American dollars there than you can at American Express or a bank. I'm very wary of this. I don't want to do anything illegal. I agree to go with him. I have no idea where we are going, and when the taxi drops us off, it is a dark, starless night. There are no streetlights, and we have only one small flashlight which Bill carries, as I walk along behind. An infrequent light from inside a build-ing guides our path. It is nearly impossible to see where we are going and we occasionally step on people sleeping on the sidewalk. Bill steps on a man. He yells out and Bill turns his flashlight on him. He raises his arms to protect his eyes from the light and curses at us. I feel like I'm in a very strange dream. Beginning to get nervous about this whole business, I take my Swiss Army knife, from my pocket, unsheathe the blade, and walk with the open knife in my hand.

We finally arrive at a small, one-room hut with a man standing outside. Bill talks to him. He goes inside, comes out, and tells us to go in. The scene resembles something out of an Indiana Jones movie. There is a lone, small shaded light hanging from the ceiling. There is a man with wooden boxes on a table in front of him. Behind him stands a husky, turbaned fellow with his arms folded across his chest. A luxurious, ocher colored Oriental rug seems out of place in the otherwise stark surroundings. Fascinated by the scene in front of me, I forget about the open knife in my hand. The fellow at the table looks at the open knife. I look at him, then the knife. He says, "You want to sell?" I laugh nervously and say, "No," and put the knife away. Bill does his business and we leave. Later, we can't stop laughing; it's all so funny. We were so scared for a few minutes; turns out it was nothing.

Katmandu, Nepal

I go to the airline office and try to change my ticket. I can only leave six days from now—the date on my ticket. I fly to Katmandu, Nepal, for a five-day visit. The plane for Katmandu is a Royal Nepalese Air Force twin-engine turbo-prop. For a snack, we are given hard candy. That's it. We have to fly over the Himalayan Mountains. The plane climbs for forty-five minutes at approximately a forty-five-degree angle. After what seems like only a few minutes of level flying, we begin a sharp-angle descent, breaking through the thick clouds about 4,000 feet above the ground. There, below us, lies a magnificent sight, a bejeweled landscape and shining oasis of lush green rice paddies all along the mountainsides, and then the magnificent city of Katmandu.

Stepping into Katmandu is like entering another world even more exotic than India. Here saffron robed Tibetan Buddhists and Hindus live side by side. All around are thousand-year-old stupas or temples with erotic sculptures of mating couples in every imaginable sexual posture. They are sort of sex manuals carved in stone. Hinduism instructs us not to suppress sexual desires but to seek them intelligently. Here is a spiritual celebration of the mystical dimension of sexual union as one would never find in the West. There are celibate Sadhus (wandering beggars) with long hair and street vendors who openly sell hashish. I try some horrible tasting hard cheese. I buy several antique items, including a silver vajras (a small round object held in the hand while meditating) inlaid with turquoise, an incense burner, and a number of ancient Tibetan prayer scrolls.

I'm standing watching the burning of a funeral ghat, when I feel someone staring at the back of my neck. Turning to look over my left shoulder, I have a shock! There is a man staring at me who has no face. He has no eyebrows, no nose, no lips, and no ears. There are only two eyes, holes where his nose should be, a slit instead of lips, and exposed teeth. He is a living skeleton, no doubt a leper. We stare at each other. I hand him some money, and he walks away without speaking. I wonder if he had a tongue.

At the airport in Katmandu, as I go through customs, I'm told I cannot take these ancient scrolls out of the country, as they are Nepalese antiquities. The plane is leaving and I have to make connections the next morning in Delhi. I cannot possibly return to where I bought the scrolls, find the man who sold them to me, and get my money back, so I leave them in the hands of the customs officers. I hope they really are genuine antiquities, which find their way into a museum, and are not sold back to the street vendors to be sold again to another naive American tourist. Who knows?

In Delhi, I have only a short night's sleep, as I need to be at the airport at six a.m. for a seven o'clock flight. I make arrangements for a cab to pick me up at five a.m. There is little traffic at this hour, and as the cabby buzzes down the dark Delhi streets, suddenly an old woman with a shawl over her head steps into the road right in front of the cab. With a sudden thud, the cabby runs right over her. Immediately, the cabby stops the car, runs around to the back, opens the door, grabs my backpack, throws it out of the cab onto the street, and demands I get out of his cab. He runs over, picks up the old woman whose moaning tells me she is still alive, throws her into the back seat of the cab, and takes off. This all happens within less than two minutes, and I'm left wondering whether he is taking her to a hospital or just somewhere to dump her.

It is not yet daylight and I do not know where I am. Before long, I hail another taxi and get to the airport. There I find some police and explain what happened. I don't have the license plate of the cab. I know he was wearing a turban and picked me up at five a.m. and I tell them the hotel where I was staying. The hotel made the arrangements with the cab company. Maybe they know something. I'm afraid I'm going to be detained by the police. Thankfully, they let me go.

It's been hard being in India; sometimes I've had difficulty breathing here. I wonder if I had an unhappy previous life in this place. Some parts of India are enchanting. There is something spiritual in Indians' eyes—something we do not have in America. The peculiar genius of the Indian people is the reverence innate in even the lowliest peasant. You cannot help but admire the Sadhus who have forsaken worldly ties to seek the divine. I appreciate the Indians' open attitude toward death. They are much less obsessed with things. Life is more clearly a dream here—sometimes a nightmare. Americans "buy" the reality of the external world. Indians "buy" the internal and thereby the eternal. Religions are also something of a "hustle" here, as it is in some of fundamentalist America. One thing is for sure; many Indians are fascinated with the wealth of the West.

Iran

At the New School I befriended a young, dark haired Iranian woman named Fatima and I asked if I might visit her in Tehran on my return from India. She said yes with hesitancy. I call Fatima from the airport, and she tells me how to find her. The steps leading up to the front door of her house are impressive. Much of the house is made of tile, marble and granite. Although not overtly ostentatious, the house is well-appointed with fine old furniture and Persian rugs. Following custom, I remove my shoes before entering. Fatima introduces me to her parents, and I shake her father's hand. (It is taboo to shake hands with Iranian women.) I don't speak Farsi, and they don't speak English, so not much is said. I'm shown to a room, and then pretty much left alone. Fatima's father is a pious Islamic man, with deep-set eyes, who prays ritually five times daily. I feel he considers me an intruder in his home. I try to be respectful. Only a curtain separates his worship and my room, so I can see his shadow and hear him praying. He acknowledges my presence with an occasional nod. I never eat with the family or engage in any conversation with Fatima's mother or father.

Tehran is under the control of the Shah. His picture is everywhere. I visit a museum where they have a display of the crown jewels. Everywhere are the minarets and the five-times-daily call to prayer. I get lost in a bazaar with miles of aisles. I try some wonderful-tasting stuff that looks like spaghetti ice cream and tastes a bit like lemon sorbet. Why don't they serve this in the States? I go to the smelly tanneries and watch the craftsmen work the leather. I go into the countryside, where workers are drying huge handmade rugs. In the evening, men are dancing in the street to the beat of a drum.

Getting around in Tehran is an adventure. Unlike the way taxis work in New York, you step out into the street and yell out your destination, like "Upper West Side!" Since the cabby can take as many passengers as the car holds, he will pick you up if he is headed in your general direction and has room. He then delivers each individual in turn to their destination, sometimes going a bit out of the way to drop someone else off first. The cab I stop is so crowded I'm nearly sitting on another man's lap. Everyone smiles politely. You can also hitchhike, if you give a tip.

The longer I'm here, the more tension I feel from Fatima's father, who does not seem happy with his westernized daughter. He is clearly suspicious of our relationship, which is in no way romantic. One evening in 1979, while watching a televised demonstration against the Ayatollah Khomeini in Iran, I'm sure I see Fatima in the forefront of a group of Iranian women demonstrators. At the end of my six days, I am anxious to arrive home. It's nice to be around friends and things familiar. I am delighted to see Judy. She is so cute and tender, and she has the sweetest voice. I'm really in love with her. I take her for a ride in Prospect Park, and we park, and it's wonderful—and frustrating, so frustrating.

CHAPTER 23

Edie and the Move Back to Manhattan
General Theological Seminary

There are no new Methodists or Protestants of any sort moving into the Windsor Terrace. I'm doing lots of funerals. I do few weddings or baptisms. I ask the members of Windsor Terrace if I can move into General Theological Seminary in New York City. I will keep my space in the parsonage in Brooklyn and spend time there, especially on the weekends. The position, however, is part-time, and living at the seminary will enable me to be close to my classes and to my teaching in the city.

General Theological Seminary occupies a full block, between 9th and 10th Avenues on the east and west, and 19th and 20th Streets on the north and south. Architecturally, it fancies itself as the Oxford of the West. The old stone buildings surrounding an inner courtyard filled with tall sycamore trees would fit well in an Oxford setting. Begun in the 1820s, most of the buildings date from the 1890s. The courtyard runs the entire length of the inner part of the seminary, with a stately chapel in the middle. Most of the faculty members live in apartments within the complex.

For $100 a month, I have a combination office/apartment at General Theological. There is only one problem. My three rooms are in a fourth-floor walkup in the Lorillard building. The only bathroom is in the basement five flights below. Still it seems like a good idea. I'm teaching at both the New School and New York University and I'm within walking distance of each. There is a nice little working fireplace in the main room. I cover the east and west walls with bookshelves and put my desk in front of the three windows facing south, out onto the courtyard and the oldest building in the complex. There is no air-conditioning, and throughout much of July and August the spongy, humid air hangs over this city like a wet circus tent.

The Methodist hierarchy wants to close Windsor Terrace and encourages its members to go to the next nearest Methodist church in Park Slope. The only convenient way to get there is to drive, and most of the members, especially the older ones, don't have cars. Around the corner from Windsor Terrace is St. Mark's, a little Lutheran church. Since the hierarchy of the

Lutheran church is looking to close St. Mark's, and the people of Windsor Terrace are more interested in community than denominational affiliation, we merge the two churches into a federation. We now have a fairly substantial congregation, larger than the one I began with five years ago. The church is renamed Windsor Terrace Community Church. We combine worship services in a way that turns out to be mostly Lutheran and requires my singing much of the liturgy. To my surprise, this is fun.

My major professor at General Theological, Dr. John Johnson, Jr., was a college football player. He has broad shoulders, big upper arms, and a neck as thick as a tree trunk. He is only eight years older than I am and therefore more of a contemporary. Dr. Johnson becomes my new guide. I can trust this man. Finally, I've found someone who can shepherd me through a doctoral program. On his recommendation, I go into therapy with Dr. Anelisa Pontis, an older Jungian psychologist, and begin keeping regular recordings of my dreams. I've read Dr. Johnson's entire bibliography while traveling, so I have a jump on the other students. This gives me an opportunity to focus on my other courses while still being able to discuss each of the books required by Dr. Johnson.

I'm on my way to teach at Highland when I hear on the car radio that Betty Taylor, president of Spiritual Frontiers Fellowship, has died while trying to flee a rapist who broke into her apartment. While the intruder was raping her roommate, Betty climbed out an eighth story window on a bed sheet. There she lost her grip and fell to her death. The news of her death is a shock. I had accepted the vice presidency of Spiritual Frontiers the previous year thinking it mostly a do-nothing position. Suddenly, I'm the President of Metropolitan New York Spiritual Frontiers Fellowship with extra responsibility added to my academic, teaching and ministerial duties.

1972—Age Twenty-Nine

I teach a course on Consciousness Expansion and Religious Experience with seventy-five students in one class. I awake one morning realizing I have performed enough funerals and done enough research into death and dying that I have sufficient material for a book. I begin putting together *Learning To Die*. I contact Laura Huxley for permission to include the letter Aldous wrote to his friends after the death of his first wife, Maria. When I mention to an executive at Spiritual Frontiers Fellowship that I have completed a book, he asks me to send him the manuscript. They would like to publish it.

I'm filled with energy—working on a doctorate, running the church, teaching and writing. In the spring, I teach nine different courses at four different universities: the New School for Social Research, New York University, the City College of New York, and Fairfield University in Connecticut. I'm teaching at least one and sometimes two classes each evening, including two two-hour classes in yoga at City College in Queens on Wednesday evenings, plus a Saturday morning class at the New School. Sundays are reserved for the church, preaching in the morning and making pastoral calls in the afternoon. There is no time for anything like a social life. If it's Tuesday evening I must be in . . .

I teach a course that includes a section on the mystical Jewish writing, the Kabbalah. Vera has heard of Rabbi Joseph Gelberman, a modern Hasid and an expert on the Kabbalah. I call and ask if he can give a lecture to my class. Rabbi is about five foot four. Slightly rotund, I've never seen him gain weight in more than thirty years. He has a friendly air about him and most people come to love him quickly. The Rabbi and I soon become friends. Rabbi Gelberman lost his wife, daughter, parents, brothers and sisters during the Holocaust. He was angry until he realized that Hitler was going to destroy him, too. So he transcended his anger through forgiveness. In time, I simply call him "Rabbi." Rabbi was born in 1912, the same year as Daddy and he comes to play a fatherly role in my life. With the Rabbi, I can talk about God and religion—things Daddy and I never talked about. It is the Rabbi who introduces me to *The Heavenly Hand,* the mystical epistle of the Baal Shem Tov (1698—1760), who encouraged people to enjoy singing, dancing and the sharing of community.

Vera wants to do what I've done so she takes off for India to spend time with Muktananda. She will later become Ma Saraswati. Though things have not always worked well for Judy Halpin and me, there is no doubt I'm in love with this lovely young woman. Judy has not started college and is not interested in doing so. I'm immersed in academia. It is impossible to get Judy to go away with me. I have the apartment at General Theological till 1978. We date off and on throughout this time; we never spend a night together.

One friend, Gene Kieffer, persuades me to read Gobi Krishna's *The Evolutionary Energy in Man.* Gene is convinced that Gobi Krishna is an enlightened being. He thinks this is what I'm looking for. I don't know. Gobi Krishna is in India. I'm impressed. I was told to come back to New York. I don't know.

I'm teaching in Greenwich village and living in Chelsea, the area just north of the village. I enjoy walking from one section to the other. There is an excitement in the air, and incense that issues from the many psychedelic shops, new age bookstores, music stores, craft shops and apartments. Many friends are enjoying a rather rebellious and liberal lifestyle. I come to have two lives: one the life of the pastor of a small parish in Brooklyn, with Judy, her family, and members of the church who have become my second family. Then, there is another more exciting life with friends who are into academia, parapsychology, consciousness expansion and the exploration of new ideas. Everything is mod and sexualized. And of course there is music, music, music.

The Beatles, it seems, are trying to strike a balance between the wild and the truly spiritual. They are saying it best: "Let It Be!" "All you need is Love—da da da da da." John Denver is also one of my favorite musicians. We are the same age. What Elvis was to the fifties, and the Beatles were to the sixties, John Denver is to the seventies: "Take me home, Country Roads," "Thank God I'm a Country Boy." The words of the Beatles and John Denver are lucid and luminous. Though I am living in the largest city in the North America, I am as Harry Truman expressed it "first and foremost a country boyfrom Missour." I know what Denver means when he sings "Rocky Mountain High," and I don't think he was on drugs when he wrote that music. It's a natural high like I experienced on the farm and on the mountain in Norway.

At the New School, I meet a lovely young woman named Lena Rodriquez who is a mixture of French, Cherokee and Cuban. She has been living with her boyfriend, Tommy. They have split. Lena is a disciple of Hilda Charleton's and has an appreciation of yoga and the Hindu tradition. She says she is using protection so I feel safe in making love with her. However, after just three dates, Lena tells me she is pregnant. I feel responsible. I don't know what to do. I do not want to marry her. If I ever get married again, I have to be sure it is love. Now, Lena is pregnant. While I'm worrying about what to do, Lena goes back to Tommy, and they marry.

A new distraction now presents itself. Her name is Edie Cadenhead. Edie is an impressive, petite, lively star on the soap opera *As the World Turns*. Her stage name is Lisa Cameron. She has long blonde hair which when she laughs, she flicks back over her shoulder like a satin shawl. God, she is gorgeous. Edie holds a master's degree in drama from Yale. She has a sharp inquisitive mind. She is an avid reader and explorer of her dreams. Edie and her husband, Ian, have recently divorced. Edie found a copy of the New School catalog lying in the top of a trashcan opened to the description of my course on Consciousness Expansion. Taking my course is a way for her to break out and expand her own consciousness. I'm so incredibly busy with my academics and teaching load, it is impossible to find time to date, so I ask her to wait for me. "When this semester is over," I say, "I'll have some time. Right now it's impossible."

My best friend is my wonderful Joyful Dog. She is so excited to see me when I get home, her whole body quakes. It's good to see her, too. I often let Joyful sleep at the foot of my bed.

At the end of the school term, I take off for Missouri. Judy Femmer and I get together for an afternoon, and we have our picture taken together in a park. It's strange. I'm clearly in love with two different women both named Judy, and now . . . now there is Edie.

Edie waits, sort of. Although she dates other men, she makes no commitments. When the semester ends, we have our chance. Edie and Ian have two sons, Bruce and Stuart. Edie and the two boys live in a brownstone on west 89th Street near Central Park West. They bought the brownstone with a loan from Ian's parents and fixed the place up with four apartments in addition to their own living space. Edie does much of the work herself, laboriously removing the old varnish on the stairs, from the top floor to the basement, breathing in the heavy fumes. Ian has a well-equipped workshop in the basement. The first floor includes a studio apartment with immediate access to the street. Edie's part of the house also includes a family room, kitchen and outdoor patio. The second floor includes a large living room and a front apartment. When the apartment becomes available, I encourage Edie to rent it to Bruce Gregory, another active member of Spiritual Frontiers. Bruce will later become a student/teacher of *A Course in Miracles*. The third floor includes three bedrooms, one for the boys, one Edie rents out and her own, which is really a "boudoir" with canopy bed, walk-in closets, and an adjoining bathroom with a sunken French marble bathtub, often used in commercial "shoots."

Ian has fallen in love with Julie, a shapely dancer with the Radio City Rocketts. He has moved out to a nearby apartment. I can't see why he has given up on Edie. To my delight he has. Edie is earning six hundred dollars a week on the soap opera and she does frequent commercials. More than one viewer has written Edie's character, Lisa Cameron, to warn her that another character on the show is out to get her. Do they think the dream world of a soap opera is real?

Edie has enough money to buy her own retreat house in the Catskill mountains, on Lake Louise Marie in Rock Hill, New York, about an hour and forty-five minutes northwest of the city. There is a large rock in the back yard on the edge of the lake where you can dive into the water. She purchases the home with difficulty, as the bank is not in favor of a woman buying a home by herself. They want her ex-husband Ian to cosign the loan. Edie sees this as an attack. Eventually, she assents, and her former in-laws cosign. The summer of '72 with Edie and her boys at the house in Rock Hill is one of the best of my life. The lake house is a great place to study. Joyful Dog loves the lake house and Edie and I are having an unbelievably wonderful time swimming in the lake, reading, and when the boys are sleeping or with their father, making very sweet love. I buy an inflatable rubber raft with two electric motors and go out into the middle of the lake, shut off the motors and drift and dream.

Kristian

With Edie, I share things, as never before. She is truly "Ma Jolie," and I know with her something I have never known with another human being—a connectedness and the sharing of our innermost selves. We lie in bed and talk for hours, and I unburden my soul and talk about my love for Brooklyn Judy and Missouri Judy as well as my quandary about Lena. Tommy and Lena want me to pay for the baby's birth. I say that I will. Kristian is born on November 17, 1972. His Cesarean delivery leaves Lena to heal in the hospital for several days. I visit her and Kristian the day he is born. I'm feeling very guilty. I take her two-dozen red roses. According to our agreement, I pay the bills. A few days later, Tommy comes to see me at General Theological. He wants me to continue to pay for raising Kristian. I agree that I will. Then, I say, "If I'm going to have the obligation of fatherhood, I would like some of the privileges. I would like to be able to see Kristian and spend time with him." Tommy will not hear of it and stamps out slamming the door. I assume I will see Lena again, as we move in some of the same circles. I will not see her or Kristian for seven years.

Shanti Rica Josephs

Edie introduces me to her friends, including a number of actors, authors and psychologists like gregarious Shanti Rica Josephs, an active Lesbian psychologist, seventeen years my senior. Shanti has always looked twenty years younger than her actual age. She and Mother share the same birthday, April Fools. Shanti is nine years younger than Mother. She can move right in and talk to anyone about anything and often does. Shanti soon becomes my companion, confidant, crisis intervention counselor, traveling partner, and explorer of different realms of consciousness. As Ann is my younger sister, Shanti now becomes my older sister.

Edie is seven years older than I am, thirty-six to my twenty-nine. Ian is around a lot. He has keys to the brownstone and comes and goes as he pleases. His frequent, unannounced intrusions don't make Edie happy. As far as Ian is concerned, however, it is still "his" house. He is there most evenings, and it is not unusual for Edie and me to be upstairs in the bedroom making love, while Ian is sawing and hammering away in the basement. Eventually, Edie and I are spending six nights a week together. Sunday evening is our one night off. On Sunday, I go to church; often having lunch with Judy, then return to the seminary in the evening rather than to Edie's. It's strange being in love with two women at the same time; yet I'm doing it. I don't know what else to do. I cannot deny the love I feel for Judy or Edie. I'm sleeping with Edie, not Judy. Still, Judy and I remain friends. I just can't break it off completely—Judy doesn't want to either. She is not developing any other relationships.

Ian is very much the father and I'm something of an outsider in someone else's home. I have few parenting skills and few rights when it comes to disciplining the boys. Edie and I look past the difference in age and other possible problems and go ahead and fall in love.

What one believes to be true either is true or becomes true within limits to be found experientially and experimentally. These limits are beliefs to be transcended. —John Lilly, M.D.

I sponsor a weekend retreat for Spiritual Frontiers with Dr. John Lilly, author of *The Center of the Cyclone,* at Holiday Hills in Pawling, New York. Dr. Lilly has worked extensively with dolphins and with psychotropics. He comes to New York with his new wife, Toni. Edie comes along for the weekend, and the four of us have a great time. I stay in touch with John and in 1973 he persuades me to read Franklin Merrell-Wolff's *Path-*

ways Through to Space. John is convinced that Franklin Merrell-Wolff is an enlightened being. I love his book and I agree he does seem to be enlightened. Is this what the voice in the cave in India said I would find in New York? Merrell-Wolff does not live in New York and you can't approach him directly. I'm not sure. Is this the path I am to follow? Is this my guru? John seems so convinced that he is.

For Christmas Edie comes to Missouri to visit my family. We decide to get married, and I announce our engagement to the church. Judy, always at church on Sundays, is amazingly civil in accepting Edie.

New York City is getting to me. I need to get back to the country—back to some quiet time and some open space. How? I hunger for the country, for soil, for rain on earth and bird songs. The openness of the Missouri prairie gives perspective that you just can't find here. The view from my apartment window is the top of the Empire State Building. Then it hits me: I can do what Daddy did. I can sell the Dodge Charger and get a small motor home, which will provide an opportunity for escape. On December 31, 1972, I become the owner of a Dodge van with a toilet, stove, refrigerator, and table that drops down to create a bed. I have a way out of the city.

1973—Age Thirty—The Parsonage is on Fire!

Spiritual Frontiers Fellowship publishes *Learning to Die*, and I'm invited to be on the Barry Farber late evening radio talk show. I take a cab to Edie's at one a.m.; I'm getting undressed when Edie's phone rings. It is a nun from the house I own in Brooklyn. I gave her Edie's number in case of an emergency, and we have an emergency! The parsonage is on fire! I drive as fast as I can, hazard lights blinking on and off on the motor home, down the Westside highway, through the Brooklyn Battery Tunnel praying as I go that no one is hurt. As I turn down the street toward the parsonage, I see a horrible sight; there are fire trucks all around, with their lights flashing and fire hoses strewn all about the street and sidewalk. Worst of all, a young man to whom I have rented a bedroom has died. He had long red hair, and it seems he fell asleep, probably drunk with a cigarette in his hand next to his head, setting his hair on fire. The fire got a good start before he awoke from his stupor and ran into the bathroom to the shower. He died in the bathtub.

Though I've moved a number of my possessions to the seminary, still I've lost numerous irreplaceable possessions; the saddest loss is a large oval shaped picture of Uncle Estel as a young man. I plummet into a sink-hole of guilt and depression. Though everyone is supportive, I feel responsible. Why have I not been more vigilant about who I let into the house? I had funny feelings about this young man from the very beginning. Why have I not paid more attention? Walking through the charred remains of the parsonage, I get a sick feeling in my stomach from the noisome stench of wet, charred wood. To this day, that smell takes me back to that horrible night. Insurance covers everything, and the parsonage is rebuilt. I'll be sick over this for a long time to come.

Wainwright House

One of my students at the New School is on the board at Wainwright House, a personal growth center in Rye, New York, an hour north of the city. He invites me to lunch at The Mobil Corporation on Forty-Second Street. He offers me a position as a part-time director of programming for Wainwright House. I will be required to put together an annual Spiritual Healing Symposium. I can also offer whatever workshops I want. It's a great opportunity. I begin regular commutes to Wainwright House for monthly business meetings and weekly classes I now offer on "The Way of the Warrior" (on the teachings of Don Juan from the Carlos Castaneda book series) along with classes on psychic development, Jung, alchemy and more. Working with me is Dr. Jean Houston, one of the most brilliant women I've ever met, and Dr. Houston Smith, who began the work of Interfaith long before most of us.

I go home to Missouri for my thirtieth birthday. I take Joyful Dog for a walk out on the farm. We're walking through the alfalfa fields, and the alfalfa is so tall Joyful can't see me except that every now and then she jumps up in the air to see where I am, each time her ears flapping like little wings, like she's trying to fly. She has the most wonderful big grin on her face. She is one happy dog this glorious day, and she has a right to be—we're on the farm in Missouri. It is May, and everything is emerald green and butter yellow, and the powder blue sky is filled with puffy white clouds with crimson underbellies. God, I love this place!

Although already published, *Learning to Die* is *officially* released at the Spiritual Frontiers Conference in Chicago in June. Edie goes with me. David and Rosie McKnight are there, along with author John White. I spend the next several months visiting several major American cities talking to Spiritual Frontiers groups. In the fall, two of the people present for my talk in Atlanta are Dr. Helen Schucman, the scribe for *A Course in Miracles,* and her colleague, Dr. William Thetford. That evening, we are introduced in someone's home. It seems important that we meet. Nothing is said about the Course.

In order to meet the monthly mortgage payments, Edie lets out a bedroom in her own part of the house. A young woman named Marianne Williamson, who is trying to make it as a nightclub singer in New York, shows up to rent Edie's room. Marianne is obviously very bright, quick-witted, and a great conversationalist. I'm immersed in teaching my courses on Consciousness Expansion, Oriental Philosophy and Psychology of Religion. Marianne and I sit and have coffee and talk about philosophy and religious experiences. Edie and I go to her performances, and clap extra loud, giving support to this aspiring young singer. It will be two years before I'm introduced to *A Course in Miracles* and four years before Marianne will pick up a copy of the Course off the coffee table in her then boyfriend, Jeff Olmsted's apartment. Jeff will, years later, become the music director for Interfaith Fellowship. Little can Marianne or I know that because of the Course, sixteen years later, our lives will begin to overlap again and again in totally miraculous ways. We often speak at the same conferences and in July 2002 I'll give a talk at her church, Unity Renaissance in Warren, Michigan.

CHAPTER 24

Prague and Russia

I'm invited to present a paper at the first International Congress on Parapsychology in Prague, followed by a trip to the Soviet Union to look into the parapsychological research going on there. I go with Dr. Stanley Krippner, known for his work in dream research, and Dr. Harold Puthoff of Stanford University, and others. Since early days on the farm, I've been interested in psychic communication between humans and animals. Uncle Estel spoke to his horses, and I always thought they understood him. It's been the same with Joyful Dog. We understand each other in some wonderful unspoken way. There is a language that does not depend upon words. In Prague, I present a paper on psychic communication between humans and animals.

I have to take Joyful Dog for walks three times a day, and I'm able to do so without a leash. She will delightedly run ahead of me. As she approaches the end of the block, I tell her to "Slow Down" and then to "Wait," and she does so perfectly. She just sits there with her tongue hanging out, smiling, and waiting for me to catch up with her. When I say "Go!" she takes off and runs across the street. I never have to worry that she might run into traffic. She knows better. She is such a good dog.

Prague is the cultural and intellectual heart of old Europe, the home of ancient alchemy and one of the architectural gems of Europe. In studying Jungian psychology, I have become fascinated with alchemy. Alchemists tried to turn base metals into gold. Alchemy was about much more than gold. It was a spiritual discipline, because first, before the alchemist could turn base substances into gold, he had to be himself *golden*—pure. Dr. Puthoff and I visit Alchemist's Row and peer into the quaint little houses where many of the alchemists lived and worked during the middle ages.

Russia is cold, unadorned, unromantic and ruthlessly pragmatic. In Moscow, I'm struck by the size of everything—the biggest bell in the world, the biggest cannon in the world, huge trucks, and big doors. The subway system is impressive. Deep inside the earth, it doubles as a bomb shelter. So far every subway system I have seen—in London, Paris, Montreal, and now Moscow—are all quieter, neater, cleaner and far superior to the one in New York City.

We stay at the Grand Hotel, a block long and a block wide with an immense courtyard. We are told it is the largest hotel in the world. Here we meet with a woman who has psychokinetic abilities—she can move things without touching them. She rolls cigarettes, cigar holders and ping-pong balls around on the top of a coffee table, simply by moving her hand over them without touching or blowing on them. She shows us how to do it, using the same kind of kinetic energy David and Rosie and I have experimented with in spiritual healing. With concentration, deliberation and practice, several of us are able to move the ping-pong balls and cigarettes. Most of us do not have this ability simply because we don't take time to develop it. It takes time, patience and practice, practice, practice.

Communism is in full swing, and wherever we go, we are treated with suspicion. At the airport, our luggage is dumped out and gone through bit by bit. Some books on psychic research are confiscated. In certain places (the subway system for one), we cannot take pictures. When we meet our psychic friends at the Grand Hotel, there are two conversations, what is being said and what is being written on notes as we are talking. A Russian was elected president of the International Congress on Parapsychology in Prague. When we say that, a note is passed around saying he is a member of the communist party.

We go to the opera house. It's all red and gold. I sit for a while in this sumptuous structure listening to dramatic Wagnerian-type performers singing in a language I cannot understand. Finding the whole thing melodramatic and incomprehensible, I excuse myself and tell my companions I will meet them back at the hotel. I head for a nearby park. It is a bright, clear August day. A young man approaches speaking Russian. When I say I don't speak Russian, in good English, he offers to sell me some marijuana. I'm not interested. When he finds out I'm from the United States, he wants to talk further. While we are talking, he lights up a joint. Two policemen are approaching, which I point out to him. He says, "They know me. They can arrest me if they want to, but they won't." And he is right. Though the air is filled with the sweet smell of his marijuana, they walk right past us. We go to a cafe filled with young people listening to American disco music. He introduces me to several friends, and we spend our time eating, drinking and comparing notes on lifestyles. Walking back to the hotel, I become increasingly aware of the number of alcoholics around the park. Vodka is everywhere.

We visit a clinic that specializes in dream research. Dr. Krippner is especially interested in this work, as the Russians are far ahead of us in this field. From Moscow, we go on to Leningrad to visit the luxurious gold-laden palace of the Czars. No wonder the people revolted. This is luxuriance and opulence outside the realm of reason.

We fly to Amsterdam and on to the States. When we get to New York, the plane cannot land because of bad weather. We fly to Boston, where again we cannot land because of bad weather. We fly back to New York, where we still cannot land. So we fly to Washington D.C., where we have to land before the plane runs out of fuel. I'm due to preach that morning at Windsor Terrace. It is now three a.m. I rent a car and hurriedly drive back to Brooklyn exhausted. By the time I arrive, the service has started. I'm just in time to deliver the message. So I tell everyone about my adventures.

I'm anxious to see Edie. When we get together, she wants to talk. What's this all about? We go to a restaurant, where she tells me she has decided she does not want to have any more children. I'm now thirty. She is thirty-seven. I'm still thinking I would like a family, so this puts me in a quandary. Slowly, very slowly, our relationship begins to cool. We drop back to five days a week together, then after a few weeks, down to four, then after a few more weeks, down to three. It is the most gradual break I ever experienced. We still love each other; we still enjoy being together. We no longer speak of marriage or a "future." We eventually get down to one night together every two weeks. Finally, we are no longer dating. Edie calls when she needs an escort to an event, or there is a party with mutual friends. We remain close. In the spring of 1974, I direct a weekend Healing Symposium at Wainwright House. Dr. Norman Shealey is to be the primary speaker. It is Judy, not Edie, who comes with me. Dr. Shealey will later found the American Holistic Medical Association and set up his practice in Springfield, Missouri. We'll be speakers at the same conference again in 2003.

The Th.D. degree requires reading proficiency in three languages, French, German and Ancient Greek. In December, I pass the doctoral qualifying exam in French. I petition the faculty to change the qualifying exam in German to computer language or Spanish. They say no; I have to take the

German exam. What use would I have for computer language? What use would I have for Spanish? I will make several trips to Mexico, Southern California and Texas. New York is filled with Spanish speaking people and I am frequently asked if I can perform weddings in Spanish. I have to learn the more "academic" German. For the next nine months, I immerse myself in German, going to the Berlitz School twice a week for lessons. German is fun; it's more like English. In September of '74, I pass the qualifying exam in German. Now I begin to work on Ancient Greek.

CHAPTER 25

Finding What I'm Looking For

1974—Age Thirty-One

I need a retreat from the city. The small Dodge camper is big enough to sleep in. There is, however, no room to walk around. I see an ad for a white, 1971 Discover 25 motorhome. The Discover 25 looks like a space ship with a pointed nose and no door up front—only in the middle on the right-hand side. There is a table that converts to a bed, a stove, refrigerator, shower, toilet, and another full size bed in back. No longer manufactured, two black Discover 25's starred in the movie *Slither*. I trade in the Dodge for the larger Discover 25. It is not a smart decision. In order to park on the street in New York City, I need to find two empty parking spaces in a row!

To top it off, we now experience a gasoline shortage. Lines are up to six miles long at open stations. Many stations are limiting purchases to two or three dollars per automobile, which means spending hours on line for only a few gallons of gas. On the positive side, I'm able to rent the motorhome out to film crews for use as an on-location dressing room. This more than enables me to make the monthly payments.

Due to all the guru worship, I've become disillusioned with Hinduism. I now focus on Buddhism. Buddhism is on the whole the most peaceful of the world's religions, much less arrogant than Christianity, Judaism and Islam. Buddhism says that our way of thinking literally makes the world we see, and the world we see, coming from an insane thought system, cannot be anything other than insane. All heavens and hells are created in our own minds. A peaceful mind perceives a peaceful world. There are remarkable similarities between Zen Buddhism and *A Course in Miracles*.

Judy and I continue to date through 1974 and 1975. She is working as a secretary in the medical offices at *Time* magazine. On Friday evenings we have dinner together in Manhattan. Judy would make a perfect Methodist minister's wife. She is pretty and perky and interested in the church and children. I'm not a perfect Methodist minister. In fact, I'm finding it more and more difficult to fit into this box called Methodism.

We must believe that some of the ancient and blessed philosophers also discovered the Truth. And it is only natural to inquire who of them found it and how we may obtain knowledge of it. —Plotinus, *Enneadss*, III: 7:1.

In the spring, I offer at the New School, for the first time, a course called "Esoteric and Mystical Philosophies." I understand esoteric philosophy to be the perceptions of a dimension of reality traditionally confined to a select group of initiates, and mysticism the belief that communication or union with the divine is achieved through intuition, faith, ecstasy, and/or revelation.

I write a letter, which is published in the Newsletter of the Transpersonal Psychology Association, in which I express interest in being in contact with anyone who is working in the fields of psychotherapy and spirituality and where these two fields converge. Dr. William Thetford sees my letter and suggests to Dr. Helen Schucman that it is a call for her to complete the writing of *Psychotherapy: Purpose, Process and Practice*, a booklet Helen received from the same source as *A Course in Miracles*.

1975—Age Thirty-Two

Helen remembers our previous meeting and agrees it is a call for her to complete the psychotherapy booklet. She calls me in April 1975 to say she has something for me. I have no idea what she is talking about. It seems important. I agree to meet her, Bill, Ken Wapnick and Father Michael, who comes along to see how they are going to present the Course to a neophyte. We meet at Ken's Spartan studio apartment on East 17th Street. The apartment consists of a day bed that doubles as a couch, a desk, chair, and a copy of the Bible. There is a teapot on the stove. In the bathroom there is a toothbrush, a towel, soap, shampoo and toilet paper. That is it! There are no modern electronics, no whatnots, no knickknacks, no novelties. It is sparser than a hotel room. There is one noticeable difference. On the wall next to the day bed is a large black obelisk made from a six-foot hollow door with the word ELOHIM (the Hebrew word for God) painted in gold upon it—a gift from Ken to Helen in keeping with one of her visionary dreams. Apparently, it is not something Helen wants in her apartment.

Helen is barely five feet tall with thick glasses and frosted hair. Bill is tall and slightly balding with fuzzy hair along the sides and a dimple in his chin. Ken is also tall and thin. He wears glasses and a great smile. Helen sits on the day bed and tells me about the Course, its development, and its effect upon the three of them. Sharp and insightful, she speaks very quickly. At the end of the evening, she gives me a copy of the manuscript *Psychotherapy: Purpose, Process and Practice.* Is this what the voice in the cave in India said I would find in New York? I have explored many different philosophies. Most of them have left me wanting. Though impressed with these people, I'm concerned that I will once again be left wanting. At the end of our meeting, it is decided that Ken and I will get together for further conversations.

I walk home with the manuscript of the psychotherapy pamphlet tucked under my arm. I feel like the most important thing that ever happened to me has just happened. I'm not at all sure what it is. Still, I feel that my spiritual life is to be connected with this material. Ken and I get together for further discussions at his place or at my office at General Theological. He tells me the story of his life, and I tell him mine. I'm not sure why we are doing this. Nevertheless, it seems important. Ken has a noticeable stutter. Over the years, he will completely overcome this problem. I'm perpetually amazed by the clarity of thought, determined purpose, and clear resolve that characterize Ken. He clearly follows each step as it is placed before him. In 1992, I write an article about Ken that I call *Impeccably on the Path.* There is no one who has been more dogged or clear in his pursuit of this teaching.

The Origin of *A Course in Miracles*

The course began in 1965, with Dr. Helen Schucman and Dr. William Thetford, both Professors of Medical Psychology at Columbia University's College of Physicians and Surgeons in New York City. Bill was head of the department, Helen his assistant. Frustrated with the competitiveness and backbiting that so often characterize academia, and frustrated with their relationship in particular, Bill turned to Helen one day and said, "There has to be another way," meaning there had to be some way people could get along without all this ego conflict. Helen uncharacteristically said, "You're right—and I'll help you find it." In many ways this was the first miracle. In this ground of joining in common purpose to heal their relationship, the seeds for the course found fertile soil and took root.

Helen has a well-trained and rigorously analytic mind. She is also intuitive and receptive to visionary and mystical experiences. She has a keen ability to tune in to the needs of others. Her chemist-metallurgist father, Sigmund Cohn, was half-Jewish—his mother was Lutheran. He was unin-

180

terested and uninvolved in religion. Her mother, also half-Jewish, was interested in Christian Science, Theosophy and Unity. Helen was raised in part by a Catholic nanny and a black Baptist housekeeper, both of whom introduced her to their religion. Helen likes the enthusiasm of the black Baptists, and she admires priests and nuns because of their dedication to their calling. Helen carries rosary beads in her purse, and she has a deep love for the Virgin Mary. Interestingly, not being a Catholic, as a child she was not allowed into Catholic churches. Helen is interested in me, in part, because I am a young Protestant minister. Most of the other primary people involved with the Course are Jewish—Judy and Bob Skutch, Ken Wapnick, later Jerry Jampolsky and still later Marianne Williamson. Helen follows no particular religious path and she likes to say of herself that she is an atheist. I *know* she is not.

In October 1965, Helen began hearing a voice, which she described as "inner dictation." The Voice began, "This is a course in miracles. Please take notes." Frightened, she called Bill and told him what had happened. He suggested they meet early the next morning to look over what she had taken down. If it was just a bunch of gibberish, they would throw it away; if it seemed important, they would take a closer look.

The Voice of the Course

The voice in the course is Jesus. If you believe that inspiration is something that happened, once and for all, a couple of thousand or more years ago, then you may not think it possible that Jesus could speak to someone in the twentieth century. Why could Jesus not speak to anyone he wants to at any time? Christians believe he spoke to Paul and the Apostles—why could he not speak to you or to me, or to Helen? The voice in the course makes several references to his life as the historical Jesus. One may also ask, who is Jesus? Do we mean a historical figure who walked upon the earth some 2,000 years ago? Yes, but is that all? To talk about Jesus is to talk about something beyond the world of birth and death. To speak of Jesus is to speak of *the* Christ, *the* Son of God, *the* Self that God created. To speak of *the* Self is also to speak of one's own true Self, which always has been and will be a part of God.

Six weeks after my introduction to the Course on May 29, 1975, Helen meets Judy Skutch. Judy decides that the Course is what she has been looking for all her life. Judy begins by distributing several photocopies of the Course, making it possible for a group of us to get an early start studying it. Judy and her husband, Bob Skutch, together with Helen, Bill and Ken, start the Foundation for Inner Peace, which becomes the publisher of the course. Bob and Judy later divorce and Judy marries William Whitson, a former army officer, professor at West Point, and author. She is now known as Judith Skutch Whitson. She has accepted as her duty in life the oversight of the many foreign language translations of *A Course in Miracles.*

I divide my course on mystical philosophies into two separate courses—one on the ancient and one on the modern period. The first course includes a study of Egyptian, Babylonian, and Greek mythology, astrology, alchemy, primitive rites of initiation, lost civilizations, and two ancient Greek religions—the Eleusinian Mysteries and the Orphics.

The Discover 25 is looking more like a white elephant than a super escape—New York City—vehicle, so I sell the motor home. Daddy has a Volkswagen camper with a pop-up roof he wants to sell so I fly home, buy his much more economical VW camper and drive it back to New York.

I think I'm supposed to start a magazine. I always admired Ben Franklin for his informative little *Poor Richard's Almanac.* One of my favorite philosophers, Soren Kierkegaard, once started a journal called *The Individual Thinker.* In early 1975 I begin, *The Individual Seeker*, a full-size magazine, jobbing out the typesetting, laying out and pasting it together as I do each year with the Annual Journal at Windsor Terrace. *Seeker* lasts for two issues. It is just too much work and too expensive to keep going without funding and help. It is a training ground for *On Course, Inspiration* and *Miracles* Magazines.

I start a weekly cable TV show called *The Individual Seeker.* I interview various spiritual leaders, psychologists and psychics. One of the first, and the one I'm most impressed with, is Dr. Stanislav Grof, author of *The Realms of the Human Unconscious.* Dr. Grof began research in psychotropics in his native Czechoslovakia in 1956 and, from 1967 to 1973, continued in this work in Baltimore as Chief of Psychiatric Research at the Maryland Psychiatric Research Center as well as research fellow at Johns Hopkins University. He is currently scholar-in-residence at Esalen Institute in Big Sur, California. He has written a number of wonderful books on the nature of consciousness and the power of the mind.

When there is no one to interview, I make up a slide lecture presentation on "The History of Alchemy." I put together a slide lecture on the life of mystical philosopher Rudolf Steiner (1861-1925) from pictures I find in the Theosophical Society library. Similar to *A Course in Miracles*, Steiner held that ascent to higher supernormal levels of thinking was possible by gradual relinquishment of the ego. I create two other slide shows, one on the Egyptians and their religion, and the other on spiritual healing through the centuries.

Vera comes back from India wearing a sari. A disciple of Swami Muktananda, she is now called Ma Saraswati. She calls and asks me to come see Baba Muktanada at his ashram on Riverside Drive. We're standing at the bottom of the stairs when he comes down. He remembers me, smiles, puts his arm around me and asks me if I've found my path yet. I tell him that I have. It's called *A Course in Miracles*. He then invites me to come into his worship hall. There are admiring disciples and curious onlookers all around. He asks me to sit next to him crossed legged on the dais as he greets each old and new disciple by lightly tapping his or her forehead or back with a peacock feather. Again his disciples encourage me to become a devotee. Muktananda tells them to leave me alone.

Jonni

In April, I'm invited to return to the Southern California School of Theology at Claremont to deliver a paper for the Academy of Religion and Psychical Research headed by Dr. J. Gordon Melton. There I speak on C.G. Jung's concept of synchronicity, or "meaningful coincidence," of outer and inner events. While there, a strangely synchronistic event occurs. There are no friends around from the sixties except for Alan Hunter, the fellow who lived next door to Dr. Heicker. I call to say hello, and he invites me to his house for lunch. There is a beautiful orange tree in bloom in his front yard. I comment on the aphrodisiac aroma of the blossoms. Mr. Hunter reaches up, pulls a few white blossoms off the tree, takes a whiff of them and hands them to me to smell. He then says, "Put them in your jacket pocket. Give them to some girl and she will fall in love with you."

I present my paper in the morning, so I'm just going to sit and listen to the other papers that afternoon. As I go into the auditorium, I notice a lovely Japanese girl. We smile, and I sit next to her. She says she enjoyed my presentation. I thank her. Reaching into my jacket pocket I find the orange blossoms and, taking them out, smell them again. She looks at me quizzically and, I hand her the blossoms. She takes a whiff. Her name is Jonni. She is half-Japanese, half-Irish, a magna cum laude graduate of the

University of Hawaii. Her mother's Japanese characteristics dominate her father's Irish—an interesting combination. She has black, black hair, a wonderful broad smile, and black eyes as dark as coal. Jonni and I spend that evening and the next day together. After I return to New York, we start writing, calling, and sending cassette tapes back and forth.

Outward Bound

The city is getting to me. Maybe if I had not grown up on the open plains, I wouldn't be so aware of the stark contrast. I need to breathe. I need to get back into the country. I need to be among trees and grass and all growing things. I sign up for an outward bound wilderness survival-training course that promises training—plus some serious time for inner reflection. Along with new acquaintances from New York City, I drive my Volkswagen camper to the Adirondack Mountains in Upstate New York. There we join six others on a seven-day training program, after which each of us will spend three days alone in the woods with no food other than what we can find. The program is educational and fun. We learn how to climb cliffs and then to rappel back down again. We learn to live off the land, and we enjoy socializing. The three days alone in the woods are particularly valuable. I make pine nettle tea and find some Indian cucumbers. That is about it. I spend most of my time fasting and sitting on a large rock in the middle of a stream with the soothing sound of water all around. Judy is an important part of my life. Now, I'm also thinking about Jonni. What am I going to do: Judy, Jonni—Jonni, Judy?

While meditating on the rock, suddenly I think, "snake"! Opening my eyes, I find a snake has slithered up onto the rock next to me. I look at him for a long, curious moment. He looks at me. We size each other up trying to decide if this is something dangerous or just something interesting. I don't think the snake is poisonous. I decide not to make any sudden moves. We stare at each other for a long time, and then he slithers off. The second night alone in the woods it rains. I try to make a lean-to by stretching my poncho across branches. It leaks. It is impossible to sleep. I just lie awake and get drenched.

There is one problem. We have two trainers, a young man and a young woman. I remember little about the man. The young woman leaves an impression on all of us. She seems out to prove herself and lays down the law like a drill sergeant. Everyone is stoic and polite, and no one says anything to her about her bossy, arrogant manner. We also never talk to each other about her, though there are occasional raised eyebrows and glances. On the day we leave, however, as we pull out of the parking lot onto the main road, everyone in the VW van bursts out laughing. For the next several minutes we are all in an uproar. No one has to say why. We are laughing from the sheer exhilaration of being free of her tyranny. The only thing we've had to drink during this expedition is chamomile tea. Ever since then, the smell of chamomile tea takes me back to that summer.

In the fall, I offer a second course on the mystical philosophies of the modern era. This course includes a look at the works of J.G. Gurdjieff, a foremost Russian esoteric philosopher of the early part of the twentieth century, and his student, author of *In Search of the Miraculous*, P.D. Ouspensky, also Rudolph Steiner, Alice Bailey, Madam Blavatsky, Ramakrishna, Yogananda, Meher Baba, Krishnamurti, Franklin Merrell-Wolff, Gobi Krishna, as well as the teachings of Mexican shaman Don Juan as told through the writings of Carlos Castaneda.

Castaneda's books are a wonderful antidote to a worldview that seems increasingly preposterous and disheartening. The Vietnam War is in full swing. Nixon is about to be re-elected. Much of our world seems to have gone crazy. Carlos is talking about turning off one's internal dialogue in order to experience an expanded reality. His is a path of the heart. I would like to go on a spiritual pilgrimage and meet a real shaman.

I live in the Lorillard building at General Theological. Across the way is the building in which *'Twas The Night Before Christmas* was written. Joyful is a nearly barkless dog. One night I'm sound asleep when she starts barking furiously. I get up and find her staring directly at the fireplace barking her head off. This event is repeated several times. You figure it out.

Long distance romance is difficult to maintain. Jonni decides she will move to New York. Unfortunately, all I have is the three rooms at the General Theological seminary and a five-flight walk to the basement bathroom. Jonni tries to help me get *Seeker* magazine off the ground, and for the next several months we struggle with our relationship. She gets a job and her own apartment in nearby Chelsea. I'm still indecisive about Judy. I'm still in love with her. I'm in such a dilemma about what to do, I go into therapy again with a Jungian analyst named Joyce who lives and works on Manhattan's Upper West Side. Again, I start keeping a record of my dreams. One Sunday, after I return from church, I go straight to Jonni's apartment. As I enter, I smell cigarette smoke. Jonni does not smoke. The aphrodisiac smell of orange blossoms brought us suddenly, magically together; now, the malodorous smell of cigarettes suddenly brings an end to our relationship. She has spent the afternoon with another man. Jonni is the only relationship I ever had that started instantaneously and ended just as instantaneously. I never saw her again.

1976—Age Thirty-Three
Memories of Helen Schucman and Bill Thetford

I take the two courses I have developed on mystical philosophies and break them into four different courses, which I teach over the two-year period of 1976 and 1977. The first course is on mythology and the ancient esoteric philosophies of the Babylonians, Egyptians and the mystery religions of the Greeks.

I sponsor several workshops, with Ken as the leader, from 1977 to 1984. Like a mother hen, Helen has a way of taking certain people under her wing, and I am fortunate to be one of her brood. Helen becomes a mother figure, mentor, guide, teacher and counselor in times of trouble. It seems I'm frequently in trouble in my relationships with women. Is it Judy or is it someone else? Judy in many ways seems to be so right, and I clearly love her. Other than the Methodist church, we don't share many interests. Helen tries to help me sort through my feelings. She is always available by phone and very supportive. She seems to intuitively know when I'm in trouble and calls to see how I'm doing. She has an incredible ability to work with people in distress, bringing a sense of serenity to the situation. During my last several years at Windsor Terrace, I repeatedly ask to be transferred to a larger and more substantial parish, preferably in the country. Each year I'm told nothing is available. I call Helen and say, "I'm quitting." Helen repeatedly says she feels it important I not quit—at least not yet. She always leaves the door open. "You can always quit later."

Whenever I am down or disheartened, Helen encourages my faith, assuring me that on a deeper level I know what to do. She is sure I will make the right decision. I break off a relationship with a woman with whom I've had only a few dates. The woman in question gets very upset and starts making insulting phone calls at all hours of the day and night. She comes to the seminary and when the guard at the door tells her I'm not in, she throws a cup of coffee in his face. I feel tremendous guilt for having entered this relationship in the first place. I'm carrying such a weight of guilt; I go to see Helen. At one point Helen says, "You know you're not guilty." I assure her that she doesn't know what she's talking about. I am indeed guilty. I have entered this relationship without clarity. I have broken off the relationship and hurt someone. Still, on a deeper level, I feel as if I know what Helen means. In the truth of the reality of who I really am, in the truth of who any of us really is in our greater reality as our true Self, I'm not guilty. That's not the way I feel right now.

The relationship with this woman has an interesting, almost miraculously happy, ending. If I wanted to get some sleep and not find an answering machine full of insults, it is necessary to take the phone off the hook each night before going to bed. One night I forget to take the phone off the hook and she starts calling. I get up and answer the phone. We talk till dawn, and we work it out. We are good friends to this day.

Helen is very direct and makes clear suggestions as to what I should do. I fall hard for a beautiful woman I meet at the New School. I'll call her Charlotte. We date off and on throughout 1976 and into early 1977. An opportunity comes up for her to move, and the question is should she go or am I going to make a better offer? Charlotte and I meet with Helen at Ken's apartment on East 17th Street. After a few minutes, Helen leans forward, touches my knee, and says, "Charlotte should go." I can't possibly see how this is the right decision. Certainly, it is not leaving me in a state of peace. After we leave, we walk down through Greenwich Village looking for a place to eat. We pass a window with the words "Psychic Reader" painted on the glass. Charlotte says, "Let's go in." I say no, that it doesn't interest me. Charlotte insists, so we go in for a reading. We are there only a few minutes when the psychic asks me to step with her into another room for a moment. There she says, "This woman who is with you. She has to move on." It has not been more than half-an-hour since Helen said the same thing.

Just Plain Bill

Bill Thetford is simple, gentle, kind and unassuming. He has a relaxed attitude toward most everything. He is usually in the background (sometimes referring to himself as "Exhibit B"). Yet, he is very present. Jerry Jampolsky said at Bill's memorial service that he, himself, came to the Course because he saw the qualities of presence and integrity in Bill Thetford. Bill could be characterized by his "nothing special-ness." I wonder if it was something like what people might have felt around Abraham Lin-

187

coln. Like Lincoln, Bill is tall, thin, and radiates confidence. He is someone you can trust, the kind of person you can safely tell things to. There is completeness, a totality and wholeness about him. Bill is not an individual with a lot of unfinished business. There is something fetching, almost melodically hypnotic about Bill's uniquely smooth, clear and comforting voice. His reading of the Course aloud made it come alive—like it is saying exactly what it is supposed to.

Bill has an inspired, philosophic sense of humor. He is a master of the pun and loves to play with words. One of the important review lessons from the Course is "I am not a body. I am free. For I am still as God created me." Bill translated it into the ego's more frequent perception: "I am a body. I am sick. Hurry, call a doctor quick." Bill is a minimalist—the less the better, whatever is necessary, that is enough. His spirit is, I think, reflective of St. Francis.

Leaving the City

I go out for walks. Once I leave the seminary, there are huge skyscrapers towering above me. I'm looking for hills and trees and finding stone and steel. Living in the city has its advantages. Still, somehow it's synthetic. I need soil, not cement, and my feet need to be bare. I begin lecturing for Unity Fellowship in Yorktown Heights, New York. One Sunday evening, I announce my intention of finding a place in the country. If anyone has any ideas, I would appreciate knowing. As one woman is leaving, she hands me a note, "Log cabin, a mile back in the woods on its own lake, near Cold Spring, New York," along with a telephone number. The next morning I call. Indeed, it is a log cabin, a mile back in the woods. The woman is going to Europe for the summer; the cost is $1,000 a month. She had it rented. The deal has fallen through, and she is leaving in two days. The best I can come up with is $400. She agrees. It is better to have someone there than to leave it abandoned. I go to see it immediately. It's a lovely, four-bedroom log cabin, with a fireplace made from fieldstone, in a large living room and a deck across the entire expanse of the front, overlooking its own small lake. All about there are wildflowers. I think I've just died and gone to heaven.

The cabin is a perfect place to study Ancient Greek. This is the same idea I had back in college when I wanted to play Thoreau for a summer. I hire David, a tutor from Columbia University, and make weekly trips to his apartment on 114th Street and Broadway, where we carefully go over each step in the process of learning this archaic language. David is tall, slim, and slightly balding. Like Ken, he lives alone in a tiny apartment. The walls in his two rooms are covered with books—floor to ceiling.

I get to know a deeply spiritual man who has found himself in the study of languages. Except for all the books, his apartment, like Ken's, is very Spartan. Like Ken, he has no television or other modern electronic marvels. David knows some thirty different languages and is focusing on Sanskrit, which he says is truly the most ancient and mystical of all. After I have mastered Greek, he says, I should begin Sanskrit. He and Ken could easily be friends. David sharpens his pencils with a pocketknife, so I surprise him on our last session with the gift of a hand cranked pencil sharpener. He takes the sharpener in his hands, turns it over looking at it carefully. He says he guesses it is all right, as it is strictly mechanical, requiring only muscles and no electricity. I learn as much about the value of a contemplative life as I do Greek from David. I thoroughly enjoy Ancient Greek. French and German have been fun because you can speak the language. Ancient Greek is something esoteric. You are able to read and appreciate something only few can.

A Course in Miracles is published on June 22, 1976. I go to see Judy Skutch and Helen at the Beresford, Judy's apartment building on 81st Street and Central Park West. Helen hands me the newly printed books and says, "I think you're supposed to teach this." In August, with people from Unity Fellowship in Yorktown Heights, I start at the cabin, near Cold Spring, what is perhaps the first study group based on *A Course in Miracles*. We sit on the deck, overlooking the lake and I read the Course out loud, stopping after each paragraph, so we can talk about what *we think* it means.

Though I still have the office/apartment at General Theological, at summer's end, I simply cannot move back to New York City, so I find a winter rental across from the lake in Mahopac. I live in Mahopac for nine months. I repeatedly ask Judy to visit me. She never does.

I plow into working on my doctoral dissertation on "problems of the ego in the encounter with death." This is exciting stuff, a mixture of psychology and theology. Edie invites me to join her and a group of friends for a party, for our country's two hundredth birthday on July 4, 1976, on the roof of a New York City apartment building next to the Hudson River. Here we easily watch fifteen tall ships and more than 200 smaller ones strutting their stuff up and down the Hudson River. It is a glorious night.

And it's wonderful to have Edie leaning back in my arms as we shout, "WOW!"—watching the unrestrained fireworks display. Edie and I celebrate the 200th Anniversary of the United States with our own fireworks! She is the best!

I offer a course on the Mystical Philosophies of the Roman and Early Christian eras including the Essenes, Phio Judaeus and Plotinus. I pass the Greek exam in December. The passage I have to translate is one with which I'm familiar. Finally, after nine years, all of the course work is done, all of the doctoral qualifying exams in foreign languages are over, and I'm well on my way with the dissertation. A year goes by before I "really" begin to understand *A Course in Miracles*; and that is foreshadowed by an experience in July of 1976, in which I'm convinced I have died.

CHAPTER 26

Holy Hell

An Account of My Visionary Journey

It is your world salvation will undo, and let you see another world
your eyes could never find. —ACIM, T-31.VI.3: 4

Shanti Rica asks me if I would like to go to Mexico to meet a shaman. My immediate answer is, "Yes!" After reading Castaneda, I'm intrigued with the possibility. In the experience that follows, I see something I have always sought, and for a moment *re-membered*. I do not expect it to be comprehensible in ordinary terms. I present it as a phenomenological experience worthy of examination. If you cannot accept it as fact, think of it as a dream or a vision. The experience *seemed* real, infinitely more real than this moment. One difference between what I am about to describe and what sometimes happens in other death experiences, is the dissolution of the ego. Many of the death experiences we read about describe the ego and the personality of the individual as still intact during and after the experience. There is often no *trauma* over having lost a body. This was not true for me. As a result of this experience, I now know that. Human consciousness is one of a great variety of other states and consciousness as a whole is a basic cosmic phenomenon related to the organization of energy. This experience was so momentous; it completely shook every aspect of my being. A new vocabulary is necessary to describe this, which I render in italics. It includes a few new words and combinations of words. This experience sounds painful, and it was; the lasting effect, however, has been positive. My life since has been an attempt to try to understand what happened.

Conditions Surrounding the Experience

The experience occurred as part of a shamanic journey in the jungles of Chiapas in Southern Mexico. It took place under the supervision of Mexican psychiatrist Dr. Salvador Roquet and his colleagues. Salvador was a shaman with an M.D. in Western Medicine—a man of compassion trained in the psychoanalytic tradition of Erich Fromm. He was a serene and gentle man. I always felt humble in his presence, as all those who worked with him did. When he was not working with us directly, he could often be found reading the Bible, the Tao Te Ching, the Rig-Veda, or a book of poetry. It was through Salvador that I developed a love for and study of the flute.

Salvador ventured into the mountains of Mexico to bring the benefits of modern Western Medicine to Mexico's native Indians. In exchange, the Indians ministered to him and taught him their ways. In time he became a shaman himself. Bringing together the two disciplines of modern medicine and shamanism, he developed a way of helping us look at the ego—not to affirm its reality, but to help us understand its nonexistence through the experience of "non-ordinary" states of consciousness. The ego is strong and filled with defenses. Traditional talking therapy takes a long time—often many years—and then you still may only have strengthened the ego rather than overcome it. Expose someone to death and see how the ego reacts. There is no faster way of getting to the truth. There are of course much gentler ways.

Getting into the Jungle

Shanti and I fly to Mexico City where we meet Salvador and his family of fourteen children; David, an American potter from Tennessee and his wife, Linda; Frank, a balding, bearded psychiatrist from San Francisco, Rick, a long, lanky, blond, intellectual assistant to Salvador, and a couple of other assistants. All of them will venture with us into the jungle. Every moment with Salvador is a learning experience. It isn't about what is going to happen when we get into the jungle. Salvador does everything deliberately, all the while preparing us for our climactic awakening.

We drive as far as we can to the jungle in a caravan of three cars. I drive a Volkswagen beetle with Shanti, David and Linda. Our destination is an Indian village somewhere in Chiapas, a two-day drive south from Mexico City. The first day we stop and spend the night in a charming hotel with a vast open courtyard with fountains and flowers. In the evening we walk around the plaza dominated by a large park in the center of which is a huge Catholic cathedral.

The next morning we visit an Indian museum. I buy an Indian flute. Then our *"caravan"* takes off. The lead driver, one of Salvador's assistants, drives with keen resolve and far too fast—as though we have to reach our destination at a certain time. That evening as we race down the streets of a Mexican village, a scrawny-looking dog steps out of the dust of the car ahead of me and sacrifices his life right in front of my eyes. I hit the brakes—there is a yelp, a quick dull thud, and a mess of fur, blood and broken bones in the dust behind the car. In a fraction of a second, an impression of the dog's red eyes staring at the headlights of the car is burned into my mind. He stopped, turned, and looked at me a second before I hit him. It is only the first death that day.

We arrive about eleven p.m. at a combination cantina, pool hall and butcher house. Exhausted from continually driving roads that have become progressively more rough, dirty and dusty, we arrive just in time to witness the slaughtering of a cow, the culminating experience of our evening. Though I do not realize it till later, it is all part of Salvador's plan. He wants us to witness this death, and the Indians have waited for our arrival before they begin their butchering.

Tied up outside the cantina where we are to spend the night is the poor cow, her eyes wide with terror, mooing and pulling on a rope tied to a tree. She knows her fate. Beyond this spot, there are no more electric lights or refrigeration. To provide themselves with meat, once a fortnight the natives butcher a cow. They begin at night, working through till morning. As a young boy, I have watched the butchering of pigs and beef cows and enjoyed the camaraderie of farmers coming together to share in a mutual task. After butchering, all shared in the spoils.

Now we are sharing with Mexican Indians in their night of slaughter. I can no longer kill anything, and I don't care to see anything killed. Shanti is, as with all things, fascinated with what is about to happen. "Oh, wow! Look at that!" Standing looking into the face of the doomed cow, an Indian steps forward and places a large pan near her throat. Another Indian walks forward and quickly cuts her throat. She begins to moo an awful, woeful wail of death as blood shoots out partly into the pan, partly splashing out of the pan, making a puddle of mud in the dusty earth, forcing us to jump back lest we become splattered with mud and blood. A few minutes later, weak from loss of blood, she falls on her front knees, then over on the ground. She kicks her legs with a violent jerk, tripping one of the Indians. She is dead.

All night long, the Indians hack and saw the carcass of the cow—talking all the while, making jokes, drinking tequila, and spitting on the floor. A dirty white sheet drawn across a wire is all that separates our sleeping quarters from their butchering. On the sheet you can see their shadows hacking away. Exhausted as we are, it is impossible to sleep. Adding to the cacophony, Salvador, who alone has the privilege of crawling up on top of the pool table, torments us by snoring the night away. I can't get the image of the poor cow with her terrified eyes out of my mind. And then there are mosquitoes celebrating their bloodthirsty rites, eating us like the specialty of the day.

Early the next morning, Indian women arrive carrying large, empty blue and white speckled enamel pans on their heads, which they fill with the meat. Covering their pans with cloth, they start their march back to their homes in the jungle. Lacking refrigeration, they will cook the meat as soon as they return. When it runs out, they will rely on local game until the next butchering.

Up and packed, we are treated to a meal of huevoes rancheros (eggs over corn tortillas with refried beans) and coffee—delicious. There is no lunch or dinner. We will not eat again until we return from the jungle. We are off, riding on top of our backpacks in the back of two-wheeled bullock carts. Salvador is taking us to a safe space. No one will happen upon us. Our destination is an island in the jungle surrounded by a swamp. The only decent means of transportation are two-wheeled bullock carts, slowly drawn by yoked oxen. The hut looks a good bit like the chicken coops on our farm, though our chickens actually fared better. There is one room with a wooden floor and a porch. Though we are on edge from lack of sleep the night before, tonight is going to be *the* night. There is no delay. Salvador's plan is to keep us on edge. Before the night is over, we are going to be pushed *over* the edge.

The Experience Itself

The Beginning—The Loss of the Body

Salvador checks everyone's blood pressure. He has never lost anyone and isn't going to now. We each go into the experience about a half-hour apart. I go first. Each in turn takes a tablet of quality LSD. We then lie down on our sleeping bags, our eyes completely covered with a black sleep mask, which is then in turn covered by a bandanna to exclude all light. External stimulation is to be kept to a minimum. Earphones cover our ears. Salvador has an extensive collection of tapes, tape recorders, mixers and enough batteries to provide us with the sounds that will take us on our journey.

About a half-hour or so into the experience, after the LSD begins to take effect, Salvador administers a shot of Ketamine. Ketamine knocks out the body. This is why it is so good in operations; the body just passes out. The mind cannot pass out because you are wide-awake on LSD. Ketamine, now, both accelerates and smoothes the trip.

At first there is nothing—only a sense of peace followed by growing apprehension. Then suddenly there is an expansion. My arms come back over my head; my heels dig into the earth below me. My whole body then arches itself upward, energy pouring through my arms and legs, as huge arching lights meet in the center, then pour back in a myriad of different colors. I experience what I can only describe as an orgasm in every cell, a supersensational edge cutting through everything. Thick juice pours from my being while intense emotions pass through me. I tell myself that I can hold on, that I can hold on, that I can . . . I cannot. I'm face to face with something uncontrollable and irreversible—a chain reaction tearing apart every aspect of my being.

Any identity I might have had is being *ripped* away. There is nothing I can do to hold on to any form of ordinary reality. The pain is intense, immense, and I'm completely insane. In one final arch, with thousands of volts of energy running through me, I slip completely out of my body. I say, "I'm dead." I'm quite dead. The acceptance comes not casually. It is a firm and clear fact.

Antimatter and the Collapse of Time

I'm being pulled by "immense energies," pivoted back and fourth from a convex—through a whip-like motion into a concave—arch. Outwardly I'm shot forward, while inwardly pulled backward faster and faster—like a logarithmic spiral, exponentially increasing speed with every step, becoming infinitely smaller as the universe opens to its maximum. Everything keeps expanding outward, then collapses inward. It's like watching cells divide. There is an inward turning—a point of condensation, then suddenly a burst, a shot forward, and a whole new world is present. The only term I can think of to define this is *Matter-Anti-Matter*.

Time collapses in a series of violent jerks. My life, my past, all dying. Turning to dust. Disappearing. I am losing my autobiography. I remember Daddy and my life on the farm, and that oh-so-ordinary reality that seems like a space of bliss. I feel the most incredible sense of connection with the earth and that man. I then experience what I would call the severing of the *genetic-ego*. The earth and every aspect of it appears before me and then is burned into a tiny crisp, and disappears in a jig-jagging line. A web or grid now delineates a very familiar universe. In fact, this is the most familiar thing there is. This is where I have always been—where we all are.

The Collapse of Ego

Again, I remember my ordinary identity and the brief statement I made in life. Then it is as though I say to myself, "Oh, yeah!—Jon Mundy." There is a giggle, a roll of laughter, and I see how puny and insignificant that identity was. My striving, my worrying about and working through problems is suddenly all absurd—even funny.

There occurs now an element that is even more difficult to describe, a point of absolute insanity in which my ego judges itself to death. This reality is then also seared, stamped out, excluded from existence. It is not that I go unconscious. Something becomes far more conscious than ever. The self that I had created, however, is burned, snuffed out, not because it is bad. It is simply that Jon Mundy, as I had known him, is unreal—or meaningless.

The Experience of a Star

I am aware of myself as a tiny point in the tail of a gigantic star, whirling itself toward the center of something, a single Point-of-Consciousness of *consciousness - feeling - knowledge,* nothing more than a tiny subsection of the continuum of something immense. I scream at the enormity of what is ahead, completely incapable of resisting the force that pulls me forward. The sensation is that of pure and raging firepower. The light becomes brighter and brighter like the light of a thousand suns. I am part of an incredible network of other Points-of-Consciousness on the tip of the tail of a star somewhere in some space. I understand with complete empathy the Thought-Feeling of every other point in this tail. I will give anything to stop this experience. I have nothing to give. Each of these Points-of-Consciousness is screaming for the experience to stop, pleading for forgiveness for having *Mistaken-Themselves,* begging for just one little moment of death, rest and unconscious nonexistence—my own voice drowning in this cacophony of sound. Caught in this cosmic maelstrom, unable to resist the intense gravity, I'm pulled relentlessly into its center.

The Merging of Multiple Minds

Now I am everywhere and everything at the same time! Any point and every point is a center. Turning inside out on myself, I focus down into a sphere surrounded by other spheres, all of which are *Coming-Moving-Away-From-Me*. Heavenly bodies float soothingly by me—all-pervading and all-seeing.

I'm merging with other consciousness. At first I think it is the consciousness of the people on earth whom I have known and loved. It is also, however, the consciousness of those I have *always* known and now *re-membered*. I cannot identify this consciousness as human. There is no longer singular ego-consciousness. There is a much broader perspective with incredible depth of perception. As a grain of wheat is ground into flour, excited and expanded with leaven, and turned into bread, so is my ego crushed, and my mind opened into a new and very familiar merging of multiple-minds.

The New Vision

I'm seeing the way I imagine a computer might see. Everything is divided into tiny cubic forms, each in turn divided into innumerable cubic forms *ad infinitum,* each a certain depth of space, each a certain gradation of color, running in all directions, forming an immense array of patterns. I can see in 360 degrees and *See-Feel* each space of depth in descending gradations and focus with a telescopic vision that comes down on, or opens up to, larger visions with amazing rapidity. The colors of these other spheres run from deep black on the outside down through dark, then light blues, reds, or greens with almost blinding red, green and blue centers—the colors all perfectly clear as there is no atmosphere that separates me from my perception—energy pulsates through everything, undulation upon undulation. Nothing is constant, everything is moving.

The language of this world is beautiful, clear, precise, and melodic—a kind of *Musical-Equation*. It is difficult to say whether the language aspect predominated over the math-music or the math-music over the language. All language has merged into one language, a language that, strangely enough, I can understand even more clearly than English or any earthly sound. I both hear and *see* elaborate expressions produced in beautiful, four-dimensional geometric design.

Like a Möbius strip, ideas turn into form, then back into ideas. I feel as though I'm *Seeing-Reality-As-It-is,* yet not seeing—*Knowing.* The brilliance with which everything fits together is beyond belief. There simply are no accidents, no coincidences. Each *Musical-Equation* is an exact and melodically logical statement that gives rise to paradoxes and results in emotional sensations. Some, I sense, are the names of authors of complicated formulas, already determined by previous generations of computer-like consciousness.

The Marketplace

A *Musical-Equation* defines the world, and once expressed, produces the experiences endured. Complicated emotional states are being "called out" by spheres from different directions. These *Musical-Equations* are made up of *Math-Musical-Equation-Points* and are combined in rapid-fire order so that a marketplace effect occurs as each *Point-of-Consciousness* calls out for various programs to be played, or responds to programs being played in another part of the galaxy. An explosion or burning of some great equation, system of belief, or personality, sends *A-Wake* through the other spheres, causing us to *Pay-Attention.*

Insight flashes upon insight. With every conclusion, I become aware of a position that stands in opposition to that conclusion, and a third position that stands between these two and thus becomes a new conclusion. Each of these *Concluding-Equations* can then be *swallowed* by a *Check-Mating-Concluding-Equation* that then might be burned into a tiny cinder to become an *Old-Truth* in a *Greater-Realization.* I or any other *Point-of-Consciousness* might call out an equation that predominates in value over the last conclusion.

I have fallen into a boundless effulgent ocean of intelligence. Huge waves of shining sea rush toward me. Visually, the experience is like looking down a kaleidoscope—watching everything fall into the middle, each old form falling off to the side, while new beauty is ever before me.

My relationship to the other *Points-of-Consciousness* depends upon who is playing the program, whether I'm being pulled toward some other program—whether the program seems pleasant or unpleasant. I try, under the elaboration of some hypothesis, to gain some temporary control. I soon wander into a *Negative-Deviation* and am instantly swallowed by a *Check-Mating-Evaluating-Equation.* For every decision I make, I'm congratulated for having reached the right conclusion—then shown the paradoxical nature of my decision. I then find myself standing over a new proposition that makes my original position seem so inconsequential I'm sure I have erred, even though it is clear I have chosen quite rightly, indeed, the only way I could have chosen. It is clear I have made the right decision, which is wrong. That is, I cannot help making the right decision, even when it is the wrong one. Each time this happens, I roll over and turn out another way. Each change of form brings a new perception and a new identity, which I begin to grasp, only to lose it to another form. It is very hard to know "what" it is that is having this experience.

I don't know how to control my thoughts in the presence of what I perceive are divine beings who have long ago figured out what I'm now seeing for the first time. I thus grasp only bits and pieces of this alternate reality, which I'm now attempting to convey on these pages. Other parts I remember momentarily in intuitive flashes when I again see a tiny piece of this puzzle obscured by a misty cloud.

For a time, in the midst of this experience, it seems I know all that is to be known. Later I conclude that I know nothing. I have become *too conscious* and know no way not to be.

An atomic explosion is going on in consciousness, always has been and will be. For a moment, I gain the ultimate insight into the absurdity of the universe and think I shall never be able to return to that merciful self-deception that is necessary for sanity. The more consciousness knows of itself, the more impossible it is to know its origin. It simply is and always will be. In this incredible world, every thought is instantly turned into form, every defective form is burned, every perfect form turned yet again into higher perfection. I have no idea if I will ever return to bodily life. There is clearly no choice or chance of ever leaving. There is only fantastic Energy-Information-Flow.

The Divine

From the "northeast" section of consciousness comes a holy sound like the very best in Gregorian chanting. As I focus on it, the pitch gets louder and absolutely deafening. God, it seems, is behind that sound. It is impossible to go that way, as the pull of the universe before me is even more intense. I further think that by following such a path, I shall lose an even greater hold on consciousness, which means going crazy faster, and it is impossible to go crazy any faster than I already am.

199

I would do anything to have something that is real in the old and ordinary sense of the term, some little piece of "sanity." I call out several times for Judy. Love is the only thing that makes sense in this experience. Yet, I have left that speck of earth, on which I at one time lived in some more unconscious and more peaceful condition. Earth is dumb and stupid, and I want to be dumb and stupid. What bliss, what joy it would be to return to my *Animal-Body*. Life, as I had known, it is precious. I lost all such reality millions of years ago.

The Burning of Karma

I say shit, *merde*, and God-damn-it in every language I know and many I do not. The sensation is like throwing up awful pieces of sandy green slime. This gives me a sense of relief. I feel clearer and more centered. While riding the tail end of the star, I beg for forgiveness, which is not forthcoming and seems undeserved. Still, I cannot help begging for it. By saying something like *Mistake-Myself,* I beg to be released from *The-Sin-of-Desiring-Ego*. Sometime after this experience, I read a dialogue between Oscar Ichazo and Dr. John Lilly in which they discuss this effect as the *Burning-of-One's-Karma*. I now realize that no darkness within is ever able to hide. There is also nothing I want to hide, and I joyfully accept my fate.

Coming to Consciousness

I become aware of myself as a tip on the peak of a high mountain. Dirt and rocks are falling off the sides as I begin to fall into form. I'm turning into a temple, and then I'm on a couch within the temple, surrounded by millions of Points-of-Consciousness. Those close to me are beginning to take on human form and begin to back away respectfully. Other points, less humanoid and more distant, begin to move more slowly. Yet I know they are increasing their level of awareness. I call upon them to pay attention and tell them they will be relieved of their ignorance and pain. This returns a sense of ego along with a sudden sense of power—followed by loneliness.

I think these other Points-of-Consciousness will have to come to consciousness just as I have. They will have to go through the same pain, and that seems so horrible. Yet it is clear that, when one breaks through, there is less pain. Also, it is clear that I am in want of greater wisdom, and I sink down into denser human form. This is a great relief, at least, though still far from what it used to be.

Regaining Ego and the Expression of Anger

By screaming *Stop-It!* And *Wait-a-Minute!* I am able to return a little more to my body. I have yet to return to flesh and bones. My molecules are still spread out over immense space. Desperate to obtain some form of identity, I lash out at the world around me. My arms move through space and I feel the air give way in millions of points of rarefied sensation. I exert more energy and the world backs away quickly and with caution. I gain some control, but it is momentary, as I immediately see my error and begin to sink down into lower form. By bringing my arms up over my body, it is now possible to tear away an outer layer of consciousness, as one might strip away an outer layer of a cocoon.

I'm *Coming-to-Consciousness* in a spaceship. The circular interior is huge. The walls all around are padded with different colored blocks. I'm not in ordinary human form—more like a cocoon of energy—more like some kind of embryo. Around me are a number of humans. Most notable is one young man who keeps saying, "Do you want to wake up?" which clearly means do I want to "get up" or "be reborn" in this other world—a world inside a space ship.

I experience this *Coming-to-Consciousness* as a formidable *ignitiation* (an instantaneous initiation by fire), in which I am being introduced to higher knowledge in an advanced stage of the future. I'm being born again in the way that a concept is born or a cocoon is unraveled; more and more clearly I see the truth of the world about me. I'm an embryo developing very rapidly—incapable of stopping the development. There is a lot of excitement about my birth. My closest friends (Edie is there!) are going to greet me and laughingly smile upon my *ignitiation* and welcome me to a higher stage they have already attained. I can't pull through. I cannot remove the veil. I let go of my struggle and sink down into a less conscious but more peaceful state.

An Ape Scientist

I'm now experiencing Coming-to-Consciousness as an ape scientist. I think I'm one of the first people ever to come to consciousness. There is a sudden pang of guilt, the thought that something has gone wrong. I'm Adam on the first morning of awakening, and I am alone. When I realize what is happening, I beg the others to stop their own endeavors and rest for a moment, for we are very near the truth. If we go more quickly, we will find ourselves passing right through it to a new form of insanity that surpasses our present one. Now, it is too late, and I begin to cry, "Who's the doctor?" Who is responsible for unleashing this atomic reaction? Who cracked this cosmic egg and unleashed these molecules of mind?

Time

The concept of time is blown apart when you enter into a black hole.
—Stephen Hawkins

The next part of this description is very important. I can only say that I am convinced that I have *Already-Not-Yet-Had* this experience in the *Future-Past*. Yet, I'm so in the present that past and future lose their significance. Perhaps I had this experience in some nightmare before I was born, certainly in some state of *Unconscious-Madness*. It is a state to which I shall have to return, to which I am even now returning, through a black hole in space, through a tunnel in time, in which everything is turned inside-out on itself. Now I understand what Nietzsche meant by *Eternal-Recurrence*. The future, like the past, pulsates, undulates, spirals, and turns over and over again. Past, present and future are simultaneous! Everything is happening in a radically loaded *Now*. One single thought is leashed forever into eternity, ever breaking itself into repeatedly more complex forms, ever being burned and then born again.

Responsibility

I'm responsible for this experience because I'm here. To accept responsibility for an irreversible chain reaction in consciousness is immense. Yet I'm also back. I'm home, in the place I always have been. My external and now lost life is a story into which I escaped in time. Time is phenomenal because it is sequential. Events seem to happen one after the other, and because of that, they are comprehensible. I live in time to learn a lesson, one I have not yet learned at the time of this experience. Ever since, I've wanted to find out what happened. I've been trying to re-member.

Sufficiently back into my body to be able to move, I get hold of a brass crucifix. Though remarkably porous it provides a sense of solidity in my hand. It is something to hang on to. Its symbolic quality means nothing, and I scream, "Who the hell is Jesus?" Perhaps he had something of this experience thousands of years ago. That information is of little use in this moment.

I pray, though I know not to what God, that this experience will never have to happen to anyone. Yet, it seems that innumerable other worlds or *Points-of-Consciousness* are having the experience in much the same way I did. I know now that the whole experience is correlated to my own state of being; therefore, what I saw, another might not see; nor do I believe it is necessary for anyone else to have the same experience. I'm going through something clearly beyond my level of perception and emotional preparedness. I'm seeing a universe so much beyond this one, there is nothing of this world left at all, save perhaps atoms, molecules, planets, asteroids, comets, and stars of deepest space—intelligent beings far more intelligent than a poor human mind can comprehend. All about me planets were exploding, new planets were being born. Suns were evaporating; new suns were being born. There are universes within universes. Universes lying side by side "existing" through each other in "different" dimension of time. It goes on endlessly and instantaneously.

I am to that world what an ant is to this one—only more so. I'm totally at the mercy of that world. An ant who turns its head up into the light and sees a gigantic being standing above him cannot possibly know what that being is. The light, the sound, the whole of that world above (I now know is within) is totally overwhelming. All my ordinary ego defenses collapse in the face of it. What lights a mystic's way blinds an ordinary man, unprepared for the light of knowledge.

Return to the Body

I get back into my body by screaming, "Stop it!" I return completely dumbfounded. I can hardly believe I have reintegrated myself into an old and familiar body. My ordinary mind by this time is wide-awake. I'm completely exhausted and can only stare. My mind has literally "been blown." For two hours I simply sit and look at my right hand. I am completely speechless because I realize that anything I say will be an attempt to put into words something, which defies words. I'm using words now because I know others have had similar experiences and can identify with what I'm saying.

Two days later, when my mind has returned a little more to its "normal" state, I sit down at a typewriter. My internal tongue is loosened, and it comes back as I have just described it.

I have translated this experience through the framework of the human brain. You see it with human eyes or hear it with human ears and translate it through your own thought system. Therefore, you gather only the smallest glimpse of what actually happened. I have painted a picture of a possibility for consciousness—the description of a world hundreds of thousands of times more real than this one.

Did I Die?

Some say I did not die. Maybe I didn't. I thought I did. I have both heard and read accounts by others who have gone through this experience, and each describes it as a death experience, including the dissolution of the ego. I had no idea it was going to be as completely shattering as it was. If I had, I might not have done it. I thought it might be like my experience with LSD back in 1966. It was more—much more! Now I am convinced to the inner core of the presence of an immense consciousness.

I will go through this experience several times. I remember this first time in more detail because of my ego's encounter with death. I remember very little of later experiences. By that time, when I saw what was coming, I just ran and jumped off the cliff. I just let go and disappeared. So the other, later experiences I don't remember, except for the very beginning and a bit of the return. The Course says that the one thing we have not *truly* done is forgotten our bodies. For a few moments I didn't just forget my body, I lost it!

CHAPTER 27

Postmortem

I meet with Helen, Ken and Judy Skutch. There I read them what you've just read. The account confirms many of the things the Course says—that we are not bodies, that there is no death, or time, and that we are making up this world. In the hours and days to follow I'm aware of the petty, ridiculous, and insignificant nature of my ordinary earthly problems. I can see through so much of the bullshit. All our problems are surface-realities that cover greater problems of security, openness, and faith. Freeing one's being from the surface realities gives rise to feelings of purity and cleanliness.

A good deal of this encounter was hellish. Had I had greater faith, say, to follow the sound of God, I am sure the experience would have been even more profound. It was already more profound than I could endure. I actually went crazy, a fact, which I later found, confirmed by Jungian psychologist Marie-Louise Von Franz:

> . . A schizophrenic episode is often prefaced by dreams of world destruction.
> In modern terms it is generally an atomic explosion, or the end of the world,
> the stars fall down—absolutely apocalyptic images. This generally announces
> that the consciousness of this human being is in a state of explosion or is
> going to explode and his reality awareness will soon disappear.
> —Creation Myths, Spring Pub. 1972, p. 11

This is exactly what happened. My reality awareness as I had come to know it disappeared, and I was left with another reality that I wasn't prepared to handle.

> What seems eternal all will have an end. The stars will disappear, and night
> and day will be no more. All things that come and go, the tides, the seasons
> and the lives of men; all things that change with time and bloom and fade
> will not return. —ACIM, T-29.VI.2:7-9

Faced with the exclusion of this "reality," I had an opportunity to look into a greater one. The experience gave me an opportunity to understand who I am, outside the little self I created.

> The self you made is not the Son of God. Therefore, this self does not exist at
> all. And anything it seems to do and think means nothing. It is neither bad
> nor good. It is unreal, and nothing more than that. —ACIM, W.I.93: 5:1-5

Illumination

In a later experience, similarly induced in 1977, I feel as though I am illuminated—pure, utterly beautiful white light, warm, radiant, perfect in beauty, and tranquility, flowing with energy and wonder—what Heaven is when we just let go and let it happen. I am ecstatically happy and filled with a great sense of well-being. I have never known a feeling like this—yet I have also always known it. Many things are clear. All of the issues and events around which I experience pain and fear are gone. I know that I am forgiven. There is nothing to do—just love, letting others be, guiding without hurting.

This "illumination" lasted until our time of processing, when a woman who had gone through a similar experience attacked me verbally. I was open and, it seems, total love until she attacked. I don't remember what the attack was about. It doesn't matter. When it happened, it was as though a nucleus someplace within defended itself. I said nothing. It all happened in the mind. The second it happened, I began to lose it. The shell began to return. It did not return quickly, as I was just too open.

Every now and then I find a description in some text that reminds me of that first experience in Mexico. This is particularly true in my reading of the physics of consciousness and *A Course in Miracles*. One section from the Course struck me particularly:

Beyond the body, beyond the sun and stars, past everything you see and yet somehow familiar, is an arc of golden light that stretches as you look into a great and shining circle. And all the circle fills with light before your eyes. The edges of the circle disappear, and what is in it is no longer contained at all. The light expands and covers everything, extending to infinity forever shining and with no break or limit anywhere. Within it everything is joined in perfect continuity. Nor is it possible to imagine that anything could be outside, for there is nowhere that this light is not. —ACIM, T-21.I.8:1-6

During the experience, I felt fear and expressed anger. I can imagine that another soul, able to release itself more freely than I, might find the experience absolutely blissful. Much of my life since this time has been an effort to find out more about that world, so that when I leave my body forever, it will not be painful. I would like to confirm these realities or see if there are yet other profound visions that await human perception. I know now that it is possible to attain such states through meditation and spiritual exercises such as those afforded by the Course.

206

Thus, the Holy Spirit operates within this temporal framework even though He knows that time and space are not real. However, He does not obliterate the belief in time and space, which would awaken us from the dream too rapidly, precipitating panic.
—Ken Wapnick, *The Vast Illusion: Time in* A Course in Miracles, p. 215

Fear not that you will be abruptly lifted up and hurled into reality. Time is kind, and if you use it on behalf of reality, It will keep gentle pace with you in your transition. —ACIM, T-16.VI.8:1-2

Using psychotropics is a bit like using dynamite to break through the doors of perception. I do not suggest that anyone do what I did. I had, in fact, been hurled into reality. I wanted to come back to "ordinary consciousness" even though I knew it meant being dumb and stupid. Things are comprehensible in this world precisely because they seem to happen sequientially.

My experiences happened in the years '76, '77, and '78. I have had no similar experiences since then and feel no need to do so. After the last experience, Salvador asked me a question I don't remember. I do remember my response. I said, "I'm already dead," to which he replied, "You don't have to do this anymore." And I never did. Given my present state of ordinary consciousness, I would appreciate a much slower much less profound awakening when I leave this body forever. It is my understanding that Salvador has died. He knew a great deal about where he was going.

Time Stopped

Can you imagine what a state of mind without illusions is? How it would feel? Try to remember when there was a time—perhaps a minute, maybe even less—when nothing came to interrupt your peace; when you were certain you were loved and safe. Then try to picture what it would be like to have that moment be extended to the end of time and to eternity. Then let the sense of quiet that you felt be multiplied a hundred times, and then be multiplied another hundred more. And now you have a hint, not more than just the faintest intimation of the state your mind will rest in when the truth has come.
—ACIM, W- p.I.107.2:1-5 & 3:1

One of the most interesting aspects of this vision is my sense that I have seen it all before. If there is something that is eternal, and this life experience is temporal, then *seeing* can be understood as returning home again, what I understand as "eternal return."

Such is each life; a seeming interval from birth to death and on to life again, a repetition of an instant gone by long ago that cannot be relived. And all of

time is but the mad belief that what is over is still here and now.
—ACIM, T.26.V.13: 3-4

I want to prepare myself for greater rest on the other side, and I think it possible to do so by dealing now with the problems I encounter in this experience. I now have a much more profound respect for schizophrenia. The good thing about the Course is that it helps us deal with our madness slowly, enabling us to awaken without going crazy.

Here are two descriptions from others that have had similar experiences with Ketamine.

I got deeper and deeper into this state, until at one point the world disappeared. I was no longer in my body. I didn't have a body. I reached a point at which I knew I was going to die. There was no question about it, no 'maybe I will' or 'perhaps I will,' and what incredible feelings that evoked!

Then I reached a point at which I felt ready to die. It wasn't a question of choice; it was just a wave that carried me higher and higher. At the same time that I was having what in my normal state I would call the horror of death. It became obvious to me that it is not at all what I anticipated death to be. Except, I knew it was death, that something was dying.

I reached a point at which I gave it all away. I just yielded, and then I entered a space in which there weren't any words. The words have been used a thousand times, at-one-with-the-universe, recognizing-your-godhead—all those words. The feeling was that I'm 'home.' I didn't want to go anywhere, and I didn't need to go anywhere.

—Reported in *Psychotropics Encyclopedia*, by Peter Stafford, Ronin Publishing, Berkeley, CA, 1992, pp. 393 & 394.

Much of this previous experience has about it qualities of what I think the Course means by a Holy Instant.

One should be lying down, because they will be unconscious of their body shortly after. As the high is coming on, there is a break in the continuity of consciousness. Soon after this point I found myself in a swirling universe. Frequently, there was no recollection of ever having been myself, been born, having a personality or body, or even knowing of planet earth. The experience was one of being in total orgasm with the universe. I felt like I was in hyperspace, simultaneously connected to all things. Billions of images and perceptions were simultaneously flowing through my circuits. I was not bound into three dimensions. I experienced backward and forward in time as well with the current moment being the center of intensity.

I felt as though there had been a major and permanent shift in the 'fabric of reality.' Sometimes I felt like a single atom or point of consciousness adrift in a swirling vortex of energies, like a single cell within a being of galactic proportion. The experience was of titanic proportion in the merging of energy,

intent, and awareness, yet lucidity articulated to the minutest spiraling details.
All the while I felt very relaxed and at home in this universe. Even though any
support of reality, identity, or stability was dissolved at the speed of light,
I did not experience any fear, as if the one who would experience fear at
losing these things was not a part of me. As the waves of experience passed
through me, I felt a bit like a kid on a roller coaster. Although he's about to
have an exhilarating experience while going over a hill, deeper in his mind
he's confident that the roller coaster will stay on its tracks. The experience
was so otherworldly that a normal mind can't even conceive of experiencing
in this manner.
—D.M. Turner, *The Essential Psychedelic Guide*, Pranther Press,
San Francisco, CA 1994, pp. 64-66.

Shanti had a totally different experience. She was apparently able to let go and simply disappear. As she entered her experience, she no doubt took the roller coaster ride. She kept saying, "Wow!" and "Oh my God!" and "Look at that!" She was apparently more accepting of death than I was.

A word about David, the young potter from Tennessee. I had completed my experience and was sitting with my back against the wall of the hut looking at David when he went into his experience. Much of this experience has about it an oceanic quality; that is, you feel as though you are melting or blending with your environment. At one point I felt as if I was a chicken cackling on the roof, at another point a pig rolling about in the mud outside the hut. We were down to our underwear, in the jungle. For some reason David was completely naked. I watched him as he went into his experience, and I saw something you wouldn't want to see too often. David's whole body contracted. He then regurgitated and defecated at the same time. Next day as we were processing our experiences, David said he became the cow we saw butchered the night before.

Back in the states, I want to share this adventure. With whom can I share it? I call Judy and try to talk to her. She has no idea what I'm talking about. How can she? I cried out for Judy in this experience, and now I can't connect with her. Or was it Judy Femmer in Missouri? Or was it just woman, the other half of me—my someday wife. Edie listens with great interest. I'll not be telling my district superintendent!

As time goes by, I do tell people I have had a death experience in the jungles of Chiapas in Mexico in the presence of a shaman. I'm reluctant to talk about the psychotropics because I'm concerned about people's phobic reactions. I mention it several times from the pulpit without describing the circumstances. No doubt, people are able to deduce that psychotropic agents were involved. This does not put me in good standing with the church. It has all happened as part of a spiritual pilgrimage from which I gained immense insight. There is a tremendous difference between the once or twice or even dozen experiences with psychotropics over a period of several years and the chronic addictive use of a drug. It would be impossible to work with psychotropics on a daily basis. Nor would you want to. You need time to process.

I return to the log cabin near Cold Spring where I'm able to observe the fabric of nature with greater clarity. There is a new way of experiencing, seeing, knowing, and connecting with everything. I am able to "feel" the trees, the flowers, and the earth. Everything is a myriad of energy and I am in everything. I am the flower; I am the sky, I am the people I meet. All my relationships become more immediate. I'm more interested in peo-ple—in getting close to them and knowing what's going on with them. It is possible to pass over much of the game playing and move more quickly into meaningful contact. As the days go by, however, I can feel the pull of the socialization process taking me back into what I was before.

One morning I wake just at dawn and go out on the cabin deck. I notice a huge owl sitting on a path to the right of the house—just sitting there. I go down and slowly walk straight up to this mighty bird. I slow down. I get closer. I'm standing now only about fifteen feet from the owl, who does not move. He just stares—his huge yellow gaze planted deep inside me. We fix our eyes on each other for the longest time. The phone rings. I'm expecting a call. I go back into the cabin. When I return to the deck, he's gone. Later, I tell a Canadian Indian about my experience and he says the Owl was there to help me not to forget the wisdom I gained in my experience.

I become a voracious reader of anything I can find on the new physics or what is sometimes called "psycho-physics." These works offer insight into what has happened. I become excited reading Dr. Fritjof Capra's *The Tao of Physics*. I make contact with Capra and offer to put together a workshop for him in New York City in September of '76. Edie has a large living room in her brownstone and volunteers the space for the workshop. It is perfect. It is also packed. I begin to more seriously desire a place where I can regularly hold workshops, preferably in the country where people can at once get away from the city and learn about the things people like Capra have to teach.

I do further work with Dr. Stanislav Grof. I sponsor workshops with Dr. Grof in New York City and at Wainwright House in Rye, New York. In May 1977, he comes to stay with me. I also sponsor a Conference on Psychophysics for the Academy of Religion and Psychical Research at Union Theological Seminary in New York City.

CHAPTER 28

High Rock Spring

1977—Age Thirty-Four

Having saved a bit of money and sold the little house I owned in Brooklyn, and my half interest in Daddy Mundy's farm to Ann and Glenn, I look for a permanent home I can also use as a retreat center for workshops. I find a completely secluded home in Katonah, New York. The former owner is a landscape architect and the two and a half-acre mini-estate includes a terraced yard, a large garden and an acre of woods. A fountain bubbles forth from a spring in the ground with a rock above carved with the words "High Rock Spring." The house has a large living room, and a great office with two-inch-thick maple bookshelves with built-in backlights covering all of two walls. A house without books is like a body without a soul. The sight of these wonderful bookshelves and the incredible grounds sells me on the place. The name High Rock Spring is perfect. It is at once uplifted, solid and new. There is enough off-street parking for twenty-five cars. The real estate agent assures me I will have no trouble using High Rock as a retreat center. It is a great place. The grounds are magnificent. Joyful Dog will be able to run to her heart's content. The selling price is $97,000. The family is anxious to move. I'm able to buy High Rock for $75,000. I think I'm in heaven. I'm also very gullible and naive.

Helen, Bill, and Leaving Things Alone

Helen has reservations about my buying High Rock, concerned that things are not going to work out as I hope. I love it and do not want to start looking again. Bill suggests to Helen that she leave me alone about her misgivings. Bill has an abiding faith that things will turn out all right and is much less prone to worry than Helen.

I'm now in upper Westchester county. I'm later to call it "upper snobsville." With my first workshop, I receive a cease and desist notice from the zoning board. I'm told I can apply for a variance. I think this is just a formality. I apply. Little do I know my neighbors have gotten up a petition against me. One of them calls my district superintendent to check up on me. He wants to know if I'm "really" a minister. A hearing is to be held by the zoning board. When I get to the hearing, *all* of my neighbors are there. It is a hot night in July, the air-conditioning in the courtroom is broken, and the windows have been painted shut. Two big, noisy industrial fans make a poor effort at clearing the thick, humid air. People have to speak extra loud to be heard over the bustling whirl of the fans.

My case, the eleventh on the docket, is not called till eleven p.m. By this time, everybody is baked, boiled, and stewing in his or her own juices. I don't have a chance. I make the mistake of saying I just want to do my own thing. One woman shouts: "Your own thing! Damn your own thing. This is OUR community!" I lose by a vote of five to four. The chairman of the zoning board casts the deciding vote. He clearly does not like me. Why could I not have won by a vote of five to four?

Helen calls the next day to see how the hearing went. I'm down in the dumps. Seems she was right in her intuition. Still, she is supportive and assures me things will work out even if I can't use High Rock as I had hoped. Although I eventually do occasional workshops, I advertise them in New York City only, not in Westchester, and keep them small and quiet. I do have this big house, however, and on my minister's salary, I can't pay for it without help. As it is more than one person can use, I let out bedrooms to help cover the mortgage. One neighbor writes a nasty letter saying he knows I'm renting out rooms, and threatens to turn me over to the zoning board, which he does. As it turns out, it's not illegal. Up to five non-related people can live together in one house in this community. I rent out the four bedrooms at High Rock and move my own bed into my large office, where I get to sleep amid my books. One of the fellows who comes to rent a room at High Rock is a young psychologist and disciple of Rajneesh who's been given the name Ulas. I start a Course in Miracles study group and sponsor Course workshops on Memorial Day and Labor Day, normal gathering days. Every Fourth of July I throw a big party and each Thanksgiving I have dinner for friends and the family, which begin to develop around High Rock.

I begin classes on transpersonal psychology with Dr. Thomas Hora. He has developed a form of counseling that enables people to transcend egoistic ways of thinking. He calls his approach "Meta-Psychiatry." The more I study *A Course in Miracles* the more it seems Dr. Hora and the Course are talking about the same thing. The truth is the truth wherever it is found.

In one of our sessions, Helen asks me if I'm seeing anyone. I say I am, that I have a new friend, Therese Quinn. Therese is a very free spirit, and a lot of fun to be with. There is also a beautiful light that comes from Therese. She is interested in mystical philosophies and she is a wonderful poetess. Our relationship is one of the most "relaxed" of all the relationships I ever enjoy. She is recently separated and not interested in a serious romance; it's more just a nice friendship. I tell Helen about Therese, and Helen says that she knows that sex is important to a young man. She leans forward, touches my knee and says, "You know, it's no big deal," meaning, I think, that we make a big deal of sex.

I buy several books on gardening and throw myself into terracing the hillside, planting every vegetable, herb, and flower I can. Each year at High Rock, I create a bigger and bigger garden. I build trails off into the surrounding woods and a meditation cave. I often spend as much as four or more hours a day in the garden. I eat very little of the produce. Most of it I give away. Gardening feeds my soul and nourishes my inner life. I enjoy showing off the gardens, fountain and woods.

I continue the series on Mystical Philosophies, with a course on Mystics of the Medieval Period. I focus on alchemy and Kabalistic cosmology, and the medieval mystics Giordano Bruno, Dominican mystic Henri Suso. We study Meister Eckart, St. Theresa of Avila, St. John of the Cross, St. Francis of Assisi, the Baal Shem Tov, Kabir, Jallaluddin Rumi, Jacob Boehm, and Emmanuel Swedenborg. I love this stuff. I complete a first reading of *A Course in Miracles*. The metaphysics of the Course are fascinating. When you begin to get the Course, a mystical thing happens—you begin to see things on another level. It's not about this world. It's not about the ego.

Interfaith

Rabbi Gelberman calls to ask if I will join him in the creation of an organization of interfaith clergy who will get together for a monthly service in New York City. I'm happy to help him in this endeavor he calls The New Light Temple. Swami Satchitananda also joins us.

Friend and fellow Miracles teacher Paul Steinberg calls and asks if I can help him and Bette Martin develop a newsletter for students of *A Course in Miracles,* called *Miracles News.* I begin writing articles and we begin keeping track of A Course in Miracles Study Groups throughout the United States.

Jim Halpin, Judy's father, a heavy smoker, dies of lung cancer. I'm with Judy and her mother in the hospital in Brooklyn. Jim keeps saying, "I don't want to die, Jon." I watch as he breathes more and more slowly. I count the seconds between breaths. It gets slower and slower. Eventually there is no breath. Judy and her mother are devastated. A few days after the death, Judy tells me she and her mother are moving to Jacksonville, Florida, to be near friends who have moved there from Brooklyn. I'm still interested in turning High Rock into a growth center and I'm considering an appeal to the zoning board. Judy wants to be in her own home, not a growth center. We have struggled off and on through our ten year relationship. We both cry. She has to get away from Brooklyn and on with her life. I'm not offering her much. It is time to let go of any fantasy that we might marry. Judy and I remain close. We call each other on our birthdays. After all, it's the same day. We call at Christmas. We call with other news. We both still say, "I love you." To this day I'm Judy's best male friend and confidant. I will forever be committed to Judy—to her happiness and her well-being.

Carol Rollinger—Sweet Medicine

A tall, blond woman with short-cropped hair shows up for every course I teach at the New School. Semester after semester, there she is sitting in the back row. Carol Rollinger has an easy smile, dancing eyebrows, twinkling eyes and a way of scrunching up her nose when she grins that is incredibly cute. She has the most knowing laugh. It is inevitable that I notice her. Carol is also a midwestern mystic. She was a high school teacher in Iowa till a recruiter for United Airlines showed up, and it was Carol, not one of her students, who decided that life as an airline stewardess might be more adventurous than the life of a school teacher.

Carol is fascinating and a truly intriguing woman. She is a rare, true mystic. The center of her life has always been the spiritual. Though raised Christian, she has always had a broader "interfaith" perspective. Carol and I share much in the way of favorite authors, activities, and interests. Carol is a paradox. On the one hand she is the most together woman I've ever met, certainly the most independent. She also doesn't quite have her feet on the ground. Flying is an appropriate occupation for Carol; she is as free as a newspaper blowing down the street. Many of her friends joke that she is an angel. They are not wrong. Carol and Therese Quinn soon become friends. It's appropriate; they are both angels and free, spiritually evolved beings.

Carol's handwriting is nearly perfect, smoothly rounded and very clear. Of all the women I bring home, Carol is Mother's favorite. She is also a simple girl from Iowa. Traveling as she does, she has chosen to spend her time alone rather than sharing hotel rooms with the other stewardesses. She is as cosmopolitan as a comet and a true citizen of the world. Staying alone in various hotels throughout the world, she has lots of time to explore, meditate, and read, and she has listened to thousands of tapes by hundreds of different spiritual leaders.

Carol accumulates enough vacation time to take several months off. She takes off for the summer to study at the Hippocrates Health Institute in Boston, learning to become a naturopathic health practitioner. Ann Wigmore, the director, is so taken by her, she asks her to stay on with the hope she might groom Carol to take over as director. Though she manages her own money well, administrative duties are not her thing. In an age of cell phones and e-mails, to this day Carol does not have her own phone number. She holds a record with United Airlines. No one else even comes close. Since 1969, she has never missed a flight!

At summer's end Carol decides to give up her apartment in New York City and calls to ask if she can come live at High Rock. There is no reason to say no. I'm not going to be able to use High Rock as a retreat center, and I need extra income for the mortgage. We're good friends. We have a great deal in common.

Carol sends a nice contribution to a Sioux Indian reservation in South Dakota. They write back and ask her to visit, which she does. She now designs her flying time so she can spend one week a month at the reservation. She becomes a student of their shamans and is initiated into their native rites and given the name Sweet Medicine. She makes a similar pilgrimage into Sufism in 1979. She goes to India and visits, as I have, with various gurus, and she becomes a student of Carolyn Myss and astrology. Carol is no dabbler. She is a serious spiritual seeker who looks deeply in many different directions. More than anything, she is a lover and a practitioner of bhakti yoga. Bhakti yoga requires a high consciousness that few people are capable of bringing to their inner worlds. The more I come to know Carol, the more I come to admire, respect and love this marvelous woman. At High Rock she begins an active life of growing and juicing wheat grass and sprouts in order to enjoy and share a chlorophyll-filled life. Though I'm fascinated by her incredibly bright light (she literally "beams") and although we develop a relationship, I do not think of Carol in terms of marriage; nor does Carol. It makes for an interesting relationship. We have a certain commitment to each other, to support the other's ideals. We become partners in a way. Still, we each live independent lives.

I sponsor a workshop at High Rock on shamanism with Dr. Michael Harner, professor of anthropology at the Graduate Faculty of the New School. His research has taken him repeatedly into the upper Amazon forests of South America, as well as to the American West and Mexico. We don't use psychotropics as we did in Mexico. We use instead a monotone, repetitive drumming and chanting to achieve a trance state. We greet the morning sun with a "quiet" drumming ceremony so as not to disturb my neighbors.

I renew my interest in the teaching of Rajneesh, in good part because of the dedication I see in Ulas and our leader Dr. Barry Farber (Swami Bodhichitta). We start using High Rock for monthly meetings of Rajneesh's disciples. We do chaotic meditations and then listen to a tape of Rajneesh, which is followed by a discussion based on his teaching led by Bodhichitta. Bodhichitta persuades me to become a disciple (a Sannyasin) of Rajneesh, and I'm given the name Nitam meaning virtue. I'm not sure if this is a curse or a blessing.

As these sessions go on, I realize my path is clearly *A Course in Miracles.* While the eastern approach is intriguing, it does not have the clarity of the Course. Rajneesh wants his disciples to wear saffron-colored clothes, and a mandala with his picture around their necks. I'm still active as a Christian minister. As much as I respect Rajneesh, if I start wearing saffron robes and beads, the church will go crazy. Just as Christianity puts Jesus on a pedestal and worships him, rather than doing what He asked us to do, there is much worship of the guru in the eastern approach. A spiritual path must focus on development of one's "inner" spiritual life, and that the Course does.

In the fall, I continue the course on Mystical Philosophies, covering the modern era, including Russian philosophers Gurdjieff and Ospensky. I meet Tom Foreman, a former student of Ospensky, and sponsor several workshops with him. We make a table that runs all the way through the dining room and the living room at High Rock by putting two four-by-eight boards on top of concrete blocks. We eat a Middle Eastern meal of couscous and lamb. Tom sits in the middle where the two tables meet and teaches, while we lounge around on the floor on pillows next to the table in this Middle Eastern manner. Afterwards, we all enjoy some Middle Eastern liquor.

CHAPTER 29

Methodist Ministry
in the Frustrating Eighties

1978—Age Thirty-Five

Bill Thetford moves to California. Helen is upset he is leaving. Still he calls her every afternoon at four p.m. . . . seven p.m. New York time. Helen and I will work together more intensely during the next three years.

Things are winding down at Windsor Terrace. I was sent here to keep the church alive as long as I could. Everything has worked fairly smoothly. There were no ego battles, no frustrating, uncooperative board of trustees, and no serious uphill battles to fight. All pastors should have it so good. Still, ten years have passed, and I need something more substantial. Each year for the last five, I ask to be transferred to a larger parish, preferably in the country. Each year I have been told nothing is available. Finally, Rev. Richard Parker, the new district superintendent, and the most decent man I ever met in the Methodist Church, offers me the opportunity to move to Central Valley United Methodist Church, about an hour north of the City, forty-five minutes due west of High Rock Spring, on the west side of the Hudson River. Although Central Valley is a small town the church *is* bigger than Windsor Terrace. A huge outlet center known as Woodbury Commons now dominates the area. It is so enormous that traffic jams are frequent and there are so many lights they illuminate the surrounding Catskill Mountains. In 1978 it was just a quiet little town.

The church has a curious steeple topped with what looks like a witch's hat. There is a well-cleaned, blue carpet against hardwood golden oak floors, and white pews with powder blue cushioned seats that match the carpeted aisles. There is an excellent organ, and an excellent organist. I'm thirty-five and very energetic. The interview goes well. I explain to the search committee that I already own my own home and (mindful of the woman in Windsor Terrace who kept an eye on my comings and goings) I do not want to live in the parsonage next to the church. I'm happy to take the position if I can live at High Rock and commute. Although it's a full-time post, the salary is the same as my part-time position at Windsor Terrace, $9,000 a year. Windsor Terrace rented out the parsonage and gave me a housing allowance. There is no housing allowance at Central Valley though they receive a monthly income from rental of the parsonage. I will be making less while working more. It *is*, however, in the country. There *is* potential here. I need a change. I make it clear that I'll have to continue part-time teaching. They agree.

I focus on building the church with personal contacts, a new youth program, quality preaching, an active program of workshops and a first-class newsletter. I have written hundreds of sermons in my ten years at Windsor Terrace. I begin to rewrite them now for the more sophisticated audience of schoolteachers and other professionals. This is going to be fun. There was turmoil in the years prior to my arrival and discontent with the older pastor. Now, everything has changed, and there is a positive, upbeat and cheerful feeling in the air. I enjoy visiting the older women. Mildred Clark stands in line each Sunday after services waiting for her weekly kiss. It is the only overt display of affection Mildred receives from a man and there she is each Sunday, beaming and waiting for a little love. I adopt moms wherever I go and Marion Tedmon becomes my mom in Central Valley.

Mexico and the Huicholi

In the summer of 1978, Shanti and I are off to Mexico to do more work with Salvador. This time we're going to take a more native approach. We do a "convivial" workshop with other leaders, including Rabbi Zelman Schachter-Shalomi. This time we are going into the mountains of Oaxaca to work with the Huicholi Indians and meet the Noachian sage, Maria Sabina. She says she does not know how old she is; only that she is more than ninety. Last time we were in Mexico, I thought our final destination was worse than our chicken coop in Missouri. The chicken coop and Maria Sabina's home are one and the same. Chickens walk in and out of her dirt floor hut as freely as she does. Again we'll be spending the night on the floor in sleeping bags. This time, we're working with mescaline (magic mushrooms).

In lightness and in laughter is sin gone, because its quaint absurdity is seen.
It is a foolish thought, a silly dream, not frightening, ridiculous perhaps...
—ACIM, W-156.6:4-5

I spend the whole night in Homeric laughter, rolling about on the floor, in an ocean of ineffable joy, my sides hurt. It's as though I've been given an opportunity to look into the absurdity of the ego and its universe—I just laugh. There is a German fellow with us named Manfred, who is looking for Don Juan, "the real one," that Castaneda wrote about. He doesn't realize that he is in the presence of a genuine shaman in Salvador. While I laugh, Manfred groans as if he's trying to pull through something. I keep repeating, "Come on, Manfred!" I'm trying to help him pass on out and get reborn already. The next day one of our companions castigates me for the way I've treated Manfred. Manfred says he understood exactly what I was doing in my "midwifery" and thanks me. I go to Missouri after Mexico to take a walk on the back pasture and wander for a while in the woods. While there I perform a wedding ceremony for my niece Erin's dolls.

I come back to New York with tremendous energy. This is one of the best years at Central Valley. Everything is new and fresh. We're running workshops and having a ball. There is a happy feeling in the air—new life and a number of new members joining the church. I break the four courses on Mystical Philosophies into six. It is now going to take three years to cover the material. At the end of that time, I plan to take these six courses and break them into eight and then take four years to cover the material, each time reviewing previous material while going ever deeper and deeper. I can easily do this for the rest of my life.

One of the most remarkable things about Helen is the way she kept herself out of the spotlight regarding the Course. Her name does not appear in early editions of the Course and was added only later to the introduction. She also avoids public lectures on the Course. The first conference on the Course is held at the Barbizon Plaza in New York City in 1978. Helen is not there. Already the Course is being misconstrued, and Helen is disquieted by these misinterpretations. Beginning students are already announcing they are in contact with the Holy Spirit and they are spouting their own messages. "The Holy Spirit told me . . . " The ego did not form in a day, and it's not an easy process to remove the blocks to an awareness of love's presence. These students jumped the gun, overlooking the hard work of the Course.

The conservative Pope John Paul II, the first non-Italian pope in over four hundred years, is elected pope. Rev. Jim Jones and 909 people of the People's Temple commit suicide in Guyana. After the catastrophe, I persuade Rabbi Gelberman to change the name of the New Light Temple to Interfaith, as it says clearly with just one word what it is we are about. I design a logo for Interfaith by superimposing the word Interfaith across images of the Eastern and Western hemispheres of the globe. I have a meeting with the new United Methodist district superintendent. He makes it clear that he is suspicious of this stuff called "New Age."

1979—Age Thirty-Six

Due to a political upheaval, Dr. Alfred Sunderwirth, the program director at Wainwright house, is fired. The old board of trustees is reconstituted with a new board and a new administration takes over with an altogether new direction. Due to my close alliance with Dr. Sunderwirth, my work at Wainwright comes to an end. Dr. John Johnson, Jr., my mentor at General Theological seminary, is fired, in part, for having experimented with psychotropics. I'm his protégé, and I have experimented with psychotropics. Now I don't stand a chance of getting the doctorate. No one else is seriously interested in the Psychology of Religion, Transpersonal Psychology, Parapsychology, Psychophysics, Mysticism, or my "theories" about space and time. I'm more interested in mystical philosophies than orthodox theology, and my adventures in the jungles in Chiapas are no secret.

I'm summoned to the Dean's office for a "chat." I have completed all my course work with A's or B's. I have passed the qualifying exams in French, German, and Ancient Greek. I have nearly completed the dissertation; yet, I'm not to be awarded the doctorate. A Th.D. is a sacred and sanctified degree. It is not to be given out lightly. It is given primarily to Episcopal scholars who plan on teaching in seminary. I have no plans to teach in a seminary—at least not an Episcopal one. I have not gone to chapel. I am hardly known by the older and more established faculty members. What is this about *A Course in Miracles?* Is this serious theology? And what is this teaching on esoteric philosophies? Is this serious theology? Ralph Waldo Emerson graduated from Harvard but received no honors, because he preferred to read what he wanted rather than assigned material. Emerson's student, Henry David Thoreau, once said that individuals by definition are at odds with institutions and are therefore inevitably regarded as a threat. The problem isn't academics. One of the members of the faculty is not sure I'm the "kind" of person they want. I'm not in with the in crowd. I'm out. I have now gone through this process twice. I have spent eleven years, thousands of hours and thousands of dollars, working on a doctorate. It is not to be, at least, not now. I understand, don't I? Do I? Jennifer Kenney, one of the librarians at General Theological, who is in on the local gossip says, "You know, you just didn't play the game."

I leave the Dean's office more than a little distressed and truly disgusted. I was counting on this. If Dr. Johnson had not been fired, he would have shepherded me through. Without his support, I'm sunk. My association with him has blocked my doctorate. Has his association with me contributed to his dismissal? I don't know. At least they can't take the love of knowledge, of reading and writing and books away from me. Many doors that would have opened are now closed.

No one at the seminary wants to look at my dissertation. I self-publish it as a book with the title *Search for the Center*. My topic is "Problems of the ego in altered states of consciousness, with particular reference to the experience of death." I distribute it free to a few friends, some of whom are good enough to read it. Some, like artist Wally Putnam, take the time to offer comments and suggestions. Wally has also been fascinated with the writings of Carlos Castaneda and has painted thirty-five pictures of scenes from the Castaneda material. In 1996, Michael Leach, my publisher at Crossroads, calls. Someone gave him a copy of *Search for the Center* and he wants to publish it. It is nearly twenty years old, and some of the ideas are now outdated. I would have to do a complete rewrite. At this point I have other projects in mind. If I had been at a California school that focused on Transpersonal Psychology, none of this would have happened. I am responsible for what I receive. The best way to handle this rejection is with grace. It isn't easy. I've done so much research, reading, writing and teaching. (Twenty-four years later, at age sixty, I'll finally earn a Ph.D.)

The End of the Season of Love

When bad ideas have nowhere else to go, they go to America and become university courses.—Frederic Raphael

With their finger ever on the prevailing pulse of the popular, the New School changes its emphasis to courses on how to make money in the stock market and real estate investing. They even offer a course on "Handicapping, or How to Make Money playing the Horses." And, they start offering courses on computers. My course on "Esoteric Philosophies of the Ancient Greek, Roman and Early Christian Eras" is undersubscribed for the first time. The head of the department says I have simply become "too esoteric." After a decade, my work at the New School comes to an end.

The seventies were a wonderful, exciting time. For ten years I've been given permission to teach whatever subjects I wanted, at one of the most progressive universities in America, in the heart of Greenwich Village, in this most diverse and exciting city. During the last five of these years I've been able to do the same thing at Wainwright House, the only major growth center in the metropolitan New York area. It's been a wonderful time. Most of that time I have lived and worked in Chelsea and Greenwich Village. Everything about the time was vibrant and exciting, alive and fresh. Something happened in the late seventies—the "sixties" came to an end. There had been vulnerability and a willingness to experiment with new ideas. Now, the doors are closing and there is a backlash to the openness of the seventies. I sincerely supported Jimmy Carter for president in 1976. I thought him a goodhearted, kind man. I'm sorry when he loses the election in 1980.

Now in the Reagan-Bush era, the United States begins a program of nuclear arms build-up. I had great sympathy for the hippie movement. Something "really different" *was* happening with the Dawning of the Age of Aquarius. The church is becoming increasingly conservative and those outside the church increasingly materialistic, with hippies becoming yuppies. Mainline Protestant churches are dying, and fundamentalist churches are shooting up in numbers and taking over on television. There is a push for mainline Protestant churches to take a more conservative stance, and the United Methodist church is caught in this right wing swing.

General Theological has ended. The New School has ended. Wainwright house has ended. I'm not going to be able to turn High Rock into a growth center. Several sources of income have dried up. I'm in the country; at least that is a relief. For the next eleven years I will try to make it as a United Methodist Minister. The first six of these years go fairly well. New members join the church and there is steady upward growth.

Rev. Randy, the previous pastor at Central Valley, had served at Windsor Terrace ahead of me. Before he leaves Central Valley, he takes me aside and warns me about a woman in the church. She was his friend and then turned on him. She had trouble with the previous pastor too. That had something to do with unrequited love. She wants to run the church. He is glad to be free of her. I should watch out. She seems to like me. I don't know what he is talking about. I don't see a problem here.

There is one positive development. I secure a position teaching Transpersonal Psychology for the Foundation for Religion and Mental Health in Briarcliff, New York. In the summer of '79 the Foundation asks me to put together two one-day Saturday seminars on Transpersonal Psychology. I do so with Father Michael, the Catholic priest who was present when Helen first told me about the Course, and with Kenneth Wapnick. Although Ken has previously met his future wife, Gloria, at a Course function on Long Island, this is the first time that I notice them smiling at each other with wide smiles. Gloria is almost glowing. Father Michael later becomes a hard-line Catholic and abjures his relationship to the Course. He also becomes something of a celebrity in the Catholic Church. I frequently see him on national Catholic television—looking much older, with his long squirrel-gray beard and matching cassock, explaining with authority the basic doctrines of the Catholic Church. I put a second Saturday workshop together with Dr. Thomas Hora on Meta-Psychiatry. Dr. Hora is talking about the principles of the Course before there is *A Course in Miracles*.

Kristian's Back

I'm in the church office on the phone with Ronnie Kahn, a musician for Interfaith services in New York City. Ronnie has written hundreds of songs. Perhaps the most popular is *Return Again*. He says, "You know, we have a mutual friend." I say, "Who's that?" and he says, "Lena Weihs." I say, "You're the first person to mention her name in seven years," and I ask him if she has ever mentioned her son Kristian. He says, "Yes, she says he's your son." I ask for her phone number and call. The conversation begins strangely with Lena saying, "The reason I called you . . ." She had just left a message on my answering machine at High Rock. Seven years to the day we call each other. She wants to use my name as a reference. Later, I realize it is a ruse to get us back in touch. She and Tommy are now divorced. I ask if she still claims that Kristian is my son and she says that he is. I ask if I can see him and she says, "Sure." I ask her if I can do so that evening and she says, "Sure."

I drive down to Park Slope in Brooklyn and find the brownstone, neatly arranged along with similar houses on a street lined with tall sycamores. Lena, Kristian and his two cousins, Jason and Richy, occupy the top floor. Lena's sister overdosed on heroin and Lena has inherited her sister's two sons. I knock and Kristian opens the door. He looks at me and his first words are, "I know you." "How," I ask, "can you know me?" "Because," he says, "you are the man with the same color hair as me." I look at Lena. She says, "I swear, I didn't put him up to that," and she has not, for he never mentions it again.

225

Lena and I become friends again. She and Kristian and the younger Richy start coming to High Rock for visits. Kristian and Richy will spend time with me each summer for the next nine years. They come for Thanksgiving and the Fourth of July. Tommy is playing the role of father in Kristian's life, so we don't tell him about his parentage. It's strange being around my own son and not being able to tell him I'm his father. It is also fine just to be able to get to know him and start to develop a relationship. Kristian will continue to play an increasingly important role in my life, coming to live with me when he is sixteen and later moving to nearby New Paltz.

As I am not going to be able to turn High Rock into a spiritual center, I have high hopes for Central Valley United Methodist. There is an energetic group of teachers in their mid-thirties to mid-forties looking for something new. I invite them to come to High Rock so we can talk about ways we can help Central Valley United Methodist become a place for spiritual development. I start *A Course in Miracles* study group at the church and sponsor a number of workshops with various leaders.

Ananda Ashram

Ananda Ashram is close to Central Valley, in nearby Harriman, so I venture up there to say hello. My time in India and my exploration of the teaching of various gurus has warmed my heart toward yoga and Hinduism. The founder of the Ashram is Dr. Mishra (Shri Brahmananda Sarasvati), a dark-skinned Indian man who is also a non-practicing medical doctor. It is not Dr. Mishra, however, but Vyasananda, a handsome, slightly balding Sanskrit scholar who becomes my friend.

Being the minister at Central Valley means being involved with the local clergy association, made up of other Protestant ministers, two parochial Catholic priests (one an unfortunate good-natured alcoholic), and the local "good to see ya," rotund little Rabbi. Not wishing to dilute the truth, as they understand it, the Baptist and other more fundamentalist congregations do not participate. After my visit to Ananda, I suggest to the clergy that there is another spiritual leader in the area, namely the head of the ashram, whom we might invite to a meeting. They agree, and the next month Vyasananda shows up and gives a talk about yoga, meditation, and life at the ashram. The next month I raise the question as to whether he should be invited to join. There is no thought of inviting him. His presentation was informative. He is not "clergy!"

226

Interested in Interfaith affairs and in improving community relations for the ashram, which is sometimes eyed with suspicion, I invite Dr. Mishra to speak at Central Valley. He shows up with a large entourage, mostly women in flowing white gowns. I must admit to feeling betrayed by Dr. Mishra. Dr. Mishra has long dark black hair. He comes to church wearing an all-red robe, carrying a black stick in his hand. Mounting the pulpit he closes his eyes and begins a long, drawn out "OM" which lasts at least ten minutes, though it seems more like twenty. Some of the congregates start to squirm uncomfortably. Some get up and walk out. One fundamentalist family flees thinking I have brought the very devil himself into the church. It's all too much. When he finishes what many think an interminable drone, he gives a nice talk about interfaith relationships.

This event blows the lid off. The next day, on Monday evening, an emergency meeting of the church board is held where it is made clear that I'm never again to ask anyone to speak from the pulpit that is not first approved by the Board. The only exception is another ordained United Methodist minister. The next day I call the conservative fellow who challenged me so ardently at the Board meeting—the one who got up and walked out of the church on Sunday. I ask if I can come by and talk. We sit on his couch facing each other. I ask him if he can look straight into my eyes without moving or saying anything. He tries. He simply cannot do it. He quits the church. Other members are glad to be free of his tyranny.

My salary at Central Valley creeps up at the rate of $1,000 a year. It is not enough to live on. I look around for part-time teaching, finding openings in introductory courses in Psychology, Sociology, Public Speaking, and Philosophy at nearby Harriman college. I begin working on the problem of money, as there never seems to be enough, and I sponsor a workshop at the church entitled, "Money and Personal Destiny." I'm determined to get at least one hundred people to attend the seminar and spend $300 on publicity. (The woman I thought my friend is outraged that I have spent so much money for promotion.) I get the local newspaper to print an article about the forthcoming workshop. One hundred people are present for the seminar and the church grosses $1,500. In the process of doing the research, I discover that a third of Jesus' parables are specifically about money. I do a sermon on each of Jesus' parables and put together a book entitled *Money and Jesus*, which I publish in the fall of '81. Only 1,000 copies are printed. They sell out within two years.

CHAPTER 30

That Was Zen—This Is Tao

A Synopsis of My Dissertation—*Search for the Center*

In order to understand *A Course in Miracles*, you can't leave the metaphysics far behind. My death experience and the reading of *The Tao of Physics* leads to a fascination with holography, and I meet and work with Itzak Bentov, sponsoring a workshop by him at High Rock. He has written a marvelous book on psychophysics entitled *Stalking the Wild Pendulum*. Itzak is tall and completely bald on top with thick dark hair along the sides. He has deep-set eyes below heavy dark eyebrows. He wears a big smile, as if he knows a secret. When he reads the account of my death experience, he laughs and tells his wife I stepped into one of the states of consciousness known in Tibetan Buddhism as "bardo." She laughingly seems to understand what he means.

A couple of weeks after the workshop, Itzak is killed when an engine on the DC-10 airliner on which he is a passenger falls off over O'Hare Airfield in Chicago. Everyone is lost. I later heard that after his death Itzak somehow contacted his wife and told her that, as he was boarding the plane he saw everything as all gray and dead looking. Yet, he deliberately boarded the plane knowing it would crash. I can only imagine that Itzak knew he was needed as a guide for these souls.

Itzak gave the following analogy as a means of understanding holography. Take a bucket of water. Hold three small balls above it. Drop the balls simultaneously into the water. When the balls hit the water, they create three rings, which move outward from the epicenter. As the waves cross, they produce ripples, resulting in an *apparent* chaotic movement on the surface of the water. If it were possible to instantaneously freeze the top half-inch of water we would have a pictogram of that surface.

Now, let's take a laser light, and shine it through that (picture) surface of the frozen ice. If we hold it up to the light and look through it, we see three balls *falling* toward ice. Even more interesting is what happens if we drop the ice on the floor, pick it up, and hold a sliver of ice before a laser light. Again we see three balls falling toward the surface. The information is recorded in the interference pattern. The whole is contained in the part.

Light waves produce the same complex wave patterns that are produced on the surface of the water. A laser—the purest form of light—sends out a beam of light in one frequency. When two laser beams meet, they produce an interference pattern. If a beam is reflected off an object and strikes a photographic plate, the plate will record the interference pattern, storing the image. When the right frequency of light strikes the plate, the original interference pattern is set up, creating a holographic image. What we see is an apparent three-dimensional form.

There are other illustrations for the holographic image such as an audio system that uses eighteen small, one-inch condenser speakers, instead of one eighteen-inch speaker to produce the same "image." Since the invention of the microscope and the telescope, we have been constructing our concepts of physical reality in a similar manner to what the biologist now knows about the structure of the DNA molecule or what the botanist knows about a seed. Seeds are transformed "through light" in a lower mode to become plants. An acorn is a hologram of an oak tree. A human zygote will prove it is a person.

Even more interesting evidence now presents itself. Physicist Alan Aspect and a team of researchers at the University of Paris have discovered that subatomic particles such as electrons are able to communicate instantaneously with each other regardless of the distance separating them. It doesn't matter if they are five feet apart or fifty billion miles apart. This violates Einstein's tenet that nothing can travel faster than the speed of light. Traveling at the speed of light is tantamount to breaking the time barrier. Of course, if there is no time, there is no time barrier to break. My death experience was an experience of a radically loaded "now." Everything was happening simultaneously rather than sequentially. Sequential time is part of a three-dimensional world. Sequential time is a way of enabling us to see points in a larger spectrum. This makes things comprehensible in our world.

Eternity or Timelessness

The dictionary defines eternity as *timelessness*. God lives in *timelessness*. Christ is *timeless*. You are *timeless*. Jesus stepped away from eternity and came into time. Yet, he never forgot eternity. When we come into this world, we, too, step away from eternity. Unlike Jesus, we get caught in time. We get caught in history. We get caught in our photograph albums and scrapbooks. We get caught in our stories, our "dreams" and we lose sight of eternity.

Each night in dreamless sleep we step back into the center. Each morning we step back into time. We step back into activity, and the soap opera of our everyday lives. Who is it that wakes us up each morning if not our ego? If everything is happening simultaneously, you could step back into any time, in any society—in any body. If I step into the twenty-first century, I see things differently than I would if I stepped into the seventeenth or the twenty-second century.

University of London physicist David Bohm says Aspect's findings imply that objective reality does not exist. Studies in subatomic physics "prove" that "objective" reality does not in fact, "cannot" exist. Everything is "subjective." Despite its apparent solidity, the universe is a hologram. The reason subatomic particles remain in contact with one another, regardless of distance, is not because they are sending signals back and forth. It's because *there is no separation!* Furthermore, it doesn't matter how far away something is because it's not really out there. It's in my mind. Knowing that one, wholly true Self, who is us and is beyond all thought of separation, brings us to the mind of God.

Christ is the link that keeps you one with God, and guarantees that separation is no more than an illusion of despair, for hope forever will abide in him.
—ACIM, W-p.II, p.431.Intro.6 2:1

Imagine an aquarium containing a fish. Now imagine that we have two different television cameras set up to monitor the fish, one camera faces the side of the aquarium, the other the front. We have two pictures of the same fish being photographed simultaneously. If you look simultaneously at two different television monitors of the same fish, you will see that when one turns the other turns at the exact same instant, though in a different direction. You might think these two fish are synchronistically moving together. The truth is, there is just one fish! There is just one God! The electrons in the human brain are connected to the subatomic particles contained in every meowing kitten, every shooting star, every beating heart, every snowflake, and every rose petal. Itzak said it's like we are all raisins in a huge cosmic bowl of jello. If the jello shakes it moves all the raisins.

In you is all of Heaven. Every leaf that falls is given life in you. Every bird that sang will sing again in you. And every flower that ever bloomed has saved its perfume and its loveliness for you. —ACIM, T-25. IV.4:10

Working independently in brain research, Karl Pribram was drawn to the holographic model by the puzzle of where memory is stored. While certain parts of the brain are clearly responsible for certain functions, such as sight, hearing, and so on, memory is within the whole brain, indeed even within the whole body. I watch on television the story of a woman who received a heart-lung transplant from an eighteen-year-old man. Later, she developed a craving for beer and chicken fingers, the young man's favorite meal.

Pribram believed memories are encoded in nerve impulses that crisscross the brain in the same way patterns of laser light interference crisscross a piece of film containing a holographic image. If one half of the brain is destroyed, half of one's memory is not destroyed. Monkeys with only two percent of brain nerve fibers can retain the information necessary for the function of the brain. The brain itself is a hologram. We need to go beyond the brain to the mind, which is independent of the body, yet ever connected to the Mind of God. The mind is the decision-maker—the brain, the machine. In human thinking, every piece of information instantly correlates with every other piece of information.

There is No World

If the concreteness of the world is a secondary reality, and what is "there" is a holograph of frequencies, and if the brain is a hologram that selects some of the frequencies out of this blur and transforms them into sensory perception, "objective" reality ceases to exist.

There is no world! This is the central thought the course attempts to teach.
—ACIM, W-p.I.132.6: 2

There is no world apart from our *interpretation* of the world. The material world is maya. Telepathy can be understood as accessing at the holographic level. People using psychotropics have accessed memories of ancient times or even reptilian brains. Mother went back to the Civil War during her death experience. The belief in separation *is* the ego. It is impossible to think a thought outside of the mind of God. Persisting in trying to do so gives birth to the ego, the body (the ego's chosen home) and the world. Trying to make our own world is our own misery. Physical birth is yet dreaming sleep. What is needed is awakening or rebirth. Unless we are born of Spirit, we are not yet fully alive.

I once asked a young man who had a number of mystical experiences how far he had gone. He answered, "Where?" My question implied there was a height to which he could ascend, or a depth or width of consciousness he might have attained. These are spatial, temporal limitations. Space and time are ego perspectives. The mystical state is timeless.

> *On this side of the bridge to timelessness you understand nothing. But as you step lightly across it, upheld by timelessness, you are directed straight to the Heart of God. At its center, and only there, you are safe forever, because you are complete forever.* —ACIM, T-16. IV.13:6

Timelessness "is" our only reality. "God and the soul," says Meister Eckhart, "are not in space-time." They belong rather to the realms that are intrinsically or essentially real. Time ends where there is no before or after. We perceive a shadow of the real, living in a world created and sustained by our own cognition.

> *It is believed by most that time passes; in actual fact, it stays where it is. This idea of passing may be called time, but it is an incorrect idea, for since one sees it only as passing, one cannot understand that it stays just where it is.* —Zen Master Dogen

Time stands still. We move. If you can totally still the mind, you can see it.

> *Now you must learn that only infinite patience produces immediate effects. This is the way in which time is exchanged for eternity. Infinite patience calls upon infinite love, and by producing results "now," it renders time unnecessary.* —ACIM, T-5.VI.12:1-3

When we don't have to live in time, when we don't have to live up to an image or be caught up in our drama, we can have a glimpse of eternity. It is possible to so live in the moment that past and future lose their significance. Each of us has *tasted* living in the moment. I had it on the farm in Missouri, and I can have it again whenever I allow it. A worried mind rehearses guilt and projects a fearful future. When we lose our body, our immediate form of identity with space and time, by necessity we look to a greater reality. If the body is not our primary reality, its past and its projected future disappear. Only the moment exists. This "is" the mystical experience.

Jesus remembers God as his father. He "is" God's Son and Heaven "is" His home. Coming home we step out of the "trap of time." It is possible to so live in the present that past and future fail to imprison us. The world of sin, guilt, and fear lock us in time—in the story. There is no guilt or fear in Heaven. Were we as centered as Jesus, we would have no guilt or fear. Jesus steps from eternity into time and teaches us about eternity. Eternity is a perfect place. It is our home. We always have been and will be eternal. I'm not suggesting reincarnation. Reincarnation is a time-bound concept. Everything outside of the present moment is a conceptual delusion.

There is no road to travel on, and no time to travel through.
—ACIM, T-13.I.7: 3

The Holy Instant

Any moment can be a holy instant of forgiveness and peace. In the holy instant, we transcend our limited view of ourselves and others, let go of our soap operas, drop our personal histories and step out of time. The only thing that dies in time is that which is mortal. The body is finite. Spirit is eternal. Jesus stepped away from the center and came into time. Unlike you and I, he never forgot the center. He never got caught up in the projection of guilt. Though dramas developed around him, he never got caught in the drama. Eternity remained alive inside him regardless of what happened on the outside. He understood there is nothing to defend.

The Sonship is not out there "somewhere." Heaven is not to be found in the future. Eternity is now, and our task is no more complicated than to joyfully "be here now." We can be happy this moment. Not for a single moment do we need to wait. What Jung referred to as "meaningful" synchronistic events occur as meaningful interference patterns collide. Miracles occur as a perfectly natural process. It is no accident that we are in contact with exactly the people who fill our lives. Mystics see the "implicit order in things" as opposed to the "explicit," or external, order. When Jesus said, "Heaven is within you," he meant it literally—not in our bodies—in the mind, which is forever connected with the Mind of God.

You are but asked to let the future go, and place it in God's Hands and you will see by your experience that you have laid the past and present in His Hands as well, Because the past will punish you no more, and future dread will now be meaningless.—ACIM, W-p I.194.4: 5-6

Through my death experience and subsequent study of the new physics or psychophysics, I am seeing things in a *wholly,* and thus more *holy,* new way. I'm trying to work in everything I've been learning from esoteric and mystical philosophies and from Dr. Itzak Bentov, Dr. John Lilly, Dr. Salvador Roquet, Dr. Stanislof Groff, Dr. Stanley Kripner, Dr. Harold Putoff, Dr. Michael Harner, Dr. Thomas Hora, Dr. John Johnson Jr., Dr. Helen Schucman, Dr. William Thetford, Dr. Ken Wapnick, and *A Course in Miracles* into my doctoral dissertation. (If only, these people could have made up my doctoral committee!) Now I have to come back to the world of work and form and function and live like an ordinary human being. The world will soon become "way too ordinary."

CHAPTER 31

Three Failed Romances

Three failed relationships in as many years are more likely to force you into awakening than three years on a desert island or shut away in your room.
—Eckhart Tolle, *The Power of Now*

1980—Age Thirty-Seven

Why do women have to be so beautiful and so enchanting? And why this sex drive? Life would be easier without it. It would also be less interesting. For me, the eighties are dominated by three heartbreaking relationships. In January, Carol moves out of High Rock and goes to live with Shanti in New York City. I will forever be committed to Carol—to her happiness and her well-being. Carol is later to become a disciple of Dr. Mishra and live at Ananda Ashram. She is still one of my best friends and the truest mystic I know.

I start dating "Susan," a recently divorced, new member at Central Valley. Susan is a brunette with long fluffy hair and the most wonderful giggle. She is seven years my senior with four daughters, each of whom is a delight. Susan is into yoga and takes to *A Course in Miracles* like a duck to water. I've now stepped back into a situation similar to the one with Edie, a woman seven years older and not interested in having any more children. Susan is a schoolteacher and we start hanging out with other schoolteacher friends. Kristian comes to stay with me. Susan falls for Kristian and the three of us have a great time together.

The eighties are a wonderful time at High Rock. I enjoy gardening and I'm able to practice early morning meditation. Edie calls to say she has fallen in love with a wonderful man, a gestalt psychologist also named Jon. They are going to be married. Can I perform the ceremony? Furthermore, they are moving to Pound Ridge, so we will be neighbors. Edie shares a love of gardening and wants to take advantage of the effulgent emerald pachysandra on the hillside at High Rock Spring. Edie and I went our separate ways because she did not want to have any more children while I did. A year into her marriage she calls to say she is pregnant. At forty-four, she gives birth to her daughter Lauren.

There are two stages of ordination in the Methodist church. In 1970 I was ordained as a Deacon. Now, ten years later I'm to be ordained an Elder. This is a bit like getting tenure. At the Annual Conference in June, just hours before the ordination ceremony, I am taken aside by my District Superintendent and told that the Board of Ordained Ministry is aware of my experiences with psychotropics. It's not a problem. All I have to do is say that I'm sorry, repent of my waywardness, and promise not to do it again. I am not sorry. It was a very important experience. Although I've not had any such experience since 1978 and never will again, I "will not promise" that I will never do it again. My candor does not go over well. I am ordained an Elder as I meet all of the other qualifications and it is really too late to start raising objections now. My defiance is not to be forgotten.

Four Methodist ministers and their families move into Central Valley and become members of the church. Each of them works for the National Board of Ministry in New York City. I become especially close to Paul and Shari Morton and their two sons. Shari becomes my secretary, and with her skills, we are able to get things done at the church as never before—especially the development of an excellent newsletter. There are also Roy and Dorothy Katayama. Roy is a Japanese-American who works for the Board of Missions. There is also an Indian man married to an American woman. They have beautiful twin girls and two younger children. Suddenly, we have an active youth group. None of these ministers are members of the New York Conference. They are all executives who commute into the city to work. They are excellent assistants on Sundays. Things are working really well at Central Valley.

Ken Wapnick moves to Gloria's house in Ardsley, New York. I go to see him for one of my annual spiritual checkups. Whenever I meet with Ken, I ask him what his next step is, and he tells me in a simple, direct fashion. He is working on a Glossary. He and Gloria are going to get married. He has decided to incorporate The Foundation for A Course in Miracles. What is amazing is his remarkable clarity and the precise manner in which he inevitably does exactly what he says he is going to do. He follows steps one, two, and three as he sees the need to take them. I ask him about setting goals. He says it is not about goals. It's about doing what you are being asked to do. "The question," he says, "is not 'Why can't I hear the voice of the Holy Spirit?' The question is, 'Why don't I do what he asks me to do, so I can follow him even better?'"

236

December 8th, one of my heroes, John Lennon, is shot to death by a crazed fan outside his residence, The Dakota, in Manhattan. A line from one of his songs, "The dream is over" echoes poignantly through my mind. I go home to Missouri for Christmas, call Judy Femmer and we meet in a country western bar. We dance together and as I hold her, we look into each other's eyes and sing, "Can I have this dance for the rest of my life? Would you be my partner every night?" We decide to get together for our twentieth high school reunion in August of 1981.

1981—Age Thirty-Eight

Helen becomes ill in 1980 and dies from pancreatic cancer on Sunday, February 9, 1981. Ken calls on Monday morning to tell me of the funeral plans. Ken said she had a wonderful look of peace on her face after her death. He is convinced Jesus came to her. Ken gives an eloquent eulogy in which he discusses Helen's devotion to God, a strange eulogy for an atheist. At the request of Helen's husband Louis, Ken never mentions *A Course in Miracles*.

After the funeral, I spend some time with Jerry Jampolsky and we drive in a small convoy of cars, to a cemetery on Staten Island. It is a gray, foggy day. The black wrought-iron fences surrounding the graves are barely visible, giving an uncanny, dreamlike quality to the moment. Helen's last words to Judy were, "You know why I'm going, don't you? I have to get out of its way." By "it," she meant the Course. It was disquieting to Helen that people were misinterpreting the Course. Helen, like the rest of us, had an ongoing dialogue with God. Hers got written out loud. Judy said there were three men Helen loved as sons. They were Ken Wapnick, Joe Jannis, and myself. There were thus, three sons and one daughter—Judy. There was never any doubt about Ken's being the number one "son." Joe Jannis was a priest. I was a protestant minister. Ken and Judy were both born Jews. I was the younger, naive, and somewhat mischievous son, whom Helen had to help sort through problems. Ken is an excellent older brother. If only I followed his advice.

High Rock Graphics and the Birth of *The Mustard Seed*

I go home to Missouri in May for my thirty-eighth birthday and I get to see Judy Femmer. We're going to our twentieth high school reunion together. What a kick this is going to be, to show up together after twenty years! Judy comes over to the house to see Mother. Mother looks at Judy and says, "Very few people get a second chance in life, Judy." Judy says, "I know." Judy's children, Jean and Jeff, are now adults. Now, maybe we really *can* get it together.

One of the families from Central Valley is moving. The father says since I write out all my sermons, he is wondering if he gives me one dollar per week, would I be willing to make a copy of the sermon, put a stamp on an envelope, and send it to him? I say I would. As long as I'm making a copy for him, I can send one to Mother, and Ann, Judy Femmer, Judy Halpin, Edie, Shanti Rica, Carol Rollinger, Myron and a few other friends. This is starting to get expensive. If anyone else wants a copy they, too, will have to give me one dollar per week.

I put three hundred dollars down on a Varityper 510 II typesetter and begin a small typesetting business called High Rock Graphics. I'm now able to produce professional-looking church newsletters and worship bulletins. When I started *Seeker* back in the mid-seventies, I realized that to be successful I would need to own typesetting equipment. I take my message from the previous Sunday. I add seasonal material, jokes, stories, poems and more. I buy church worship bulletins and use them for covers. Slowly, slowly, *The Mustard Seed* begins to grow. I'm doing most of the work myself along with one full-time and two part-time employees. Other than Sheri Morton, no one at Central Valley is interested in my inspirational magazine.

The woman the former pastor warned me about seems to be a good friend. She got quite excited about my coming to Central Valley. Things change. In the summer of '81 she calls the district superintendent to tell him a teenage boy has called her and told her he and other friends have decided to spend their summer following Susan and me about. They saw us making love in the woods and thought she should know about it. Why would teenage boys, ones I do not know and who do not know me, and who have no knowledge of my erratic schedule, want to take the time to follow Susan and me about? Don't they have more important things to do? Susan isn't even a high school teacher. She teaches kindergarten, first and second grades. Her students would not be interested in her activities. It doesn't make any sense. Why would they call *this* particular woman, of all people?

Susan and I are dating openly. Our relationship is not a state secret. Yet, the Methodist church has a policy. Single ministers are to remain celibate. This is one policy with which I'm never in agreement. Sexuality is a wonderful way for a man and a woman to get to know each other. Celibacy is great for monks who willingly take such vows. I am not a monk. I'm now charged with violating the policy of the United Methodist church, and a trial is held, conducted by the district superintendent and the members of the board of trustees of the church.

I'm acquitted because the boys who have charged me with this transgression never gave their names and never show up as accusers. Therefore, all there is is hearsay. I do not understand, *at first*, that the boys never existed. The strange part is Susan and I did make love in the woods, in exactly the place reported to the district superintendent. It was some twenty miles' distance from the church. It was a long walk from the road. For someone to have seen us in that remote spot, they would have had to have followed us. Though I'm acquitted, the trial has its effect. My relationship with the district superintendent, already on shaky ground, slips precariously. I've about had it with the church. Susan and I are both single adults. What we do on our own private time is no one else's business.

Susan is not happy about my going to Missouri to take an old girlfriend to our twentieth high school reunion. Just days before I'm to return to Missouri, Judy calls and says she has other plans. She is going to Texas with friends. We will not be going to the reunion together. She goes to the reunion with Larry Campbell, a former basketball player from high school. They later marry and, after a few years, divorce.

Rabbi Gelberman comes up with another creative idea. He wants to start an Interfaith Seminary, which he plans to call The New Seminary. As with the beginning of Interfaith in 1977, I'm not sure it will work. Again I say I will help out. As it turns out, Rabbi is a major visionary. He has put his finger on something important. There are lots of adults who feel called to be involved in ministry. They do not have the time to go through a three-year, full-time residential program, and are not interested in being ordained through a traditional Christian denomination. They need another approach to ministry. Rabbi finds that way.

The United Nations declares 1981 "The Year of the Child," and a number of observances are planned. Some people at the United Nations hear of Interfaith. They come to meet with the Rabbi, myself and members of our executive committee. A celebration is planned at the Beacon theater on Broadway. As the program of speakers and musicians develops, it is decided that as the main producer for the event, I will be the emcee. It is a spectacular event, the biggest thing Interfaith has ever been involved in. Many of the better-known swamis, rabbis, priests and ministers are invited. An unfortunate thing happens. Dr. Mishra is among those invited to speak. At the proper time he goes out onto the stage, sits down and he goes into one of his long OM drones.

At events like this, everything is planned to the minute, and each speaker or musician only has a few minutes. Dr. Mishra is going on and on, oming away. His time is up and he still hasn't said anything. A petite Japanese woman, a stage director for the event, and an official from the United Nations, starts repeating, "What *is* he doing?" What he is doing is "his thing," the same thing he did at Central Valley. She insists that the curtain be dropped. After a little commotion, it is dropped. When it falls, it nearly hits the still oming Dr. Mishra. His disciples now get upset, thinking I'm the one who ordered the curtain dropped. I'm unable to assuage or in any way appease their anger. So much for my working on positive community relations with the ashram. Many of my friends love and respect Dr. Mishra. They've spent a lot more time with him than I did. I certainly love and respect them and the choices they've made in life. Dr. Mishra dies in September 1993. I go to his funeral. I'm sorry I did not know him better. Dr. Mishra never appointed a successor. After his death, a board of trustees runs the Ashram. They get caught in a power struggle.

I come home one evening from a church board meeting. As I open the door at High Rock, Joyful Dog awakes from her sleep and jumps off the couch to come greet me. As she jumps, she falls and twists her back and begins barking looking to be in great pain. I run to her, and as I touch her, she bites my hand, tearing away the flesh between my thumb and fingers. I'm bleeding so badly I have to take care of my own wound first. I call an emergency veterinarian service and take her to a vet who tells me she has ruptured a disk in her back. It's not clear what to do. He can put her down, or there is a chance she will come out of it. He is not sure. I cannot put her down. She can no longer walk; only drag her back end with her front legs. I take a log-carrying device Mother made and hold her in it so that her front and back legs just touch the floor. I try to get her to use her back legs again. I place her food away from her across the room so she will have to drag herself over to the bowl. I keep working with her in the wood carrier and eventually, slowly, like an indomitable old turtle, she begins to walk. Her running and jumping days are over.

October the 4, 1981 is the 800th birthday of St. Francis of Assisi. I've put together a slide show on the life of St. Francis as seen through great works of art, which I produce for Interfaith at Christ Church United Methodist on 60th St. and Park Ave in New York City. At the end of the service an older man with brilliant white hair, wearing a leather vest and a white shirt, comes up to me with a large manila envelope in which he has a picture. It is clearly a picture of Jesus. There is just no other possibility. It is, however, a photograph, not a painting. He tells me that he took a picture of an altar of a church in California. When he developed the photo this picture of Jesus came out. He says I'm supposed to have it. I have it to this day on the wall next to my desk. I never see the man again.

Susan and I grow closer after the trial. It's interesting being mutually persecuted. Despite what has happened, everyone is genuinely supportive. Most people understand what *really* happened. Susan holds a surprise party for my twentieth anniversary in the ministry. All the members of the church are invited. It seems like a payoff for what had happened. It is a delightfully positive time. The choir writes two songs just for the occasion. I remember a few lines. One peppy song based on a Broadway tune runs, "Consider yourself, at home . . . Consider yourself, part of the family...." Another runs, "We used to see empty pews, congregational blues, my, my." The pews are filling up. Things are looking up.

1982—Age Thirty-Nine

The well-known folk singer, Odetta, comes to Interfaith, and I get her to give a concert at Central Valley, which packs the church, bolstering our presence in the community. We are growing and glowing. For the next few years only the larger churches in Middletown and Newburgh will report greater additions to their church rolls.

Harriman college closes and I transfer to Mercy College in Dobbs Ferry, New York, and I start teaching in Sing-Sing, Taconic, Down State, Otisville and Bedford Hills Correctional Institution for Women. Mercy College lets me go back to teaching courses on the Psychology of Religion and World Religions. Gone are the days, however, when I can make up my own courses. Working with people who have been through hard knocks is rewarding. We teachers do not know our students' crimes. "Lisa," signs up for each of the different classes that I teach. She is bright and energetic. She not only reads the books I assign, she reads even more than I ask. She is an A+ student. She always sits in the front row, and we enjoy sparring with each other with little intellectual jokes and jabs. My class seems to be the highlight of her week. One evening I ask another of the teachers if she has Lisa as a student. She says she does and isn't she wonderful. Then she says, "You know she drowned her daughter in a bathtub." I am taken aback. Would I have been so free of judgment, if I had known her crime, before I got to know and admire her?

In 1996 governor George Pataki rescinds funding for prisons. People were concerned that tax money was being used to teach prisoners. Courses in philosophy, religion, and psychology are important in helping them deal with their incarceration, giving them something "worthwhile" to do and helping restore a sense of self-esteem.

I take a two-day seminar on time management. We are assigned a partner for the weekend. My partner is Ken Blanchard. He shows me a book he has written called *The One-Minute Manager*. During the breaks he's on the phone talking to a radio station and his manager. It always appears that he uses his time wisely. He gives me an autographed copy of his book and tells me that before the end of the year it is going to be on the bestseller list. In October, *The One-Minute Manager* hits the bestseller list and it stays there for ten years, with innumerable spin-offs.

1983—Age Forty

Whenever we are at the changing of a year or the changing of an age (especially when passing a milestone), we think about change ourselves. Approaching my fortieth birthday, I need to be more honest with Susan. Though I love this vibrant, radiant woman, she is seven years older than I am, and I'm still thinking about having children other than Kristian—children that I might grow up with myself.

Without a clear-cut, positive goal, set at the outset, the situation just seems to happen, and makes no sense until it has already happened. No goal was set with which to bring the means in line. And now the only judgment left to make is whether or not the ego likes it; is it acceptable, or does it call for vengeance? —ACIM, T-17.VI.3: 1-4:2

I went into this relationship without serious forethought. I never expected our relationship to evolve into marriage. In May of '83, Myron and I hold a party at High Rock for our fortieth birthdays. Susan is not happy. At the party she accuses me of flirting with another woman. I'm unable to conciliate her anger and she leaves the party in a huff. She is right. Our time has come to an end.

242

Susan isn't the only loss. I also lose my love—my Joyful Dog. Her arthritis has gotten really bad. She's been going deaf and blind for some time, and now she's got cancer. I hold on to her for as long as I can, actually too long. I just don't want to let go. Now, she's in pain. I finally resolve that tomorrow I will take her to the vet and have her put down. She dies during the night, and I find her cold body on her bed next to the wood burning stove. I bury her by the rock that says High Rock Spring. As I dig the grave, I'm crying so hard I cannot see, my eyes so filled with tears.

I've been looking for a way to become more involved with the Methodist hierarchy, thinking it might improve my relationship with the church. When an opening becomes available on the conference communications committee, I volunteer. A few months later I become the editor of *Update,* the conference newsletter for the United Methodist church of New York. Being involved with the newsletter means I now have my finger on the goings-ons of the New York Conference of the United Methodist Church. With my typesetting equipment I'm able to give the conference newsletter a more "professional" look. I enjoy this work. I'm even reimbursed ninety dollars per issue, for expenses.

I sponsor another workshop with Ken Wapnick in New York City and another at High Rock. There is a terrible infestation of gypsy moths that devours nearly all the leaves on the trees in the Northeast. As we sit outside at High Rock listening to Ken, the droppings from tens of thousands of these little creatures fall so constantly it sounds like gently falling rain.

Doris

Susan and I split on my fortieth birthday in May. In June, I meet "Doris" while leading *A Course in Miracles* Workshop at Ananda Ashram. The reason I'm protecting her privacy will soon be clear. Though I have not seen or talked to her since 1985 when she moved to California, I assume that she is out there somewhere, and it is my prayer that she is leading a happy and fulfilling life.

Doris is tall, blonde, one of the most beautiful women I have ever met. She is bright. She is good with children. She is also a deeply troubled manic-depressive. I'm later to discover that her father horribly abused her. She is to tell me stories so appalling, I cannot repeat them. Suffice it to say that she was abused from her earliest memories until the time she was eighteen and married to escape her father. She didn't tell me about this abuse in the beginning, and we were together for several weeks before I learned the cause of her deep disturbance.

She also keeps from me her dependency on a variety of prescription drugs, which she keeps in a small blue overnight case. She is going to two different psychiatrists at the same time, getting different drugs from each. The first time we go away together I get a look into her blue case. It is filled with pills. On the positive side there are vitamins, minerals and herbs. There are also antidepressants to keep her from getting too high, mood elevators to keep her from getting too low, and tranquilizers to even her out. She takes a Xanax every few hours. She is high or low or somewhere in between. It is hard to know where. She suffers from PMS, something I have no prior knowledge of, and panic attacks. She has candida, yeast infections, and severe allergies. She is especially allergic to mold spores. High Rock is built on a slab and is often damp, so the environment of my home is impossible for her. She later tells me that the first day she walked into High Rock, she knew she would never be able to stay there.

From the middle of 1983 to early 1985, Doris dominates much of my life, as I fall rather precipitously in love with this tantalizing beauty. There is much that is exciting about her. For the first time in my life I go skiing. I love being out in the bright sunlight and snow. Doris received her divorce from her first husband a few weeks prior to our meeting. She has her own apartment in Nanuet, New York. Though it is high and dry on the second floor and has wooden floors, she has to keep air-purifying equipment running in each of the rooms. She is working as a teacher for learning disabled students. She has great empathy for the kids, and I think she might make a good mother. As she cannot stay at High Rock, I visit her often.

My romance with Doris is rocky almost from the beginning. On evenings when I do not have to be at a church meeting or I'm not teaching, I go to see her. I never know *whom* I'm going to see. One evening it is a wonderful, together woman who has a candlelight dinner waiting. The next day there is no thought of dinner, the house is a mess, and the woman I meet at the door has disheveled hair. She's wearing a bathrobe and spewing out observations about the various flaws she notices in my character. Her ex-husband, Dan, later tells me this is one of the strangest parts of their relationship—never knowing which Doris you are coming home to. I later learn that she was suffering from disassociative identity disorder, fairly common among the severely abused.

Intelligent and beamingly beautiful, many things are right on the surface. I want very much for this relationship to work. I keep hanging in because the together woman is so wonderful. Doris is seven years younger than I am. She has never had any children, and wants to. A few weeks into the relationship, I have one of my annual conversations with Ken. He says he understands I'm in a new relationship, congratulating me, and asks if this is "it." I assure him that "it" is.

1984—Age Forty-One

I sponsor another workshop with Ken. Concerned about suspicious neighbors, at the last minute, I move the workshop to a friend's home in order to avoid a possible violation notice from the zoning board. I still want to have a center and continue to look for a better place. I find a possible place in Crompond, New York. The main house has been added onto many times, with extensions running out along the back right and left side of the house around a swimming pool. It is closer to Central Valley and will cut my commuting time in half. There is not a lot of parking. There is plenty of room inside for offices and workshops. I put High Rock on the market. A buyer doesn't show. Later, I'm talking to Ken. He is still working from Gloria's house in Ardsley. He needs a place where he can run his workshops. He has put a binder on just such a place in Crompond. It is, of course, the place I'm aiming for.

I take Doris to Missouri for Christmas of 1983, and the following August we venture back again. From Missouri, we swing down through Kentucky, finding opportunities for horseback riding and exploring Mammoth cave, then north for a tour of Washington, D.C. We leave Washington, D.C. on Labor Day and head back to New York. Doris is particularly unhappy about having to go back to work. Shortly after breakfast, she lays into me and does not stop all the way home. I'm trapped in the car with no way to get away from a five-hour diatribe. I try answering her. Soon I see it is futile, so I say nothing. There is nothing I can say. Fighting back would be unproductive. It would only make her angrier than she already is. Her eyes have a wild fire in them—like a mad dog. She is completely out of control and knows it. She cannot stand the fact that I have so little money. Dan had money. She is used to having money. Why don't I quit the damn church and get a "real" job? I will never write the books I want to write—why don't I quit kidding myself. I grin and bear it.

*Tolerance for pain may be high, but it is not without limit. Eventually every-one begins to recognize, however, dimly, that there **must** be a better way. As this recognition becomes more firmly established, It becomes a turning point.*
—ACIM, T-2.III.3: 5-6

I come to an internal resolve. I have to get out of this relationship. There is no way I can help her. I'm too immersed in this monstrous mess to know how to help. Loving her isn't enough. No matter how gentle I am, there are always problems. I have come to respect Dan. I understand why he *had* to leave. How did I get myself into this mess?

As Doris unlocks the door to her apartment, the phone is ringing. It is my sister Ann. Daddy has died. I have to come home immediately. As upsetting as it is to hear that Daddy has died, I feel a sense of relief. I'm going to go home to Missouri without Doris. I can take a walk in the back pasture. Maybe I can find some clarity. At home en route to Daddy's fu-neral, Mother looks at me and says, "Jon, Doris—No!" That's all she says. I have already made up my mind. Mother just adds the exclamation mark.

Doris does not want me to leave and suggests we go into therapy to-gether, which we do. One Friday evening in early December, we go to see a well-known couples therapist in Manhattan. Doris is very high on something. I do not know what. She probably doesn't know either. The therapist tries to talk her down without much success. Afterward, at a nearby Mexican restaurant, she has not one, nor two, but three margaritas. This I know is not a good idea. Her conversation becomes animated and explosive. She starts a harangue about what an idiot the therapist is and decides that after our meal we are going back to his office to tell him just exactly what kind of an s.o.b. he is. I beg her not to do this, to no avail. As soon as the meal is over, she storms out of the restaurant, down the street, through his waiting room, and straight into his office without knocking. He has someone else in session. That makes no difference. She tells him exactly what she thinks of him. I keep begging her to stop.

On the way home she falls sound asleep in the car. When we get to her apartment, she starts in on me. Impetuously, she swings and hits me. I had not expected to be hit. That one blow knocks me to the floor. She now starts kicking me, flailing her arms and legs with her elbows tucked in next to her body—like someone inadequately electrocuted. I lie on the floor in a fetal position, with my arms up over my face trying to protect myself. I keep saying, "Stop it, baby! Stop it, baby!" She stops, goes into the bedroom and collapses on the bed. Within minutes, seconds even, she is sound asleep. I'm not seriously hurt. I go in and lie down beside her. Sleep is impossible.

I finally sleep for an hour or so near morning. I awake knowing she will sleep through the morning. Tomorrow is Sunday, and I have to prepare. I write a note, and go back to my office at High Rock. At one p.m. she calls, mad as hell that I have gone. I try reason, saying I have work to do and she needed the rest. She now threatens suicide. She has enough pills. She is just going to kill herself. She hangs up the phone. I call back. There is no answer. She might do it! She might actually do it! She tried it before with Dan. I call the police in Nanuet and tell them the story. I hop into my car and drive as fast as I can to her apartment, a good forty minutes from High Rock. When I get there, an ambulance and a police car are parked in front of her apartment building. They are taking Doris out of the apartment strapped down on a stretcher. She is as hysterical as a tree full of chickens, shrieking and screaming obscenities. Like something out of the exorcist, she disgorges her vitriolic madness out onto everyone nearby, oblivious to the neighbors watching from their windows or standing around with folded arms. I'm terribly embarrassed and keep apologizing. Doris spends the next two weeks locked in a mental ward. Dan and I visit at the same time. Afterward, we go out for dinner together. He predicts that this will happen again. I hope not. This is definitely the end for me.

1985—Age Forty-Two

Bishop "Black" takes over as head of the New York Conference. I receive a letter dismissing me as editor of *Update*. No explanation is given. Bishop Black looks a great deal like Chief Supreme Court Chief Justice William Rehnquist. At a Spring Retreat for Methodist ministers I seek him out and take him aside. I want to see if I can get back onboard. I have ideas about how to improve the newsletter. It is soon clear that we march to the beat of different drummers. He is not interested in my ideas. His eyes narrowed, his jaw is set so tight, it's a wonder it doesn't lock. He is as unemotional as an umpire and he's clearly just waiting for me to stop. My words falling on deaf ears, I stop. This man, whom I have never met before, has made up his mind. Nothing I say matters. I excuse myself and leave. I'm so upset that I leave the retreat altogether. I need to drive, to try to think. He and the district superintendent are friends. The district superintendent does not approve of my unorthodox approach to ministry. He probably told him about the incident with Susan. Little do I realize how menaced he is by my teaching of *A Course in Miracles*. And my relationship with Doris, as far as the hierarchy of the church is concerned, is just another misadventure. On this point, they are right!

I once heard John Gray, author of *Men are from Mars, Women are from Venus,* say that mid-life crisis hits about the age of forty-two. It's safe to say that at forty-two I'm in my "terrible forty-twos" and clearly in a mid-life crisis. I am not prepared to continue to see myself as a small-church pastor, locked into a low-paying profession. Over a six-year period, my salary has risen from $9,000 to $15,000 a year, a half to a third of what the teachers at Central Valley, with the same number of years of experience (and even less education) are earning.

I still have my study group on *A Course in Miracles* at High Rock and I'm enjoying the work on *The Mustard Seed*. I'm enjoying teaching at Sing Sing and the women's prison in Bedford, New York. I always begin the class with a joke and enjoy teasing various students. The students at Bedford honor me at the end of the term with an award as "most popular teacher."

I feel as if I'm supposed to be doing something more. Pastoral success is measured in commitment to the denomination and to the numbers: membership, attendance, budget, offerings, building programs. The reward is an increase: higher salary and more perks. From the time I turn forty and each year thereafter, I ask for a larger and more substantial church. Year after year I'm told nothing is available, even when something is.

The surface of the earth is soft and impermissible by the feet of men; and so with the paths, which the mind travels. How worn and dusty, then, must be the highways of the world, How Deep the ruts of tradition and conformity!
—Henry David Thoreau, *Walden*

Routines as such are dangerous, because they easily become gods in their own right, threatening the very goals for which they were set up. —ACIM, M.16.2:5

I'm naive in assuming that it will be easy to change things in Central Valley. The degree to which tradition rules is astonishing, and small towns do not easily accept what they do not understand. I failed to recognize the tribal nature of my setting, its lines of authority and boundaries. I plan programs that, I think, are worthwhile. I have lots of enthusiasm and ideas about what we can do to make this an exciting church. That's fine. Some of my ideas, are a little too innovative. Committees do everything. There are reasons why certain things cannot or should not be done. How many Methodists does it take to change a light bulb? The answer is fifteen, one to change the light bulb, and two committees to approve the change. Though I am the pastor, I'm still an outsider. As a woman once told Rev. John Shelby Spong, "Son, this church was here long before you came, and it will be here long after you are departed."

> *You are not at peace because you are not fulfilling your function.*
> —ACIM, T- 4.I. 9:4

Once the preoccupation with the relationship with Doris ends, I'm able to get back to working on a book about *A Course in Miracles.* I've been "off course." I've not been doing what I've been called to do. If you don't know what you are supposed to be doing that is one thing. If you do know and you're not doing it, it's another matter all together. When it comes to the Course, I think of my life as that of Jonah and the whale. The call could not have been clearer. It came from Helen herself—actually it came from Jesus! I have allowed for a million distractions. Ken, it seems, is clearly listening to his inner guidance, doing what he is called to do. Though I've heard the call, I've been diverted.

I dig in and get to work. I put together the first draft of *Awaken to Your Own Call,* a book that will finally see its way to the light in 1993. At last I'm doing what I'm supposed to do. I have no idea how or when it will be published. I have faith that it will. I send Myron the chapters as I finish them. He edits and sends them back my way. In order to take *The Mustard Seed* to a higher level, I hire a new employee—Jackie Bolander. Jackie has a big head of light blonde hair and a wonderful smile. She looks a bit like the actress Doris Day. Neat, well organized and a good artist, she will become another good friend.

Though we are no longer dating, the connection with Doris goes on mostly via the phone, mostly just as friends. Then she takes off for California to make amends with her parents. There she becomes pregnant by a man who works for her father in the carpet laying business. She calls and asks to borrow $500. I send it her way. I know it's a gift—not a loan. I later hear that when she got pregnant, her doctors told her that unless she gave up drugs she would not have a normal baby. Apparently, she went cold turkey and it straightened her out. I hope so. I heard she had a beautiful, blond baby boy. She is a beautiful, sensitive woman who deserves much more happiness than she was experiencing. I am sorry for whatever pain I caused her.

Out of the Frying Pan into the Fire

After the dust of the disaster of Doris has cleared, I take a deep breath and date no one for a while. Then, one day after church, I notice "Jane" standing and smiling a very pretty smile. Jane had been a member at Central Valley but dropped out to join a fundamentalist church. She has returned to Central Valley, I think because she knows I'm not dating anyone.

I don't have much of an opportunity to meet anyone outside of the church. I'm an idiot when it comes to women, and I'm clearly not listening to inner guidance when I go into this relationship. Jane is the divorced mother of three adolescent daughters. Again, I'm in a situation similar to that with Susan, only I got along well with Susan's daughters. Jane's daughters give me the cold shoulder. Jane is as delicate and as fair as moonlight. She has thin light brown hair as soft as thistle down. She is sweet—very sweet,—a beautiful woman. She is my Achilles heel.

Jane is charming, and for a while we have a nice time together. She is something of a mystic. Her spirituality, however, tends to be conservative; in fact it is becoming progressively fundamentalist. It is difficult being with someone you care about and not being able to speak the same language. Some of the time, of course, we do speak the same language—in fact, remarkably well. I come to love Jane dearly. Though we do not connect "conceptually"—we do connect in bed. She is a wonderful lover. In this sense it is one of the best relationships I've ever had. There is an incredibly coy way she looks at me, and her passion makes lovemaking very exciting. She gives herself so totally to the experience. Nothing is more exciting for a man than for a woman to get excited.

We are clearly on different wavelengths when it comes to religion. I'm reminded of Archie Bunker turning to Edith and saying, "The problem is that I'm speaking to you in English and you're listening in dingbat." I'm not suggesting that Jane is a dingbat. Jane actually detests the Course. She once says it can't be true because she never sees any miracles. Of course, she is thinking about something supernatural, something extravagant as in the Bible, not the miracle the Course means as a changing of one's mind and moving from fear to love.

I don't think Jane's adolescent daughters would have liked any man who might be taking away their mother's affections. For Thanksgiving, I'm invited to Jane's mother's house for dinner with her family. There is a blackout leaving us to eat by candlelight, which makes it more interesting.

When I go to get into my car to go home, I notice that her daughters have placed pitted green olives on the car seat, hoping I won't notice and sit on them.

1986—Age Forty-Three

I gradually back away from Jane while trying to remain her friend. I'm sorry I started the relationship. Unless one's intentions are marriage from the very beginning, a minister should never date someone in his congregation. I come to this wisdom the hard way. Why can't I find the woman who is to be my wife? I'm sure I will recognize her when I see her.

I get a call from Lena. Kristian is now thirteen. Lena's ex-husband Tommy is a successful photographer. Kristian often stays at his apartment in New York City. Kristian is sleeping in his bedroom at Tommy's house. Tommy and his girlfriend are sitting on the couch in the living room. Tommy turns to his girlfriend and says, "I have a horrible pain in my chest, and I think I'm going to die." And he does! Lena calls me immediately. I go to Tommy's funeral. I stay in the background. He was only thirty-four. He had a promising career before him. It is a tragedy. After the funeral, Lena, Kristian, and Richy come to spend the weekend at High Rock. Though we try to make the best of it, it is a very difficult weekend, especially for Kristian.

Mother, Ann, Glenn, my nephew Sean and niece Erin all come to visit New York. We make the rounds of sites in the City and invite people over to celebrate Mother's seventieth birthday. On a trip to Sturbridge, Massachusetts, I invite Jane to come along. Afterwards, Mother says Jane surprised her. She doesn't think Jane is my type. When it comes to women, Mother is always right. I still have occasional dreams about Jane. She always has that diffident smile. Every now and then, I'll see Jane driving her car. One day at a stoplight, I turn to see her sitting in her car next to me. I roll down the window. She rolls down hers. She says, "You look good." I say, "So do you." The light changes. She turns right. I go left. It's the story of our lives.

I rent out a room at High Rock to Frank Gruder, a German fellow employed at the IBM think tank in nearby Yorktown Heights. Frank is a redheaded, square-jawed genius who is working on "fractals" formulas that describe the pattern of leaves, or the patterns that sound waves make. After reading the description of my death experience, he says the images sound a great deal like the impressions seen in his work. I don't date anyone for

251

awhile. Instead, I find a friend in Frank. Perhaps it is good that I do not have a girlfriend. Maybe I'm going to be a bachelor forever. It is better, for a while at least, that I just have a buddy. I need a rest from romance.

CHAPTER 32

The Inn and the End of
My Methodist Ministry

One often meets his destiny on the road he takes to avoid it. —French Proverb

I go through the next two years living life out loud. When there are too many emotional pressures—too much feeling, too much sensitivity, too much pain and heartache—something has to give. A woman once told me God spoke to her after a bout of delirious ranting and raving (seems she got his attention). When she calmed down, a message came to her. Try it some day. There is no guarantee of success. It might work. These experiences do not usually come until we reach the point of exhaustion—when we crash and burn and finally surrender. When all the defenses are down, finally we can receive an answer.

Life is like playing a violin in public and learning the instrument as one goes on. —Samuel Butler

The Church and the Course

Over the years, I've come to believe that the church provides a kind of *inoculation* against religious experience. It gives enough experience so you feel as though you've got something. It is somehow also not "the" experience. The *illusion* of spirituality lulls people into a haven of false peace. We go to church and get a vaccination to protect ourselves against the real thing.

A fellow from Texas went to England. While he was there, he went to the Anglican Church. Suddenly, in the middle of the sermon he shouts, "Amen Brother!" Everyone turns and looks at him. After awhile he shouts out again, "Amen Brother!" One of the ushers walks over and tells him not to talk out loud in Church. "Yes," he says, "but I've got religion." "Well," says the usher. "you didn't get it here!"

Despite its profound message, to my surprise, the Course interests few ministers. For fourteen years, from 1975 to 1989, I actively preach from the Course and try to make a marriage between the Course and traditional Christianity. I'm convinced that the author of the Course is who He says He is, namely, Jesus. If this is so, should we not pay attention to these words? Ken keeps telling me I will never succeed in bringing the Course into the church. I persist.

Are we ministers not looking for the truth? Once we find it, should we not focus on it? I am sure it will be just a matter of time before other ministers begin to preach the Course. Other ministers do not come along and I find myself floating alone in a sea of suspicion. Yet I persist in thinking that the Methodist church is open-minded and that one should be able to find God, however one finds Him. The Course is meant as a correction for traditional Christianity and traditional Christianity does not want to be corrected . . . thank you very much! I am progressively viewed as someone who is trying to circumvent and disrupt the established order. This is not a position I want or enjoy.

I think I would do well in a college town where I could do further studies while exploring my second love—teaching. The United Methodist Church in New Paltz is available. New Paltz is home to one of the many SUNY (State University of New York) campuses. I cannot interview for New Paltz. The United Methodist church in Woodstock, New York, an artsy new age community near New Paltz and the home of the Woodstock Festival of '69, is available. I cannot interview for Woodstock. The United Methodist Church in Katonah, where I live, is available. I have made a number of friends in Katonah, mostly people active in the humanistic psychology movement. Katonah is perfect. I cannot interview for Katonah. I am blocked down each avenue I pursue. I'm *dead in the water*. My interest in *A Course in Miracles*, my experiences with psychotropics, and my inability to settle down as a married man are all getting in the way. I am not to be appointed to any position larger than Central Valley.

More and more I'm disenfranchised and at odds with how the church is being run. I cannot be an agent of change within the church on a local or a hierarchical level. There is no sense in putting down the church. The idea is to bring illusions to the truth not to give truth to illusions. It is also important to pay attention to an inner call and not to sell oneself short or settle for being someone we're not. Individuation is stifled if "the system" overwhelms us. There is a cartoon of a man standing at a party talking to another man and saying, "All my life I wanted to be somebody, and now I am somebody but it isn't me." If we can't be ourselves, what good is it?

1987—Age Forty-Four

High Rock also peaks. I have grown the graphic arts business as far as it can and still be working from the house. Jackie Bolander is working full time. I have two part-time employees. In order to expand I would have to have more employees. *The Mustard Seed* is becoming a more substantial magazine. I want to do something innovative and creative. I'm still dreaming of a growth center. I make one last attempt to obtain a more substantial church at the annual conference in June of 1987. When that effort is also rebuffed, I give up completely and focus on developing *The Mustard Seed.*

I go home to Missouri for Christmas 1987. I call Judy Femmer and go to see her in Columbia, Missouri. My hometown church, First Christian Church of Mexico, is looking for a new minister, and I consider returning to Missouri. The salary is $45,000 a year plus a parsonage and a number of perks. That is three times what I'm earning at Central Valley! I have been in New York too long. As much as I love Missouri, you can't go home again. Still, I feel sure things are going to change. They have to change. Change is coming. I can feel it. Where? How? When?

1988—Age Forty-Five

A graphic arts customer absolutely loves High Rock. The price of real estate in the area has gone though the roof. My home is now worth $300,000 and I know it. So I tell him I will sell High Rock for $300,000—not a penny less—and he says, "Sold!" (In 2001 I'm back in Katonah. I take a walk through the village. I stop in front of a real estate office to look at a picture of a house in the window. It's High Rock, and it's for sale for $635,000!).

How fickle fortune is. I have a $225,000 profit. What I could have done with it! Although I'm going nowhere in the Methodist church, I still have the ministry at Central Valley. Needing to do something more, something inventive, my first thought is to find land and build a center.

I'm in a real estate office and ask if by chance there is an inn for sale in the area. If I bought a going concern that is already making money, I could slowly turn it into a center by offering workshops and developing a bookstore. There is just such a place for sale called The Golden Inn in Monroe, the next town over from Central Valley. I look at it as a "golden opportunity." I know the inn. I have been there for TGIF parties with Susan and other teachers. Within six months I'm the owner of the inn.

255

Jesus said:

The world is a place of transition, full of examples: Be pilgrims therein,
and take warning by the traces of those that have gone before.
—James Robinson, *Christ in Islam*

I change the name to Pilgrims Inn, keeping within the theme of spiritual seeking. The inn consists of a 100-seat restaurant—seventy-seats in one room and thirty in another—separated by a lobby and a bar. You can have a party in one section and keep the other opened for dinner guests. The owners, Bill and Mary Golden, are tired of all the work and want a break. They have built a house next door and moved out of the apartment that covers the third floor of the inn. They are willing to hold the biggest part of a mortgage. Fifty thousand is to be held by a mortgage company.

There are nine rental units in the inn, a three-family house next door, which I will also own, and a small three-room house out back. If all the rooms are rented all the time, it looks good. Furthermore, there is the restaurant. I have the money. I have to do something. I'm not entirely rational. My friends, Frank Gruder in particular, are worried that I'm getting in over my head. I have to make a move. I have lots of energy. I sell at the top. I also buy at the top, paying $465,000 for the place. It is near Central Valley. It will be easier to administer the church and no more commuting.

Edie calls, having heard about my move. She knows about all the trouble I've had with the zoning board in Katonah. "Finally," she says, "you're going to get the center you've dreamed about." She wants to take me out to lunch to celebrate my forty-fifth birthday and to say good-bye, as I will no longer be living in Westchester. There she is flipping that long blonde hair back over her shoulder again. We sit on the porch of a restaurant in Mt. Kisco, with wisteria growing up along the railing. It's like stepping back in time being with this beautiful woman whom I dearly love. A couple of years earlier Edie had a mastectomy. The cancer has now returned; in fact, it's in her lungs. She knows. She doesn't tell me. She wants this to be a happy day for me. On my birthday, one year later, perhaps the most hellish day of my life, Edie will die.

In June, The New Seminary awards me an honorary doctorate at a ceremony at St. Paul's Cathedral at Columbia University in New York City. I go to see Ken for my annual spiritual check-up. Ken is in the process of buying a "real" center in the Catskill mountains. We are both moving at the same time, in the same direction, to the west across the Hudson

River. Again he asks me if I'm sure about my decision. Do I really know what I'm doing? I assure him I do.

I remembered the tiny Spartan studio apartment that used to be Ken's home. It is incredible to watch him move. At each step he exquisitely and flawlessly follows the Course, doing what he is called to do, impeccable in his research, moving ever deeper into the Course and into his amazing clarity as a teacher. Never does he seem to worry about money. A smart move at this point would have been to go with Ken; after all, I have the money. I need, however, to do something on my own. Now is the time. This midlife crisis has to end.

I've come to love High Rock. Lots of wonderful things have happened here. Every Fourth of July, almost every Thanksgiving and many New Year's Eves I've thrown a party. Although I only occasionally got to use High Rock as a growth center, a whole community of consciousness developed with High Rock as the center. Kristian comes to help me move to the inn.

We're going to California ain't we? All right then let's go to California.
—Ma Joad, in *The Grapes of Wrath* by John Steinbeck

Leaving the driveway, with the last truckload of furniture, I'm determined; I don't look back. I become owner of Pilgrims Inn on July 11, 1988. The Goldens have arranged for a graduation party of the local academy for the training of New York State correctional officers that evening. There is plenty of money that first evening. The inn is closed on Mondays, and opened for just such special occasions. For nineteen dollars a person, we can provide hors d'oeuvres and all the beer they want. Hard liquor has to be purchased. I'm probably the only Methodist minister who ever owned a liquor license. With $900 in the cash register and a check for a thousand dollars, the first evening looks good. I go to bed exhausted. I'm looking forward to this adventure. Most days thereafter it's downhill.

Kristian moves to the inn with me. He is sixteen and looking handsome. He looks, I think, a bit like the actor Robbie Benson. He becomes a waiter and, on the rare occasions when the restaurant is busy, the maitre d'. Tommy has been gone for three years and Lena and I decide the time has come to tell Kristian about his parentage. The three of us sit on the porch in captain's chairs around a table with a red and white-checkered tablecloth and a citronella candle. We are concerned about how he will respond. Will he be angry with us for having kept this secret for so long? It all goes amazingly well. He responds positively with, "that's cool." He asks us a few questions and, then, after a few minutes asks if he can be excused. He obviously wants to think. He gets on his bicycle and goes for a ride. Finally, he knows. It is a bright spot in what is about to become the darkest year of my life. Lena will go on to become the devotee of a Tibetan Buddhist. Kristian will go to SUNY in nearby New Paltz, New York.

The toughest part of Pilgrims Inn are the rooms. If the rooms had worked, I think the restaurant would have succeeded. It was just a matter of time for developing a reputation for good food and a pleasant atmosphere. We serve American food, like Mother used to make, with corn bread served at every meal. We serve navy beans, fried breaded okra, catfish and collard greens—pure Missouri. I try to make it healthy, including a selection of vegetarian offerings. I also keep the main entrees the inn is known for, particularly its prime rib. And I add my favorite—grilled salmon—as a regular feature.

Two rooms are occupied by long-timers whose rent is forty dollars per week, paid weekly. Every other room is rented to someone who is a day laborer, on welfare, disability or social security. Several construction workers have jobs in the summertime; once winter comes around, no job and no money. I allow one of my tenants, a seemingly good-natured, somewhat mentally challenged fellow, to stay and eat free, as he swears he has no money. He nervously tells me that if I should read something someday in the papers about him, I should not believe it. A few days after he moves out, I read in the paper that he has been arrested for making love to a corpse!

One tenant, a professional thief, comes into my apartment, steals checks from the back of my checkbook, and forges $2,500 before checks start bouncing and I figure out what is happening. Trying to collect weekly rents is an adventure. Most of the tenants are abusing drugs and alcohol. Whatever money they have is going up their noses or up in smoke or both. No wonder Bill and Mary wanted to get rid of this place.

The worst is the three-family house next door. Two girls I'll call Denise and Peggy show up with $1,200 in cash, $600 for the first month's rent and $600 for the deposit. They beg me not to call their previous landlord, as he is an s.o.b. They are happy to have met a Christian minister who can save them. I should trust and believe in them. They will pay their rent on time. I need the money. It is the last money I see from them. There is always some reason why they cannot or will not pay—until I fix the front steps or the bathroom, or a leak in the roof. I try to tar the roof and get covered in the stuff. I fix whatever they ask and then they point out another problem, which I have to fix, before they will pay. Or one of them gets sick. And then Denise loses her job and they have drunken fights that bring the police in the middle of the night. What a sap I am. Why didn't I check their references!?

1989—Age Forty-Six

One positive change takes place on January 1, 1989. During the move to the inn I received a letter from Diane Berke complimenting me on *The Mustard Seed.* I appreciate her letter and keep it. I have had no time to respond during the move. In December 1988, I give a talk for the New Seminary in New York City. As I'm leaving, Diane introduces herself. Diane is attractive and energetic with a thick head of black hair. She has large beautiful dark velvet eyes. She was at one time a ballroom dancer and works hard to stay in shape. I've not had a date in more than six months. I'm headed home for Christmas and suggest a date on New Years Day. Diane is the best thing that has happened to me in a long time. Diane will become one of my major teachers. During the winter and spring of 1989, as the inn begins to collapse, Diane comes to play more and more of a role in my life. Within a few months we are spending nearly every weekend together. Although I'm not falling in love, we develop a caring and loving relationship based on mutual respect and friendship.

Diane is working as a psychotherapist in private practice in Manhattan. The year before, she completed the New Seminary. She is responsible, committed, dedicated, and perhaps the smartest woman I have ever met. She is highly organized, and has as beautiful a hand at writing as I've ever seen. Diane knows how to jump right in and get to work. She begins reading the Course and the book I'm writing on the Course. She's interested in everything I'm doing and she wants to help. Diane is Jewish. I'm Protestant. We are both interested and involved in Interfaith activities, and we have a number of mutual friends in the city. The Rabbi is like a father to both of us.

The little house behind the inn is almost as bad as the three-family house. I have to replace the furnace and broken pipes. On January 3rd, I crawl around under this little house in minus three-degree bone hurting cold. It is so cold that my breath seems to freeze inside. Drenched in sewage dripping down from the bathroom above is an experience I hope never to repeat.

259

If there is hell on earth, I think this is it, except this hell is filthy, half-frozen, fetid feces. Ugh!

Finally, the girls are so far behind in their rent I go to court to get them evicted. Surprise! The judge has seen them before for the same reason. I win the case. When the sheriff shows up to throw them out, it is snowing. They beg me to let them stay. How can I possibly put them out in the snow? They are right. I can't do it. I rescind the order, which means I have to go to court all over again to have them evicted. Shortly thereafter Peggy buys a brand new little red truck. Where did she get the money? If she can afford a new truck, how about paying their rent? They never pay!

I get behind on the oil bill and the oil company takes me to court. I take the girls to court again and both cases wind up on the same docket the same day. I am a defendant and a plaintiff in one case right after the other. The oil company wins the judgment against me. Then immediately—next case! I win my case against the girls. The owner of the oil company apologizes saying if he had known what a mess I was in with the girls, we could have worked something out. Peggy's wages are attached. My lawyer is first in line to get paid and what little return there is goes to him. Over a year later, I get a check for ninety dollars. Before long Peggy is fired from her job so that is the end of it. As a businessman I learned an important and very expensive lesson. Never try to make money working with people who do not handle money responsibly, or have no money. Experience would be a better teacher if she did not charge so much for tuition.

I'm less and less capable of paying the bills and slipping deeper and deeper into debt. The first budget to go is advertising. I have to pay salaries, supplies and insurance. I do not have to advertise. Slowly, there are fewer and fewer patrons in the restaurant. The room situation continues to deteriorate. Aware of the fact that I'm going under, two tenants decide to ride it down with me. Instead of paying, they will just stay and move when the place closes.

It's Not Over Till the Fat Lady Sings

And now comes the end of the church. A new, conservative family from Georgia moves into Central Valley. The woman is bouncy, energetic, and an opera singer. She always wears a pasted on "glad to meet ya" smile. At first she likes me, then she decides I'm not speaking her language.

Truth is—I'm *not* speaking her language. On Mother's Day 1989, every-thing changes. She gets up to sing a solo. Mother's Day is like Easter or Christmas in the church, everyone is there—and their mothers. She pauses before she sings, saying there is something she wants to say. She proceeds to say that the message she needs to hear preached every Sunday is the message of the saving grace of the sacrificial blood of our Lord and Savior Jesus Christ, and she is not hearing that message coming from this pulpit. She is right. I have never preached sacrificial blood. It is one concept that didn't make sense to me even before *A Course in Miracles* came along. At least now I understand why it doesn't make sense. God does not punish! Salvation is not a "bloody" affair!

Janice Nimetz, our petite, perceptive Jewish organist, drops her music and has to go scrambling for it. People in the congregation turn and ask one another if she just said what they think she just said. You can hardly hear her singing as everyone is distracted by the chatter that now fills the pews. Diane and I have been dating for five months. In fact, Diane is there this fateful day. The opera singer has made friends with Jane and persuaded her to write a letter to the Bishop Black, telling him that we slept together. This is not exactly a secret. Our relationship was known to all. Now Jane, menaced by the presence of Diane at Sunday services, agrees to help the opera singer and she dashes off her telling letter. The district superintendent says that in all my years in the ministry they never received a single call or complaint from a member of the congregation. Now, there are two letters in one week. Though twenty-four letters of support follow, it makes no difference.

Before the week is over, I'm in Bishop Black's office. As I drive to his office, I make up a little mantra based on the Course. I keep saying over and over again, "Do not attack this man and do not defend yourself." "Do not attack. Do not defend." I have tried, ever since I made this mantra, to live by it. My reception is cold and matter-of-fact. It offends people when you don't buy into their beliefs and Bishop Black is "off-ended" by my teaching of *A Course in Miracles*. I talk about my call into the ministry. He is a farm boy from Iowa. Maybe there is a bit of midwestern mystic in him. If there is, I can't find it. He actually abhors me. I'm an anathema to him—the opposite of what he is. Somehow a New Ager got into his tent and he is about to throw me out. He's been gunning for me for some time and lacked the ammunition. Now, waving Jane's and the opera singer's letters in his hand, he is clear—he wants me out—out like a damned spot.

He "suggests" a leave of absence. I think of something to say and then think, "No, that is an attack." Then I think of something else and then think, "No, that is a defense." So I say what he wants to hear me say, the only thing that is not an attack or a defense. I say "Good-bye." To stay I would have to recant my teaching of the Course and promise to toe the line of the United Methodist Church. To abjure the Course would to me be blasphemy.

Bishop Black says there might be some money available if I would like to get a "retread" for another profession. There is another minister, a former insurance salesman, who is willing to help me get into selling life insurance. The idea of quitting the ministry to sell insurance strikes me as ludicrous. It is insurance I'm interested in but not the earthly kind. The insurance I have in mind looks more like peace of mind. At this moment, however, I don't have much peace of mind myself. No money was withheld for unemployment so I'm really out, no job and no unemployment insurance. The opera singer did her dig on Mother's Day. He gives me till Father's Day to clear out.

I badly need to talk to someone. The only person I can think of is Rabbi Gelberman. For twenty-eight years I've been a minister and the only person I can think of is a Rabbi. I drive into Manhattan and straight to his apartment. Though he is frequently on the road or with clients, he is home alone. I tell him what has happened. His immediate response is that I should start my own church. He says he will give me the basement synagogue in Greenwich Village free of charge for services. I don't know how I will make a living. I no longer have a paycheck and there is nothing to fall back on. Now, it is certain that the inn will soon fail. I have quite literally grown up in the church. Leaving the church is like rejecting a parent. Though I love my own parents, I must admit to a love/hate relationship with the church, and this parent is throwing me out—out like Brier Rabbit—into the briar patch.

Inside the Belly of the Whale or When it Rains, it Pours

This week will easily be the worst of my life. On Monday after Mother's Day my whole world turns dark. Clouds fill the sky and it begins to rain and it rains and rains and rains, as if all of nature is crying. Tuesday, May 16, is my forty-sixth birthday. I do not feel like celebrating. It rains for two whole days. The inn is built over an underground stream and I have to keep a sump pump running constantly. The sump pump goes into a slump and refuses to pump. Overnight the basement fills with water, clear to the top step that leads down into the basement. Everything is flooded. I open the door to the basement and see paper cups and plates floating around on the surface. Below all that water there is the furnace, the hot water heater, and supplies for the restaurant. Everything is gone.

Then there comes the straw that breaks the camel's back. I'm in the kitchen fussing with the broken dishwasher when the phone rings. It is Ziva Quitney, Edie's closest friend. Edie is dead. She is only fifty-one and she is gone. My eyes immediately fill with tears.

> *Letting fall his bow and arrows, he sank down in his chariot,*
> *his soul overcome by despair and grief.*
> —*Bhagavada Gita,* 1:47; based on Juan Mascaro 1962

I drop the phone and collapse on the floor, in a corner behind the bar screaming, "No! No! No! Not Edie!"

The roof is leaking and it's still raining. Climbing a ladder up into the attic, I look up at the tortured timbers that support the roof above. The roof looks like it is weeping. Water is sadly seeping in and running slowly down along the beams then dripping onto the ceiling below. I have said that I felt like Jonah and the whale in relationship to the Course. Looking up, the huge arching beams look like ribs holding a decaying carcass. Water is dripping everywhere and there is a stench of rot and rain. This monster has swallowed me. Why did I so willingly step into this mess? Will I ever get out of this hell? Is there any way out?

I am in the Slough of Despond—an absolute abyss. I climb out of the attic—completely defeated. All my swans are geese. Everything has fallen apart—the church—the inn—I'm on the verge of bankruptcy. Every time the phone rings, it's someone asking for money and I don't know what to tell them. The mortgage company is beginning to yell—foreclosure! I look about and see things as I have not seen them before. The only good thing is Diane and I'm not at all sure I can make the kind of commitment I think she wants from me. I'm acutely aware of the part I have played in this tragedy. I'm far from guiltless. It is especially grievous to think that I have hurt the people in Central Valley.

Only you can deprive yourself of anything. Do not oppose this realization, for it is truly the beginning of the dawn of light. This is a crucial step in the reawakening. Remember also that the denial of this simple fact takes many forms, and these you must learn to recognize and to oppose steadfastly, without exception. This is a crucial step in the reawakening. The beginning phases of this reversal are often quite painful, for as blame is withdrawn from without, there is a strong tendency to harbor it within. It is difficult at first to realize that this is exactly the same thing, for there is no distinction between within and without.—ACIM, T-11.IV.4:1-6

I'm going to have to do what I can to fix the furnace and hot water heater. I cannot afford to fix the roof. This is the bottom of the bottom of the pit of despair. I go to my desk and collapse, placing my head down on my folded arms. There must be another way. Nothing is working. I utter the most sincere prayer of my life. I scream out, "Help!" I truly mean it. I really need help. Lying there sobbing, feeling exhausted and not knowing what I'm going to do, I have one of those rare experiences similar to the one in the cave in India. I hear a voice, "Haven't I always taken care of you?" That is all that it says. I sit up and look about. Of course, there is no one there.

I now realize that this same voice speaks to each of us, all the time. It is always the same message though it may take many different forms. "Be Comforted." "Be still." "I am always with you." "Haven't I always taken care of you?" A sense of confidence comes over me, and an inner connection with something deeper. I have always thought that things would work out. Here I am on my forty-sixth birthday, an incredible failure, completely broke, no job, a crumbling inn falling in on itself and an indefinite future. Yet, all this tragedy *must* be for a higher reason. I have no idea how I'm going to get out of this mess. It is true. I have always been taken care of. I have never gone hungry; in fact, I'm sometimes the only patron in my own restaurant.

To be thrown upon one's own resources is to be cast into the very lap of fortune, for our faculties then undergo a development and display an energy of which they were previously unsusceptible. —Benjamin Franklin

Though encouraged by the voice, I do not know what I'm going to do. I go into a period of deep soul searching. I'm back to doing the lessons in the Course. I make time for silence. Somehow I want to develop an Interfaith ministry. I almost get a job as a director of a retreat center. If I get the job, how will I be able to develop an Interfaith ministry? I'm supposed to be an entrepreneurial minister. How? I have no money.

The last Sunday at Central Valley every seat is filled. Everyone except Jane and the opera singer are there. Instead of a sermon, I go around the room saying something to each person, thanking them for believing in and supporting me. There are, of course, many tears. There is a farewell party after services. On the way out the back door, Betsy Borg, whom I have always liked, comes running after me, grabs my shirtsleeve and in a commanding voice says, "Go back to writing, Jon!"

When it is dark enough, you can see the stars. —Charles Beard

CHAPTER 33

The Birth of Interfaith Fellowship and *On Course* Magazine

"He who has a 'why' can forbear any 'how.'" —Nietzsche

Just as a boomerang comes back to a hunter "only" when it has missed its target, so do we return to ourselves when we miss our mission and fail to find our purpose in life. I put everything I had into running the inn. And I lost nearly everything I had (financially speaking). This close encounter with bankruptcy also brings me back to myself. It literally gets me back *on course,* back ever more clearly to a ministry to which I had always felt called and to which I had not yet responded deeply enough. Losing one's money is not a tragedy when it brings one back to the Self. A setback in the physical world is just a setback in the physical world. Failure in this world is reversed in Heaven. There is no learning in pain. There *is* learning, however, in the overcoming of pain.

I need a break. To escape it all and get some perspective, Diane and I drive home to Missouri for a visit with Mother. I need to take a walk on the farm. Bishop Black is my greatest friend. He knew I wasn't a Methodist even before I did. Whoever *wrestles* with us hones our nerve and strengthens our skill. Bishop Black pushes me onward and upward, to become who I'm meant to be. He helps me fulfill my destiny. Diane, Mother and I drive up to Nauvoo, Illinois, the site of an early settlement of the Mormon Church. There we stand looking at an enormous floor-to-ceiling picture of Joseph Smith, founder of the Mormon Church. There is a caption below the picture saying that God has asked him to become the founder of *The One True Church.* Diane and I want to do something to establish a place where people of different faiths and backgrounds can come together for worship and sharing. We will not call it *the one true church.*

Driving back to New York, unemployed and watching the eighteen-wheelers buzzing down the road, I toy with the idea of becoming a truck driver. It must be a freeing experience to be out on the road. It must also be lonely. I did not come here to drive a truck. I shake it off. I want to get back to publishing the magazine, and somehow to the publication of my book on the Course. I truly dread the last day's drive back to the inn.

I know I'm going back to a mess. Bill Golden looks after the inn for me while I'm in Missouri. There has been little business and I return to bounced checks and huge bills.

I call Ken and drive up to his center in Roscoe, New York. Perhaps it will give me some perspective. It does. As always, Ken helps get me back on track. On September 15, 1989, I close the restaurant for good. Maybe I can just turn the whole inn into rented rooms? Maybe I can find a partner? Maybe? Maybe what? One thing is for sure: I have to get out myself. By getting out, I can rent out my own apartment within the inn. I find a relatively new house with four bedrooms. By letting out three of the bedrooms to single men like myself, I have enough for the rent.

When I gave up the typesetting at High Rock, I continued writing resumes, as it is one of the more lucrative aspects of the business. I can write a resume in about an hour, two at the most, and receive thirty-five to fifty dollars. Even during the time at the inn, I did this. I place an ad in the Yellow Pages for Action Resumes. Action comes first in the alphabet, so it is the first listing. It also suggests a resume filled with action verbs for active people. I put the typesetting equipment in the basement of the new house. I'm going underground, and with the aid of this machine, I'm going to work myself back up out of this mess.

The Mustard Seed existed while I was at the inn, just barely. I was late getting it out and had to scale back the size of the production. Now I have to start again. I choose the name *On Course* because it has a dual meaning, on course as with a pilgrim on a journey and, of course, on the Course in Miracles. I begin just as I had with *The Mustard Seed.* I add seasonal material, jokes, quotes, and inspirational stories.

I find two part-time teaching jobs, one a course in Sociology at Sussex Community College in northern New Jersey, the other in Public Speaking at Orange County Community College. One friend sends me $100 a week for twelve weeks. With it I buy gasoline and groceries.

> In the midst of winter, I finally learned that there is in me
> an invincible summer. —Albert Camus

Though things are very bleak, I'm free to do what I want, and free to be who I am. I have never been good at playing churchman. It was difficult trying to live according to the mandates of the Methodists. There is no reason to blame Bishop Black or the church for what has happened. I'm grateful to him. He was right. Regardless of the quality of my ministry,

I'm not a good Methodist. I'm not a victim. I'm liberated! Now I can get on with my life.

Those that make you return, for whatever reason, to God's solitude, be grateful to them. Worry about the others, who give you delicious comforts that keep you from prayer. Friends are enemies sometimes and enemies friends. —Rumi

The United Misfits

Accusations against the church for having frustrated and thwarted my career, or attempts to accuse others for putting obstructions in my path would be fraudulent. I have no one to blame except myself. If I believe the Course, I don't even have myself to blame. All forgiveness is ultimately self-forgiveness or self-understanding. Despite twenty-two years of working with them, my heart has never been truly Methodist. There are good principles here and good people. The creeds and dogmas, however, are restrictive and unrealistic. In 2000, the United Methodist Church conducts an image survey and finds that former United Methodists say the church is too bureaucratic and too heavily laden with doctrine.

I find solace and a sense of direction in reading Ralph Waldo Emerson's *Self-Reliance.*

Let me admonish you, first of all, to go alone; to refuse the good models, even those which are sacred in the imagination of men, and dare to lov God without mediator or veil. Friends enough you shall find to hold up to your emulation, Wesleys and Oberlins, saints and prophets. Thank God for these good men and say, "I am a man. Imitation cannot go above its model. The imitator dooms himself to hopeless mediocrity." When we have broken with our God of tradition and ceased from our God of rhetoric, then may God fire your heart with his presence. —Ralph Waldo Emerson,
Address to Divinity Students, Harvard University, July 15, 1838

I'm forced out of the church founded by John Wesley, and Emerson is saying I should do what John Wesley did? Wesley never wanted to start another church. On his deathbed he was still resisting the inevitable. William Ellery Channing, founder of Unitarianism in the United States, never wanted to start the Unitarian Church, concerned that it would become bureaucratic like the Congregational Church. Luther never intended to start the Protestant Reformation. The response to Luther was excommunication. We live in a more enlightened age. You don't get excommunicated—you just get fired. Luther was young, smart, energetic, and a truly spiritual man. He didn't have any choice. Rome broke with him, so he had to go off on his own. I have been a maverick; I have not submitted to all the rules and regulations of the Methodist Church. Joe Horner, a friend from Central Valley, making a play on United Methodist, jokingly says I should call our new church the United Mavericks or the United Misfits. Diane wants to call our church Another Way, simply to indicate another, different way. I want to call our new church Interfaith Fellowship.

You can take the boy out of the farm. You can't take the farm out of the boy. You can take a minister out of the church. You can't take the ministry out of the minister. On the Sunday after Labor Day in 1989, nine months after Diane and I had our first date, Interfaith Fellowship begins in the basement of a synagogue in Greenwich Village. We truly start as an "underground" movement in Greenwich Village. We send out a notice to our friends telling them what we are going to do. Thirty-five people show up for our first service and we are encouraged. Only ten people show up the next week. It seems, that the first week a number of friends showed up to say, "Although we support you in what you are doing, don't expect us to be here every Sunday."

Diane comes up to Monroe on Thursday afternoons. We work together on *On Course* and prepare for Sunday services. We go into New York City on Sunday mornings and return to Monroe on Sunday afternoons where we begin a *Course in Miracles* study group. Dr. Robert Weltman, a gray-bearded balding Jewish fellow nearing retirement and chief psychologist at Mid-Hudson Psychiatric, an institution for the criminally insane, joins us in this endeavor. Dr. Weltman is delightful. He is a true mystic and to this day one of my best friends, confidants and guides. His perceptive poetry adds much to life.

I look at every possible way I might be able to make a success of a failing inn, and wonder if I should sell it at a loss. How big a loss? I'm offered $425,000 for the place. I should have taken it. A grinning loan shark with big teeth comes swimming around. From my office window, I see his black chauffeur-driven limousine sneaking into the parking lot. I go out and sit in his car. He doesn't want to come inside. Rather, he invites me into his lair, or is it liar? I sit in the limousine and we talk. Suave and debonair, he smells of old spice shaving lotion. He can give me the money to save the inn. I know that he will later take the inn from me, and leave me with even greater debt. I've made a mistake here. I don't need to compound this error.

Sometimes you have to chew your leg off to get out of one of life's traps. Bill Golden offers to buy the inn back for $365,000, $100,000 less than I paid for it eighteen months earlier. In essence, Bill makes $100,000 in eighteen months. Bill is good about the whole business with the inn. He tried to help me make it a success. He often tended bar without pay and was a great troubleshooter. When the icemaker didn't work or the dishwasher broke down, Bill had some ideas about how to wire them back together again. Many another former owner would just have disappeared and then foreclosed when payments started coming in late. On the first day of winter 1989, Bill and Mary buy back the inn. Mary, I can see, is not happy. After the closing I call Mother and just keep saying, "It's over, thank God, it's all over."

A great weight has been lifted from me. Bill does not have any more luck than I did at collecting rents and finally sells the inn for good. Nine other people try to make it at the inn during the next fifteen years. They all fail. The parking lot has now been paved. It's been fixed up—some of the things I wanted to do have been done. To my knowledge it is still a working restaurant and inn.

I'm left with $45,000 from my original $225,000. I have some money. I give all I have to the project of building Interfaith Fellowship and *On Course* magazine. The exciting thing is that I'm free—free from the white whale that nearly devoured me. I can now be an entrepreneurial minister, no more committees, and no more board of trustees! I can proceed, as I feel guided. This will be fun.

Birds sing after a storm. Why shouldn't people feel as free to delight in whatever remains to them? —Rose Kennedy

I throw everything I have into making a success of *On Course* magazine and Interfaith Fellowship. It's all for a good cause, one I fully believe will work. Slowly, it begins to happen. Ruth Murphy, who proves a godsend, joins us in the production of the magazine. Ruth is in our Sunday evening miracles study group, and when I find out she knows DBASE, I ask if she can help us part-time to manage the database and bookkeeping. I can now focus on the magazine and the other aspects of our ministry.

Several events suggest that the fearful conservatism of the eighties is cooling and a new openness is developing. Communism is defeated in Poland and Lech Walesa is elected president. The Chinese revolt at Tiananmen Square. The Soviets pull out of Afghanistan, and on November 10, 1989, the Berlin wall comes tumbling down and with it Communism in Russia and the Eastern Block countries. The whole communist empire falls apart and dissolves without violence. We do not have to destroy anything. The coming down of the Berlin wall seems like a planetary affirmation of the coming down of the wall of separateness.

1990—Age Forty-Seven

There is more good news. Nelson Mandela is freed from prison and the Soviet Union votes to put aside seventy years of religious suppression and drafts a bill calling for freedom of belief. Now is the time for Interfaith and we are not alone in our thinking. A lot of people want to see more openness and inclusiveness in religion.

My Aunt Sue Carter, Daddy's sister, has Alzheimer's, like Daddy. Her husband, my Uncle Sam Carter, was smart in his handling of money. He always used to ask me "Are you saving any money?" To him it was important. He made a number of wise investments. His estate is worth more than one million. Six of us will someday be equal heirs. We are to be given $10,000 each per year as long as the estate earns enough to comfortably support Aunt Sue. I give the entire $10,000 to Interfaith. Each year for the next ten years this godsend will arrive each February and I will give it all to Interfaith. It stops in 2001 because of the bad market. There isn't enough money anymore.

I am free and able to talk about *A Course in Miracles* all I want. I can preach on the Course every Sunday and no one objects; in fact, they applaud. We create a wonderful Interfaith worship service with inspirational readings and meditations from the world's different religious traditions. There is a wealth of music available, not just the old Christian hymns.

If men can run the world, why can't they stop wearing neckties? How intelligent is it to start the day by tying a little noose around your neck?
—Linda Ellerbee in *The Seattle Post-Intelligencer*

I stopped wearing robes when I was a Methodist minister. Now, I stop wearing a tie. A tie is a noose and will hang a man if he is not careful. Where did neckties come from anyhow? Who thought of that? I keep records of how many people attend each Sunday and what the offering is. On March 25, there are forty-five people and eighty-two dollars. That same day Julie and Jeff Olmsted attend service. Jeff is a marvelous musician and becomes our music director, and Julie, who is going through the New Seminary, becomes our associate minister. We begin to grow. Though the next several years are lean and it is necessary to tighten the belt and work hard, the results are rewarding.

July 4, 1990, we have a party at the house in Monroe, and six of us sign our papers of incorporation. We choose that date because everyone is going to be at the party and we can all sign at the same time. It just happens that it is on the Fourth of July that we declare our independence as a church. A lawyer friend is to take the papers to the county clerk's office for validation. He doesn't get around to it right away. The date on which Interfaith is officially recognized as a nonprofit corporation or church is Reformation Day—October 31, 1990. October 31, 1517, is the date that Martin Luther tacked his 95 Theses to the church door in Wittenburg. The nineties will be for us a time of incredible growth.

In August 1990, Diane and I again return to Missouri. After, we attend A Course in Miracles retreat weekend on a farm in Southern Indiana. We arrive after the program has started. We're sitting in the back row, when this marvelous young woman gets up and starts to sing. We listen to her incredibly sweet voice. We turn and look at each other and say, "Who's that?" We've both fallen in love with Donna Cary. All the way back to New York we listen to her tapes in the car. Before long we'll be sponsoring concerts with her in Manhattan.

In one year we have outgrown the basement synagogue. Marianne Williamson has started the Manhattan Center for Living. It is a place where people with AIDS and other life-threatening diseases can come to find support. There is a large meeting room with oversize oval-shaped Palladian windows facing Broadway. We can have it for only fifty dollars per Sunday. Marianne is actively involved in teaching the Course and it seems like a good match. We are there only five months when a new director comes on board who is opposed to religious services at the center. We are given one month to vacate, so we scramble and find an even more appropriate place—the Amsterdam Room in the Dorot Building on 85th Street and Amsterdam on Manhattan's Upper West Side. Racked with power struggles and personality conflicts, the Manhattan Center for Living soon closes. The Dorot is a more appropriate space. It is larger. It was once a Jewish Temple and there are stained glass windows along one wall. It is perfect—for now.

Ever since I heard that voice at the inn saying, "Haven't I always taken care of you?" I've had incredible faith. From now on I'm going to trust God. I'm going to do what I think He wants me to do and I'm not going to worry about money. *On Course* continues to grow. With each workshop and conference there are more and more subscribers. I still have the type-setting machine. There is no spell checker. Type has to be processed through a chemical bath, and then hung up to dry. Then it has to be cut into appropriate pieces and pasted together. It starts as a weekly production and I charge one dollar per week. I make copies of eight pages on a copy machine, fold, staple, and mail each piece myself. Every penny I have from whatever resource—Aunt Sue's inheritance, teaching, writing resumes, weddings—all goes into the magazine. I sit in the evening and put address labels on individual copies. Passing my hand over each name I send out a blessing. It works.

1991—Age Forty-Eight

In January, I expand *On Course* to 24 pages. By the middle of the year I'm able to take *On Course* to a printer. Paul Ferrini sponsors a National Conference for *A Course in Miracles* students at the Omega Institute near Rhinebeck, New York. We are surprised to find that a bus, plus several carloads of Course students from Wisconsin, show up and literally take over the conference. Here is a large group of people, living in a community, following the teaching of one man who calls himself Master Teacher. It "looks" like a cult. When I get home I immediately call Ken to ask, "Do you know what's going on?" He reassures me with a passage from the Old Testament: "If this be of God there is nothing you can do to stop it. If it is not of God, it will come to naught."

Dr. Weltman, who has proven such a godsend, calls to say that he has a friend, Meribeth Seaman, who is looking for work as a graphic artist and is it possible that I could use some part-time help? I turn more and more of the work of the magazine over to Meribeth.

I read Wes "Scoop" Nisker's *Crazy Wisdom*. I've always used humor in my lectures and sermons and I've collected quite a large repertoire of jokes. At one of the Miracle conferences, we meet Steve Bhaerman, who does standup comedy as Swami Beyondananda. He is hilarious. Most of his jokes are puns and plays on words, spoofs on the new age, psychology, religion, philosophers, gurus, self-help groups, vegetarians, activists, fundamentalists, liberals, *A Course in Miracles* students—everybody—mostly ourselves. I try my hand at standup comedy at a Course in Miracles conference in Bethel, Maine, as Swami Baba Ji Whiz. That is Ji Whiz not Cheese Whiz. I bill myself as an Interfaith Swami. I worship all of the "isms" Hinduism, Taoism, Protestantism. I worship two girls. That is called Jainism and Judaism. I claim to be a follower of Jon Mundy. His Philosophy is called Mundanism. This is a lot of fun.

1992—Age Forty-Nine

Each January, I make some kind of improvement in *On Course*. I now expand to thirty-two pages. I'm growing the magazine very slowly, consistently working from a profitable base. Paul Ferrini sponsors another conference at Manassas, Virginia. Donna Cary is there, and I meet Robert Perry for the first time. Robert is, without a doubt, after Ken, the most scholarly of the Course students and teachers. He comes back to New York with us to lead some workshops. I drive Robert up to Roscoe so he and Ken can have a private session.

I have a vision. Vision has nothing to do with the body's eyes. It is rather a sudden expansion, or delimitation, of one's own awareness. Someday there will be an Interfaith Center. Diane has great spiritual gifts and the warmth and ability to convey them. I am not, however, thinking about marriage. On Christmas of 1992, our worship service overflows, people have to stand and we turn people away.

CHAPTER 34

Why is the Church so
Threatened by the Course?

In an attempt to discredit my work, the minister who replaces me at Central Valley distributes a pamphlet explaining why *A Course in Miracles* is heretical. In 1992, *The United Methodist Reporter,* prints an article listing various reasons why *A Course in Miracles* is not to be studied in United Methodist churches.

Monism or Dualism?

The Course is monistic. The Course says that all there is is Heaven. This world is an illusion, a dream or fantasy. It is actually impossible for us to be separated from God. We live in a fantasy that we are isolated egos. We try to make our own world in which God is a fantasy. We've got things backward: Heaven seems like a fantasy and this world seems like reality. It's the other way around. Heaven *is* reality and this world is the dream.

Traditional Christianity is dualistic. Accordingly, there is indeed a Heaven. There is also a hell (a place of *eternal* punishment for sinners) and a devil, both quite real and to be feared. The devil is roughly equivalent to the ego. However, as the ego ultimately does not exist, neither does the devil. Even as a young minister, the idea of a devil never made any sense to me. How can someone be sent into the eternal fires of hell just because they failed in the course of one short lifetime to come to profess Jesus as their savior? Must we go to hell because we're immature?

Sin, Guilt and Fear

One Sunday a man goes to church without his wife. When he returns home, she asks him what the preacher talked about. He replies, "Sin." "Well," says the wife, "what does he say about it?" "He's against it," replies her husband. The church has always been against sin. As Billy Sunday, the famous evangelist from the early part of the twentieth century said, and Burt Lancaster, in the movie *Elmer Gantry* so eloquently repeated: "I'm against sin; I'll kick it as long as I've got a boot. And I'll fight it as long as I've got a fist. I'll butt it as long as I've got a head and I'll

275

bite it as long as I've got a tooth. And, when I'm old and fistless and footless and toothless, I'll gum it to death."

Tell a traditional Christian that there is no sin and he will assure you there is plenty of sin—all you have to do is look around you. Furthermore, he says, if you say there is no sin then you can just do whatever you want without worrying about the consequences. We behave not because we are innately good, we behave because we are afraid of God's wrath. The "belief" in sin is necessary in order to keep us in line. This idea is based on a belief that our basic nature is evil and needs to be held in check.

> *There is no stone in all the ego's embattled citadel that is more heavily defended than the idea that sin is real...*—ACIM, T-19.II.7:1

The ego is basically centered on three premises on which it builds its defense: the belief in sin, guilt and fear. As Ken has pointed out, "This unholy trinity is a psychological hell and constitutes the ego" (*Forgiveness and Jesus*). To understand the interweaving of these three ideas is to understand the structure of the ego. I once asked Ken why he thought the Course had come into existence now? Why not in the nineteenth century or the twenty-second? He said he wasn't sure. He was certain, however, that the Course could not have come into existence until after Freud, because it wasn't until Freud that we had an ego-based psychology. The ego in Course terminology is the belief in the reality of a separated or false self, made as a substitute for the Self that God created. This use of the word "ego" is broader than the way Freud defined it, although similarities exist. Freud understood the ego very well. He described in detail its defense mechanisms. Ego defense mechanisms, like denial and projection are a means of further backing into a sense of separation, rather than moving toward God. The use of the word "ego" in the Course is actually closer to the use of the word in Hinduism and Buddhism, meaning the opposite to the true Self.

> *A major tenet in the ego's insane religion is that sin is not error but truth...*
> —ACIM, T-19.II.4:1

The word "sin" as Jesus uses it in the New Testament means, "missing the mark." If we sin, we miss being centered in God. We are instead ego-centered. Sin is "lack of love" (ACIM, T- 1 IV 3.1). Sin is thus a *mistake* to be *corrected* rather than an *evil* to be *punished*.

Swami Baba Ji Whiz tells a story about *A Course in Miracles* student who was also a Catholic girl. She came to Swami and told him that he had to forgive her for she had sinned. "My goodness," said the Swami,

"What is your sin?" "I have committed," she said, "the sin of vanity." "Well, how is that?" said Swami. "Well," she said. "Each day I go and look at myself in the mirror and I say, you are so gorgeous you are absolutely beautiful." So, Swami had to tell her, "Look dear, that's not a sin—no, no, it's just a mistake."

When we see the word "sin" we can substitute the word "separation." Sin is the belief that we have separated ourselves from God and set up a self in opposition to our true Self. The Self is synonymous with Christ. Once we believe we have committed the sin of separation, it is impossible not to feel guilty. Once we feel guilty, it is impossible for us not to fear punishment *for what we think* we have done.

Sin is an illusion because the ego is an illusion. It's not who we are. Who each of us is—always has been and will be—is a Child of God. What God creates must be like Himself. His creation is the extension of His being. You are part of God, a Thought in the Mind of God. This is not arrogance. It does not mean that you are God.

Yet where He is, there must be holiness as well as life. No attribute of His remains unshared by everything that lives. What lives is holy as Himself, because what shares His life is part of Holiness, and could no more be sinful than the sun could choose to be made of ice; the sea elect to be apart from water, or the grass to grow with roots suspended in the air.
—ACIM, W. pt. I.156.3: 1-3

Management theory suggests two ways to manage. One way is to focus on who is doing things wrong, who is sloughing off, who is incompetent, and then either correct or get rid of them. Ken Blanchard, in *The One Minute Manager,* explores another, more profitable method of management—namely, to catch people doing things right. You thus support and encourage them to do even better. Not only is it more effective, it's also more fun. The methodology of the church is to seek out sin, provide testimony to its reality, and then try to overlook it by forgiving it. What we make real we cannot overlook and the fact that we make it real means we cannot overlook it (ACIM, T-9.IV.4: 6). You can be for or against something. It's more fun to be for than against.

If you attack error in another, you will hurt yourself.
You cannot know your brother when you attack him. —ACIM, T-3.III.7:1-2

Error or Truth?

To say that sin is not sin, only error, causes the ego to jump to its defense. The idea of sin is sacrosanct to the ego's thought system and essential to its existence. "It is the most 'holy' concept in the ego's system…" (ACIM, T-19.II.5:1-3).

Saying that sin is an error in thinking or perception doesn't mean that we condone what we call "sinful behavior." It simply means that such behavior is the inevitable outgrowth and expression of a false belief about our own identity and that of others. We have forgotten who we really are. We have misidentified ourselves as abandoned, unloved, unlovable, alone, and vulnerable. We have mistaken one another for enemies and thus justify unloving treatment. We justify condemnation and cruelty in the name of righteousness. Since judgment, condemnation, and punishment only reinforce our mistaken beliefs, there cannot be a real solution to the problem.

To say there is no sin does not mean that we can do whatever we want. The most basic law in the universe is the law of cause and effect. For every action there is a reaction. Thoughts are real. Not only does everything we do have its effect, everything we "think" has its effect. Obviously, then, we should be aware of our thoughts. What are we projecting? What are we seeing? As we give, so do we receive. As we forgive, so are we forgiven.

Once we no longer perpetuate error, we are free—no longer obsessed or possessed by something that does not become us in the first place—because it isn't us. To awaken to our own call is to awaken to who we really are, as a Son or Daughter of God not as some sniffling, whining little ego caught in illusions. Search out the devil and what do you find? Search out Heaven and what do you find?

The Atonement

In many ways, the most important difference between traditional Christianity and the Course has to do with the concept of the atonement. The opera singer at Central Valley said that the message she needed to hear every Sunday was that of the saving grace of the sacrificial blood of our Lord and Savior Jesus Christ. There was no sacrificial blood! Jesus never sacrificed anything! This is one idea in traditional Christianity I could not understand even before the Course. I had no explanation as to why this concept was so dear to the church, and I didn't preach it.

One of the Church's objections to the Course is its claim that the
is Gnostic and, therefore, heretical. To say that something is *heretical* me
it is *unorthodox,* or *contrary to accepted dogma.* The word gnosis mean
knowledge. It means *spiritual knowledge.* It is possible, according to Gnosticism, for us to *know* what Jesus *knew* and *to see* what *he saw.* It is
inevitable that each of us will come to the Vision of Christ—we already
have. Salvation in the traditional Christian perspective is based on *belief,*
not *knowledge.* Why should we not know what Jesus knew? Why not see
what he saw—do what he did? This is not blasphemy. This is affirmation
of life. Jesus in the Gospels says that even greater things than he has done
we can do. So why don't we?

I still believe that the Course will revolutionize the church by turning
the focus away from sin, guilt and fear to love, forgiveness and peace. I
now realize that this change is going to come from lay seekers and clerical
seekers alike who are rediscovering the heart of Christianity as expressed
in the Course. The Course may yet provide a Copernican revolution in
Christianity because reality does not revolve around institutional systems
of belief. It revolves around the truth.

> *Many are the paths of men. They all in the end come to Me.*
> —Bhagavada Gita, 4:11 based on Juan Mascaro, 1962

A Course in Miracles works for hundreds of thousands of people. There
are lots of ways of awakening. Still, there is one mountain, one God—one
peak experience. I may journey up the mountain from the west while you
climb from the east. It makes no difference which side of the mountain
we climb. We all begin from where we are. The more clearly each of us
pursues our own unique path—the closer we get to the top, the more we
realize how similar our paths have been.

CHAPTER 35

A Golden Year

1993—Age Fifty

I resolve that my book on the Course will be published by the time I'm fifty. I'm writing all the time. I have no idea how the book is going to be published. I have no connections with the publishing community. Still, I keep writing. Tom Kemnitz, the printer for *On Course* and later *Miracles* magazines, gives the best clue to successful writing. He says, "Just keep writing." He's right. It works. I'm driving home from Manhattan late one evening wondering how *is* the book going to get published. I ask for guidance and I hear a voice say, "The answer is in *On Course*." That's all it says. It assures me that I am on the right track.

Joan Ryan, a subscriber to *On Course,* is on the commuter train from New York City to her home in southern Connecticut. Sitting next to her is a man reading *A Course in Miracles.* He leans over her shoulder and notices that her little magazine is on *A Course in Miracles.* They talk. He subscribes. I think it is interesting that Michael Leach of Crossroads Publishing in New York City should be subscribing. Not only does he subscribe, he reads the magazine!

Diane writes an editorial, in which she mentions that I'm working on a manuscript on *A Course in Miracles.* Michael reads it and calls to ask if he can see my manuscript. I send it his way. In the meantime, we have outgrown the Dorot, so I look around and find an incredible place. On the first Sunday in March of 1993, we move to Cami Hall, directly across the street from Carnegie Hall on 57th Street and 7th Avenue. I send out a bunch of announcements, and that first day, the place is packed. That same day, Michael Leach comes to services. After the service, he comes up on stage and hands me a contract for my book to be entitled *Awaken To Your Own Call.* Two incredibly positive events occur on the same day.

A map on the wall of my office shows a 75-mile radius around New York City. The spot used for the center of the map is Columbus Circle—only a block and a half from Cami Hall. I take a pushpin and stick it in the spot where Cami Hall is and measure. It is four inches to the Hudson River, and four inches to the East River, eighteen inches to the bottom of Manhattan, and eighteen inches to the top of Manhattan. Eighteen inches to the west takes us well into New Jersey and eighteen inches to the east takes us well into Long Island. Our church has found its home in the center of New York City. There are many Protestants, Catholics, Jews, and Muslims here. I'm living in the country, so I have the best of both worlds. People are willing to come into the city from Queens, Brooklyn, Long Island, New Jersey, Westchester, and Connecticut. It would not work the other way around. Many New Yorkers do not have cars. They could not go to the suburbs. It is perfect; we are where the people are. Subscribers to *On Course* and visitors from all over the world can easily find us. All you have to do is to find Carnegie Hall, and everyone knows how to get to Carnegie Hall.

Mother must undergo a serious operation. Not only does she need a triple bypass, she also has a huge aortic aneurysm. Her chances of making it safely through the operation are fifty-fifty. I fly to Missouri to be with her. Judy Femmer lives in Columbia where Mother is having her surgery. I make several calls. I leave messages on her answering machine. We never connect.

Mother's courage in the face of what she is about to go through is impressive. First thing every morning she reads through and listens to *The Daily Word* devotion on tape. Her pastor says of her that she is not only a leader of their church in the usual sense (having been a deacon, elder and, for many years, president of the women's society), she is a spiritual leader as well, a fact made apparent by her daily life.

If it is her time to go, she is ready. Ann and I are not ready and neither are her grandchildren, Sean and Erin, or anybody among her family or friends. Ann and I are sitting on either side of her bed prior to her going into the operating room. She holds our hands and says, "I have been so lucky." Ann says, "We are the lucky ones." She said her meditation for the day is: "I go to meet my good." (What does that mean?) I break down in tears, hug her and say, "I love you so much." She replies, "I love you, too, sweetie." Love is all there is. It is the only thing that matters. Mother recovers and does just fine. She will, however, need another heart operation in 2000.

Back in New York, Interfaith throws me a fiftieth birthday party and I get a new computer. Finally, I'm free of the old typesetter. I sit down at my new computer to write a sermon on peace. I have to name the file so

281

I decide to simply call it *Peace*. I type in the letters P-E-A-C-E and hit Enter. Immediately it pops up on the computer screen. "Peace does not exist. Would you like to create it?" "Yes" or "Cancel." I choose "Yes."

Diane and I work well together and the fellowship continues to prosper, as does *On Course* magazine. Sadly, our relationship doesn't hold the same romantic quality for me that it does for Diane. Once again I have stepped into a relationship without perfect clarity. Diane came along just at the right time. She saw me through the very difficult time with the inn and the leaving of the Methodist church. Together we have built a church in New York City. I'm not able to make the commitment to a lifetime together. Diane is not happy with our relationship either. We both now agree that we came together to give birth to Interfaith Fellowship. I sometimes look at couples who come together and have a child or two and then split. I wonder if maybe they came together just so those people could be born. I ask Diane what she wants for Christmas and she says, "A ring." Then she adds, "After five years together, it is time to get engaged or to finally have an honest conversation about why not."

There is something about the changing of a year, which often correlates with the changing of certain ages in our life. I broke off with Susan on my fortieth birthday. I'm now fifty. Lying awake in bed at Mother's house early on Christmas morning, I make a vow to change things in the new year. I will be more honest with Diane, no matter how much it hurts, no matter how inevitable the tears. It will not be easy.

CHAPTER 36

Finally, Dolores
Love, Marriage and Family Life

1994—Age Fifty-One

Diane and I began our relationship on January 1, 1989. Five years later, the first week of January 1994, it comes to an end. The day after the decision is made, Diane tells the congregation from the pulpit on Sunday morning. If we have learned anything from the Course, it is that forgiveness works. Despite our separation, our mutual commitment to the Fellowship and to each other is strong. I admire and respect Diane greatly and it seems to be mutual. She has always been for me a "wise advisor" and friend. Now we can love each other as we are. In March, Diane begins to date Dr. Tony Zito, a New York City psychiatrist who began attending services the previous fall. Before long he and Diane are a regular number. They are looking at each other with big smiles, wide-open eyes and lots of love.

Life as a Methodist minister was desperate. Now life is full of hope. 1994 will easily qualify as one of the best years of my life. This is the year that I meet my wife, Dolores, *Awaken to Your Own Call* is published, and I buy a badly needed new car. Overwhelmed with the task of producing *On Course* on a weekly schedule and receiving feedback that it comes out too often. I increase the number of pages from thirty-two to forty-eight and cut production to every other week.

I turn most of the resume writing business over to Ruth Murphy, splitting the revenues. We don't write many resumes, maybe two or three per week. It provides some income for groceries and gasoline and helps to make up for a low salary. One afternoon Ruth has an appointment to write a resume and is called home to care for her children. She tells me I will have to take care of the appointment. I have forgotten about it when abruptly the doorbell rings. Answering the door, I'm standing face to face with the most stunningly beautiful woman I have ever seen. Her face is open and shining like sunlight, and I soon discover that she is gorgeous through and through. To this day, every time I look at her I think—"gorgeous!"

Dolores is unique, enchanting, free spirited. She is also *just* a nice person—a "real" human being. Dolores is a tall Irish girl with long, thick, red hair that risks being mistaken for a sunrise, dark eyes that sparkle like diamonds, and tiny freckles on an impish face. She has a winning smile as wide as it is wonderful, and a laugh like moonlight on water. She is as good, and as beautiful, as an angel. I am drawn to her like steel to a magnet. I am, as they say, "smitten." I look at her and think, "Where have you been all my life?" I don't say it. For all I know she is married.

Mother once observed that there are interesting similarities between Dolores, Judy Femmer, and Judy Halpin. They are each beautiful with cute little noses, wonderful overbites and sexy rabbit-type teeth. Each of their fathers was an alcoholic. They each have interesting, wonderful quirks like a fear of mice and other critters. Each has a delightful and enchanting chuckle that can roll on for a long time laughing. Judy Femmer and Dolores both enjoy chess, and they are both "addicted" to reading and classical music.

I help Dolores write her resume, gathering lots of information in short order. When I get to the end I look at her and say, "Do you want to put down any personal information? For example, are you married?" She looks at me with shy surveying eyes. "No," she says after a pause. "I'm divorced." I do not let the sun set before I call and ask for a date. Dolores and her ex-husband Lenny had owned a small seafood restaurant called the Sea Shanty. Seven years earlier they adopted an infant daughter Sarah.

I not only helped Dolores write her resume, I also write her a glowing reference. Dolores has always been a professional secretary. She decides that working for a public school might be an excellent job. Although she would still have to work summers, she would get off on the same school holidays as Sarah. In the fall Dolores starts working as secretary to the principal of Valley Central Middle School.

On our first date we go to The Rainbow Room, a northern Italian restaurant in Monroe, and then for a walk around the Goose Pond, in the center of town. We sit on a yellow park bench near a weeping willow tree and a small waterfall over the spillway. God, this moment is perfect. The silver moon, like a huge oval spotlight, is shining down on the mirror of a lake below. It is an outstanding night. And then—our first kiss. Dolores has a radiance about her that reaches inside and seizes my soul and speaks to me in words too tender to repeat. There is a gentleness about Dolo-

284

res—and an ease in relating. I am completely enamored. I will do everything I can to please her. I've fallen in love again—and this time I feel it will last.

Dolores owns a quaint, thirteen hundred square foot blue-gray house with a yard full of large chestnut trees. Each evening now I venture to her house. Her home is ordered and clean—plain, not ostentatious. Like Mother, Dolores has an "eye" for color and a flair for interior decorating. As I open her door, the sound of some operatic or modern instrumental music greets me. Dolores comes to the door with a big kiss before we go into the kitchen to talk and finish fixing dinner. I'm sure Dolores is the woman I want to marry. I want both of us to be sure so I try not to come on too strong too fast. Lenny and Dolores are in daily contact, and it is a source of constant conflict. Lenny now lives in an apartment in Washingtonville. We take Sarah there a couple of times each week, giving us a chance to be alone.

In July my nephew, Sean, and his fiancée, Cindy, are married. Sarah stays with Lenny while Dolores and I fly to Missouri for the wedding and an opportunity for Mother, Ann, and Glenn to meet Dolores. Ann falls for Dolores first and Mother comes a-tumbling after.

Dolores and I take a walk on the farm, in the pasture of my regeneration. We take along a blanket and lay it out on the ground in the tall grasses, near the woods and Daddy's bass pond. We lie back looking at puffy white clouds drifting along. I often did this as a young man. Now I'm sharing this, "my heavenly spot," with my future wife. God, this is a beautiful place! What a beautiful day! What a beautiful woman! I turn and look at Dolores. She is covered with ticks, and not just one or two. There are dozens and dozens of them are crawling all over her clothes and beautiful red hair. I look at my own clothes. I too, am covered. We hurry home and repeatedly comb each other's hair, removing more and more ticks. We then shower and shower again. Fortunately, they are wood ticks, not the deer ticks that carry Lyme disease.

1995—Age Fifty-Two

I increase the number of pages in *On Course* from forty-eight to sixty-four. We are growing very slowly and very nicely, working consistently from a profitable base. On the average we take in $5,600 per month in new subscriptions and renewals with another $3,800 in book sales. With the addition of an occasional unexpected donation from a subscriber we're grossing in excess of $10,000 a month from the magazine. With the addition of Aunt Sue's $10,000 each February, it's easy paying the bills. My long held dream for a magazine has come true. Next step? I want to see it on the newsstands.

With the able assistance of our music director, Jeff Olmsted, Interfaith sponsors a number of concerts with Donna Cary, Scott Kalechstein and other musicians. Jeff produces his first CD, *Step into the Light* with The Interfaith Fellowship Choir. We sponsor workshops with a variety of leaders: Alan Cohen, Jerry Jampolsky, Lee Coit, Robert Perry, Tom and Linda Carpenter and others. I'm doing more traveling and lecturing. In June I'm invited to Anchorage, Alaska, for a speaking tour of Unity and Religious Science Churches and Miracles studies groups. I take a helicopter tour up into the mountains where we land next to a glacier and we see bears, eagles, moose and, out over the sea, white Beluga Whales.

At the end of *Awaken to Your Own Call,* I ask if anything is missing. And I say "Yes," there is a lot more that could be said about the role of the Holy Spirit in the Course; so much you could write a book about it. As soon as *Awaken* is done, I begin writing *Listening to Your Inner Guide.* I send it off to Ken. He writes back offering his comments and says his favorite chapter is the one entitled *Missouri Mystic.* I decide to someday take that chapter and make a book of it. It takes only a year to write *Listening to Your Inner Guide.* Dedicated to Dolores, it is published by Crossroad in 1995. With two books out, I begin to do even more traveling, speaking in Unity churches and for a variety of Course in Miracles groups and conferences.

On Thanksgiving Day, Dolores says she will marry me. I don't have enough money for a ring so we wait till St. Patrick's day of 1996 when I'm finally able to make the purchase.

December 19, 1995, Dolores and I have both fallen asleep on the couch. Suddenly, the phone rings, startling us awake. Dolores answers the phone and immediately starts screaming, "No! No! No!" She is down on her knees on the kitchen floor screaming "Noooo!!!" The caller is Ned, Dolores' best friend's husband. He works at the local hospital. Lenny is dead. He choked to death on a piece of meat while having dinner at a friend's house. He was only forty-five. The next few months are rough. Dolores still loved Lenny, though she could not make a life with him. Lenny has died the same way Daddy did.

1996—Age Fifty-Three

I increase the number of pages in *On Course* to eighty per issue and cut back to one issue per month. I'm giving lectures at more and more conferences and workshops in a variety of cities. I hand out a number of free magazines. Our subscription base is growing from the variety of Course in Miracles students I'm meeting around the country.

There is snow on the ground constantly from November of 1995 to April of 1996. In March we experience the worst blizzard to hit New York City since 1888. What's bad in the city is worse in the country. One Sunday morning there is a terrific snowstorm. The Methodist churches in the city close. The Catholic church gives special dispensation so people do not have to attend church. I leave an hour earlier than usual. With the Jeep it's not too bad. We open as usual and seventy people show up for services. Although the roads are a mess—the subways are open.

A wonderful lady named Julie Tyler comes to work for us, helping with the mailings and book sales. She slowly develops a ministry corresponding with prisoners, sending money to help them with art supplies, sneakers and typewriters and shipping books to prisons throughout the United States. Julie says she only needs to earn $200 a week. She is, however, working nearly full time.

In May, Diane and Tony are married. Rabbi Gelberman and I perform the ceremony in the courtyard of Barbetta's restaurant in the theater district in Manhattan. I get to pronounce them "husband and wife."

I do a speaking tour of the Midwest that includes Unity of Chicago. In Chicago, I meet Charlotte Foster, a friend from high school, and her husband for dinner. Charlotte, her then boyfriend Butch Church, Judy Femmer and I used to double date. While we are eating and reminiscing about high school days, Charlotte says, "When Judy got pregnant and ran off with Jim. . . " I drop my fork on my plate. It had never occurred to me that Judy was pregnant when she married. I was celibate and assumed that Judy was a virgin. That is why I could not dissuade her. That is why she had to go through with it. Back in New York, I call her, and she tells me she deliberately got pregnant with Jim. "Damn it, Jon, I needed to get away from home! And you were not asking me to marry!"

Ruth Murphy, who's been handling our database and the bookkeeping, informs me that her husband has been offered a position in Massachusetts, so she has to move. This is very sad. Ruth has been a godsend. She is so neat, methodical, organized and thorough. She is an active student of *A Course in Miracles* and a deeply spiritual and committed woman. It will be difficult to replace her. In fact, it will be impossible.

A New Home

Dolores' house is too small to be both a home for the three of us and an office for Interfaith Fellowship. We need to find a new home. Diane and I take little in the way of salary. I have no reserves since the loss of the inn and cannot afford a house. With the sale of Dolores' home, however, we'll have enough money for a down payment on a decent home. The house will be in her name. We decide to celebrate my fifty-third birthday with a trip to Mohonk Mountain house near New Paltz, New York. First we meet with a realtor to visit a two-story heritage-blue cedar colonial.

There is a perfect space for an office in an area over the garage, a beautiful bay window and a balcony looking down to the family room below. Part of the basement can be used for producing *On Course*, and an extra bedroom will act as a second office. A deck at back of the house covers the entire length of the house. The neighborhood is perfect for Sarah. She can safely bicycle and roller blade around the mile-long circle and attached cul-de-sacs. There is a community pool less than a quarter of a mile from the house. Sarah is now ten, and there is a ten-year-old girl in the house next door. There is an apartment in the basement, which means that Ted Sosler, who lives with me in Monroe can come live with us. His rent can help with the mortgage. Ted is the kindest, gentlest, sweetest man you could meet. He is a mister fix-it, a great help in maintaining the place in Monroe and he's willing to help maintain the new house.

During lunch at Mohonk and while we stroll in the beautiful spring gardens, we dream together. What would it be like if "that place" could be our home? At $269,000 the price is too high. Back in Monroe I hear that the place is sold, so I keep looking at other possibilities. I never find anything so appropriate. One evening, on our way out for dinner, we drive by again just to look at the house from the outside. There is a new sign out front saying, "for sale by Owner" with a phone number. I call right away. The place is still for sale and the price is reduced. We move in September.

My niece, Erin, after several years of trying, becomes Miss Missouri. Mother flies to New York for a few days' visit. Then we all go to the Miss America pageant. Erin is a lovely young woman, and we want to support her in the pursuit of her dream. On the final evening of the pageant, Dolores and I are sitting directly in front of the parents of Miss Oklahoma, who becomes the next Miss America. I'm able to turn and snap several great pictures of their faces as the count increasingly comes down to their daughter—a stirring experience, itself worth the price of admission.

1997—Age Fifty-four

Meribeth has been working for *On Course* and Interfaith part-time for the last five years. If she's to continue, she needs to be full time. Meribeth now becomes the managing editor for *On Course* magazine so I have more time to work on the development of Interfaith.

In January, we start producing a ninety-six-page *On Course*. In August, I take another good look at *On Course*. We have two thousand paid subscribers. It's time to take it to a higher level by going to a full-size magazine format with a colored cover. We will never get on the newsstands using church worship bulletins for covers. I decide to change the name to *Inspiration*. Diane likes it and the change is made. A magazine should say in one word what it's about if it can; *Time, Life, Look, Money*. What we are about is *Inspiration*. The subtitle for *On Course* has always been *Inspiration for the Inner Journey*. With the full-size format we immediately begin to attract more advertisers and subscribers.

The Interfaith Center

The only drawback to our new home is a rather small driveway, both in comparison to the other homes in the community and in comparison to my previous home in Monroe, which means shuffling cars around. Furthermore, people who come to see me for counseling or for help with resume writing have to park on the street. This is not too big a problem until a neighbor complains to the zoning board that I'm running a business from my home and that we have an illegal apartment. This results in a visit from the building inspector, who says I will have to shut down my office and get rid of Ted. There is nothing illegal about my having an office in my home. I cannot, however, have employees and we now have four.

I have always worked from home. I never had any trouble at the house in Monroe. There was also plenty of off-street parking in Monroe, and more importantly, no one ever complained. This visit from the building inspector seems like another setback, a bit of bad luck. Twenty years after my unpleasant experience with the zoning board at High Rock, it's happening again. Once again, it seems the world is coming in and trying to impose itself on our happy situation. We have just gotten settled and things are working out well.

I soon find an 800 square-foot space in Washingtonville, that we can use as an office and bookstore for only $500 per month. It's in the basement again. It is, however, a move outside the house. We've been selling books through *Inspiration* magazine. We might as well sell them off the shelves. This will be fun. I had envisioned an Interfaith Center. Here it is: The Interfaith Center and Inner Journey Books! My dream has come true. We begin to decorate the place and add a few appropriate gift items. Dr. Weltman's Miracles Group starts meeting at the center, and Therese Quinn forms a women's group. A young man from Ananda Ashram, Justin Davis, starts a yoga class. I start monthly lectures and we sponsor workshops and concerts with Jimmy Twyman, Scott Kalechstein, Donna Cary and others. We expand the bookstore and gift shop. And, lo and behold, I discover as I did at High Rock that it's not illegal to have an extra apartment. Ted can live with us!

Our Wedding Day

On July 5th, Dolores and I are married at the Bulls Head Inn, just a mile from our house. There is a garden and fountains and it's a perfect day for our wedding. Ann and Glenn and Mother drive up from Missouri and stay with us in our new home. There, before family and friends we affirm our commitment to spend our lives together. Diane performs the ceremony along with our associate ministers, Julie Olmsted and Sara Emrie. Father Giles Spoonhour, instrumental in helping set up the New Seminary, and Rabbi Gelberman give their blessings. Diane pronounces us husband and wife. It's perfect. It is a splendid, sunny, mild July day. It hits a high of 80 degrees. Everyone is there—all of Dolores's sisters—Barbara, Susan and Maureen, their husbands and children, my family and our closest friends. Myron is my best man.

One of the subscribers to *Inspiration* from St. John in the Virgin Islands tells me she can get me a great deal, a villa called "Pistarkle." It's on the side of a mountain at the farthest point on the east end of St. John's, a forty-five minute drive from Cruz Bay, all for only $100 per day. To get to the villa we have to travel on twisting mountain roads, accessible by means of a little four wheel drive Suzuki Sidekick—just about the only

290

kind of car on St. John. The roads make Dolores nervous. She is right. It is treacherous!

From the full-length deck of the villa we can see no house in any direction. All we can see are the British Virgin Islands across the way. Because we are closer to the equator, at night the stars are clearer than I've ever seen them, even on the farm in Missouri. We are alone—completely away from everything. Though there is a television and a telephone we hardly touch either. Waves crash up against the huge rocks of an inlet some 800 feet below—while we make love. I am sure that I have died and gone to Heaven. It is also a retreat, a time of refreshment and restoration. Much of our time is spent looking out across the ocean at the other islands. It proves to be a great time to read—to meditate and go within.

Dolores and I get closer and closer. Marriage is the right move. It's good to finally be settled, contented—committed. I appreciate marriage, in part because I waited for it so long. It is wonderful to have a partner with whom I can share a home, a daughter, meals, work, play, movies—life. Marriage offers opportunities for sharing that no other human relationship can equal. It deepens and enriches every facet of life. We are each other's lover, confidant, teacher, listener, reflector and friend. Sarah becomes more and more my daughter. We develop the ability to kid and joke while respecting each other. It's fun being a dad. I wish I had more of an opportunity with Kristian; now he has moved back to New York and we begin to spend more time together. With Dolores and Sarah happiness is fuller; memories are fresher. Everything is more fun—more complete. Joy must be shared to make it a full experience.

John Denver, another of my heroes, dies in a small plane crash off the coast of California. We were born the same year. I so identified with his "Thank God I'm a Country Boy" and his "Take Me Home, Country Roads." I keep singing the lyrics, "Hey it's good to be back home again…." His Colorado was my Missouri.

1998—Age Fifty-Five—An Opening of the Heart

Diane and Tony's apartment is on the 14th floor of the Century Building in Manhattan, across the street from Cental Park. The experience of dawn, of night and the moonlight over the city can be marvelous from this spot. We begin holding monthly meetings at their apartment to help define Interfaith's mission and basic tenets. Interfaith receives an unexpected windfall and I expand the Interfaith Center into another room. We now have

1,300 square feet so I can separate the office from the bookstore and workshop space. I'm building more and more bookcases. The Center is growing nicely.

In April, Dolores and Sarah accompany me to the International Attitudinal Healing Conference in Orlando, Florida—of course, there is Disney world. My altered ego, Swami Baba Ji Whiz shows up! This is getting to be fun. I could make a career of this. Robin Williams, Billy Crystal and Whoopi Goldberg have, I think, some of the best jobs in the world. There is nothing more fun than making people laugh, and if you can work in metaphysics, mysticism and miracles, so much the better. Jesus was a storyteller. I'll bet that among those stories there were many good laughs. There are certainly ironies. As my teacher, Swami Beyondananda says, "Seeing a doctor will not cure you of irony deficiency. But seeing a paradox will."

Heart disease is an inherent problem in my family. Mother had a triple bypass at seventy-seven. Her father Carl and her sister, Marie, each died of heart attacks in their fifties. I have been experiencing high blood pressure for several years. I've been trying to correct it through medication, meditation, diet and exercise—without significant improvement. My doctor sets up a date for a stress test. A few days before the test, I have an *incident,* after swimming laps in our community pool. I develop a number of flu-like symptoms including nausea and a weak and listless feeling. I talk with Judy Halpin in Florida and she advises me to cease all exercise till I've had the stress test. I stop exercising. The cardiologist says, "Judy probably saved your life."

After a few minutes the cardiologist stops the test, takes me into his office and puts me under some real stress by saying I am a candidate for a major heart attack in the near future. Less than a week later I undergo quadruple bypass surgery. Open-heart surgery is a humbling experience. I know I will survive. I'm still relatively young. I have lots of energy. Still, open-heart surgery gives one the opportunity to look at death a little. I do not have a will. It's silly not to, as I now have a family. So I make out a will.

After the cardiologist said I was a candidate for a major heart attack, he added, "I have to tell you that your chances of not surviving the operation are one in a thousand." I check into Manhattan's Columbia Presbyterian on Monday. I don't go into surgery until five p.m. on Wednesday as five heart transplants come in ahead of me, taking priority. Sitting and waiting costs $3,500! While waiting I read *Tuesdays with Morrie*. The anesthesiologist who pilots me into the operating room says, "I have to tell you your chances of not making it are one in five hundred." "Wait a minute," I say. "the cardiologist said one in a thousand." To which he responds, "I'm being more realistic." I tell him to "knock me out good—and we will talk about it in the morning."

The next thing I know it's morning and I am regurgitating ether while someone is pulling a tube out of my throat. I've had better mornings. Still, it isn't all that bad. Indeed, I was never in any really great pain, only discomfort. The anesthesiologist must have knocked me out "good." Next morning I have a number of bumps on the back of my head and I am left to this day with a dent in my skull and tinnitus (constant ringing in my ears). A line from *A Course in Miracles* serves as a reminder that whatever we experience we have chosen.

> *Remember that no one is where he is by accident, and chance plays no part in God's plan. —ACIM, M-9.1:3*

My surgeon is Dr. Mehmet Oz, just like the Wizard of Oz. A strong believer in alternative therapies, he has written a new book called *Healing from the Heart,* which I read while I am in recovery. His method is to incorporate ancient methods like yoga and prayer along with ultramodern approaches to healing. My surgical team were all skilled surgeons working together like a precision orchestra, doing what they needed to do over a period of six hours. My job is to practice what I preach—to relax in faith and trust in God. I went into this operation with a good deal of faith, knowing that everything was going to work out. I'm in the hands of well-trained professionals. I have one of the best surgeons in one of the finest hospitals in the United States. Interestingly, Columbia Presbyterian is where much of *A Course in Miracles* was written.

There is a wonderful nurse named Ellen. The day after my surgery I'm told there is fluid in one of my lungs, which requires putting a hole in my side, a tube in my chest, and a pump to drain out the fluid. Ellen stands on the left side of my bed and holds my hand while they perform this procedure. There is such love and compassion coming from her. Thank God for all those who work in this wonderful profession!

I am not a body. I am free, for I am still as God created me. —ACIM, W.199

Ken calls twice while I am in the hospital and once when I get home. I'm grateful to him. On the occasion of his first call, while I am still in post-op, I say, "I'm not a body, right, Ken?" He says that he thought he had read that somewhere, giving me an opportunity to laugh while holding a pillow against my stitches. After the experience, I want to hang on longer on the phone with various friends. I want to know more about how *they* are doing. I'm back at my desk in five days and while recuperating I start writing this book. Dolores says, "You miss your horse, don't you, country boy?" I'm back in the Jeep and on the road after three weeks.

Mystery is the true art and science. He who can no longer pause to wonder and stand rapt in awe is as good as dead. —Albert Einstein

I'm to spend some time walking every day. I stop and look at the white ladies mantle, black-eyed Susan and the blue bachelor buttons, all with bees busily buzzing about. Being alive is to be wondered at and celebrated! There is so much love coming from neighbors, from the community that has formed around the Interfaith Center, the Fellowship and subscribers to *Inspiration.* I give an address to the Phoenix Society in Connecticut—exactly one month from the day of the operation.

Myron is constantly writing, determined not to let his disability destroy his life. He writes a play, *Chronic Joy,* about his experience of coming to terms with MS. I see to it that a reading is done before friends at Cami Hall.

I've been working on *The Ten Laws of Happiness*, based on the ten characteristics of a Teacher of God as described in the Manual for Teachers of *A Course in Miracles.* I decide to publish it with the help of Tom Kemnitz of Royal Fireworks, who does the printing for *Inspiration.* All the money from the sale of the book goes to Interfaith, which is okay. Still, I need a better system.

1999—Age Fifty-Six

I dream that Judy Halpin in Florida is getting married. I see clearly the white gown she is wearing. Her mother is wearing the same style of dress. I'm performing the ceremony in Windsor Terrace. The dream is so vivid; I call and leave a message on her answering machine. Two weeks later she calls. She is incredibly happy. My dream is coming true.

Rabbi Gelberman, at eighty-seven, retires as the head of the New Seminary and Diane takes over. Diane is immensely capable. I'm sure she will do a good job. In September, we celebrate Interfaith's tenth anniversary with a $100 per person fund raising banquet with 120 people, in the wood-paneled City Athletic Club in Manhattan. The next day we have a full house for our Sunday service and an afternoon talent show.

Each decade has brought a major change. The forties and fifties were spent on the farm. The sixties were the decade of education and travel. The seventies were the time of Brooklyn, teaching, doctoral studies and Wainwright House. The eighties were the time of High Rock Spring and Central Valley. The nineties were the time of Interfaith Fellowship and *On Course* (*Inspiration*) magazine. Now, as the twentieth century comes to a close, once again everything comes to an end.

CHAPTER 37

New Life in the Twenty-First Century

2000—Age Fifty-Seven

In February, Revs. Tony Ponticello and Larry Bedini of the Community Miracles in San Francisco hold a wonderfully well-thought-out Course in Miracles Conference with many of the major ACIM leaders. I sign on several new subscribers for *Inspiration* magazine. There are over 400 participants, and it is so successful, and so well organized that John Nagy and Bob Sandoe of The Quest Foundation in Boston and I announce that we will hold the next Miracles Conference in New York City. Staff at the The Interfaith Center can work on the production and *Inspiration* magazine can provide much of the promotion.

*I **am** responsible for what I see. I choose the feelings I experience, and I decide upon the goal I would achieve. And everything that seems to happen to me I ask for, and receive as I have asked. —ACIM, T- 21.II.2: 3-5*

I've run Interfaith as an entrepreneurial ministry. I've handled most of the administration along with our office staff, Silita, our bookkeeper/database manager, Julie Tyler, who handles the book sales and mailings, Phyllis DeNoyles, who helps in every way possible, Meribeth Seamen, who edits the magazine, Diane Berke and an administrative council that oversees our accounts and supervises our program planning. A new board of trustees is now established. We start holding meetings twice a month in the city. I felt spirit guided; now we're committee directed. There is a new way of doing things.

I go to England to give lectures sponsored by Miracles leader Ian Patrick. Before I leave, I turn over all of our records to the new board. They want to do some reorganizing. Ever since the voice back at the Inn said, "Haven't I always taken care of you?" I've had incredible faith. I am sure that trust is the way to go. If you do the right thing—the money will be there. The money has always been there. Interfaith Fellowship and *Inspiration* magazine are what I'm meant to do. For the past eleven years the bills have been paid. We've put out 265 editions of the magazine—all of them paid for. Though Diane and I have sometimes taken weeks without pay, our staff has always been paid. We had gross receipts in excess of $250,000 in 1998 and again in 1999. We have a debt of $18,000. That is less than 7% of our yearly income. We have no credit card debt and no loans. We have a number of different lines of income and thus cash flow—and at Christmas and Easter it flows very well. The new board says that they love me. They want to make things better. We should be carrying no debt at all. A few cutbacks would probably be a good idea.

We now experience micromanaging in the extreme and lots of cuts. The Center in Washingtonville is not "itself" self-supporting. Our main source of income, however, comes from the donations of subscribers to the magazine and our office generates this income. I must make cuts. The number of telephone lines is decreased. I close off the room where we started. Staff must be reduced. The work is to be picked up by volunteers. Who will volunteer? The first to go is our database manager and bookkeeper, Sileta, then Julie Tyler—who has been so helpful—who has worked for so little—who believes so strongly in what we are doing—whom Dolores and I have come to love so much. Julie is an integral part of the Center and one of the sweetest human beings to ever visit this planet.

All promotional expenses are stopped. Just like at Pilgrims Inn, this starts a downward spiral. We stop sending out "missed you Sunday" letters. We stop sending birthday greetings to members and subscribers. Copies of the magazine are not mailed free to absentee members and prospective subscribers. We stop sending *Inspiration* to the magazine distributors, as they are not paying us in a timely fashion. I want to send *Inspiration* magazines to a Miracles Conference in California. This would, I know, result in many new subscriptions. I cannot. Half of the magazines printed are not distributed.

I am told that *Inspiration* magazine is sacrosanct and will not be touched. The Center itself, however, must be closed. Staff is reduced to Meribeth only. Volunteers do not come forward. Renewal notices are not being sent out. Book orders cannot be filled. To avoid bank charges we stop accepting credit card purchases. This is, I think a huge mistake as so much income came in this way. Cash flow slows and crawls down to a trickle. In the meantime, no fundraising plans are in the works. We cut, and cut, and cut, and cut, and it is way too much. We cut to the bone and sever the arteries, which fed our heart and gave us life. With continuing expenses and no staff or programs to generate revenues, our debt increases.

Beware of the temptation to see yourself unfairly treated. —ACIM, T-26.X.4:1

I've often said that if you could get one idea in the Course, you could get the whole Course. If you really get "I am not a victim of the world I see" (W-pI.31), you get the whole Course. I do not want to see myself as a victim in the dissolution of the Center. This must be happening for a higher reason. We teach what we need to learn. I give a sermon on the importance of not being a victim and another on being appreciative of those who test us and make us stronger. Why do churches "have" to go through this? It seems it's all about power. Who has it and who wants it? I'm beginning not to want it.

I drive up to Roscoe to see Ken and Gloria Wapnick. I tell Ken what has happened. He asks me who I am now in relationship to Interfaith and I tell him that I am now essentially an employee. I am no longer "the director." When I finish, he sits silently for a moment looking at me. Then just as Helen used to do when she wanted to tell me something important, he leans forward and says that he is sorry but he thinks I will have to quit the Fellowship. I tell him "No!" I'm sure he is wrong. The situation is not "that bad." He smiles sympathetically and says he is sorry.

In July, Dolores, Sarah and I go home to Missouri for my niece Erin's wedding. It's a reprieve from the upheaval that now dominates our dear Fellowship. Erin marries Michael Englemeyer, a charming six-foot-eight professional outdoor photographer. I pronounce them husband and wife, slowly drawing out the announcement so it gets a laugh. I get to talk at Mexico Central Christian on Sunday morning, and I make it a tribute to Mother. I want her to know how loved she is. I will not wait till the day of her funeral to give this talk.

Sunday afternoon Dolores and I drive out Sunrise Christian Church Road. We stop at the country church and visit the grave of my great-grandparents Jonathan and Jenny Mundy and Aunt Bertha. I must also kneel for a moment at the grave of my first guides in life, Uncle Estel and Aunt Jessie. We swing back by the farm I grew up on, then around to the Monglers. Surprise of surprises, my old friend Clifford, his brother Ricky and his sister Dee are all home visiting with their mother, Lillis. It's been forty years since I've seen them. Always chubby as a kid, Clifford looks wonderfully trim. He's wearing a beard, bib overalls and a cap with the word NAVY on it to protect his baldhead. He still has a simple, easy air and a down-to-earth Missouri farmer philosophy. Live and let live—be at peace with your neighbor. God, it is good to see him! He's such a decent human being. Then it's back to New York.

Four of the members of the new administration are recent graduates of the New Seminary and they begin to take turns preaching on Sunday mornings. My own speaking schedule is reduced to one Sunday per month. I have always felt called to be a minister, a preacher, and a teacher. I have been doing it since I was eighteen. I am still convinced that it is what I am here to do. I shall do it till I die. Friends, who have come to services to hear me speak, now quit the Fellowship. Others decide to come to services only on the Sunday that I'm there. I call Judy Skutch Whitson and she says that she has watched the same thing happen with two of the organizations she has worked with. The leader is out and a board is now running things.

I'm asked to be a speaker at The Great Lakes Retreat in Michigan. There I receive a reading from a psychic. I ask about the current situation with Interfaith. I'm hopeful that the dismantling is over. I'm told no, there are more changes to come.

Interfaith is no longer sponsoring workshops, concerts or seminars and there are no fundraising activities in the works. With none of the income we used to have, my salary, Diane's and Jeff's are stopped completely for three months. Then we begin to receive $100 per week as "parsonage allowance." Of course you can't live on $100 per week. I need an income. I send out proposal packages to several Unity and Religious Science churches looking for speaking opportunities and the opportunities begin to present themselves.

In September, the Interfaith Center is closed for good. Books I purchased to sell in the store are handed out on the streets of Manhattan in exchange for whatever donation people want to give. This is my third failure at trying to start a Center. Is this what that psychic was talking about so many years ago—three failures—and I bounce back from each? I guess the real "center" is just wherever I am, wherever any of us is.

2001—Age Fifty-Eight

Now comes the toughest blow of all. *Inspiration* magazine is stopped and Meribeth, too, is dismissed. I break into tears. The main income for the Fellowship came from subscribers to *Inspiration*! How many magazines have been suspended and never renewed? Except for ever-faithful David Perle, who volunteers his time helping with computer problems, everyone is gone. Ironically, Meribeth's computer dies.

I'm alone. I have to get quiet. It is time to stop—to think. I start the workbook lessons of the Course over again. *Inspiration* was my baby—my form of creativity. I gave birth to it. Much of the money I inherited and earned went into it. We were just beginning to have some success in getting it distributed through a couple of distributors. A month before *Inspiration* is suspended, I have an experience I had dreamed of for years. I'm standing looking at magazines at a magazine stand in New York City and I see a copy of *Inspiration*. I buy it. It is after all a souvenir. It is the last one I will ever see.

As a further irony, I receive calls from Atlantic Distributing in New York City and from a Canadian distributor, both saying they have received requests for *Inspiration* and want to put it on newsstands throughout the United States and Canada. Subscribers are disappointed. *Inspiration* provided a sense of community for the larger Miracles community. A guidepost for that community is now lost. Friends start calling offering their condolences and their hope that someday it will return. That would be a *Miracle*! The Dalai Lama once said that when everything is falling apart, something better is trying to be born. What is being born? I must believe that what is happening is for a greater good.

Hope is not the conviction that something will turn out well, but the certainty that something makes sense, regardless of how it turns out.
—Vaclav Havel

By appealing to the same subscribers who have for years been the mainstay of Interfaith and by cutting almost all expenses, our new treasurer is able to announce that we are debt free, although there are still some unknown unpaid taxes. About the only income now comes in the Sunday morning offering. There are still major bills to pay like rent for Cami Hall. While the Fellowship is going through this changing of the guard, I'm enjoying my work with John Nagy and Bob Sandoe of The Quest Foundation putting together the International Miracles Conference for February 2003.

Members of the Fellowship, who are there essentially because I am, ask me to break away and start another church. I do not want to split the Fellowship. I look around for local work and find a part-time position as a lecturer in the Philosophy Department at nearby Marist College. It's good to be teaching again. Marist lets me go back to teaching courses in the Psychology of Religion, The History of Philosophy and World Religions and my favorite, The History of Mysticism.

A year ago there were four people helping in the administration of the Center, the Fellowship and the production and distribution of *Inspiration* magazine. With the exception of Sunday morning services, everything I've spent the last twelve years building has been dismantled.

CHAPTER 38

The Classroom Called Cancer

Sometimes the greatest miracles
come in the ugliest packages.

Dolores has been after me to have a colonoscopy, and I finally get one. They find cancer. On May 7, 2001, a tumor the size of a lemon and eighteen inches of colon are removed along with eight lymph nodes, five of which are cancerous. The doctors are concerned. They feel sure that there is cancer in other lymph nodes, and possibly other organs. I'm still convinced that everything is part of a divine plan even when it doesn't look that way. I'm not saying that things like wars and disease are part of God's plan. I'm sure they are part of the ego's plan, and the ego's plan has a built-in self-destruction mechanism. At some point it will implode. When it fails, God's plan automatically takes over.

When cancer comes up, it's inevitable that we ask, "Why me?" My friend, Rabbi Hershel Jaffey wrote a book after his experience with cancer entitled, *Why Me? Why Anyone?* When Rabbi Gelberman called the first thing he said was: "This doesn't sound like you." I had to agree with him. It doesn't "sound" like me. No one wants to hear that they have cancer. I've never been afraid of cancer. I never thought it would happen to me. Daddy was terrified of cancer because he watched both his parents die from it.

How can a student of *A Course in Miracles* get cancer? As much as I understand the Course, I've never claimed to be enlightened. Until we are enlightened, none of us can be sure how much *stuff* is buried inside us, how much is "eating" us. Even "enlightened" beings die. Ramakrishna and Ramana Maharishi both died from cancer. My most invaluable guide in life, Dr. Robert Weltman, upon hearing the news asked, "What's been eating you?" According to Louise Hay, colon cancer comes from difficulties in letting go. In the past year-and-a-half, I've had lots of letting go to do. There is almost no income now. Due to the bad stock market, this year, the annual $10,000 from Aunt Sue does not come through. Things are very bleak. There is a lot of sadness and now—now cancer!

An Awakening Experience—The Day Seeking Stopped

If you know you're going to be hung in the morning,
it helps to concentrate the mind. —Dr. Johnson.

I awake at four a.m. the morning after the doctor gave me the news that the cancer had spread. I am wide-awake! The doctors want to do another colonoscopy, and start chemotherapy. The only light in the room comes from the hallway. My roommate is fast asleep. The curtains are drawn between us. To my left, the window curtains are open and it is dark out. There is a pine tree next to my window, and out past the pine is the hospital parking lot with its lights all-ablaze. A light fog hangs in the night sky making the lights look misty. I lie there in the dark, staring at the night sky thinking about what the doctors said, and think: "You know you could die. You could actually die!" Tears come to my eyes, and I am overwhelmed for a moment.

Maybe the story is played out? Maybe it's over. I had a good friend, George O'Kelley, who was the lawyer for Interfaith, a graduate of the New Seminary, a student of *A Course in Miracles,* and a spiritual healer. He was diagnosed with cancer in November of 1998, and the next November, he died. I lie there thinking, "Maybe I'm going to leave. If so—so what?" Dolores once said, "I'm not afraid of dying. It just means I don't have to get up in the morning." I'm not afraid of dying—by thinking that's the end of things—I know better. I have accumulated, in the course of this life, far too much evidence to the contrary.

When your body and your ego and your dreams are gone, you will know that you will last forever. Perhaps you think this is accomplished through death, but nothing is accomplished through death, because death is nothing. Everything is accomplished through life, and life is of the mind and in the mind. The body neither lives nor dies, because it cannot contain you who are life.
—ACIM, T-6.V.A.1:1-4

What Does Dying Mean?

I imagine that loss of the body is going to be an interesting adventure. In some ways I'm ready to go. The ringing in my ears will stop. I'll be so grateful for that! A lot of wonderful things have happened. This life has also been a bit of a struggle. Right now I'm broke, sick and tired. Maybe it's time to go.

Dying means letting go of everything of this world—all hopes and dreams. I begin to let go of all of what you might call "good" things and "bad" things. Maybe whatever it was I thought I was supposed to do with my life, I'm not going to get to do. Maybe I've already done it. Maybe *Missouri Mystic* will never be published. I decide to take a good look at death—to give up completely as there might be no other choice. I'm not going to "fight" for my body as people sometimes do in a "panicky" way when they hear that they have cancer. I'm not going to "beg" God to spare my body. That's not real prayer. That is not saying "Thy will be done." Prayer is a shift in perception, and a changing of one's mind about a situation, rather than changing the situation. I understand that what is needed now is a change of mind. Either I am going to survive or I am not. If it's my time to go—I'm going. I still think I have unfinished business to fulfill. Maybe I'm wrong. God knows best.

Interfaith and *Inspiration*

Lying there in the hospital, looking out the window at the lights in the parking lot, I decide it doesn't make any difference what happens with Interfaith Fellowship. I let it all go. I drop all expectations. The difficulties we've gone through over the course of the past year pale and fade away. Interfaith is out of my hands now. I completely let go of *Inspiration* magazine as well. It's a dream, which is more than thirty years old and has manifested itself in four different magazines—*Seeker, The Mustard Seed, On Course* and *Inspiration*. The magazine is just something of this world. It doesn't have to happen. I open *A Course in Miracles* and read lesson 189—*I Feel the Love of God Within Me Now*. And Jesus tells me:

> *Simply do this: be still, and lay aside all thoughts of what you are and what God is; all concepts you have learned about the world; all images you hold about yourself. Empty your mind of everything you think is either true or false, or good or bad, of every thought it judges worthy, and all the ideas of which it is ashamed. Hold onto nothing. Do not bring with you one thought the past has taught, nor one belief you have ever learned before from anything. Forget this world. Forget this course, and come with wholly empty hands unto your God.* —ACIM—W-pI.189. 7:1-5

I Don't Give a Damn

I keep letting go. I let go of entanglements, hang-ups, regrets and remorse—all the nostalgia about what might have been—relationships that did not turn out better—the Methodist Church—the belief that anything "had" to happen—even everything I've been ashamed of. I go deeper and deeper. I take a good look at my secret sins and hidden hates. And then comes the last thing, the biggest thing of all. I even forgive myself for not having done a better job.

Lying there in the dark, I become *empty* in a way I've not been *empty* before. I don't mean to sound crude but I take a deep breath, sigh and then say, "I don't give a damn!" Whatever will be will be. It's clearly out of my hands now. I enter into a place of no will, no energy, no feeling, no experience—nothing. I am so nothing, I wonder, what is it that thinks, talks, walks? I become empty of desire and anger and I understand, in a way in which I had previously only understood "intellectually," what Buddha meant when he said that the loss of desire is the key to enlightenment. I achieve, by this profound "letting go," some sort of objectivity. How incredibly manipulative I've been, I've tried to make things work out—my way. The theme song of the ego is *I'll Do It My Way*.

When a man surrenders all desires that come to the heart, and by the grace of
God finds the joy of God in himself, then his soul has indeed found peace.
—Bhagavada Gita 3:30

When there's nothing more to lose, we see who we are behind who *we thought* we were. And now, a deep peace comes over me, a peace that comes when we give *everything* away, a peace that comes when we take a good look at Friend death. I am now transported out of my body. Unlike the experience in 1976, this time it's perfectly peaceful. In fact, I'm still aware of my body. I simply lose my attachment to it. This time, I am not "hurled" into Reality. Whatever happens is okay. Dying is perfectly acceptable. I say okay to death—I say, "okay, come get me" and then an amazing thing happens. You don't die. You just keep going on.

I know that I don't "really" exist in an individual way. There is no subject and object. There is just oneness. The Mind that is thinking everything is one mind completely outside of time. Realization requires no effort! Seeking is unnecessary! No path is the right path. Finding can only happen without interference! We are born enlightened. To try to achieve something which already is is absurd. There is nothing to achieve. There is nowhere to go. There is nothing to be done. We are already divine just the way we are. Problems are all just so much nonsense. Problems do not "actually" exist. There are no worries because all worries are concerned with life. When you are going to die, why worry? We are everything and nothing. I am that I am! What is needed is to be deeply involved in life, while unattached to the "drama." I'm happy with what I have. I love Mother,

Ann, Dolores, Sarah, Kristian, and my many friends. I love my work and I love you!

The acceptance of death brings an incredible awareness. When there is nothing left but God, you find that God is all you need. And now something I never would have guessed, an unexpected manifestation of intense compassion. Tears come to my eyes and *LOVE* in all its glory intoxicates my heart. I think of those who closed the Center and stopped *Inspiration*. I feel the greatest love for them and I thank them for giving me the opportunity of loving them so much. Everyone did exactly what he or she was supposed to do. I cannot be mad at anyone. As Martin Luther King Jr. once said, "I cannot at heart be the enemy of any man." I love the Course and believe in the Course. Anger "is" never justified. Everyone did what he or she did thinking that it was best. It was the best! Then I begin to laugh, and laugh, and laugh, and laugh. I laugh a really uproarious laugh. Ken is right. I am a bliss ninny.

To know yourself as the Being underneath the thinker, the stillness underneath the mental noise, the love and joy underneath the pain, is freedom, salvation, and enlightenment. —Eckhart Tolle

What I Learned from Cancer

Truth is always simple. We always learn really simple things.

1. Love is all there is—it's all that matters. The end result of realization is love, compassion and humility, and the love of everything is the love of Self.

2. We take so much for granted.

The day I come home from the hospital—just watching our cat, Pockets, walk across the deck, listening to our neighbor mow his lawn, and saying grace together around the dinner table brings tears to my eyes.

Sometimes when you are feeling jaded or blasé, you can revive your sense of wonder by merely saying to yourself: suppose this were the only time.
Suppose this sunset, this moonrise, this symphony, this buttered toast, this sleeping child, this flag against the sky.
Suppose you would never experience these things again!
Few things are commonplace in themselves.
It's our reaction to them that grows dull.
—Arthur Gordon

Happiness is one more walk with Dolores. It's one more driving lesson with Sarah, one more lunch with Kristian or one more chat on the phone with one of you.

3. Your Life is none of your business. Life is God's business. The sooner we turn it over the better.

After I come home from the hospital, I do a two-week vegetable juice cleansing fast and I begin a daily diet of detox tea, along with a long list of vitamins, minerals and herbs. I also begin a thirty-week session of chemo. I now know that I got cancer just so I could have that experience in the hospital. I needed to engage in a deep, total let go. The only way to do it was to look at death. Something in me died that day never to be born again. I am free. You can never lose an experience of the eternal. It may fade but it is never forgotten. My lectures now take on a different, dimension. I can feel it. The words come easier than ever. Others can feel it as well—or so they say.

CHAPTER 39

This is It!

There comes a tide in the affairs of men which if taken at the flood leads on to fortune. —William Shakespeare

There is a story about a soldier who is walking around his army camp picking up bits of paper, looking at each bit and saying, "This isn't it." He then throws it down, finds another piece of paper, picks it up, looks at it and says, "This isn't it." He keeps doing this and his supervising officer decides he is probably crazy so he sends him to an army psychologist for testing. The psychologist decides that he is indeed deranged so he writes out a discharge from the army for the guy. He hands the guy the letter. He takes it, looks at it and says, "This is it!"

Ken and Gloria Move to California

Ken and Gloria Wapnick move the Foundation for *A Course in Miracles* to Temecula, California. In June, I'm invited to be a speaker at the Miracles Conference in Anaheim, California, and I visit Ken's new facility out in the desert. Temecula is an all-new, twenty-first century city with new roads, houses and stores. The town blossomed from 15,000 people in 1990 to over 30,000 during the last decade of the century. Ken has always been on top of technology. He's now developing more of a presence on the Internet. Ken and Gloria are glad to be free of the "hotel" end of their business. From now on, it's just lectures, books, and more and more CD's, tapes and videos. Ken is the most prolific individual who ever walked the face of this planet. This is not an understatement. Almost every lecture is recorded, made into audiotapes and CD's and transcribed into books. I love listening to Ken's tapes.

Chemotherapy is not fun. My hair becomes much thinner. I lose my eyebrows, and eyelashes, my eyes water constantly and I wake up with nosebleeds every morning. Mostly, chemo makes you sick. Despite my depleted condition, I'm trying to carry out my usual schedule.

September 11, 2001, I'm sitting down at my desk at 8:45 a.m. when I hear, "Turn on the television. There is news." An airplane has just hit the first of the twin towers in New York City. I keep repeating a line from the Course; "This *is* an insane world, and do not underestimate the extent of its insanity." (ACIM, T-14.I.2:6) The ego is capable of really insane things like flying airplanes into skyscrapers, and screaming as one goes, "Vengeance is mine, saith the Lord." My neighor across the street, Kevin is a New York City fireman. He was walking toward the second tower when it began to collapse. He had to run for his life. He said he felt as if he were a character in a bad movie. It was just too grotesque, too nightmarish, too surreal and too unbelievable. His wife said: "He saw too much." The days after 9/11 in New York City are truly different. People are looking each other in the eye and saying hello. Lampposts all around the city are covered with pictures of missing people with a note saying, "Have you seen . . .?" followed by a phone number. Members of the Fellowship volunteer to help with the disaster. When humans experience disaster, they are at their best and are often quite noble. Churches all across the country are filled the Sunday after 9/11. A deeper awareness has been attained at least temporarily. During the next several months I will run several workshop on "Healing the T(error)ist Within."

Sunday, December 2, 2001: Today is my 40th Anniversary as a minister. I give the message at Interfaith and I talk about the changes I've seen in the church, our world, and myself.

In Memory of Mother—Milly Mundy

I receive a call from Ann on Christmas Eve morning. Mother's aortic aneurysm is tearing. It was repaired in 1993, and again in 2000. This time there is no repair. The doctor told her she only had two days to live. She went home to die. Ann puts Mother on the phone and I tell her I'm going to come home to see her. My last words to her: "I love you!" Her last words to me: "I love you too, Sweetie!" A chaplain from hospice came to see her. He sang *Amazing Grace* to her. She loved him. She said to Ann, "I can't believe I'm going to die in two days." I arrive at her bedside on Christmas Day.

I sit by her bedside and keep saying, "Mother, it's Jon, I'm here!" I don't know if she hears me or not. Everyone thinks that she has waited till I arrived to let go. I love Mother dearly, deeply, clearly, and completely—so does Ann. There is something about the loss of your mother. Somehow, you lose your connection with the earth. No one has known you longer, loved you more or forgiven you more often. I cry for several days. I know she is in a better place. I know she is free of the pains of the body and this world. I know that she is with me now more than ever.

I still miss her! I don't care how old you are when your parents die. I don't care how old they are. When you lose your mother, you lose it. If you don't lose it—why don't you?

Mother asked that her casket not be opened for the funeral service. The evening before her funeral we go to the funeral home. They bring out Mother's body. I reach out and touch her. She is ice cold. They must keep bodies in refrigeration. I look at her corpse and think, "That's not her." I look up at a picture of her on top of the coffin. She is smiling and bright eyed. "That," I think, "is her." That is the way I choose to remember her. I continue to talk to her till this day. She is just fine. I knew she would be. She was a very spirited lady. I was truly blessed to have her as my mother.

2001 has been an incredible year. In January, I lost *Inspiration* magazine. I no longer have a paycheck from the Fellowship. I now have cancer. The whole world went into a spin after 9/11 and now on Christmas Day I've lost my mother. It has also been a year of astonishing revelation.

2002—Age Fifty-Nine

Again, members of the Fellowship come asking me to please start another church. Again, I say "No." I gave talks in twenty-five different churches in 2001. I will make presentations in fifty different churches and several centers in 2002. I'm having fun on the road. The thing which is not fun, is chemotherapy. I do a tour of Florida in early January with ten lectures in eleven days. I did not realize, at the time I did this planning, that this would not be a smart move. There is such a massive accumulation of chemo in my system, I am so sick, I can hardly fulfill my speaking obligations. I can't eat anything without throwing it right back up. I'm depleted, dehydrated and sleep deprived. I get on the stage in Orlando and begin by saying; "I'm feeling quite sick right now, so if you see me suddenly run off the stage in the direction of the men's room, I hope you will understand." Somehow, I make it through. I am not at my best. I don't know where my energy comes from. It's not coming from food or sleep. Now, however, thank God, the chemo is stopped.

Inspiration is revived as a quarterly newsletter for the church. I am no longer the editor. The new editors are not Miracles students and it is no longer "my baby." I miss being in contact with friends as I was with *Inspiration* and *On Course*. I still feel called to have a Course based magazine. I need to let people know about my workshop and lecture schedule and I want to start the publicity for the miracles conference coming up in New York next February. I put together 300 copies of eight pages of *Miracles* magazine. I run it off on my copy machine, fold, collate and staple by hand just as I did with *On Course* in 1989. I pass my hand over each address, blessing each name as I attach each label to the little magazine. Once again, it works.

April 1, 2002: Mother would have been 86 today and Shanti is 75. I get a call from the oncologist. My latest CAT scan came back clean! I am cancer free! Yippee! The power of the mind, eating the right foods, taking vitamins, minerals and herbs along with chemo can heal. I know some of these things are magic. If you have a headache you take a magic pill called an aspirin. I have gone through a magic purging called chemotherapy.

Diane resigns as the Director of the New Seminary and with the assistance of Dr. Joyce Liechtenstein, begins her own seminary called One Spirit Interfaith Seminary. Diane is a wise wonderful and kind-hearted woman. I am sure that she will succeed.

I put together a Sunday afternoon Fundraising Fun Day of Cosmic Comedy and Healing Humor with Swami Beyondananda, Swami Baba Ji Whiz and Laraaji with his *Laughing Meditation* for Interfaith. It's the end of my promotion of events for the Fellowship. By December *Miracles* magazine is growing so well, I'm able to hire a part-time assistant.

2003—Age Sixty—Golden Handcuffs

The sage does not retire from life. He retires from unhappiness.
—William Martin in *The Sages Tao Te Ching*

There cannot be two captains on one ship. Interfaith has new leadership and it's going in a different direction than what I had charted. There is now little emphasis on the Course. Again, friends come and ask me to break away and start another church. I won't do it. They are, however, right. There needs to be a change.

Sometimes forgiving means letting go of the physical. Sometimes it means letting go of space—time and history. Sometimes, letting go means divorce. Sometimes you have to give up everything for something you believe in. It's time to step out of the dream of myself as a minister in midtown Manhattan. It's time to wake up. It's time to get up. It's time to get out. It's time to move on. Even if you get broadsided, if you forgive, the pain goes away. It's a miracle! True forgiveness is the way to break the pattern and awaken from this dream.

Politics is for the moment. I'm interested in eternity.—Albert Einstein.

Organized religion IS politics. Fortunately, *A Course in Miracles* is a self-study course and does not require organized religion. That's why there should not be *A Course in Miracles* churches. Keep the ego out of it folks— now and forever! Although I'm enjoying working with The Quest Foundation, I have become progressively disenchanted with all organizations, even those with the best intentions—even those I have founded!

It's been three years since the new administration took over. The mystics I've been studying say that they are happy because their lives are unencumbered. A.H. Almas says that to reach enlightenment one must be free of all "entanglements," "embroilments," and "perplexities." Soap operas are blocks to the awareness of love's presence. They reinforce the illusion. They do not provide freedom from it. Why muck about in the illusion? Why not be free of it? I'll be sixty soon. I don't know how many "productive" years I have left. I do know that I want to spend those years happily having fun—doing what I enjoy. I like going places where people enjoy hearing the message of the Course. I enjoy receiving a check at the end of the day. I then return home and whatever "soap opera" may be going on in a local church is not something in which I am involved.

Monday January 27, 2003. I send in my letter of resignation. Immediately, a feeling of release and freedom comes over me. Nothing fills the soul like freedom. Freedom is choice. Choice is what makes us human. I'm not saying "No" to Interfaith. I'm saying "Yes" to life. Thirty e-mails soon fill my mailbox saying Hurrah!!!!!!!!, Good for You!!!, Terrific!!!!!!!!!!, I'm behind you 100%!, I am SOOOOOOoooooo HAPPY for you! and Congratulations!!!!. Interfaith is an idea whose time has come. It feels good to have played some part in the beginning of a new deeper— broader—clearer way of understanding.

In September, Diane also resigns and becomes like myself, Senior Minister Emeritus. Then one by one, the various members of the "new board" who saw to the closing of the Interfaith Center and Inner Journey Bookstore, and the dissolution of *Inspiration* magazine, each in turn, also resigns. It's hard for someone to come along and try to fulfill someone else's dream. In June 2004, Interfaith Fellowship discontinues services altogether.

Truth, being limitless, unconditioned, unapproachable by any path whatsoever, cannot be organized; nor should any organization be formed to lead or coerce people along a particular path. The moment you follow someone you cease to follow Truth. I am concerning myself with only one essential thing: to set man free. I desire to free him from all cages, from all fears, and not to found religions, new sects, nor to establish new theories and new philosophy.
My only concern is to set men absolutely, unconditionally free.
—J. Krishnamurti

Or as one of my favorite teachers, Jesuit mystic Anthony de Mello expressed it.

Religion is a fruitless effort to mark a pathway on the shifting stands of the desert. The infinite cannot be trapped, described or noted. We are One with the infinite even as we pretend that we are not.

Loss is always followed by new opportunities. When you close one door it is "inevitable" that another will open in front of you. When Ken has moved, I've moved. We both moved from New York City to Westchester in the late seventies. In 1988 we both moved west across the Hudson River into the foothills of the Catskill Mountains. He bought the Center in Roscoe; at the same time I bought Pilgrims Inn. Now, he's gone to California, and I'm stepping away from Sundays in New York City to a Senior Minister Emeritus position. While Ken stays put, I move. Ken is the mountain. Go visit the mountain. I get to be a missionary.

Now has our ministry begun at last, to carry round the world the joyous news that truth has no illusions, and the peace of God, through us, belongs to everyone.—ACIM W. 151, 17:3

I am literally stepping off the stage in New York City and on to a bigger stage. I am going to take Swami Baba Ji Whiz and we're going to take this show on the road. I have a large map of the United States on the wall in my office. I make a label, which says, "My Parish." I go over and put it on top of the map. My church, the people I minister to, are the subscribers to *Miracles* magazine and the folks who come to my lectures and workshop, who read my books and listen to my CD's. Jesus was a traveling itinerant holy man, and his church was the world. After Ralph Waldo Emerson left the church, he became an itinerant preacher, speaking almost every Sunday someplace in New England. John Wesley, the founder of the Methodist Church, once said that his church was the world. My church is "the world"—wherever I happen to find myself on a Sunday morning is fine.

313

Once a month and on every major holiday, I stay home or go hiking, bicycling, or on some other adventure with Dolores and Sarah. I run workshops in New York City, New Jersey and the Hudson Valley. Otherwise, I go wherever I am invited. I develop a regular returning relationship with cities within easy reach—Albany, Philadelphia, Boston, Harrisburg, Hartford and New Haven. There is a small International Airport only ten minutes from our home. It provides easy access to Chicago, Atlanta, Orlando, Cincinnati, Pittsburgh, Washington, D.C., and from these cities anyplace in the world.

At each workshop and conference, I pass out free copies of *Miracles* Magazine. *Miracles* is growing miraculously. In less than two years it surpasses *Inspiration* magazine in sales and distribution. It is appropriate that I have a peripatetic ministry. I have always been a pilgrim. I love being at home with Dolores and Sarah. I'm also at home on the open road. Though the Course needs no proselytizing, I carry its message of love, forgiveness, and appreciation wherever I'm invited. Despite all the failures, despite cancer and heart disease, I'm a lucky and happy man. Dolores is a witty, wise and wonderful woman. We enjoy fixing up our home and relaxing together. Sarah is turning into a beautiful young woman. Kristian is now a fine young scholar. I have my family in Missouri and my many good friends. I thoroughly enjoy my work and feel clearly that it's what I'm called to do. I go back and finish writing this book. The rest is, as they say, history.

314

CHAPTER 40

Something Wonderful Is Going To Happen

Interfaith, *A Course in Miracles* and the Twenty-First Century

Wandering into a Christian bookstore in a large shopping center, I go over to a prophecy section and begin to go through the tables of contents of different books and read occasional paragraphs. The books are all on the apocalypse, the last judgment, a third world war, Armageddon, and the end of the world. Based mostly on Revelations and the prophets of the Old Testament, each book predicts some sort of catastrophe for humankind. Everyone is to be annihilated, except those Christians who have been washed in the redemptive blood of Jesus. After several minutes of going through this material, I say to myself: WAIT A MINUTE!

- Maybe there is no devil.

- Maybe the devil is only our own fearful projection.

- Maybe we've had enough of fear-rooted images.

- Maybe the emotional climate of the earth is changing.

- Maybe we can see more positive developments.

- Maybe there is a Happy Dream instead of one of doom and gloom.

- Maybe the twenty-first century will be different.

- Maybe we can see peace instead of this.

Motivation based on fear has never gotten this earth anything except war and rumors of war, sadness, sorrow and suffering. The truth of God reflects a love not of this world. That love speaks to us of our *real* home—Heaven. Buckminster Fuller says we are citizens of a regenerative universe. The human mind, he says, *is designed to know the design* and when we know the design, we will see there is nothing to be afraid of.

Though a long time coming, positive change has been happening all around. Slavery ceased to exist in this country in the 1860s. Though the struggle for freedom continues, positive changes did occur in the nineteenth and twentieth centuries. During the last quarter of the twentieth century, three men—at one time political prisoners—became president of their countries—Lech Walesa in Poland, Vaclav Havel in Czechoslovakia and Nelson Mandela in South Africa. On the occasion of Mandela's election, De Klerk said, "The people of South Africa today transcended themselves."

The Death of the Church and the Dawning of Aquarius

All about, we see the falling off of the old and the birth of something new. Mainline Protestantism experienced a precipitous decline during the last half of the twentieth century. In the twenty-five year period between 1965 and 1990, while the population of the United States grew by 50 million, mainline Protestant churches lost 37 percent of their membership and 55 percent of their Sunday School enrollment! Bishop Richard B. Wilke of the United Methodist Church writes in his book *Are We Yet Alive?* "Our sickness is more serious than we first suspected. We are in trouble—you and I and our Methodist Church. We thought we were just drifting like a sailboat on a dreamy day. Instead, we are wasting away like a leukemia victim when the blood transfusions no longer work."

Rev. Jerry Falwell used to speak of a silent majority of conservative Americans. There is another larger, silent segment of society that simply walked out the doors of the church, never to return, because they were unsatisfied in their search for spiritual fulfillment. Not knowing where to go, they went nowhere, or they went shopping, or jogging or fishing, or they stayed home, had breakfast in bed, and read the Sunday paper.

Rev. Lyle Schaffer says that mainline Protestantism is dying because Protestantism lacks *freshness, vigor, energy, vitality,* and *wholesomeness.* People are looking for something new and they're receiving the same guilt ridden philosophy that has been scaring people away for decades. As the average age in Protestant churches increases, churches become more traditional, rigid and restrictive. This is not to say that there are no inspired individuals working within the church. They have, however, uphill battles to fight. The process is thwarted and slow going.

The church is also on the decline because of its intolerance of non-Christians and its refusal to be open to the rich diversity of religious experience. There was even a debate at the annual meeting of the Dutch

Reformed Church, in 1998, as to whether or not it was possible to admit into Christian theology the *idea* that non-Christians might be saved and go to Heaven! Traditional Christianity often condemns other religions as inferior at best, at worst the work of the devil. If you demonize another's religion you must then be at war with them.

Catholicism, too, is in Crisis

Fewer and fewer men are entering the priesthood and there are fewer nuns, due in good part to the refusal to allow for divorce, clergy to marry, women to be ordained, and the hard-line stance on abortion and birth control. Headlines in the newspaper in the summer of 1994 read, "The Pope says there will never be women priests." There will be women priests, and I feel safe in prophesying that it will happen in the twenty-first century. These issues of the Church all focus around sexuality. As revelations of recent years have shown, the Church's repression of sex means that sexuality then finds outlets in secretive and deviant forms. The sexist position of the church cannot forever be maintained. Meanwhile, an already besieged Catholic Church will continue to decline.

George Gallup, Jr., (of the Gallup Polls) in his book *The People's Religion*, predicts that America will become progressively more religiously pluralistic and less Christian in character. The trend, he said, clearly points in the direction of the growth of nonwestern religions and those who claim no religious affiliation. According to Gerald Celente, director of the Trends Research Institute, the twenty-first century will see a new faith developing based on universally common themes like the principle of personal spiritual development.

An article in *USA Today* in the last days of the twentieth century announced, "Spirituality is replacing church-based faith." According to a USA Today/CNN/Gallup Poll, God has been detached from "religion." More and more people regard themselves as "spiritual"—not religious. People are saying, "I believe in God. I just don't believe in the institution." The National Opinion Research Center at the University of Chicago found that the number of people who claim no religious preference climbed from six percent in 1972 to fourteen percent in 1998. Despite this fact, on September 5, 2000, the pope issued an encyclical reaffirming its position that the Catholic Church is the one and only true church.

What is Interfaith?

Interfaith is *a genuine movement*—a collective effort by a large number of people who are trying to achieve something new. Interfaith has no dogmas, no canons, no statutes, and no creeds. Thank God! What a relief not to have to carry around a bunch of heavy tablets filled with rules and dogma. If you say that people *have to* believe in a particular path—then you must castigate, scourge, reject, or think less of those who do not think the way you do.

Interfaith seeks through listening and exchange, through openness and cross-fertilization, the development of a deeper connection with God and all of humankind. Interfaith seeks to bring into focus the joy, serenity and wisdom that exist as the foundation of all the world religious traditions. What we need is not a new theology. A universal theology after all is impossible (ACIM, C-In.2:5). What is needed is an *experience* of the consciousness of love.

Interfaith is not interested in disputing or debating; trying to convert another; proving someone else wrong or focusing on that which makes us different. Interfaith is interested in facilitating spiritual growth; getting in touch with the seeker of truth that lies deep within; fostering a universal experience of God; remembering that ineffable something which makes us one, and experiencing inner peace. Interfaith is inclusive rather than exclusive. Opening ourselves to the wisdom and beauty of the world's sacred scriptures and meditations, and songs and chants deepens our own understanding of the universality of religious experience and brings us closer to the spirit residing within. I love Tibetan bells, Gregorian chant, Hindu melodies and the mystic poems of Rumi. It makes me richer. It restores my soul.

For fourteen years, I tried to bring *A Course in Miracles* into the Church thinking it would revolutionize the church. The church does not want to be revolutionized. The older the institution, the more solidified in its position, the more filled with magic and superstition—the less likely it is to change. If you build a castle, you must then defend your castle. If you build an institution, then you must defend the institution. If you build an ego, you defend the ego. So we create defense mechanisms to support the ego. Once the structure is built, be it a church, a denomination, a country, or a political party, or an ego, its defense is maintained—right or wrong, truth or not. The Catholic Church supports the contradictory doctrine of

318

annulment, which says that two people (even if they lived together for forty years and had six children) were never married. In June 2000, the Southern Baptist Church, in a literal interpretation of the scriptures, declared that women couldn't be pastors of its churches. Beauty and meaning are lost when tradition becomes the truth, even in the face of glaring discrepancies.

You don't change the old by resisting it. You change the old by making it obsolete through superior methodology. —Buckminster Fuller

What is needed is not *revolution*. What we need is *revelation*. Mystics are interested in an *experience* of God, not in creating dogmas or building cathedrals.

Our first task in approaching another people, another country, another religion is to take off our shoes, for the place we are aproaching is holy. Else we may find ourselves treading on another's dream. More serious still, we may forget...that God was there before our arrival. —Author Unknown

Along with our many freedoms, comes the obligation to practice "tolerance" for those who "think" differently than we do.

Only appreciation is an appropriate response to your brother. Gratitude is due him for both his loving thoughts and his appeals for help.—ACIM, T-12.I.6:1-2

The rigidity of the fundamentalist lifestyle is not one in which I could live happily. A fundamentalist has, however, as much right to be a fundamentalist as I have to be a student of *A Course in Miracles*.

Things They Are A Changing—Then and Now

Five hundred years ago the ox cart that went by your house the day you were born looked like the ox cart that went by your house the day you died. Things were, however, changing in the minds of inspired people like Galileo and Luther. The *revolutions* of human history have always first and foremost been preceded by *revelations* that took place within the minds of inspired individuals.

Five hundred years ago, *the* biggest change in the western world was the Protestant Reformation. Luther was able to do what he did because of the many mystics who came before him. By the time of Luther, there were so many people pressing for change that the German princes intervened and saved Luther from being burned at the stake.

Five hundred years ago an incredible advance was also taking place in consciousness because of discoveries in science. Circumnavigation of the world had proven that it was round. Galileo then focused his telescope on the heavens and realized that Copernicus was correct in his assertion that the earth moved around the sun. Consciousness then had to expand from an egocentric, geocentric view, to one that was much more inclusive. Change did not come quickly. Galileo was forced to recant and forbidden to teach. It was, however, too late. The cat was out of the bag. Galileo was right! Five hundred years after the birth of the Protestant Reformation, we are ready to transcend the limitations of denomination. God is after all, too big to fit inside one religion.

The Second Coming—The Last Judgment —Omega

"Each individual," says Teilhard, "is a member of one body." Through the complexification of consciousness, we are ever more interactive with the whole. Teilhard felt we were approaching a quantum jump, which he described as *Omega*. Barbara Marx Hubbard talks of a *Planetary Pentecost*. Christ's Second Coming is the return to sanity. It is that which "restores what was never lost and re-establishes what is forever true" (ACIM, W-pII.9.1:2). It is the willingness to let forgiveness rest on all things. The Second Coming is the time when all minds are given to Christ and returned to Spirit. The Final Judgment will not come until it is no longer associated with fear. It will then be a final healing, not a final punishment. The Final Judgment comes as we realize that all is forgiven and our seeming sins are part of a bad dream. Outside the limited realms of time and space, it is possible to love everything in complete openness, as God does, without judgment and condemnation.

You have no idea of the tremendous release and deep peace that comes from meeting yourself and your brothers totally without judgment.
— ACIM, T-3.VI.3:1

How Will the World End?

When the purpose of forgiveness is fulfilled, when guilt is laid aside, the illusions of this world will merely "cease to seem to be" (M-14. 2:11). What do you lose when you lose an illusion? When we awaken from fearful dreams, there is no regret, no looking backward. We are then just glad that we are now awake. There is simply gratitude that our nightmares are over.

The world will end in joy, because it is a place of sorrow. When joy has come, the purpose of the world has gone. The world will end in peace, because it is a place of war. When peace has come, what is the purpose of the world? The world will end in laughter, because it is a place of tears.

320

Where there is laughter, who can longer weep? And only complete forgiveness brings all this to bless the world. —ACIM, M-14.4:1-5

In the twenty-first century we shall inevitably experience an increasingly global and inclusive view. I predict that within the twenty-first century, we shall experience new dimensions of consciousness, including contact with extraterrestrial life. Our limited minds can only begin to guess about this. We will not, however, be open to other dimensions of consciousness until we move beyond the limits of the *human point of view.* There are layers and dimensions of consciousness awaiting our perception that will make our present worldly perspective insignificant. There are dimensions of awareness and perception so far beyond ours that, from where we stand, even if we were to look at that next dimension, we would not be able to see it or have any idea what it is till we experienced it firsthand.

The next jump in consciousness calls upon us to do what Jesus did, to see as he saw, to move from being a child of God to being heirs of God. The next jump calls for our discovery of Christ Consciousness or Cosmic Consciousness or whatever term feels comfortable for you. Consciousness does not care what you call it. It doesn't have a name. It's time to move from an earth ruled by fear to an earth reflecting Heaven.

I Believe

- that the more we look within, the more we will discover a well-spring of spiritual energy ready to be shared with the entire world.

- that we are going to experience the coming together of the planet, the awakening of the members of the body as one living system.

- that even in the face of tragedy, it is possible to experience hope.

- that our purpose here is to promote inner peace.

- that our task is to seek to be the servant of all, and the enemy of none.

- that universal principles of truth are more important than rites and ritual.

- that "happiness" will characterize the psychology of the Twenty-First Century.

- that we will witness an awakening that will dissolve fearful projections.

- that Pierre Teilhard de Chardin was right
  —we are ready for an experience at a collective level.

- that there is nothing to be afraid of in the change we're beginning to experience.

We are now poised to witness the most beautiful spectacle ever to grace time.

What Are the Things that Make for Peace?

The major transformations which have taken place in humankind, have not occurred where the sound of marching soldiers was the loudest, nor in corporate boardrooms. The great changes have occurred when holy men and women of vision, out of their great love for humankind, demonstrated by their lives that there is another, better and more loving way of seeing.

Where shall we look for change in the twenty-first century? How shall we experience a healing of the divisiveness that has separated people of different religions? Who is to take up the cause of peace? Shall we rely on politicians? Shall we rely on the military? Or, shall we move in the direction where real significant change has always occurred—within the hearts and minds of mystics and seers, and everyday seekers—spiritual men and women who are the first to be open to a bigger picture?

We're All Just People Here

Sitting in a restaurant with a friend, waiting for our dinner, I cannot help overhearing the conversation between an older man and woman at the next table. The man has had a revelatory experience, and he keeps trying to tell the woman about it. He keeps saying, "You know, we are all just people here." The woman, clearly not hearing what he has to say, responds to his statements with something of her own agenda. After a minute or two he tries again to tell her about his revelation. He keeps saying: "You know, we are all just people here." My job is to relay his message—*We are all just people here*!

Jesus said that we could do far greater works than He has done. We are just beginning to find out how. I believe at the beginning of the 21st Century we stand poised to experience something tangibly different, something wonderful beyond all previous human experience. There are many that have gone on ahead, already preparing the way and sowing seeds of Spirit. The last line at the end of the movie 2010 is, "Something wonderful is going to happen." Something wonderful *is* going to happen. We are making way for love—real love—happy energy dancing across the face of the earth.

Something Wonderful is going to Happen. It already has!

Postscript

For Thanksgiving of 1999, Dolores, Sarah, and I go home to Missouri to stay with Ann and Glenn on the farm. The Saturday after Thanksgiving is a sunny day in the upper 60s. Dolores takes a picture of me sitting on a bale of hay in front of the pump house (the picture which is on the cover of this book). I want to take Sarah to see the farm where I grew up. Sarah doesn't want to go. She's watching a Spice Girls movie on television and doesn't want to see an old farm. Sarah is thirteen. How could she possibly understand how important this is to me? I go alone.

Once again, I get to walk on the back pasture. Once again, I see the beauty and richness. It is an absolutely beautiful day—too warm for a coat. I walk back to the bass pond where Daddy went fishing on Sunday mornings. A whitetail doe bolts from the bushes and I watch her beautiful back end bounding over the field. She makes one, two, three, four zigzagging bounds, and then she stops and turns to look inquisitively back my way. Above, a hawk reiterates its insistent cry. There is no one else around, not even the clattery critters whose sounds I'm accustomed to hearing in August. The sumac is a beautiful dark red velvet. I break off a few branches for the bouquet Dolores made yesterday from dried flowers she collected on the back of Ann and Glenn's farm. I let myself fall backwards in the tall grass and just lie there, the sun gently warming my face. My attraction to this land is as strong as ever. I have traveled far, but I have never come across this same beauty. This is the place where the love of God first filled my heart. What a crystal clear beautiful day! There is a richness here that, for me, can be found no place else.

Thank God for Missouri! I am so very lucky! I am so blessed!